Social Archeology
Beyond Subsistence
and Dating

This is a volume in

Studies in Archeology

A complete list of titles in this series appears at the end of this volume.

Social Archeology
Beyond Subsistence and Dating

EDITED BY

Charles L. Redman

Department of Anthropology
State University of New York at
  Binghamton
Binghamton, New York

Mary Jane Berman

Department of Anthropology
State University of New York at
  Binghamton
Binghamton, New York

Edward V. Curtin

Department of Anthropology
State University of New York at
  Binghamton
Binghamton, New York

William T. Langhorne, Jr.

The Museum
Michigan State University
East Lansing, Michigan

Nina M. Versaggi

Department of Anthropology
State University of New York at
  Binghamton
Binghamton, New York

Jeffery C. Wanser

Department of Anthropology
State University of New York at
  Binghamton
Binghamton, New York

ACADEMIC PRESS   New York   San Francisco   London
A Subsidiary of Harcourt Brace Jovanovich, Publishers

ACADEMIC PRESS, INC.
111 Fifth Avenue, New York, New York 10003

United Kingdom Edition published by
ACADEMIC PRESS, INC. (LONDON) LTD.
24/28 Oval Road, London NW1 7DX

Library of Congress Cataloging in Publication Data

Main entry under title:

Social archeology:
    Beyond subsistence and dating.

    (Studies in archeology)
    Includes bibliographies.
    1. Archaeology--Methodology--Addresses, essays,
lectures. 2. Man, Prehistoric--Addresses, essays,
lectures. I. Redman, Charles L. II. Berman, Mary Jane.
III. Curtin, Edward V. IV. Langhorne, Jr. William T.
V. Versaggi, Nina M. VI. Wanser, Jeffery C.
CC75.7.S6   930'.1 028   78--16390
ISBN 0--12--585150--2

Contents

v

chapter 12
Environmental Perturbations and the
Origin of the Andean State   303
WILLIAM H. ISBELL

chapter 13
The Archeological Study of
Andean Exchange Systems   315
CRAIG MORRIS

chapter 14
Mesopotamian Urban Ecology:
The Systemic Context of the Emergence of Urbanism   329
CHARLES L. REDMAN

chapter 15
The Keresan Bridge:
An Ecological and Archeological Account   349
FRED PLOG

chapter **16**
Le Projet du Garbàge 1975:
Historic Trade-offs   **373**
WILLIAM L. RATHJE

chapter **17**
Prehistoric Populations of the Dinaric Alps:
An Investigation of Interregional Interaction   **381**
EUGENE L. STERUD

PART **III**
Cultural Resource Management   **409**

chapter **18**
Cultural Resource Management—Archeology Plus   **415**
CHARLES R. McGIMSEY III

chapter **19**
Cultural Resource Management and the "New Archeology"   **421**
FRED PLOG

List of Contributors

Margaret W. Conkey (61), Department of Anthropology, State University of New York at Binghamton, Binghamton, New York 13901

Edward V. Curtin (1), Department of Anthropology, State University of New York at Binghamton, Binghamton, New York 13901

Robert K. Evans (113), National Museum of Natural History, Smithsonian Institution, Washington, D. C. 20560

John M. Fritz (37), Department of Anthropology, State University of New York at Binghamton, Binghamton, New York 13901

William H. Isbell (303), Department of Anthropology, State University of New York at Binghamton, Binghamton, New York 13901

Gregory A. Johnson (87), Department of Anthropology, Hunter College of C.U.N.Y., New York, New York 10021

Thomas F. King* (225, 431), Office of Archeology and Historic Preservation, National Park Service, Washington, D. C. 20005

Mark P. Leone (25), Department of Anthropology, University of Maryland, College Park, Maryland 20742

Charles R. McGimsey III (415), Arkansas Archeological Survey Coordinating Office, Department of Anthropology, University of Arkansas Museum, Fayetteville, Arkansas 72701

Craig Morris (315), Department of Anthropology, American Museum of Natural History, New York, New York 10024

Fred Plog (349, 421), Department of Anthropology, Arizona State University, Tempe, Arizona 85281

* Present address: Micronesian Archeological Survey, Division of Lands and Surveys, Trust Territory of the Pacific Islands, Saipan, Mariana Islands 96950.

William L. Rathje (373), Department of Anthropology, University of Arizona, Tucson, Arizona 85721

Charles L. Redman (1, 159, 329), Department of Anthropology, State University of New York at Binghamton, Binghamton, New York 13901

William T. Sanders (249), Department of Anthropology, The Pennsylvania State University, University Park, Pennsylvania 16802

Eugene L. Sterud (381), Archaeological Institute of America, New York, New York 10007

Nina M. Versaggi (1), Department of Anthropology, State University of New York at Binghamton, Binghamton, New York 13901

Jeffery C. Wanser (1), Department of Anthropology, State University of New York at Binghamton, Binghamton, New York 13901

Patty Jo Watson (131), Department of Anthropology, Washington University, St. Louis, Missouri 63130

David Webster (249), Department of Anthropology, The Pennsylvania State University, University Park, Pennsylvania 16802

Rex L. Wilson (439), Office of Archeology and Historic Preservation, National Park Service, Washington, D. C. 20240

Gary A. Wright (201), Department of Anthropology, State University of New York at Albany, Albany, New York 12222

Preface

Archeology is an active, growing, and constantly changing discipline. The work of archeologists has taken many different directions, each claimed to be useful and innovative. Out of this diversity of efforts, we identify a basic overall trend and for the sake of communication give it a name, *social archeology*. The essential aspect of this trend is the combination of increasing methodological rigor and sophistication with a concern for addressing meaningful cultural questions. The authors of each of the chapters in this volume do not necessarily agree with this abstraction, but we, the editors, identify their works as contributing to the overall trend.

Each of the following chapters is published here for the first time. Shorter versions of most of the chapters were presented as parts of three symposia organized to characterize the advancement of archeology. Two of the symposia, "Archeology in Anthropology I: Changing Organization Structure" and "Archeology in Anthropology II: Broadening Subject Matter" were organized by Charles L. Redman for the 74th Annual Meeting of the American Anthropological Association. The third symposium, "Problems in Archeology: Studies of Process and Social Differentiation" was organized by all of the editors of this volume and held at the State University of New York at Binghamton. The Department of Anthropology, associated graduate organization, and university administration were generous in their support of this symposium.

Our special thanks go to the authors of each of the chapters and to the many other scholars who have dedicated themselves to improving the conduct of archeology and to making it an exciting discipline.

chapter 1

Social Archeology: The Future of the Past

CHARLES L. REDMAN, EDWARD CURTIN,
NINA VERSAGGI, JEFFERY WANSER

The roots of social archeology extend into the substrate of archeological history. Its fundamental elements are not new, but we believe that this volume is among the first to express this in an integrated, published form. We perceive of social archeology as a diverse, yet integratable, approach for bringing together the new goals and advanced techniques of contemporary archeologists by operationalizing methods that have hitherto only been discussed on paper. *Hence, it is the combination of increasing methodological expertise and meaningful interpretations that characterize social archeology.*

There is a growing concern to explicate methods, expand interpretive scope, and contribute substantively to social science. Applications of hypothesis testing, systems theory, geographic and economic models, statistics, and other formal techniques are some of the approaches being employed. The focus on methods in social archeology has demanded a multiple-factor approach to deal with the complexities of the societies being investigated and the related archeological data base. In order to put the substantive examples of social archeology contained in this volume

1

Social Archeology:
Beyond Subsistence and Dating

into a historical context, we describe our perspective on the nature of frustrations that stimulated social archeological thinking, present some of the past achievements of archeologists who have escaped the implicit limitations of traditional kinds of research, and offer several recent examples of studies that we consider to be social archeology.

Some may ask why there is a development toward social archeology. We perceive the emerging trends in this direction as a response by the discipline to the frustrations building during the past decades. By frustration, we refer to the feeling of many archeologists that the discipline isn't doing enough, that it isn't saying enough about our subject matter, and that archeologists aren't being listened to by the rest of anthropology. Archeologists have found it particularly difficult to understand nonmaterial aspects of past sociocultural systems. Part of this problem derives from the historical orientation of our discipline.

Many archeological studies of the mid-twentieth century (ca. 1935–1960) were concerned with the artifact as an entity separate from meaningful cultural context. Analysis focused on compilations of traits and comparisons among sequences. Other works examined the artifact within its regional context and analyzed similarities and differences among these geographic cultures. The scope of research narrowed in subsequent studies to microvariations of artifact traits over time and space. As the artifact took on more interpretational significance for inferring human behavior, the concentration shifted to techniques of analysis. Perfecting methods of extracting and interpreting information from artifacts and their local and regional contexts presently consumes much of the research energies of archeologists.

By dealing primarily with results of direct observation, archeologists often restricted themselves to the more mundane aspects of past social systems—chronology, the history of technology, and subsistence. In this way archeologists have made major substantive contributions to the overall understanding of hunting and gathering societies where other sources of information are limited. The more complex the society's organization, moving from hunting and gathering to state societies, the less archeologists seem to say about their subjects, leaving major cultural insights to be derived from other disciplines. This tendency has been compounded by the stress on technology and environment, both in the nature of archeological data recovery and our major interpretive framework, culture evolutionism. Consequently, our explanations and interpretations often involved simplistic models of linear causality related to environment or technology, only tangentially dealing with "social" factors.

The results of this orientation have been a proliferation of studies that lack interesting interpretive content by not convincingly relating archeological research results to questions of general anthropological importance. Studies that concentrate on rigorous techniques of data recovery and analysis frequently have not been conducted within a meaningful anthropological framework. Their results can go no farther than demonstrating technical sophistication. At the other extreme, many studies that do address general anthropological issues cannot concretely support their conclusions on the basis of their research.

For much of the history of archeology, explicitly justified research methods have been lacking (Clarke 1968:xiii). Archeologists have inferred causal relationships on the basis of simple analogies instead of explicitly defined testable models, intuitive generalizations rather than systematic documentation, and plausible reconstructions as opposed to rigorous testing. While the problem of adequate methodology has to some extent been alleviated by the critical self-consciousness of the 1960s, the full applicability of the methods has yet to be explored. This, we feel, is just occurring now.

The frustrations felt by many archeologists during the last 30 years were voiced long ago by Walter Taylor in A *Study of Archaeology* (1948). Taylor was critical of American archeology of the 1940s, its preoccupation with time–space systematics, its artifact orientation, its lack of integration with the rest of anthropology, and its seeming inability to deal with the nonmaterial aspects of culture. As a result, he created a programmatic statement of goals and approaches, which he called "the Conjunctive Approach," stressing the relationships among artifacts rather than the artifacts themselves, and the notion of culture as an integrated whole instead of as a list of traits. The statement suffered, unfortunately, by the lack of immediate follow-up studies using those concepts. A *Study of Archaeology* did, however, have an enormous intellectual impact on later works, among others those of Lewis Binford (1962, 1965).

Christopher Hawkes' (1954) perception of the nature of archeology was more resigned to the concept of a limited archeology. In creating a graded scale of difficulty of reasoning and inference, he noted the following series of data categories with which archeologists concern themselves:

1. Technology—relatively easy to make inferences about, but tedious to study
2. Subsistence economics—fairly easy to infer, but laborious
3. Sociopolitical institutions—considerably harder to interpret
4. Religious institutions and spiritual life—the most difficult kind of inference.

Because, by his estimation, the latter two categories are nearly impossible to approach systematically in archeology, the discipline would be forever concerned with the mundane aspects of society.

Grahame Clark (1957), in *Archaeology and Society*, put forth a viewpoint contrasting with Hawkes by expressing an optimism about the ability of the discipline to understand nonmaterial aspects of culture:

> Prehistorians may well envy their anthropological colleagues their ability to study directly the social organization of the living "primitive" peoples with whom they are concerned, but they need not despair of recovering at least some information in this crucial matter [p. 219].

In spite of this optimism, however, technology, subsistence, and chronology remained the primary focus of archeologists either by choice or constraint.

Another positive approach, although also lacking a rigorous methodology, was offered by William Sears (1961). In his criticism of the archeological discipline, he stated

> Through a sort of feed-back reaction that causes archaeologists already engaged in this work (time–space systematics) to see only more problems of the same sort, the known content of many archaeological "cultures" in the United States is limited entirely to ceramic types, or includes only a few types of artifacts [p. 223].

Unfortunately, Sears accepted MacWhite's (1956) premise that the more complex and processual questions should be studied only after an adequate chronology, consisting of an outline of the development and diffusion of types, had been achieved. This attitude in particular has been very damaging to systematic research into the nonmaterial aspects of culture; it simply puts off the question until some later date.

Sears, however, saw a hopeful approach in the settlement pattern studies of the time (Sanders 1956; Willey 1956), especially in their regional view and problem orientation. He also offered a number of interesting techniques for dealing with problems of social and religious organization (the burial mound as a fossilized ceremony, concept of the community pattern). Once again, ethnographic analogy and plausible reconstruction were offered as the overarching methodology linking an aggregate of separate techniques. Nevertheless, Sears was confident that new approaches would be discovered:

> A prehistoric social system cannot be excavated like a house, nor can it be studied with the techniques used to define ceramic complexes or to erect ceramic chonologies. Through excavation and other methods, archaeologists can collect and record evidence that can be used in the study of social systems, and they can develop techniques for such study if their research is oriented toward social problems [p. 225].

More recently, David Clarke (1968) expressed his concern over inexplicitly formulated methodology: "Archaeology is an undisciplined empirical discipline [xiii]." Without new methods of analysis, he felt, archeological theory could not expand efficiently, since a modern empirical discipline ought to be able to aim at more rewarding results than the piling up of data and a steady output of imitation history. While Clarke refers to all of archeological research, it is painfully evident in his book that archeologists have dealt least effectively with that portion of the discipline concerned with nonmaterial aspects of culture. Clarke proposed a systematic and elaborate conceptual framework, aimed at making methods more operable.

One of the most pointed of recent criticisms of archeology's ability to understand more than subsistence and chronology is Edmund Leach's "Concluding Address" in *The Explanation of Culture Change: Models in Prehistory* (Renfrew 1973). Leach labeled "new" archeology as an essentially functional and behavioristic approach, similar to Malinowski's work of 50 years ago. Just as Malinowski had difficulty with religion and symbolism, so must functionalist archeologists have in focusing more on the problems of economics and demography. Leach then compared archeological inference to the cybernetic "black box," the inner workings of which cannot be discerned. Leach's key point is that the irrational and unpredictable nature of human behavior leaves the archeologist with nothing more to know except what goes into the black box and what comes out.

Leach's cynicism is much different from the frustrations felt by most archeologists. According to Leach, archeologists attempt too much rather than not enough. He emphasizes the inherent differences between studies of contemporary versus past societies. We acknowledge differences but deny that they irrevocably limit the inferences of the archeologists. No social anthropologist or archeologist has ever seen a social structure. Both may make inferences about social structure based on controlled observations, and both can contribute to social science.

Albert Spaulding (1973) suggests that the problem is not that archeologists do too much or too little, but that they rely too heavily on "mouth talk" (Service 1969). That is, archeologists' methodological rigor has too often been subject to standards archeologists as a body have derived from intuitive and often mistaken beliefs about science, rather than to an objective and informed perception of scientific method. Spaulding suggests that archeologists be careful, explicit, informed, and logical, as well as innovative; his comments agree to a large extent with our idea of social archeology, as related in the following discussion.

In spite of the frustrations archeologists have had and still have with regard to the extraction of information from their data base, this set of resources is unique in its potential utility to social science. First, because of their geographic range and time depth, archeological examples increase the number of societies in which behavioral patterns can be examined. Archeology is neither restricted to recorded history nor the ethnographic present. Second, because of the great time depth involved, archeologists can study long-term processes of sociocultural evolution and change over many years or lifetimes. Fred Plog (1974) has emphasized the potential of this aspect of research. In *The Study of Prehistoric Change*, Plog states, "I believe that the basic question to which we should address ourselves is: Why do cultures change as they do? Why are some instances of change slow and others rapid? Why are some accomplished with great ease and others with only the greatest difficulty [p. 9]?"

Robert Braidwood (1968) has also strongly suggested this avenue by outlining several important, prehistoric cultural transformations of major concern. These transformations are nonrecurrent phenomena in the evolution of *Homo sapiens*. Braidwood outlines them: (*a*) the appearance and evolution of man as a toolmaker; (*b*) the appearance and evolution of anatomically modern *Homo sapiens*; (*c*) the transformation from food collecting to food producing and the origin and spread of early farming villages; (*d*) the growth of urbanism and origins of civilization; and (*e*) the characteristics and spread of early civilization.

The combination of disappointingly mundane research results with the unrealized potential of archeology's unique resource base has led to considerable disillusionment among concerned scholars. The interpretive inadequacies of archeology can also be related to self-imposed restriction engendered by choice of subject matter and explanatory frameworks. In situations where archeologists have employed sophisticated methods and have attempted far-reaching interpretations, the mode of explanation often relied on linear causality with the situations being confined to "simpler" societies. For these societies it is often implicitly believed that fewer variables come into play, therefore presenting a more understandable system for interpretation. As a result, model-building and nomothetic techniques of analysis have been concentrated on remains of hunter–gatherers and primitive agriculturalists, leaving issues concerning more "complex" archeological societies impoverished in method and theory. This means that archeology has been bypassing many opportunities to perform studies and obtain results of direct relevance to problems in the world today. We believe that one of the most significant orientations of social archeologists is to remedy this situation.

At the present time, social archeology can be more accurately characterized than defined. Primarily, social archeology is a growing awareness of the critical importance of the application of careful and explicit methods to substantive problems of widespread interest. This position holds that successful archeology is evaluated on the content and applicability of its results. The logic of science requires that procedures are at all points explicit, including clear statements of goals, problems, methods, techniques, and interpretations. Speculation is diminished, and aspects of the procedures are coherently linked, leaving a minimum to the imagination of the observer.

The essence of the recent controversy over archeological epistemology has been over whether or not explicitly scientific methodology is either sufficient or necessary to understanding in archeology. There are two results from this quandry:

1. Many archeologists have offered theoretical statements that far outstrip the sophistication of archeological methods.
2. Interpretations of data are often qualified as speculative and tentative.

Frequently, it is felt that not enough data are available to make strong theoretical statements. The idea that we should not interpret the information at hand until more data have accrued has been with us for a long time, representing archeology as a theoretically timid discipline on too many occasions. This juxtaposition of archeologists of the "theoretically bold" and "theoretically timid" varieties is important, in light of the growth of methodological sophistication. Methodological sophistication is the necessary element in making theories supportable while at the same time militating against speculative formulations.

Through the recent conduct of archeology, the foundations of social archeology have appeared without there being a name for this emerging set of aims, methodologies, and governing principles. There was a common feeling that archeology was inadequately dealing with the social aspects of past societies. Nevertheless, archeology suffered with the rest of anthropology in not having clear, working ideas about how to study social phenomena (Martin, Longacre, Hill 1967).

As early as 1935, V. Gordon Childe proposed that the study of past societies should be the aim of archeology. In his later writings (1951, 1958) he recognized a direction of great significance to the discipline. Childe believed that by concentrating on the study of social systems, important patterns and regularities could be discerned.

Lamenting that the archeology of their day was not living up to its potential, Steward and Setzler (1938) suggested that a study of greater scope was desirable and achievable: "Candor would seem to compel the admission that archaeology could be made much more pertinent to gen-

eral cultural studies if we paused to take stock of its possibilities [p. 6]."
Steward and Setzler argued that it was necessary for archeologists to
attempt to answer some of the "great questions" facing anthropological
research. Concern with the relatively undirected study of taxonomic
minutiae would make no significant impact on the discipline in the long
run, save to provide a sense of classificatory elegance. Nevertheless,
much energy went into such activities. Steward and Setzler suggested that
if archeologists ceased to view systematics as the intellectual end of their
endeavors, sociocultural phenomena could be more directly approached.

Grahame Clark also made early efforts at interpreting archeological
phenomena in a social mode, asking more of the archeological record
than spatial diffusions and chronological sequences (Clark 1939, 1947,
1957). His work reveals a history of interpretation derived from various
lines of reasoning: ethnographic analogy, environmental reconstructions,
and studies of technology. Clark's aim has continually been the observation of interrelationships among the factors in human sociocultural adaptation, to the extent that he has been able to discern them in the
archeological record (cf. Clark 1970).

Further efforts were made by Willey and Phillips (1958) to develop
an interpretive context. Their statement "American archaeology is anthropology or it is nothing [p. 2]" set the mood for greater achievements
by unequivocally categorizing archeology as a generalizing social science. However, nothing was necessarily gained by making archeology
into anthropology. In proposing that archeologists ask why, Willey and
Phillips made the discipline take serious note of its intentions. Nevertheless, the focus of most archeologists remained the study of normality. For
both archeology and anthropology, the important processes in continuity
and change could not be studied without a proper context for describing
and explaining variability within and among the various units of analysis.

One step in this direction during the early 1960s was Lewis Binford's
rigorous approach to the question of "archeology as anthropology" (1962,
1965, 1968). Binford outlined an analytical approach to the study of
sociocultural phenomena in general while at the same time being keenly
aware of the utility and role of anthropological studies in understanding
human behavior. In discussing his three major classes of artifacts—
technomic, sociotechnic, and ideotechnic—he identified social subsystems of the total cultural system as important targets for studying the
relationships between technology and changing social organization
within a society.

> I would consider the study of the establishment of correlations between types
> of social structure classified on the basis of behavioral attributes and structural
> types of material elements as one of the major areas of anthropological
> research yet to be developed [1962:220].

Binford (1965), in "Archaeological Systematics and the Study of Culture Process," criticized the "normative" approach in archeology, taking his contemporaries to task for characterizing episodes of cultural change and continuity by means of changes in the most "typical" classes of artifacts, or their assumed behavioral correlates. His assertion that culture is not so much shared as participated in differentially has far-reaching implications for social archeology.

During the last decade, attempts have been made to bring together theory and techniques in order to gain a fuller understanding of the important issues reflected in archeology's data base. We have characterized this trend toward increasing methodological expertise combined with meaningful interpretations as *social archeology*. Currently, we see five components of social archeology: (a) the use of explicit models; (b) the integration of single-cause and multivariate explanations; (c) the recognition of a broader data base; (d) research into the importance of both the individual and normative factors in society; and (e) the application of quantitative techniques and simulation models. These five areas are largely methodological trends. Although much of the pioneering work in these areas was carried out by "new archeologists," we believe that contributions to social archeology include a wider spectrum of scholars.

Social archeologists rely heavily on the use of *explicit models* to organize theoretical, methodological, and interpretive approaches to specific research problems. Frequently the structure or form of these models is borrowed from a sister discipline and is modified to fit archeological goals, problems, and data. Modifications may be warranted by the model being tested in a new geographic or ecological context, due to the fact that the data are derived from an extinct cultural adaptation. The application of an already formulated model to an archeological context should not be construed as uninteresting because almost always the reuse will add new dimensions to the explanatory value of the original idea. Some of the important explicit models recently used by archeologists include decision models (Jochim 1976, Wright 1969); locational models (Crumley 1976, G. Johnson 1972; F. Plog and Hill 1971; style or design interaction models (Deetz 1965; Hill 1970; Longacre 1970; S. Plog 1976; Whallon 1972); cognitive process models (Kehoe and Kehoe 1973) and information theoretic models (Justeson 1973).

Decision models have been used to specify hierarchical relations in the organization or implementation of labor (Wright 1969) or to isolate factors that may be used in weighting a model for site locations and functions (Jochim 1976). In testing such a model, it is found that many kinds of data are required—locational, faunal, lithic, or ceramic, for instance—and that auxiliary techniques may be required for operationalizing the implications of the model. This was very much the case for Jochim, who relied on faunal, locational, and lithic data to test a model based on hunter–gatherer behavior and animal ethology, and for Wright, who relied heavily on ceramic analysis and literary sources.

Similarly, the locational research design devised by Fred Plog and James Hill (1971) intended not only to identify the determinants of site location but to provide a standardized form for the observation and comparison of intraregional land use and interaction. Gregory Johnson's (1972) central place model allows the observation of the growth of urban systems in Mesopotamia in a formal, systematic mode, although questions of economic, political, and ritual behavior are only dealt with indirectly. Carole Crumley (1976) argues that it is difficult to apply central place models to nonmodern examples and that there are many criteria (e.g., economic, political, and ritual) for defining the "central" nature of a site. Crumley proposes a typology of settlements related to state levels of organization. She defines concepts of functional center and functional lattice in relation to the specific processes through which they interact, such as, trading, agricultural production, religion, or military activity.

Explicit models are also being employed in ceramic studies. The results of new applications of ceramic studies are widely felt because of the traditional recognition of the importance of ceramics in chronological studies and the roles of potsherds as transmitters of "influence" or the hallmarks of "contact." The essential question for both traditional and social perspectives is, What do ceramic styles tell us about processes? Early design element studies aimed at constructing models of change (i.e., Deetz 1965; Hill 1970; Longacre 1970); borrowed the concepts of tradition, enculturation, residence, and group membership from social anthropology. Confidence was lost, at least in the conclusions of these studies, when their assumptions and methods were called into question. The relevance of design element studies is not obviated by the shortcomings of these early studies, and refinement and reorientation of the approach continues (S. Plog 1976).

Drawing on many methods and seeking diverse behavioral information facilitates the *multivariate explanation* of cultural phenomena under investigation. An attempt to apply this approach to solve an old problem has been made by Wright and Johnson (1975). Wright and Johnson propose a model of state formation that emphasizes interaction and exchange between centers and satellites, administrative development, and boundary maintenance among political systems. Another multivariate approach has been taken by Kent Flannery and his coworkers in *The Early Mesoamerican Village*. Flannery (1976) has explicitly identified units of analysis, such as the household, the community, the catchment area, and the region, studying the integration of scales in many dimensions (exchange, social interaction, ritual) to provide a comprehensive view of Formative adaptations in Mesoamerica.

Recent directions that are *broadening archeology's subject matter* include ethnoarcheology (ethnographic work testing essentially archeological models) and experimental archeology (the replication of technology, and processes such as tool manufacture or extractive techniques, providing controls for assumptions about and reconstructions of past behaviors). These new sources of data available to social archeologists may be used to generate new models or to clarify ambiguities in existing models. Illustrating the latter instance, multivariate ceramic studies based on explicit models have been used to broaden our understanding of the meaning of ceramic variability. Investigating the ways in which modern potters manufacture their wares, plus the ways in which modern populations use and discard pots provides information about contexts and conditions of ceramic-related behavior (Friedrich 1970; Schiffer 1976; Stanislawski 1969a, b; Stanislawski, Hitchcock, and Stanislawski 1976). Nicholas David's (1971, 1972; David and Hennig 1972) investigations of contemporary Fulani raise questions for the analyses of both settlement patterns and ceramics. For ceramics, David provided a controlled example for measuring the rate of discarding broken pots; in addition, the observations included in his study allowed him to make significant statements about the training and identity of potters, the statuses of potters, and the correlation of wares with ethnic groups and means of exchange. The works of Stanislawski, Friedrich and David refine archeologists' assumptions about ceramics and their uses and help to clarify the relevance of ceramics as data. Ethnoarcheological work has pointed archeological ceramic studies in directions that indicate how certain classifications and descriptions of contexts mask the observation of the processes under study. Additionally, some measure of confidence has been demonstrated for the utility of an archeological perspective in technical–sociological studies.

The premise that archeological methods are directly applicable to studying the "material culture" of the present and recent past has directed innovative research. Bert Salwen's (1973) investigations of dorm room arrangements and grocery sales patterns are clearly archeological and provide insight into modern behavior. William Rathje's nationally famous "Garbage Project" has shown similarly interesting patterns of household consumption and waste (Chapter 16, this volume). The use of such studies may be profitable for marketing strategies as well as for individual household kitchen economy or the use of living space.

Ethnoarcheological research into the mode of community organization provides information on the ways in which various people use space and materials. Mark Leone's (1973) study of house locations and fence patterns has much to say about frontier ecology and Mormon ideology. Carol Kramer's (1976) and Patty Jo Watson's (Chapter 7, this volume) research leads to conclusions about the use of household space, building structures, and socioeconomic classes in a Middle Eastern farming village.

Replicative experiments have appeared in recent years also, especially in the area of lithic analysis. Following Semenov (1964), microscopic analysis of wear patterns is employed in experiments in order to provide information on variables such as properties of raw materials, effects of abrasive agents, frequency of tool use, type of use, and motor habits in manufacture and use. Tringham, Cooper, Odell, Voyteck and Whitman (1974) have devised detailed experimental procedures as well as classes of edge damage and use modification. Another approach, complementary to wear analysis, is the statistical simulation of lithic assemblages under various conditions (Ammerman and Feldman 1974).

The study of the manufacture, allocation, use, and disuse of materials ranging from flint tools and clay pots to houses and gardens enhances the ability of the archeologist to make assumptions about tradition, enculturation, economy of materials, economy of effort, and so on (Schiffer 1976). The exploration of more contemporary and experimental data is providing archeologists with interpretive insights and hypothesis test implications not available in the analysis of materials from long-abandoned sites.

Not only are archeologists exploring a broader range of data, but also the foci of study are being enlarged. Of late, several attempts have been made to study the *role of the individual* and the functions of rule systems in prehistoric societies (Hill and Gunn 1977). James Hill (1977) is using ceramic decoration in an attempt to correlate stresses on individual potters with external environmental perturbations, hypothesizing that potters would err in their work more often with an increase in environmental stress. Robert McC. Adams (1974) has also examined the individual initiative in order to understand the roles of entrepreneurs and interest groups in the communication and initiation of sociocultural change in the formation of urban society. The question of whether the activities of any single individual can ever be identified in archeology may or may not be answered, but archeologists may agree that analytical units on an analogous scale to the individual could prove effective (Redman 1977).

In addition to investigating the role of the individual in culture change, some archeologists are attempting to delineate the impact of *belief systems* on ancient societies. Robert Hall (1976) has used a comparison of widely held beliefs concerning the effects of circles and water on ghosts to suggest implications for site structures (the positions of houses, earthworks, and graveyards) in Eastern Woodland archeology. Hall's arguments are based on the recognition that social norms and beliefs exert tremendous control over organized behavior, and that the affects of belief systems and normative behavior leave recognizable patterning in the archeological record. Cautions concerning dabbling in "paleopsychology" or the limited effectiveness of studying normative behavior should not disuade archeologists from realizing the important ramifications of cognitive or rule systems models, so long as they are testable and systematically formulated.

Another cognitive study has been done by Kehoe and Kehoe (1973), which focuses on burial practices in the eastern woodlands. They argue that the least effective normalizing aspect of burial studies has been archeological typologizing. Burial practices will be better understood when archeologists realize that although some conservative, regulating factors operate in burial customs, they are not transmitted to all groups in the same way over time and space. Change occurs when environmental factors and differential modes of participation provide altered stimuli in the formation of so-called cognitive maps, thus affecting the definition of appropriate behavior.

Multivariate approaches are enhanced by *quantitative techniques*, especially as these techniques are used to construct simulation models. Archeologists have always been concerned with quantification to some extent, and in the mid-1970s this trend resulted in the publication of statistical textbooks for archeologists (Doran and Hodson 1975; Thomas 1976). Techniques range from counts and percentages to multivariate statistics and computer methods. Quantification substantiates scientific statements in an explicit manner. Modeling techniques, such as computer simulation, facilitate the construction of multivariate models as well as test implications for evaluation.

Among the best known archeological simulation models are those of Thomas (1972), Wobst (1974), and Zubrow (1971). The Wobst study determined the minimal band size in a dynamic equilibrium system for paleolithic hunter–gatherers. Marriage rules, diet, birth rate, territory, and death rate were variables that specified the conditions of the system. Zubrow examined another dynamic equilibrium system, considering population growth and carrying capacity for a population of prehistoric southwestern agriculturalists. His simulation showed population overshooting carrying capacity at a time immediately before other evidence shows that the region was abandoned. Thomas (1972, 1973) investigated the relations among the seasonal importance of scheduling behavior, site locations, and group compositions. The latter two factors appear as constants, however, and the actual simulations were run on variables defined in the subsistence strategy. Thomas's work supported in large part the ethnohistorical reconstruction of Julian Steward (1938) while reconstructing the precontact situation. Simulation techniques are a quantitative method for constructing multivariate models. Models may also be drawn from tested situations in other disciplines, or from archeology's expanding awareness of the content and uses of its own data base.

Social archeology is not meant to be exclusionist, nor is it proposed in opposition to previous approaches. Rather, we view it as a still loosely defined direction toward which many researchers are moving in order to remedy some of the shortcomings of previous research. Which of the aspects of social archeology we have outlined will prove to be successful and which will be discarded must be based on reliable interpretative results that are of interest to a broad spectrum of scholars. We believe that the investigations described here and the chapters in this volume are, among others, the test cases of social archeology.

REFERENCES

Adams, Robert McC.
    1974   Anthropological perspectives on ancient trade. *Current Anthropology* 15: 239–258.
Ammerman, Albert J., and Marcus W. Feldman
    1974   On the "making" of an assemblage of stone tools. *American Antiquity* 39: 610–616.
Binford, Lewis R.
    1962   Archaeology as anthropology. *American Antiquity* 28: 217–225.
    1965   Archaeological systematics and the study of culture process. *American Antiquity* 31: 203–210.
    1968   Post-Pleistocene adaptations. In *New perspectives in archeology*, edited by L. R. Binford and S. Binford. Chicago: Aldine. Pp. 314–342.
Braidwood, Robert J.
    1968   Archeology: An introduction. *Encyclopaedia Britannica* 2: 225–227.
Childe, V. Gordon
    1951   *Man makes himself.* New York: Mentor.
    1958   *The prehistory of European society.* London: Penguin.
Clark, Grahame
    1939   *Archaeology and society.* London: Methuen.
    1947   *Archaeology and society.* (2nd ed.) London: Methuen.
    1957   *Archaeology and society.* (3rd ed.) London: Methuen.
    1970   *Aspects of prehistory.* Berkeley, Calif.: University of California Press.
Clarke, David
    1968   *Analytical archaeology.* London: Methuen.
Crumley, Carole L.
    1976   Toward a locational definition of state systems of settlement. *American Anthropologist* 78: 59–73.

David, Nicholas
1971 The Fulani compound and the archaeologist. *World Archaeology* 3(2): 111–131.
1972 On the lifespan of pottery, type frequencies, and archaeological inference. *American Antiquity* 37: 141–142.
David, Nicholas, and Hilke Hennig
1972 The ethnography of pottery: A Fulani case seen in archaeological perspective. *Addison-Wesley Module* No. 21.
Deetz, James
1965 The dynamics of stylistic change in Arikara ceramics. Urbana, Ill.: Univ. of Illinois Press.
Doran, J. E., and F. R. Hodson
1975 *Mathematics and computers in archaeology*. Cambridge, Mass.: Harvard Univ. Press.
Flannery, Kent V. (Ed.)
1976 *The early Mesoamerican village*. New York: Academic.
Freidrich, Margaret Hardin
1970 Design structure and social interaction: Archaeological implications of an ethnographic analysis. *American Antiquity* 35: 332–343.
Hall, Robert L.
1976 Ghosts, water barriers, corn, and sacred enclosures in the eastern woodlands. *American Antiquity* 41: 360–364.
Hawkes, Christopher
1954 Archaeological theory and method: Some suggestions from the Old World. *American Anthropologist* 56: 155–168.
Hill, James N.
1970 *Broken K pueblo: Prehistoric social organization in the American Southwest. Anthropological Papers of the University of Arizona* No. 18.
1977 Individual variability in ceramics and the study of prehistoric social organization. In *The Individual in Prehistory*, edited by J. N. Hill and J. Gunn. New York: Academic. Pp. 55–108.
Hill, James N., and Joel Gunn (Eds.)
1977 *The individual in prehistory*. New York: Academic.
Jochim, Michael A.
1976 Hunter–gatherer subsistence and settlement. New York: Academic.
Johnson, Gregory A.
1972 A test of the utility of central place theory in archaeology. In *Man, settlement and urbanism*, edited by P. J. Ucko, R. Tringham, and G. W. Dimbleby. London: Duckworth. Pp. 769–785.
Justeson, John S.
1973 Limitations of archaeological inference: an information-theoretic approach with application in methodology. *American Antiquity* 38: 131–149.
Kehoe, Alice B., and Thomas F. Kehoe
1973 Cognitive models for archaeological interpretation. *American Antiquity* 38: 150–154.
Kramer, Carol
1976 An archaeological view of a contemporary Kurdish village. Paper presented in the symposium "Ethnoarchaeology: Implications of ethnography for archaeology," organized by Carol Kramer for the 75th annual meeting of the American Anthropological Association, Washington, D. C., November 17–21, 1976.
Leach, Edmund R.
1973 Concluding address. In *The explanation of culture change*, edited by C. Renfrew. London: Duckworth.

Leone, Mark P.
   1973   Archeology as the science of technology: Mormon town plans and fences. In
           Research and theory in current archaeology, edited by C. L. Redman. New York:
           Wiley-Interscience. Pp. 125–150.
Longacre, William A.
   1970   Archaeology as anthropology: A case study. Anthropological Papers of the Univer-
           sity of Arizona No. 17.
MacWhite, Eoin
   1956   On the interpretation of archaeological evidence in historical and sociological
           terms. American Anthropologist 58: 26–39.
Martin, Paul S., William A. Longacre, and James N. Hill
   1967   Chapters in the prehistory of eastern Arizona, III. Fieldiana, Anthropology 57.
           Chicago: Field Museum of Natural History.
Plog, Fred T.
   1974   The study of prehistoric change. New York: Academic.
Plog, Fred T., and James N. Hill
   1971   Explaining variability in the distribution of sites. In The distribution of prehistoric
           population aggregates, edited by G. J. Gumerman. Anthropological Reports No.
           1. Prescott, Ariz. Prescott College Press. Pp. 7–36.
Plog, Stephen
   1976   Measurement of prehistoric interaction between communities. In The early
           Mesoamerican village, edited by K. V. Flannery. New York: Academic. Pp.
           255–272.
Redman, Charles L.
   1977   The "analytical individual" and prehistoric style variability. In The individual in
           prehistory, edited by J. N. Hill and J. Gunn. New York: Academic. Pp. 41–53.
Renfrew, Colin (Ed.)
   1973   The explanation of culture change. London: Duckworth.
Salwen, Bert
   1973   Archeology in megalopolis. In Research and theory in current archeology, edited
           by C. L. Redman. New York: Wiley-Interscience. Pp. 151–163.
Sanders, William T.
   1956   The Central Mexican Symbiotic Region. In Prehistoric Settlement Patterns in the
           New World, edited by G. R. Willey. New York: Viking Fund Publications in
           Anthropology No. 23.
Schiffer, Michael
   1976   Behavioral archeology. New York: Academic.
Sears, William H.
   1961   The study of social and religious systems in North American archaeology. Current
           Anthropology 2: 223–246.
Semenov, S. A.
   1964   Prehistoric technology. Bath, Great Britain: Adams and Dart.
Service, Elman R.
   1969   Models for the methodology of mouthtalk. Southwestern Journal of Anthropology
           25: 68–80.
Spaulding, Albert C.
   1973   Archeology in the active voice: The new anthropology. In Research and theory in
           current archeology, edited by C. L. Redman. New York: Wiley-Interscience. Pp.
           337–354.
Stanislawski, Michael B.
   1969a   The ethno-archaeology of Hopi pottery making. Plateau 42: 27–33.

1969b   What good is a broken pot? An experiment in Hopi-Tewa ethnoarchaeology. *Southwestern Lore 35:* 11–18.
Stanislawski, Michael B., Ann Hitchcock, and Barbara B. Stanislawski
1976   Identification marks on Hopi and Hopi-Tewa pottery. *Plateau 48:* 47–66.
Steward, Julian H.
1938   *Basin–plateau aboriginal sociopolitical groups.* Bureau of American Ethnology Bulletin No. 120. Smithsonian Institute.
Steward, Julian H., and Frank M. Setzler
1938   Function and configuration in archaeology. *American Antiquity 4:* 4–10.
Taylor, Walter W.
1948   *A study of archaeology. American Anthropological Association Memoir* No. 69.
Thomas, David H.
1972   A computer simulation model of Great Basin Shoshonean subsistence and settlement patterns. In *Models in archaeology,* edited by D. L. Clarke. London: Methuen. Pp. 671–704.
1973   An empirical test for Steward's model of Great Basin settlement patterns. *American Antiquity 38:* 155–176.
1976   *Figuring anthropology: First principles of probability and statistics.* New York: Holt, Rinehart and Winston.
Tringham, Ruth, Glenn Cooper, George Odell, Barbara Voyteck, and Anne Whitman
1974   Experimentation in the formation of edge damage: A new approach to lithic analysis. *Journal of Field Archaeology 1:* 171–196.
Whallon, Robert, Jr.
1972   A new approach to pottery typology. *American Antiquity 37:* 13–33.
Willey, Gordon R. (Ed.)
1956   *Prehistoric settlement patterns in the New World.* New York: *Viking Fund Publications in Anthropology* No. 23.
Willey, Gordon R., and Phillip Phillips
1958   *Method and theory in American archaeology.* Chicago: Univ. of Chicago Press.
Wobst, H. Martin
1974   Boundary conditions for Paleolithic social systems: A simulation approach. *American Antiquity 39:* 147–178.
Wright, Henry T.
1969   *The administration of rural production in an early Mesopotamian town. Museum of Anthropology University of Michigan Anthropological Papers* No. 38.
Wright, Henry T. and Gregory A. Johnson
1975   Population, exchange, and early state formation in southwestern Iran. *American Anthropologist 77:* 267–289.
Zubrow, Ezra B. W.
1971   Carrying capacity and dynamic equilibrium in the prehistoric Southwest. *American Antiquity 36:* 127–138.

PART I

Methodology

The seven chapters of this section illustrate methodological approaches currently being used by social archeologists in their analyses and interpretations of past social systems. Although these approaches deal with a variety of data bases and the archaeologists who use them have varying theoretical orientations, the approaches themselves emphasize one key phenomenon: information. This emphasis on information has three general foci. First, information is seen as a knowledge of contemporary peasant settlement patterns and population dynamics. From this knowledge ethnoarcheological models of settlement patterns and population dynamics can be developed for Neolithic groups inhabiting similar environmental zones. Second, information is conceived of as the maximal product of an analytical system that utilizes aspects of both the empiricist and the positivist approaches to one's research. Third, information, or more specifically information theory, is utilized as an organizational and communicational system in itself, through which one can analyze the evolutionary aspects of past cultural systems. Each of these foci is illustrated in greater detail in the following chapters.

Mark P. Leone presents in Chapter 2 a new interpretation of the concept of time in archeology, based on a reevaluation of the concepts of *ideotechnic* and *ideotechnic artifacts*. Leone introduces his presentation with a discussion of materialistic approaches to anthropology. He maintains that in classless societies there is no need for ideology and therefore ideotechnic artifacts. It's only with the development of stratified societies that there is a need for ideology to mask the true relationships of production. Leone further maintains that in complex societies ideotechnic artifacts are indicative of a conscious attempt to provide misinformation about the true relationships of production. Based upon these preliminary discussions, Leone explores the concept of time as an ideotechnic artifact constructed by the archeologist. This exploration provides a valuable insight into the conceptualization of time by the professional prehistorian.

John M. Fritz, in Chapter 3, explores the roles that ideational systems play in human societies as adaptive mechanisms. He believes that ideational systems contain culturally coded adaptive information that is triggered into action when the values of key variables reach critical limits. Fritz maintains that architecture is both a product and a component of ideational systems; it is a product of ideationally organized action, which in turn organizes the action and perception of those who experience it. He develops and explores these concepts further through an analysis of architecture in Chaco Canyon.

In Chapter 4, Margaret Conkey also deals with information theory and cultural evolution. She maintains that the development of stylistic behavior is an adaptive strategy employed by human groups to encode and decode information necessary to the integration and survival of the group. Conkey also believes that this development of stylistic behavior signals the beginning of the cultural evolution of *Homo sapiens sapiens* as we know the species today. She offers several examples to support her theory and stresses a need for the development of approaches to deal with stylistic behavior on the Paleolithic, an area that has previously been devoid of such studies.

Gregory A. Johnson (Chapter 5) uses information theory to develop a model for the evaluation of hierarchical decision-making organizations. He incorporates the concepts of information transfer and processing, requisite variety, and cost–benefit optimization to produce a model that enables him to analyze social organizations with varying degrees of complexity. Johnson then tests the model on both ethnological and archeological data. The results of these tests are highly suggestive of the value of using information-based models to study the evolution of both simple and complex societies.

Robert Evans' (Chapter 6) discusses the origin of craft specialization as an indicator of the evolution of complex society. He believes that the craft specialist would have at his disposal specific information that the large majority of the population would not have. In order to utilize this information, however, the craft specialist would have to withdraw from other activities, notably subsistence. Therefore, Evans feels that social differentiation as well as some form of social organization would develop to enable the craft specialist and his products to be integrated into the society. Evans explores this problem during the Chalcolithic period in the Balkans.

Patty Jo Watson (Chapter 7) presents an ethnoarcheological study that compares observations made on a contemporary Iranian peasant village with those made from a variety of archeological sites in Mesopotamia and Anatolia. In pursuing this research, Watson deals with what she believes are critical variables to the understanding of intravillage (intrasite) social organization. These variables fall broadly under the headings of spatial organization (size and shape of rooms, size and shape of entire dwelling, activity areas, etc.), population (humans per dwelling, humans per village, animals per dwelling, etc.) and status indicators (quality of dwellings, status artifacts, kerosene lamps, etc.). The application of a model developed from Watson's ethnographic study, which deals with these variables, to the archeological material enables her to draw conclusions about the basic residential–economic unit and about intravillage organization during the Neolithic period.

In Chapter 8, Charles L. Redman deals with information processing for the archeologist through a multivariate approach to artifact analysis. He maintains that processual archeologists have been limited by outdated methods for classifying and analyzing data. In order to obtain a maximum amount of information from recovered artifacts, current systems of classification and analysis must be reevaluated and restructured. To demonstrate this, Redman presents two organizational strategies that he used to derive organizational information from ceramic variability as discovered in a series of prehistoric pueblos in the American Southwest and in a medieval town in northern Morocco. Although he emphasizes that these procedures were developed for the two projects under discussion and should not be applied in a cookbook fashion to all sites, he believes that the principles underlying these organizational strategies are applicable to a wide range of investigations.

Although the chapters in this section emphasize information, they do so in a variety of ways. This variety is representative of several problem areas currently being addressed by members of the profession. First, there is a growing emphasis on further refinement of our model-building techniques through a more rigorous use of ethnoarcheological observations. Second, our analytical systems must be revised to obtain a maximal amount of information from the data. This problem area is given greater impetus because of the rapid destruction of our archeological resource base. Third, the growing use of information theory as a methodological tool is enabling greater insights into the evolution of complex societies. It is also providing insights into the evolution of human culture, writ large, and into the manner in which the archeologist interprets the past.

Taken together, the chapters in this section are indicative of the search for new methodological techniques. This search is characteristic of the growing concern on the part of social archeologists to develop and operationalize new methodologies in order to increase their interpretive scope and thus contribute substantively to social science. The methodologies presented in this section are examples of the social archeologist's ongoing commitment to the explanation of cultural processes.

chapter 2

Time in American Archeology

MARK P. LEONE ·

Archeology exists within our society's concepts of time and space, and all our findings take on meaning as a function of these vectors, not independently of them. We rarely examine how past societies conceived these dimensions, and we never ask how our own definitions of time and space influence our interpretations of other societies. Such an investigation, if done, would have to be vast and would be enormously worthwhile; here I want to raise some questions both about how archeological societies viewed time and about how our own society, the one that is parent to our own archeological interpretations, views the same dimension.

Although I want to concentrate on the meanings time can be given, I do not yet want to face the issue of whether or not all the notions of time we discover in the past are merely our own reflections. At least to begin with, I want to maintain the "objective" distinction between us and those who used to be. And to do that, I think we can begin by trying to extend Lewis Binford's now famous ideas on the levels of reality extant in any archeological society. Binford saw that society could be divided into levels

25

Social Archeology:
Beyond Subsistence and Dating

(i.e., economic, social, and ideological), and that productions—things, social relations, and ideas—were created in all these levels and took their function and meaning from how they operated in them. When applied to dead societies, this logic held that a society's artifacts, the only range of its productions still extant, must represent far more than mere utilitarian function. From this reasoning Binford created his now famous categories for recognizing levels of society in the archeological record: technomic, sociotechnic, ideotechnic. His distinction between primary and secondary function added the understanding that an artifact could have operated at more than one level in a culture. The whole pyramid of logic was created to conclude that an artifact has the potential to be used by archeologists to make statements about any level of an extinct society: It did not include all artifacts, but none were excluded a priori. We now had far greater accessibility to the past than we had ever had before.

This syllogism and a great deal of creative thinking produced very significant archeological analyses during the 1960s and 1970s. Some of the most controversial ideas came from people who identified sociotechnic items and attempted reconstructions of social relations. That effort was not, however, accompanied by any similar effort using the idea of an ideotechnic item to try a reconstruction of ideology. Part of the reason for this was that there was no definition of ideology except the old seat-of-the-pants notion that it was religion or philosophy or some other explicit code that was more or less epiphenomenal.

Since Binford's assumptions are materialist, we can go back to that tradition for a definition of ideology. And the term of importance first encountered in the search is not ideology but superstructure, which means "jurisdiction (acts and laws), institutions (amongst others the state)," as well as what we know conventionally as ideologies. All are in contradistinction to structure, which means "social relations, both structured and structural, determined by the basis and determining relations of ownership [Lefebvre 1971:31]." Although we can see that ideology is only a part of superstructure, it is not the contrast with its co-members that is important but the meaning given to it as a discrete entity that is useful for us here. For that I want to turn to Louis Althusser's adaptation of Marx's usage.

Althusser (1971) suggests that

> we can say the following: all ideology represents . . . not the existing relations of production . . . but above all the (imaginary) relationship of individuals to the relations of production. . . . What is represented in ideology is therefore not the system of the real relations which govern the existence of individuals, but the imaginary relation of those individuals to the real relations in which they live [p. 165].

Ideology is a mask and is not easily seen. To be sure, part of ideology is public and conscious belief—religion, philosophy, law, and so forth—but the major role of such explicit material is to disguise implicit ideology: Those notions and habits called the "obvious," the "given," the "taken for granted," and the "natural." Inside these domains, so difficult to pierce, reside the crucial assumptions that hide the real conditions of existence from any native. This is what ideology is.

Obviously, then, ideology can only exist when the real conditions of existence must remain hidden in order for the relations of production to remain intact. Ideology in the Marxist sense simply does not exist in societies without classes. Ideotechnic artifacts can not be identified as such or distinguished from sociotechnic items among hunter–gatherers or simple agriculturalists because there is no class conflict (and among hunter–gatherers no classes at all), consequently there is little or no need to hide or misrepresent any group's relationship to production. Ideotechnic items do not exist among societies studied by most new archeologists or most traditional ones either.

This is not to say that such societies do not have religion; they rather obviously do, but it is to say that such systems of representation, although they represent an imaginary world (Rappaport 1971) that is a reflection of the living world, do not misrepresent relationships in the living world. Religion in class or complex societies, however, contains within it a system of misrepresentation as well as a set of statements and practices that are true to standard sociological and anthropological insights. This structure of misrepresentation comes into existence only with classes, and, I suspect, ideotechnic items can be first found as isolable units with its occurrence. Ideotechnic artifacts are the artifacts of misrecognition or misidentification. In simpler societies a religious artifact stands for a supernatural or unempirical phenomenon and in turn is a reflection of the egalitarian or two-class (chief or priest and all others) social relationships that created it. Even though an artifact symbolizes the unempirical, that symbolization does not misspeak social and economic reality.

Upper Paleolithic cave art, which André Leroi-Gourhan (1968) has clearly shown is a complete and profound statement of world view, is instructive. It is an ideotechnic "item" but probably does not represent the masking function of ideology; it is most likely a direct reflection of socioeconomic relationships and as such would be extremely hard to segregate from sociotechnic items. As such, it is not that ideotechnic artifacts do not exist in unstratified societies, it is that they are amalgamated into the same class as sociotechnic items by the very structure of those societies. For analytical purposes, then, ideotechnic items can only be identified clearly with the emergence of a class structure.

In class societies, ideology's masking functions exist for the first time, and those functions sometimes take on a concrete form that can be identified in the archeological record. Here I do not mean that when we find a temple, shrine, or church, we have found an ideotechnic item, a crucifix or statue of a supernatural. These are no different from their analogues in simpler societies. Rather, the question is: What are the material remains of the given, the natural, and obvious? What are the material remains of masking and misrecognition? These are ideotechnic items and, once identified, will form a class recognizably distinct from those artifacts whose division between sociotechnic or ideotechnic we now remain unsure of.

The categories of ideology I would like to explore are our subdivisions of time: past, present, and future. The construction of times apart from the present moment is part of a more general phenomenon: the construction of a dual world. Such a world consists of the present, which is immediate and directly available to the senses, and another world, which is not so readily available but a view of which is well articulated and which is distinct from the here and now. Robert Bellah (1970:32–36) thinks that the dual world first appeared with the great historic religions, such as Buddhism and Christianity, but more precisely emerged with a general shift to hierarchical multiclass social structure: Complex societies have dual worlds and consequently ideology in the Marxist sense.

> The cosmological monism of [simpler societies] is more or less completely broken through and an entirely different realm of universal reality, having for religious man the highest value, is proclaimed. The criterion that distinguishes the historic religions . . . is that [they] are all in some sense transcendental. [The] supernatural realm [is] "above" this world in terms of both value and control . . . [and] for the masses, at least, the new dualism is expressed in the difference between this world and the life after death. Religious concern, focused on this life in primitive and archaic religions, now tends to focus on life in the other realm, which may be either infinitely superior or, in certain situations with the emergence of various conceptions of hell, infinitely worse. Under these circumstances the religious goal of salvation (or enlightenment, release, and so forth) is for the first time the central religious preoccupation [p. 32].

The dual world marks the invention of ideology as defined here and of one of its basic units, the segmented construct of time, which we are all familiar with. Time in the linear sense initially appears as a coherent future world. Future reality is utterly different and normally superior; it is that to which one heads, which one earns, and into which one escapes or seeks release. It has two important traits. In heading toward it or earning it, one reinterprets—misinterprets, if you want to think like a Marxist, but in any case, tolerates—the conditions of daily life as something other than what they really are. The other trait is the ability of the transcendental world to comment on the empirical one: It legitimizes or condemns; it is a reflection of reality both as status quo and as evil when the latter appears. People are given a sense that they can know where they stand: This may be false and frequently is, but it may also be true in terms of economic and political reality.

Societies invariably provide visions of the future or the heavenly sphere. They traditionally do this using architecture and literature. The *Koran* contains a marvelous view of heaven, and the dome, as well as other vast enclosures in the ancient world, served the same purpose architecturally.

Bellah's typology of religious evolution allows a further insight into those religions that keep faith in the transmundane world.

> From the point of view of these religions [those maintaining faith in the transmundane world] a man is no longer defined in terms of what tribe or clan he comes from or what particular god he serves but rather as a being capable of salvation. That is to say that it is for the first time possible to conceive of man as such [p. 33].

Man conceived as mankind and as individuals or as citizens assumes a separateness from the rest of nature and the living world as well as from all other men. The gods now look like men and women, and for their part men and women now look at themselves in mirrors, portraits, and in the depictions of other living peoples. All these items, true ideotechnic artifacts, now appear in the archeoloigcal record for the first time. These artifacts of faith indicate the potential inability of a person to see his real relationship to his conditions of existence. Consequently, archeologists who dig in class societies often reassemble the structure of misrecognition, not of everyday life in the ancient world.

The creators of such items recognized and valued the self, personal idiosyncracies as well as what others could say about the self. What is hidden behind the beliefs and practices that such artifacts are an index to? Ultimately the answer must be the social relations of production, the real relationship of classes to one another. The self is highlighted and celebrated because it has become the locus of what must be controlled (through self-control) if a class society is to be kept in equilibrium. Each self maintains its economic and social role by believing in an ideology that postulates an earned future state of bliss or terror on the basis of individual performance. Man as a being headed for salvation is also a being misunderstanding his economic state because he sees himself as a self, for example, in a mirror or a portrait or reflected in his vision of a different group of people. This self's major identity is derived from its putative role in a future state, belief in whose existence has real consequences for earthly behavior. Potential conflict is thus masked by ideology that is a structure of misrecognition and is accompanied by material items like mirrors and more static depictions that in their very mirroring, disguise.

Past time, time segregated from the present and thought to be accessible but with a different degree of certainty from the present, is also a dual or alternative world and as such continues to be a form of ideology. The rise of the past as an entity systematically related to the present as we now understand it and entry into it via history and archeology coincide with the decline of the heavenly world as the realm in which life was thought to be fulfilled. With this change the very identity of reality changed, and the touchstone for understanding the present became the past. From Hume to Freud, what is is what was: You are what you were.[1] Awareness and identity were achieved, no longer through what one was to become, but through what had been. The past became indespensable to the present, and concern with it became a major preoccupation.

The past as a form of duality must leave concrete evidence especially, since, realistically, the past's fragments do exist. What are the ideotechnic items that interest us here? To discover them, we merely have to admit what we all know: The past is a cultural construction, no different from heaven. As an ideal our conception of the past came into being at a certain time and place for certain reasons. This is not to say that the past is a fiction, but it is to say that whenever we look back and describe the view as "history" or "prehistory," such a view has to be understood as our creation or, minimally, as our selection and interpretation of the range of all those things that actually happened. We now know that our view of the past derives its effectiveness from what appears to be its separateness and integrity, characteristics that we have established for it. To discover what ideotechnic items representing past time look like, we can look at archeology directly. One way to begin is to examine what we suppose archeology accomplishes. It provides entrance into the past for the society in which it exists and as such is structurally like history. Our society makes it possible for an individual to immerse himself in an archeological set that is supposed to make the past accessible and in which time is overcome, change halted, and uncertainty resolved. That time cannot be overcome, change halted, and uncertainty resolved is forgotten in the set where ideology is taken for reality and misrecognition for what is real. We as professional archeologists have been particularly concerned for the last

---

[1] I am indebted to R. Christian Johnson for this insight.

15 years with providing such entry with ever greater accuracy, which is translated in the everyday world as greater believability and authenticity, therefore making the dual world more effective and harder to pierce. Archeologists believe in what they do and help their fellow citizens do the same, and all operate inside ideology as a result.

The unreflective stance of the profession concerning its place in society and its social uses is the ultimate reason for our inability to discover ideotechnic items. We make them. History and prehistory are ideology and turn out the substantiating materials for them. It is our very work, including our dedication to accuracy, that produces all the concrete items that verify the prehistory, protohistory, and full history society consumes so much of. It is the business of our profession to make the very ideotechnic items that we as professionals have not been able to discover and that "verify" the interpretations imposed on the past. Indeed, anything labeled archeology is automatically an ideotechnic item, and anything proving the separate existence of the past would be.

John Rowe (1965) suggested that past and present time were discovered at the same time, during the Italian Renaissance. In discussing the foundations of archeology, Rowe, borrowing from Momigliano, said that the idea of the past as wholly separate from the present, as an integrated whole and one from which the present might learn, is essentially a product of the Renaissance in Italy, the fourteenth and fifteenth centuries. Before this the whole of past time was a tangled set of similitudes and allegories where everything reflected everthing else merely to be repeated in the present. Knowledge prior to and even into the Renaissance was plethoric, limitless, and poverty-striken.

> Resemblance [the basis of knowledge prior to the Renaissance] never remains stable within itself; it can be fixed only if it refers back to another similitude, which then, refers to others; each resemblance, therefore, has value only from the accumulation of all the others, and the whole world must be explored if even the slightest of analogies is to be justified and finally take on the appearance of certainty. It is therefore a knowledge that can, and must, proceed by the infinite accumulation of confirmations all dependent on one another. . . . By positing resemblance as the link between signs and what they indicate (thus making resemblance both a third force and a sole power, it resides in both the mark and the content in identical fashion), . . . knowledge condemned itself to never knowing anything but the same thing, and to knowing that thing, only at the unattainable end of an endless journey [Foucault 1973:30].

During the Renaissance and its immediate aftermath the past was segregated from the present, was reasoned to be accessible but with a different level of certainty from that with which we know the present, and

was given a new and reflective relationship to the present. We also learn
from Rowe (1965) that by the dawn of the sixteenth century knowledge of
other living peoples took on a new definition. No longer simply fearsome,
despised, or allegorical, living others were regarded as distinct, coherent,
and useful because they aided self-definition and self-understanding. The
past and the living other were called into being more or less simultaneously, and with them came new and alternative forms of the dual world.

When we think of the present, two forms of it are distinguishable:
other peoples and the self. Complex societies, believing, with varying
levels of awareness, that they can gain a hold on themselves and some
control over their futures, value knowledge of people apart from themselves. Travellers, missionaries, and ethnographers all produce this kind
of knowledge, but beyond this what is thought to be foreign and other is
experienced vicariously through imported artifacts: foods, clothes, luxury
items, and so on. Archeologists often identify these as status items, but
almost always fail to see them as samples of authentic otherness, an
attempt to transcend place and time. The imported item is not just a
luxury or sumptuary item, it is also an ideological item representing part
of the structure of misrecognition. It allows its possessor, user, viewer,
etc., to think he can escape the confines of his own cultural circumstances (MacCannell 1976) and enter a place or time he knows to be
essentially inaccessible and to experience the impossible. This is not
different in kind from aiming at heaven and missing the misery of earth,
but it is more difficult to pierce because the material item possesses such
concreteness its illusionary meaning is difficult to see. Here we begin to
notice the importance of curiosity cabinets and ethnographic collections,
zoos, and ambassadors and ambassadorial etiquette at foreign courts (do
as the Romans do, but since everybody knows that is impossible, an
obliging visitor will highlight the host's traits for all involved by continually tripping over what he can not understand or assimilate).

The rise of the future witnessed the rise of the self, but only in a
fragmentary and incomplete way. The notion of the individual and of the
self is also a product of the same Renaissance idea that produced our
modern conception of the past and the living other. The idea that encompasses the past, the living other, and the self is called *perspective
distance*, and is the major hallmark of Renaissance art. It silhouetted the
individual against his background and pointed out, not just mankind, but
an individual person: the self. Perspective as a general concept brought
the past, the living other, and the self into focus for the first time,
identifying each as separate and worthy worlds that could be contrasted
with the present. The living other and the self constituted the subdivisions
of the present and produced concrete ideotechnic items, such as por-

traits, self-portraits, full-length portraits, and full-length mirrors; a place for the virtuoso, prima donna, the organ with its solo player, who orchestrates a whole world, and so on.

The full development of the self constituting a form of dualism was reached in the late nineteenth century with the "discovery" of the unconscious. With this idea each person was given a fully constituted dual other world, another living present inside the self. This is the ultimately difficult piece of ideology to pierce, although its use in fitting psychoanalytic patients more effectively into society has been pointed out by Marxists for a long time.

When we take subdivisions of time as ideology, as has been done so far here, it is possible to see their material manifestations—that is, ideotechnic items—and to assume that our job as archeologists is intact. With this definition we may reconstruct past societies more fully and even comment on the place of our profession in the operation of ideology. Once we agree on the existence of a dual world and of its manifestations as past, future, self, and living other, we can begin to apply these categories to our traditional subject matter and see if they illuminate anything more clearly. They probably will, and the search for other society's conception of time and the conflicts masked will inevitably tell us something important.

However, such an approach neglects one very serious problem: We know almost nothing about our own notions of time. Before discovering how other and dead societies thought about the past or future, we might examine the very segments we take for granted. David Clarke (1973) has had some insight into this problem, although he kept it within a cross-cultural perspective.

> Archaeological entities, processes and explanations are bound by metaphysical concepts of time and space. . . . Time and space are relative to some observed system, and a key step in archaeological interpretation is a model approach toward the meaning of time and space for the inmates of particular systems. . . . The exposure of archaeological metaphysics to critical appraisal allows us the self-conscious capacity to consider the possibilities of altering or rejecting current disciplinary concepts in favor of some alternative forms [p. 13].

Regardless of the possibility of discovering the metaphysics of a dead society, Clarke highlights the search the discipline might undertake into its own and presumably its parent society's ideas on time and space. Clarke would then turn this self-knowledge onto other societies in order to guarantee them a more accurate treatment at our hands. I would suggest that the self-appraisal he suggests, but gives no method for achiev-

ing, be realized by examining our interpretations and reconstructions of
dead societies, since these encode within them the very "metaphysical
concepts of time and space" he would like us to raise to awareness before
we even begin looking into other societies. Whether or not we can ever
understand that "the mobile Paleolithic band presents a very different
time and space surface from . . . Iron Age society [p. 13]" is beside the
point. But right to the point is our own segregation of temporal and spatial
reality and the other allied ideas of time that we have little direct knowledge of.

To approach our own view of time, the concepts used in archeology
and those used by laymen in America need to be segregated. Let me
suggest that there are three aspects or traits in the construct of time in
archeology.[2]

1. Time is segmentable in an almost infinite variety of ways; it can be
   made into discrete units:
2. Time is also seen as (a) continuous, and (b) progressive. Process
   emphasizes the sweep of time, and evolution the growth of complexity accompanying its passage.
3. Studies of a moment in time, normally called functionalism, and
   studies of the sweep of time, called evolution, are functions of
   each other. Archeologists tend to think of these two approaches as
   antithetical, and to some degree that is true, since something can
   be viewed as either stopped or in motion but not both simultaneously.

Nonetheless, our view of linear time, which is usually expressed as
segments, inevitably invites the question: What links the segments?
Therefore it sponsors our notion of continuous time. This makes new and
traditional archeology functions of each other and complementary, since
they both operate within the same assumptions of what constitutes time,
and the more fully either accomplishes its task, the more likely each will
sponsor the rise of the other.

As opposed to an archeologist's conception of time, lay Americans
give a different view. Americans certainly see time both as segmentable
and also as in some sort of motion. But beyond that agreement with
archeology, laymen bring rather more or at least different assumptions
about living in time. Americans think that time can be controlled, the
future can be managed, other living peoples governed, and the past
commanded into existence. American belief states that we have freed

[2] I owe the essence of as well as some specific points in the following discussion to
Russell G. Handsman.

ourselves from the past in the form of the burdensome mistakes that comprise European history and even from the genetic inadequacies of biological evolution. However, Americans also see that freedom from the past destroys the past as a world from which to take identity. With the destruction of history that comes with an emphasis on each individual's ability to begin afresh without attention to any of his past, an American is left with the need to re-create some realistic tie to the past.[3] That tie is both created and destroyed in archeological sites among many other places. When one enters them, one possesses past time, and with frequent possession comes the realization that it is not separate or distinct but is a function of the present. The past is reentered so frequently Americans have begun to glimpse the real source of life in the past: the present. That realization severely compromises the idea that those segments of time that have elapsed are separate, distinct, and dead. American laymen have begun to sense that the segments of time are arbitrary, and they have done that be seeing themselves in the past. This is a lay understanding of standard archeological epistemology, which asserts that all knowledge of the past is derived from the present, but it is more sophisticated because it includes the basic notion that the content of a segment of time as well as the segmentation of time itself is a creation stemming from a cultural assumption about what time is.

The second discrepancy between archeological concepts of time and those of lay Americans, I suggest, is over continuity. Archeologists subscribe half-willingly to the idea of predictability. Continuous time expressed through evolution, with process as the mechanism for change, assumes change to be orderly, lawlike, and consequently predictable. Faith in this idea within the discipline has never been high, but the faith itself stems from the more or less complete conviction that culture develops complexity over time, especially, it is said, in its technological aspect. Perhaps because Americans do not bother with the idea of culture, or possibly for some other reason, the idea of inevitability or even predictability in social affairs has little currency. Individual effort may pay off but not social engineering or social planning. Certainly no one believes that because time is moving, we can tell where it is moving to; common sense forbids such a subscription. This is a somewhat different sight from an archeological perspective, where we say we want to know the past in order to tell the future. Laymen do not really agree with that, and they do not because they have a different idea of time.

And that idea, I suspect, is based on the notion that an individual *makes* time pass at different rates under different circumstances: with

---

[3] I am grateful to Jean-Paul Dumont for posing the problem this way and for his comments on the first draft of this chapter.

different moods during a day or with different stages in a lifetime. It also at some level holds that our imagination and fantasies cast us back into the past or forward into the future and that although some sciences can aid, prompt, and direct with their work, entry into other times is a musing, not a real movement.

It is quite probable, too, that the laymen who has realized that time moves with varying swiftness for himself also knows, although without thinking directly about it, that it moves at varying rates for others as well. He therefore has some understanding that time passes at different rates for everybody, that those differing rates are equally true, but that his neighbor nonetheless agrees it's six o'clock and Wednesday and getting dark. That knowledge of relativity and simultaneous agreement on convention puts the laymen in a different place from the professional prehistorian and suggests that since we professionals are also laymen in the same world, we should discover how we think.

REFERENCES

Althusser, Louis
    1971   Ideology and ideological state apparatuses. In *Lenin and philosophy*. New York: Monthly Review Press.
Bellah, Robert N.
    1970   Religious evolution. In *Beyond belief*. New York: Harper & Row.
Binford, Lewis R.
    1962   Archaeology as anthropology. *American Antiquity* 28:217–225.
Clarke, David
    1973   Archaeology: The loss of innocence. *Antiquity* XLVII: 6–18.
Foucault, Michel
    1973   *The order of things*. New York: Vintage Books.
Leroi-Gourhan, André
    1968   The evolution of Palcolithic art. *Scientific American*.
Lefebvre, Henri
    1971   *Everyday life in the modern world*. New York: Harper & Row.
MacCannell, Dean
    1976   *The tourist*. New York: Schocken.
Rappaport, Roy A.
    1971   Ritual, sanctity, and cybernetics. *American Anthropologist* 73:59–76.
Rowe, John H.
    1965   The Renaissance foundations of anthropology. *American Anthropologist* 67:1–20.

chapter 3

Paleopsychology Today: Ideational Systems and Human Adaptation in Prehistory

JOHN M. FRITZ

INTRODUCTION

In 1965 L. R. Binford published a massive attack on that body of theory and interpretative propositions that he termed the "normative view" of culture. This view was characterized by "the study (of) the ideational basis for varying ways of human life—culture [1965:203]." Following David Aberle's (1960) critical analysis of the "Influence of Linguistics on Early Culture and Personality Theory," Binford argued that an archeologist employing normative theory could account for sociocultural variation either by reference to antecedent events—that is, to history—or to psychological characteristics of individuals and groups. The former would account for the flow of ideas in space and time and the latter for the invention, acceptance, or rejection of these ideas by particular individuals and groups. Archeologists having the normative view became culture historians by default; they were poorly trained to be "paleopsychologists (Binford 1965:204)."

Social Archeology:
Beyond Subsistence and Dating

Binford's attack has had effects that, in my opinion, have increased the scope and sophistication of the theory that directs research and explanation in archeology. Normative theory justifiably can be criticized for limiting too narrowly both the phenomena considered and the mechanisms responsible for initiating and directing their flow and for eschewing explanation in either the historical or scientific sense. Psychologistic explanations reduce the cultural phenomena that archeologists investigate to units of innate tendency or attitude and direct explanatory concern inward. Demographic, economic, and ecological phenomena play second fiddle to mental states and the particularistic and individual experiences that produced them. Binford's critique has led to the salutory result of focusing research on the material and social means by which past human communities adapted to their natural and social environments and on the general processes indicated by particular adaptations.

As desirable as this outcome is, in throwing out the bath water, archeology came close to losing an infant of considerable promise. Many of the phenomena that attract us as humanists to the study of humankind—art, religion, philosophy—are ignored or are classed as epiphenomenal. But why do human communities, the behavior of which is seen to be governed by adaptive strategies in material domains of life, elaborate complex ideational and related behavioral systems? Some cultural anthropologists have come to believe that ideational systems play a necessary and central role in human adaptation. The works of Gregory Bateson (1972a), Marvin Harris (1968), and Roy Rappaport (1968, 1970, 1971) are pioneering examples of research that attempts to understand the adaptive role of culture conceived ideationally. This new synthesis finds supporters in archeology. Theoretical statements by Drennan (1976), Flannery (1972), and Leone (1972, 1973) and research on the socially integrative role of sanctified loci (e.g., Longacre 1966), on iconic and artistic systems (e.g., Friedrich 1970; Fritz n.d; Washburn 1977), and on cosmology (e.g., Aveni 1975, Flannery and Marcus 1976, Isbell 1976) indirectly or directly relate ideational systems to adaptive strategies. I see, then, a renewed concern for "paleopsychology"—but one that is part of a very different theoretical system and that defines different events and processes.

IDEATION AND ADAPTATION

How do ideational systems contribute to human adaptation? Rappaport (1971) suggests that such systems are analogous to the memories of automatic control devices. That is, they encode a set of reference values that trigger homeostatic responses when internally or externally induced perturbations threaten to change the values of critical variables beyond predetermined limits. In this sense, these phenomena are critical components of those subsystems by which the behavioral systems of a human community are organized and managed. Thus, although human physical (kinetic) behavior is necessary to and effects the flow of forms of matter, energy, and information through sociocultural systems, these flows are initiated and channeled, are speeded and slowed, are merged and separated, by varieties of information that are culturally encoded.

Ideational systems organize information at two distinguishable levels of specificity. First, they define the organizational frameworks, the elementary structures, on which content of greater specificity is hung. These frame works may be structures underlying all levels and modes of expression of information. And they may be more complex, for example, hierarchical structures, that underlie individual or particularistic modes of expression. Second, ideational systems provide specific content—the knowledge and perhaps wisdom (*sensu* Bateson 1972b:147) by which humans survive. Information specified at this level codifies elements and relations of nature and of society both within and among human communities. It is particularly characteristic of humans that elements and relations of the sacred are also specified. Further, information codifies and regulates the effect of human action on nature through the means of production, on other humans through social systems, and on the phenomena—the beings, the forces, the causative principles—embodied in or lying beyond the empirical world through ritual. The content of information ranges from rules that highly specify expected behavior to symbols that embody "systems of meaning," that is, that link, through ramifying connections, forms to meanings and meanings to meanings. Of particular theoretical significance is the suggestion (Rappaport 1971) that more highly specified action is regulated through an hierarchy of controls that have decreasing empirical content but increasing sanctity.

Archeologists, as anthropologists of human culture, can seek to understand ideational systems at both of these levels. We can investigate the structures and processes that manifest ideational organization and the systems of rules and systems of meanings that are embodied in symbols. I suggest that these understandings may be gained through the analysis of the formal and contextual properties of various classes of archeological data. A class of particular interest here is prehistoric architecture.

ARCHITECTURE: A COMPONENT OF IDEATIONAL SYSTEMS

Architecture is the set of alterations of the natural environment that create artificial textures, physical morphologies, and spaces. Architecture is information. It is information by virtue of the form and relation of its surfaces, volumes, and included features and by virtue of its being experienced temporally as a sequence of forms, as a process. One moves toward, around, through architecture and in so doing experiences changing morphologies and relationships.

Architecture is both product and component of ideational systems. It is a product of action organized and regulated by such systems, and it organizes the action and perception of those who experience it. It may express structural patterns and principles, and it may produce a sequence of experience that is governed by or expresses particular rules. And as a whole and/or in the forms and relations of its constituent elements architecture may constitute a corpus of material symbols, more or less arbitrary forms to which meanings cohere.

Architecture as symbol is mythic. Myth, in contrast to folk tale, which has "a cognitive or cerebral quality (in that actions follow rationally out of each other in a narrative logic)," may denote little about the rational relations of phenomena (Colby 1975:916). Highly symbolic, myth connotes richly. A cross or four-letter word is merely a physical morphology or sound sequence. Yet the information linked to and transmitted by each is great. And the elements within this body of meaning need not be coherent or synonymous.

Architecture—in particular that architecture that is a component of such complex connotative and behavioral systems as religious systems—is rich in reference. A hemisphere is a hemisphere. But the dome of a basilica moves us upward and outward from earthly boundaries while it places us at the center of heavenly concern.

I suggest that prehistoric architecture is one of several empirical domains that functioned, among other things, in prehistoric ideational systems. Further, I suggest that attributes of the former can be used to observe attributes of the latter. For example, ideational systems may be indicated by sets of rules that governed the sequence of construction or alteration of structures or sets of structures. They may be indicated by the sequence of experiences that were created in past observers as they moved through spaces defined by architectural elements. Or they may be indicated simply by the placement of elements in relation to natural features and/or to other elements. The analysis of architectural design in the last sense is part of the emerging field of iconics, which attempts to understand the "grammatical rules for 'languages' composed of design elements" in phenomena as diverse as alphabets and woven goods (Colby 1975:916).

CHACO CANYON: WORLD VIEW IN
ARCHITECTURAL DESIGN

I turn now to an illustration of the application of this perspective and of its significance to the study of human adaptation. The illustration explicates the strengths and weaknesses of this perspective in general and in archeology as applied to a particular prehistoric sociocultural system, that of Chaco Canyon.

Chaco Canyon is located in northwestern New Mexico (see Figure 3.1); it has long been recognized as containing one of the most spectacular arrays of archeological features in the American Southwest. Archeological research has been carried out in the area for over half a century and has been sponsored most recently by the Chaco Center of the National Park Service, Robert Lister, director. Archeological research in Chaco suggests that a complex social and cultural system evolved there beginning by the ninth century A.D., which continued until the abandonment of the valley in the twelfth or thirteenth century. The ideational system considered here existed at about mid-eleventh century. By this time most of the major architectural features of the valley had been constructed, and the most impressive features as well as many less impressive ones were in use.

I suggest that these features expressed through their forms and placement in space a particular world view, an ideational system that, following Clifford Geertz (1957), embodied for prehistoric Chacoans their most general concepts of order. I suggest further, that this world view, by encoding information about their world and about human action taken in relation to their world, contributed to the survival and growth of the prehistoric population of Chaco Canyon. It may have contributed to the collapse of the sociocultural system of Chaco as well.

Most generally, Chacoan world view conceived a cosmos composed of differentiated elements the relations of which were dynamic yet bounded and restrained. These relations were expressed by events and relations in space. Symmetrical crosscut asymmetrical relations. The former were expressed by phenomena located in the east and west and were defined by axes aligned roughly north–south. The latter were expressed by phenomena located in the north and south and were defined by axes aligned roughly east–west. Through the incorporation of directional symbolism, relations of identity and nonidentity, of openness and closedness, of sequence and rank, and of balance and equilibrium were given concrete geometric expression.

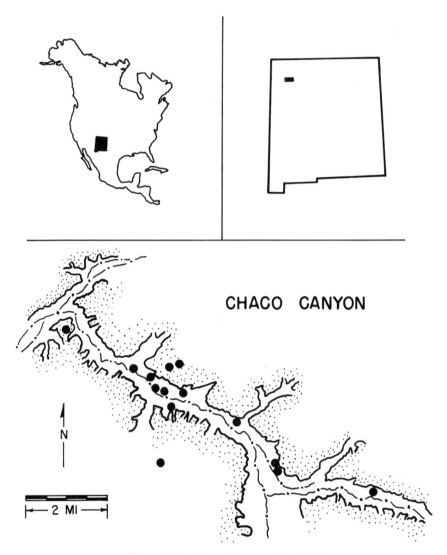

Figure 3.1. Chaco Canyon, New Mexico.

Three types of symmetry occur in the architecture of Chaco, namely, translation, reflection, and bifold rotation (see Figure 3.2). In each case symmetry can be defined by (*a*) the motion necessary to superimpose one element on another, and (*b*) a point or line in relation to which this motion occurs (Washburn 1977). Translated elements are

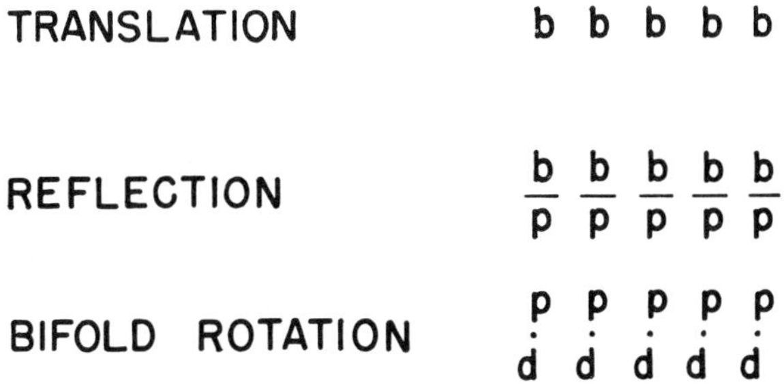

TRANSLATION   b b b b b

REFLECTION $\dfrac{b \quad b \quad b \quad b \quad b}{p \quad p \quad p \quad p \quad p}$

BIFOLD ROTATION $\dfrac{p \quad p \quad p \quad p \quad p}{d \quad d \quad d \quad d \quad d}$

Figure 3.2. Types of symmetry.

moved laterally along an axis; reflected elements are reflected or folded across an axis; in bifold rotation elements are moved 180° about a point.

Chacoan architecture expresses these symmetrical principles at three scales—that of individual spaces, of aggregated spaces, and of the inner Chacoan region, or that known as the "central group of ruins."

Reflective symmetry occurs at all three scales. For example, the interior of the great kiva of Casa Rinconada is divided into two symmetrical halves by an axis defined by the northern and southern entries and by a set of interior floor features that straddle or lie on either side of this axis (Figure 3.3). The town known as Pueblo Bonito is divided into two symmetrical halves by a series of rooms (Figure 3.4). In both cases the alignment of the axis of symmetry is roughly north–south, whereas the elements related through reflection lie in the west and in the east. I suggest that this same principle, although less well executed, underlay the organization of architectural features that constitute the central group (Figure 3.5). An axis extending roughly north–south divides the group into an eastern and western set of features. Four towns are located in the eastern set (from east to west they are Wijiji, Una Vida, Hungo Pavi, and Chetro Ketl) as is an isolated great kiva located near Una Vida (Kin Nahasbas). Five towns are located in the western set (from west to east they are: Penasco Blanco, Casa Chiquita, Kin Kletso, Pueblo del Arroyo, and Pueblo Bonito). Roughly in balance here is the number of towns and, to a lesser degree, the outer boundaries of the groups. Thus, the distance from the axis to the town farthest to the west is approximately 3.4 miles, whereas that to the town farthest to the east is 6.0 miles. Each set also includes a feature that has been termed a "shrine" (Hayes and Windes 1974). These semicircular, low masonry walls are located on high points to the south of the valley, one to the west (Site 423) and one to the east (Site 706).

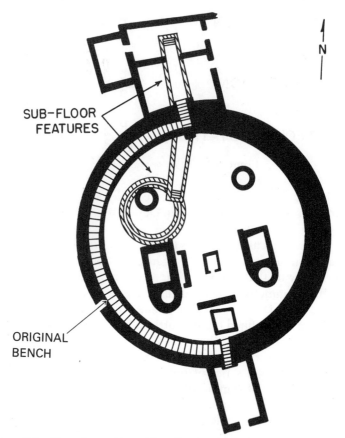

Figure 3.3. Plan of great kiva of Casa Rinconada. Redrawn from Vivian and Reiter 1960: Figure 4.

The axis of reflection is defined by at least four features that lie on or very close to it. From north to south, they are Pueblo Alto, Casa Rinconada, a shrine (Site 1207), and the town Tsin Kletzin. This axis bisects the space between the towns closest to it, namely Pueblo Bonito and Chetro Ketl (Figure 3.6).

Translational symmetry is evident within each set of features. Neither the morphologies of the architectural aggregates nor the distances between them are equivalent. Rather, it is the fact of being an aggregate and, in all but one case, of being a town that is translated. The line along which elements having these qualities are translated is not straight but is defined along most of its extent by the center of the valley. It intersects the heights bounding the southwestern end of the valley to include the town of Penasco Blanco.

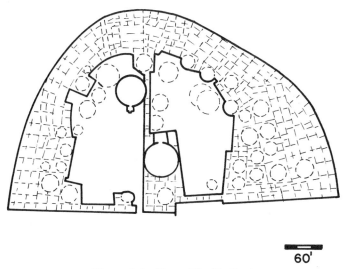

Figure 3.4.   Plan of Pueblo Bonito.

Rotational symmetry occurs at the level of towns and the inner region. In the former case it is most evident at Pueblo Bonito (Figure 3.5). There, two great kivas lie on either side of the axis of reflection. However, one can only be superimposed on the other by rotating it about a point midway between them and lying on the axis. The overall shape rather than the internal placement of features is superimposed. The same relation, although less well maifested, holds between Pueblo Bonito and Chetro Ketl (Figure 3.7). Both pueblos are roughly semicircular in plan. In Pueblo Bonito the curved outer wall is located to the north and the straight side to the south. In Chetro Ketl the curved outer wall is located to the south closing an E-shaped plan. The straight spine of the E is located to the north. Either town could be rotated about a point halfway between them to create superimposition. This line lies on the axis that defines reflective symmetry within the central group. At both levels, then, within a general pattern of reflective symmetry, architectural units located closest to the axis of symmetry are related by bifold rotational symmetry. And in both cases one element lies in the east and the other in the west.

Asymmetry characterizes the design at all three levels. The interior of Casa Rinconada (Figure 3.3) is divided into two half circles by a line described by the northern sides of the masonry vaults. With the exception of the masonry-lined seating pits that held roof posts and the bench that encircles the interior, the number and types of features are not equivalent. The southern half contains two vaults, a firebox located between them, a fire screen located south of the box, and a subfloor enclosure

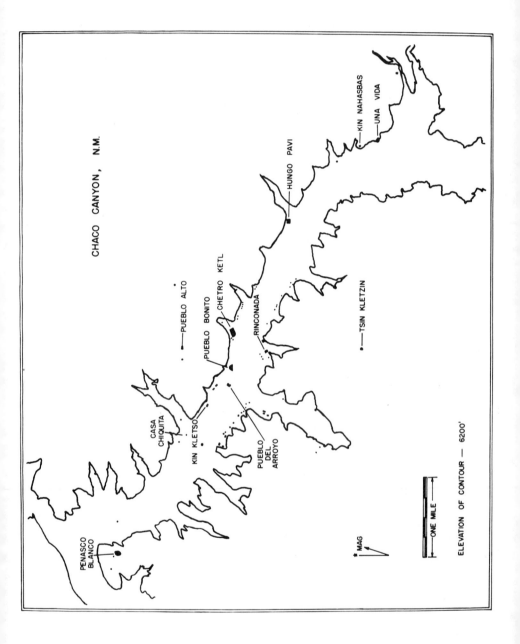

CHACO CANYON, N.M.

PENASCO BLANCO

CASA CHIQUITA

KIN KLETSO

PUEBLO DEL ARROYO

PUEBLO ALTO

PUEBLO BONITO

CHETRO KETL

RINCONADA

TSIN KLETZIN

HUNGO PAVI

KIN NAHASBAS

UNA VIDA

MAG

ONE MILE

ELEVATION OF CONTOUR — 6200'

located between the screen and the southern wall and entry. The northern half is virtually empty. It contains a circular groove that encircles the northeastern seating pit and an underground passage that leads from an outer room on the north of the kiva, under the floor to the space within the circle. It has been suggested that this space was enclosed at times by a portable screen that was set into the groove and rested against the post. Thus, the northern half contained either no features or a space within the space of the kiva. The south contained the great majority of features, in particular the hearth—the chief source of heat and light for the kiva interior.

Asymmetry characterizes the design of towns. For example, at Chetro Ketl and Pueblo Bonito the northern side or rim predominantly contains residential and associated storage spaces. Open public space and great kivas are located to the south or south-center. They are associated with rooms that plausibly were used for storage and for activities that were associated with those occurring in the great kivas. Smaller kivas are placed in intermediate locations at the juncture of residential and public areas.

The features of the inner Chaco region are also asymmetrical to the north and south. The northern side contains nine towns and one isolated great kiva. The southern side contains two towns and one isolated great kiva. One of these towns (Penasco Blanco) can be included in the northern group because it lies on the same axis of translation as do the others. Elaborate water control facilities and prepared agricultural fields associated with them are located primarily on the surfaces above the north side of the valley or are located on the valley floor to the north of the wash (Vivian 1970). Few such features are located to the south of the wash. It has been suggested that a dry farming technique using runoff from the cliffs that form the southern valley margins was used there (Vivian 1968). If so, striking asymmetry in the mode of agricultural production would have existed. Most of the 200 to 400 villages or hamlets that are estimated to have been constructed at Chaco are located on the south side of the valley (Vivian 1970). A major intersection of a system of prepared roads that link Chaco to its "hinterland" is located above the northern side of the valley, immediately to the east of Pueblo Alto (Vivian 1972). Finally, the greatest percentage of large, elaborated, and enclosed religious space—that is, great kivas—and of architecturally defined public space—that is, plazas—is associated with the towns on the northern side.

Figure 3.5. Chaco Canyon. Towns, villages, and great kivas of the central group. Elevation of contour = 6200 feet.

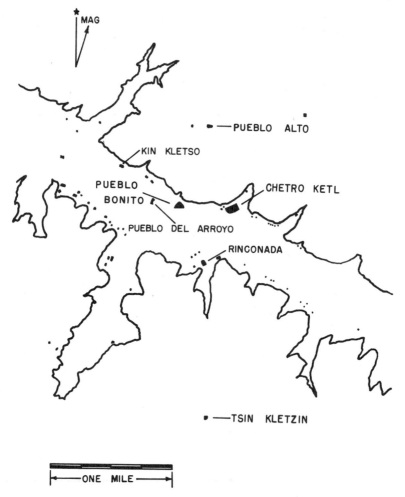

Figure 3.6. Central group. Towns, villages, and great kivas of the core area.

In summary, certain simple principles of design organize the relationship or architectural elements lying in the east and west and in the north and south. The axes that define these relations crosscut one another and create a dynamic balance not only among the elements related but also among the relationships themselves. I suggest that these elements and relations were components in an ideational system that expressed in material form elements and relations of a world view. Architectural design was a metaphor of the elements and relations of nature,

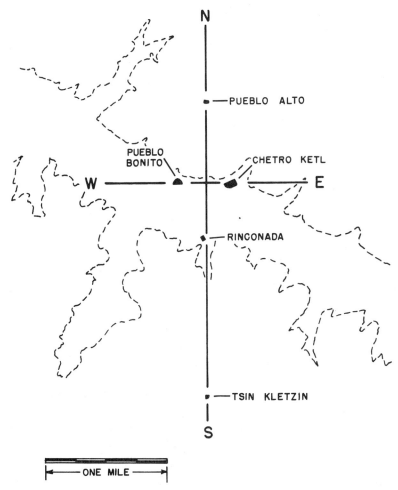

Figure 3.7. Central group. Axis of reflection and point of bifold rotation.

society, and the sacred. Design within each domain of the system of world view was symbolically resonant with that in others.

This argument can be amplified and illustrated by considering the elements and relations of the social system that were encoded in the archiecture of Chaco. I suggest, first, that translational symmetry expressed the social equivalence of social aggregates, that is, towns, and the openness of the social system of which these aggregates were a part, That is, within each set an indefinite number of elements could be added, constrained only by their placement along the organizing axis. Second, I suggest that reflective symmetry expressed social equivalence of social aggregates linked in a *closed* system of balanced duality. The aggregates were (a) participators or observers in activities occurring in kivas, (b) occupants of towns, and (c) occupants of the inner Chaco region. In each case these aggregates were organized into two groups by the placement or relation of architectural features. Their relation was closed in that alterations of number, position, and presumably other attributes of one group could not be changed without concomitant change in the other.

Analysis of the systems of measurement that appear to have been employed in the construction of walls and rooms at Pueblo Bonito supports the suggestion that two distinct social aggregates existed there during at least one period of construction. In an innovative analysis, Hudson (1972) shows that the systems of measurement employed in the construction of rooms in the east and west wings involved scales of length that were internally consistent but markedly different from one another (approximately 20 inches in the west and 29 inches in the east wing). This construction is characterized by a distinctive masonry style (type III as defined by Judd [1964: 78, Plate 10] and is believed to have occurred in one episode. Significantly, construction in this style along the central, north–south axis of the settlement includes both scales of measure.

Assuming that the designer–builders of each wing also resided there, then the conceptual systems for distance and/or the technical means that were created to define them and were employed by the residents of each wing would have been distinctive. This could indicate "drift" away from a previously shared standard among relatively isolated social aggregates, conscious stylistic differentiation, or, simply, the independent selection of standards. All suggest the independent, although coordinated, activity of (at least) the leaders of each aggregate.

If eastern and western social aggregates were balanced by reflective symmetry, rotational symmetry expressed sequential alteration within a closed system, that is, cyclical change. It is plausible that the change expressed was the rotation of authority and responsibility for management of the affairs of towns and of the valley itself. Such a pattern characterizes at least some of the contemporary Pueblo in the Rio Grande Valley, such as the Tewa (Ortiz 1969). And it would have been a relatively simple organizational structure for the population that occupied the Chaco area.

Social asymmetry is most clearly indicated in the central group. Features in the north indicate considerable capital investment and considerable planning. Features in the south are neither elaborate nor formally planned internally or in relation to one another. They suggest opportunistic and individualistic decision making, whereas those in the north suggest central planning in design and execution. It is plausible that this asymmetry represented an asymmetry of control within an hierarchically organized social system. Those occupying the upper levels, those who participated in the management of the entire social system, were located symbolically and in fact in the northern side of the valley. In contrast, those whose actions were managed were located in the southern side.

These suggestions are generally consonant with those made by Grebinger (1973) and by Martin and Plog (1973). The latter suggest that "A chiefdom type of social organization may have been present [at Chaco] with the elite controlling and distributing the food supplies [p. 305]." Grebinger suggests that the population of the entire valley was organized according to a principle of ranking. Although he disavows the suggestion that a "chiefdom" as an evolutionary type, as defined, for instance, by Service (1962:142–174), existed in Chaco, he does suggest that individuals of higher rank redistributed agricultural and other goods, stimulated the production of specialized goods by craft specialists, and eventually developed water control systems for agriculture. He locates these individuals in the towns, that is, predominantly to the north.

Grebinger contrasts his position to that of Vivian (1970:78–83), who suggests that two types of social organization existed simultaneously during the later occupation of the valley. Localized corporate lineages would have organized the populations of villages, whereas nonexogamous moieties would have organized the populations of towns.

The models presented by Vivian and Grebinger are not necessarily irreconcilable. Lineages could have been organized into moieties in both town and villages, and individuals within lineages and lineages (or other social units) within moieties could have had different ranks. Settlement plans of villages do in some cases imperfectly express a principle of duality, for instance, through reflective symmetry (see Bannister 1973: Figures 4,6,9).

Whatever the details of Chacoan social organization may have been, the predominant location of individuals and social aggregates having greatest political and economic power in northern settlements is agreed upon by these authors. I suggest that the symbolic locations of these individuals and aggregates also was to the north.

Great kivas and large, carefully planned kivas as well as large public spaces that may have held religious ceremonies are located preponderantly in the north. I suggest that this asymmetrical distribution of religious space expressed asymmetry of religious power. Thus, if in religious space the relation between the sacred and profane is mediated, then those who control this space and perhaps organize the rituals occurring within it control the interaction of the sacred and those who experience it. To the degree that these managers, that is, priests, partook of this power, the locus of a sacred power would have been in the north.

The asymmetrical distribution of sacred power is indicated by an insightful analysis of kiva wall niches by Reyman (1976b). He shows that 265 niches in 92 kivas from Chico Canyon, Mesa Verde, and Aztec Ruin are predominantly located to the north (141) and least frequently to the south (21). Here the sections of walls assigned to directional classes are demarked by axes defined by solstice sun rise–set points at the latitude at which each kiva is located. Because axes thus defined do not describe arcs of wall of equal length, the differences in frequency may in part be attributable to the method of definition. However, when axes are placed perpendicularly and oriented 45° away from the central axes of the kiva so that arcs of wall of equal length are described, 50% of the niches are still located in the north. Niches located in the eastern and western walls are not equal in frequency but are similar in magnitude in comparison to the frequencies in other directions. When directions are defined according to solstice points, 63 occur in the east and 40, in the west. It should be noted that this asymmetry does not characterize the distribution of niches at Casa Rinconada. However, antechambers, plausibly used in part for storage of ritual paraphernalia, are located predominantly on the north side of the kiva. If items employed in or otherwise symbolic of the rituals that occurred in kivas were stored or housed in these facilities, then their sacred qualities would have been linked to their spatial position in the north. Further, if through these items and/or through actions related to the facilities that contained them, linkage was made between the sacred and the celebrants of kiva ritual, then these items and facilities plausibly expressed the northerly locus of that which and those who were instrumental in this linkage.

These relations are expressed by other features of the design of Casa Rinconada. I suggest that the southern half of the interior expressed the world of everyday experience. Like this world it is an architectural environment, full of masonry facilities. And like this world it is the locus of the source of heat and light—the sun. In northern temperate latitudes the sun does not move out of its southerly location in the heavens even at its zenith at the summer solstice. I suggest that the southerly placement of the hearth and illuminated fire screen expressed through their function and placement the location of the sun. In the world of experience, the sun's light casts the northern side of objects into darkness. And, in general, areas lying to the north of the observer receive less light than those lying to the south. So, too, in the great kiva the northern half is relatively dark. It is plausible that this relatively dark and featureless area was the place of assembly and initial enactment of ritual activities. It is linked both by an underground passage and by a staircase to the antechambers to the north. In addition to storage these plausibly were the location of preparation and assembly for celebrants of kiva rituals. Their number—disproportionate to those on the southern side of the kiva (four or five to one)—recalls the disproportionate distribution of wall niches in the analysis of Reyman (1976b). The northern half of the kiva was a stage on which those impersonating elements of the sacred could perform and from which they could move symbolically into the light and the world of the everyday. This movement from a region of darkness to one of light is also expressed by the underground passage. This passage can be understood as a conduit along which those expressing elements of the sacred could move from rooms to the north of the kiva chamber to the south, where they would emerge from the underground into the lighted chamber. At the completion of their activities they could have returned to the north by way of the underground chamber or by the northern stairway. This north–south movement finds striking parallel in origin myths of the contemporary Pueblo. In these, the Puebloan peoples came out of the underworld at a spot located to the north and moved to their present locations in the south (e.g., see Ortiz 1969). It is conceivable that the underground passage was a component of rituals that expressed origin and return.

The location and characteristics of human burials in Chaco Canyon indicate asymmetrical distribution of social control, priestly function, and, perhaps, the symbolic relation of the dead to the north. "High status" burials are associated with the towns and thus tend to be located on the northern side of the valley, whereas those the impoverished contents of which indicate "low status" are predominantly associated with villages and thus tend to be located on the southern side of the valley (Vivian 1970). Grebinger (1973:11–12) reviews burial data from Pueblo Bonito and suggests that it supports the existence of ascriptive social ranking as defined by Fried (1967). These data include the inclusion of goods of exceptional quality and/or quantity and the inclusion of exotic goods in the burials of children. The most elaborate of adult burials (numbers 13 and 14) include items of plausible religious and ritual significances: beads and pendants of shell, stone, and turquoise; elaborately decorated flutes; and staves or sticks of "ceremonial" significance (Pepper 1909). These goods were placed on a board floor with 12 human skulls and other bones, the whole overlying the burials themselves. This array plausibly indicates the presence of burial ritual rich with symbolic and religious meaning.

If death and return to an underworld were linked symbolically to the north as in many contemporary Pueblo cosmologies (e.g., see Ortiz 1969) and if this linkage was expressed in rituals of interment, then the much noted relative paucity of burials at Pueblo Bonito and other sites in the valley may be accounted for. That is, interments predominantly would have been located to the north of the settlements rather than to the south, where trash mounds, frequently the repository of burials in the Southwest, are predominantly located. "North" here may have included areas outside but adjacent to the walls of the pueblo, hence in areas to the east and west of some parts of the room blocks, or areas at greater distance from the pueblos. This discovery of such burials would provide strong confirmitory support to the model presented here.

The design of Pueblo Bonito would seem to counter this argument. Residential units are located to the north and religious spaces to the south. However, if those who resided in the northern units were identified with mediation with the sacred and with sacred power—that is, if they were in whole or part a resident priesthood—then the design, like that of the valley, would express the northerly locus of sacred power. The features to the south and center would express the experienced world and the articulation of this world with the unexperienced world of the sacred. Just as ritual celebrants moved from north to south in Casa Rinconada, they moved from their residences in the north to the great kivas and public spaces to the south in Pueblo Bonito. It is plausible that great kivas expressed the sun and its significance for the support of human life. Thus, the hearth at Casa Rinconada was to the kiva as the great kivas in Pueblo Bonito (and, presumably, other towns) were to the town as a whole. This relation can be seen at a more encompassing scale: The great kiva of Casa Rinconada was to the inner Chacoan region as was its hearth to it. The southerly placement of Casa Rinconada is thus not fortuitous or anachronistic. It expresses the articulation of the sacred and the everyday for the region.

If these relations obtained, a measure of balance was created between those residing in the north and south. Whereas the former instigated and managed activities of the region and were expressive of the locus of sacred power, the latter were the recipient of this power through ritual and through the productivity of the natural world. If the north managed, the south invoked. In short, architectural asymmetry expressed the organizational basis for theocratic control, yet it also expressed the necessary role of the provision for those who were controlled.

The location of Burials 13 and 14 in Pueblo Bonito support these arguments. They were placed in a room (33) that is located on the northern side of the pueblo in the second row of rooms from the plaza, that is, to the south of the room block (see Judd 1954; Pepper 1909). At the time of its construction—that producing masonry style I—this room lay very close to the axis of reflective symmetry of the town. Thus, these individuals who commanded in death, as presumably in life, considerable goods of great scarcity and quality were located at the apex of social and sacred power. This location is at the junctures of the social aggregates to the east and west, of residential and storage spaces to the north and public and ceremonial spaces to the south, and, at a larger scale, of sacred being to the north and everyday activity—for example, agriculture—to the south. Thus, this location can be understood as symbolizing the fusion and perhaps mediation of these oppositions. If these individuals occupied roles in life in which they also mediated the relations between these domains, their secular and sacred power would have been great. The presence of two individuals may be symbolic of the dualities that they mediated and that they may have represented. And it may indicate that even at the apex of power a dynamic balance within and among social and other phenomena were maintained, for instance, by the rotation of control.

ARCHITECTURE AND ADAPTATION

In the model sketched in the preceding discussion, I have considered aspects of a system of world view that plausibly were symbolized in the architecture of Chaco Canyon. Although I have focused on social aspects, I recognize that other aspects of the everyday and sacred worlds were encoded in architecture as well. Many of these can be expected to have been linked to and resonant with these described here. The prehistoric astronomical system that is being elucidated by the work of Reyman (1976a); Williamson, Fisher, and O'Flynn (1977); and Williamson, Fisher, Williamson, and Cochran (1975) is an important example.

The adaptive function of the system of meanings symbolized by Chacoan architectural design seems clear. It identified the social aggregates that performed essential operations in the sacred world (mediation, invocation) and in the everyday world (production, exchange, organization). Equally as significant, it defined the structure of economic, political, and ceremonial relations that obtained between and among these aggregates. In particular, it defined and gave religious sanction to those who were at the top of the hierarchy of control, and it expressed for both the time and place of origin of this control. Thus, Chacoan architecture was an essential component of the memory of Chacoan culture, referents encoded in stone and space, the organizing principles of secular and sacred existence. In short, I have attempted to show that the ideational system of Chaco Canyon is neither unobservable nor adaptively epiphenominal. Rather it was a critical component of those means by which information was obtained, manipulated, and dispersed.

Although the ideational system of Chaco was critical to the perpetuation of the sociocultural system present in the canyon and may have been critical to the development of this system, it was not effective enough. It is of no little theoretical interest that Chaco was a system that ultimately failed. How it rose and fell are problems of considerable historical and evolutionary importance. An understanding of the role of this ideational system must depend on a better understanding of the variables critical to Chacoan adaptation and of the perturbations that the ideational system controlled, attempted to control, and ultimately did not control.

Various suggestions have been made—for example, deterioration of the habitat or the decline of economic ties with Mesoamerica (di Peso 1972; Reyman 1971). In the latter case it is significant that the *relation* of architectural elements, but not the elements themselves, appears to be Mesoamerican rather than southwestern (see also Ferdon 1955). Thus, the city of Teotihuacan, designed 1000 years earlier than Chaco, is organized about a north–south axis with many elements placed symmetrically to the east and west and with the north, in contrast with the south, containing an architectural environment displaying greatest planning capital investment, and provision for ritual activities (see Millon 1974).

It is plausible that sociopolitical dynamics within the Chacoan system or between it and surrounding systems set up uncontrolled perturbation. These may have included internal conflict between those whose labor constituted the basis of production and those in control of the means and modes of production. Conflict among those who controlled production and sacred activities may be pertinent (Flannery 1972) or internal growth of the Chacoan system, or the establishment of economic and other ties may have attracted population from a hinterland that ultimately could not be integrated or supported. Many of these processes may have interacted in complex ways as the Chacoan system disintegrated. Whatever the outcome of research on these problems, it is clear to me that the understanding of the prehistoric ideational system of Chaco Canyon is of the utmost importance to the understanding of this human experiment in adaptation.

ACKNOWLEDGMENTS

I gratefully acknowledge the contributions of Robert Churchill, who prepared the figures and Stephen Payne, an undergraduate at the University of California, Santa Cruz, who in a late afternoon conversation in my office helped to catalize the understanding of Chacoan architectural design that is described here.

REFERENCES

Aberle, David F.
  1960 The influence of linguistics on early culture and personality theory. In *Essays in the science of culture: In honor of Leslie A. White*, edited by Gertrude Dole and Robert Carneiro. New York: Crowell. Pp. 1–49.
Aveni, Anthony F. (Ed.)
  1975 Archaeolstronomy in pre-Columbian America. Austin, Tex.: Univ. of Texas Press.
Bannister, Bryant
  1973 Tree-ring dating of the archeological sites in the Chaco Canyon region, New Mexico. *Southwest Parks and Monuments Association, Technical Series* 6(2).
Bateson, Gregory
  1972a Steps to an ecology of mind. New York: Ballantine.
  1972b Style, grace and information in primitive art. In *Steps to an ecology of mind*, edited by Gregory Bateson. New York: Ballantine. Pp. 128–152.
Binford, Lewis R.
  1965 Archaeological systematics and the study of cultural process. *American Antiquity* 31(2):203–210.
Colby, Benjamin
  1975 Culture grammars. *Science* 187(4180):913–919.
Di Peso, Charles C.
  1972 Casas Grandes and the Gran Chichimeca. Reprinted from *El Palacio* 75(4).
Drennan, Robert D.
  1976 Religion and social evolution in formative Mesoamerica. In *Early Mesoamerican village* edited by Kent V. Flannery. New York: Academic Press. Pp. 345–368.
Ferdon, Edwin N.
  1955 A trail survey of Mexican–Southwestern architectural parallels. *School of American Research, Museum of New Mexico Press, Monograph* 2.
Flannery, K. V.
  1972 The cultural evolution of civilizations. In *Annual review of ecology and systematics 3*. Palo Alto, Calif.: Annual Reviews, Inc. Pp. 399–456.
Flannery, Kent V., and Joyce Marcus
  1976 Formative Oxaca and the Zapotec cosmos. *American Scientist* 64(4): 374–383.
Fried, Morton H.
  1967 The evolution of political society: An essay in political anthropology. New York: Random House.
Friedrich, Margaret
  1970 Design variability among Magdalenian assemblages of engraved bones from graphic analysis. *American Antiquity* 35(3): 332–343.
Fritz, Margaret Conkey
  n.d. Design variability among Magdalenian assemblages of engraved bones from Cantabrian Spain. *Proceedings of IX Congrès d'Union Internationale des Science Prehistoriques et Protohistoriques, Nice, France*, edited by H. deLumley. Centre National de Recherch Scientifique, Paris. (In press.)
Geertz, Clifford
  1957 Ethos, world view and the analysis of sacred symbols. *Antioch Review* 17:421–437.

Grebinger, Paul
  1973   Prehistoric social organization in Chaco Canyon, New Mexico. *The Kiva* 39(1): 3–23.
Harris, Marvin
  1968   The rise of anthropological theory. New York: Crowell.
Hayes, Alden, and Thomas C. Windes
  1974   An Anasazi shrine in Chaco Canyon. In *Collected papers in honor of Florence Hawley Ellis*, edited by Theodore R. Frisbie. *Papers of the Archaeological Society of New Mexico 2*: 143–156.
Hudson, Dee T.
  1972   Anasazi measurement systems at Chaco Canyon, New Mexico. *The Kiva* 38(1): 27–42.
Isbell, William H.
  1976   Cosmological order expressed in prehistoric ceremonial centers. Paper given in Andean Symbolism Symposium, Part I: Space, Time and Mythology. International Congress of Americanists, Paris.
Judd, Neil M.
  1954   The material culture of Pueblo Bonito. *Smithsonian Miscellaneous Collections* 138(1).
  1964   The architecture of Pueblo Bonito. *Smithsonian Miscellaneous Collections* 147(1).
Leone, Mark P.
  1972   Issues in anthropological archaeology. In *Contemporary archaeology. A guide to theory and contributions*, edited by Mark P. Leone. Carbondale, Ill.: Southern Illinois Univ. Press. Pp. 14–27.
  1973   Archeology as the science of technology: Morman town plans and fences. In *Research and theory in current archeology*, edited by Charles L. Redman. New York: Wiley-Interscience. Pp. 125–150.
Longacre, William A.
  1966   Changing patterns of social integration: A prehistoric example from the American Southwest. *American Anthropologist* 68(1): 94–102.
Martin, Paul S., and Fred T. Plog
  1973   The archaeology of Arizona: A study of the southwest region. Garden City, N.Y.: Doubleday/Natural History Press.
Millon, Rene
  1974   The study of urbanism at Teotihuacán, Mexico. In *Mesoamerican archeology*, edited by Norman Hammond, Austin Tex.: Univ. of Texas.
Ortiz, Alfonso
  1969   The Tewa world. Chicago: Univ. of Chicago Press.
Pepper, G. H.
  1909   The exploration of a burial room in Pueblo Bonito, New Mexico. *Putnam Aniversary Volume:* 196–252. New York.
Rappaport, Roy A.
  1968   *Pigs for the ancestors: Ritual in the ecology of a New Guinea people*. New Haven, Conn.: Yale Univ. Press.
  1970   Sanctity and adaptation. *Io* 7: 46–71.
  1971   The sacred in human evolution. *Annual Review of Ecology and Systematics* 2:23–42.
Reyman, Jonathan E.
  1971   Mexican influence on southwestern ceremonialism. Ph.D. dissertation, Southern Illinois Univ. Ann Arbor, Mich.: University Microfilms.

1976a Astronomy, architecture, and adaptation at Pueblo Bonito. *Science* 193 (4257): 957–962.

1976b The emics and etics of Kiva wall niche location. *Journal of the Steward Anthropological Society* 7(1): 107–129.

Service, Elman R.
1962 Primitive social organization: An evolutionary perspective. New York: Random House.

Vivian, Gordon and Paul Reiter
1960 *The great kivas of Chaco Canyon and their relationships.* Monographs of The School of American Research and The Museum of New Mexico, 22. Santa Fe, New Mexico: The School of American Research.

Vivian, R. Gwinn
1968 A proposed reconstruction of prehistoric social organization in Chaco Canyon, New Mexico. Unpublished manuscript, Arizona State Museum, Tucson.

1970 An inquiry into prehistoric society in Chaco Canyon, New Mexico. In *Reconstructing prehistoric pueblo societies*, edited by William A. Longacre. Albuquerque, N.M.: Univ. of New Mexico Press. Pp. 59–83.

1972 Final technical letter report for prehistoric water conservation in Chaco Canyon. NSF Grant No. GS-3100, July 1, 1970, to June 30, 1971. Manuscript, Arizona State Museum, Tucson.

Washburn, Dorothy Koster
1977 A symmetry analysis of upper Gila area ceramic design. In *Peabody Museum Papers 68*. Cambridge, Mass.: Peabody Museum of Archaeology and Ethnography, Harvard University.

Williamson, Ray A., Howard J. Fisher, and Donnel O'Flynn
1977 Anasazi solar observatories. In *Native American astronomy*, edited by Anthony F. Aveni. Austin, Tex.: Univ. of Texas Press. Pp. 203–218.

Williamson, Ray, H. J. Fisher, A. F. Williamson, and C. Cochran
1975 The astronomical record of Chaco Canyon, New Mexico. In *Archaeoastronomy in Pre-Columbia America*, edited by A. F. Aveni. Austin, Tex.: Univ. of Texas Press. Pp. 33–42.

chapter **4**

Style and Information in Cultural Evolution: Toward a Predictive Model for the Paleolithic

MARGARET W. CONKEY

This chapter is an attempt to build a perspective on Paleolithic socioecological systems that will allow us to look for variability among certain classes of Paleolithic material culture that could be interpreted as stylistic variability. Neither the demonstration of styles or "style zones" among even Upper Paleolithic assemblages, nor the development of detailed hypotheses that would predict such style have yet been presented in any depth. This chapter will focus on the latter. It is argued that prior to testing any class of material culture for stylistic variability, analysts must understand (*a*) the potential sources of variability among the products of the particular sociocultural system in question, such that stylistic behavior would be a plausible source, and (*b*) in which classes and in what attributes of material culture that stylistic treatment would be most plausibly manifest, and why. It should be noted that in dealing with not only presapiens populations but also other past sociocultural systems, one cannot de facto expect that stylistic behavior, particularly that which informs on boundaries and delineations of sociocultural entities, was

61

operative and is manifest in those components of the archeological record that we most often have to analyze.

The discussion will focus on two aspects of human cultural evolution: style and information transmission. These are obviously not mutually exclusive topics for consideration. In fact, since the original formulation of most of the ideas contained in this chapter (Conkey 1973), at least one archeologist (Wobst 1977) has explicitly proposed a definition of style in terms of the processes of information exchange. One cannot, I would argue, separate an understanding of stylistic behavior and/or information transmission among bioculturally evolving hominids of the Pleistocene without a tertiary concern, namely the evolution of symbolic behavior. Although such topics are not often a central part of the repertoire of the Paleolithic archeologist's interpretative framework, it can be argued that a discussion of style, information transmission, and the evolution of symbolic behavior during the Paleolithic is really another way of approaching a very acceptable domain of archeological research. That is, this is a chapter concerning the nature and significance of variability in the archeological record. I would like to speculate on the relationship between style and the evolution of symbolic behavior and suggest that the first demonstrable appearance of style or stylistic behavior comes at a certain point in the evolution of human symbolic behavior. And further, that this appearance of style among human material cultural systems is an integral component of the evolution and expansion of the processes of information exchange and transmission among hominids. At the present state of knowledge in prehistoric and wider anthropological research, I would argue that this appearance of style does not come until the Late, or Upper, Pleistocene and perhaps not until the appearance of anatomically modern humans, *Homo sapiens sapiens*. In order to explore the plausibility of this, we will need to understand what is meant by style and how this relates to information exchange, and then to look at the behaviors indicated by the archeological record. We will also need to explore some aspects of what is involved in symbolic behavior. I would like to argue that the evolution of style was a part of a multivariate process involving the selection of *predictability* in the context of (*a*) the increasingly complex social geography of the Upper Pleistocene (L. Binford 1972a); (*b*) increasing self-awareness and hence individuality within a group that needed to be reduced in order to maintain social cohesion (Rappaport 1971); and (*c*) the increasing dependence on and participation in symbolic modes of communication, including, of course, language—the very openness or arbitrariness of which demanded restraints.

I have always thought it was not a mere coincidence that the flowering of Paleolithic art appears with the rise of *Homo sapiens sapiens*. The origins of this art have not yet been satisfactorily explained, although in the past many felt that the mere appearance of anatomically modern humans was enough to account for it. This, of course, is a "vitalistic" explanation (Simpson 1967), which is not an explanation at all. It is granted that a certain "cognitive matrix" (cf. D'Aquili 1972) must have been reached, but this alone would not automatically produce the art of the cave walls, the figurines, the thousands of intricately engraved bones and antlers. Clearly some selective pressures were operating, and most likely they were of both a social and cognitive nature.

The beginning of a solution involves one's understanding what art is all about. That art is an essential domain for anthropological study is summed up in Levi-Strauss's statement (in Charbonnier 1969): "Art constitutes to the highest degree that takeover of nature by culture which is essentially the type of phenomenon studied by anthropologists [p. 107]." And just as Geertz (1966) has discussed religion as a cultural system, a system of meanings embodied in symbols, it can be suggested that art is also. Art involves "culturally standardized systems of visual representation" that "function as mechanisms for ordering experience and segmenting it into manageable categories [Munn 1966: 436]." The production of art forms obviously takes time and energy on the part of at least some members of the group; as such, it competes with other systems of activities for the limited time and energy of these individuals. It therefore follows that participation in the production of art forms would have at least some adaptive value for the individual as well as for the group to the extent that other potential activities are not engaged in. It cannot be reduced merely to the existence of leisure time; recent studies of hunter–gatherers suggest that leisure time is not a sufficient cause for the production of elaborate material culture (Lee and DeVore 1968). In the context of human cognitve evolution all ritual behavior, whether verbal (i.e., language) or not (e.g., art, religion), can be viewed as part of the means by which human groups organize themselves and adapt to their environment (cf. Leach 1966:405). Human cultural behavior can be seen as being an adaptive mechanism (cf. White 1949) involving "systems of meanings embodied in symbols [Geertz 1966]." To engage in such symbolic behavior, including art—which is based on the process of conceptualization—evolving human groups must have at least obtained the "cognitive matrix" that allows this kind of behavior. But it is more than just having the cognitive capacities; what are the selective pressures that demanded not just sporadic but regular symbolic behavior to the point of its being the primary means of adaptation? Both Geertz (1962) and D'Aquili (1972) have noted that the evolution of the human nervous system *does* demand the existence of culture, or a "public symbol system [Geertz 1962]," due to the very generalized nature of our intrinsic information. "Just as there would not be culture without men, there would be no men without culture [Geertz 1962]." But as Douglas (1970) has shown in the case of religious behavior there are different kinds and degrees of symbol systems developed by different groups; possibly this is related to specific sociocultural conditions. But whatever the nature of the symbol systems involved—whether kinship terminologies, marriage rules, art, or religion—they do act to codify, classify, and articulate the world of experience, both conscious and unconscious.

From this general concept of art, one can proceed to a most discussed aspect of art: style. From a general and anthropological perspective, a concept of style is based on at least four components, which are here presented as assumptions made explicit. Art is a conceptual process, and it is precisely because all art is conceptual that representations are recognizable by their style (Gombrich 1961). As presented by Gombrich, the artistic process may be one of "finding–making–matching," and images are derived from conceptions or "coded schematic conventions [Kubler 1971:167]" rather than from direct perception or mere observation of nature. The coded and classified perceptions and sensations form the conceptual basis for "finding" the code, which necessarily precedes the "making" of an image. "Matching" this image against nature, or correction, may take place, but this seems to be a characteristic primarily of Western art since the "Greek Revolution." Making, Gombrich argues, not only precedes matching, but is dominant over it. If art is seen as a conceptual process, it follows that a given style reflects similarities in at least the "finding" processes of its producers. Thus we can characterize style as reflecting common encoding and decoding strategies.

A second component of an anthropological concept of style suggests that art is in part a projective technique, so that a given style reflects the projection of similar thoughts, feelings, and orientational constructs that tend to characterize those participating in the sociocultural context of production. A style may embody the projection of the codes in terms of which experience is categorized (cf. Adams 1973). Since there exist "family resemblances" among the ways of thinking and feeling that characterize an identity conscious social group (and that constitute their "public symbol system"), it is suggested that such a group will tend to exhibit "family resemblances" in the production of art forms. This concept of "family resemblances" suggests an art style is not shared by its producers, but is participated in, and often differentially (cf. Friedrich 1970).

The third component suggests that to those engaged in the social context of manufacture a given style will elicit a similar response. On the one hand, this means that participation, especially on the part of artists, in a decoding strategy that is mutually recognizable and comprehensible will facilitate learning the style, which in turn will contribute to its maintenance and perpetuation. This enhances the role of a style as a potential integrating mechanism. It can be argued that it is only with intense interaction that all or part of a given decoding strategy can diffuse (cf. Friedrich 1970). This does not mean that art forms produced in other sociocultural contexts cannot be aesthetically appreciated (cf. Child and Siroto 1965). Bateson (1972) has suggested that this cross-cultural appreciation may be related to the success of a style or form in achieving "grace," or psychic integration.

On the other hand, participation in the sociocultural context of production also facilitates the effectiveness of the style. To understand, or "read," the significance of an image or in order that an image *will* elicit a similar response among its viewers, a process may be involved that Gombrich (1961) refers to as "an extension of class [p. 110]." His two examples, a Neolithic molded skull from Jericho and Picasso's baboon sculpture, are presented to illustrate that cowrie shells and toy cars are extensions of the classes of eyes and baboon faces, respectively. Each belong to the appropriate class because they elicit a similar response. "The test of an image is not its lifelikeness but its *efficacy within a context of action* [Gombrich 1961:110, italics added]." Anthropologists have been concerned with this aspect of symbol systems (e.g., Douglas 1966:58–72; Levi-Strauss 1963:186–205; Munn 1969), but the following Nunivak Alaskan Eskimo story is testimony to this concept as it related to visual images:

> Once there was a man whose grandmother was a powerful magician. The man often had trouble with his kayak, which kept capsizing, and so when his grandmother died, he had the idea of using the powers that were in her to stabilize his kayak. He flayed her corpse and fixed the skin with outspread arms and legs under the boat—and lo, it never capsized again. Unfortunately, however, the skin decayed and wore off, and so the pious grandson replaced it by an image that turned out to have the same effect. And to this very day, kayaks in these regions are adorned with schematic images that keep them in balance. [As quoted in Gombrich 1961:11]

This leads into the fourth component, which deals with why a viable concept of style must be anthropological. It is predictable that the Jericho skull with its cowrie shell "eyes" would elicit cross-cultural recognition as a human face that is indeed "looking at us," but if any additional dimensions of meaning were attached to this representational mode, it is within the *sociocultural context* of manufacture and/or use that additional and "appropriate" responses would most readily be elicited, as in the case of the much less universal use of schematic images of magical grandmothers to balance kayaks. Because of a sociocultural basis from which the "code" is derived, from which conceptualization and its expression (i.e., the "making" of an image) are derived, within which the efficacy of the image is established, and within which the image or artifact operates, an analysis of art and style must be anthropological. Lewis Binford (1962:220; 1965:208) has been arguing for at least a decade that stylistic variability refers to those formal attributes that vary with the social context of manufacture exclusive of the variability related to the function or use of an item. Wobst (1977) has, however, argued that a strict reading of Binford's definition can yield a negative concept of style, whereby stylistic attributes are identified as those that are not functional. This approach tends to deny stylistic objects a function in the cultural system. It should be made apparent in this discussion of style in the Paleolithic that stylistic behavior is very much viewed as an adaptive strategy employed by some Paleolithic human groups.

Further, Wobst (1977) also critiques archeological concepts of style as being derived "almost exclusively from the communication contexts of enculturation and acculturation" such that style is "given already before an artifact is made [p. 318]." In other words, archeologists perhaps overemphasize the component of style that focuses on the sociocultural context of manufacture. I would argue, however, that enculturation, as an important, if not vital, process of information transmission, has been underestimated in the study of the evolving cultural systems of the Paleolithic. It is worth exploring the adaptive advantages that may have been conferred upon those prehistoric populations that maximized the transmission of both the amount and kind of information to future generations, whether by increased life spans, delayed maturational processes, and/or encoding strategies—including not only the manufacture but also the stylistic treatment of material culture. We will return to these points.

In summary, style may be viewed as a conceptual process, a cultural code that produces variability in the formal attributes of material culture and that relates to the social context of manufacture and use. The existence of stylistic variability implies not only the participation in a similar cultural encoding and decoding strategy but the *transformation* of that code into material culture. This transformation, itself a form of communication, is based on a mutually intelligible communication system and produces material culture exhibiting "family resemblances" or some degree of standardization. Further, any standardization in the informational content borne by that material culture is enhanced, if not facilitated, by these "family resemblances." That is, as mentioned previously, participation in a common cultural encoding strategy and the transmission of this code via stylistic treatment of artifacts may be viewed as a cultural integrating mechanism. This is so because participation in a style enhances the predictability of a message by restraining it. Arbitrariness and even ambiguity are restrained in favor of redundancy. Just as participation in a style may serve as an integrating device, it may also serve as an isolating mechanism such that the message of the art form or even the meaning of the code may not readily be translated out of the cultural context (cf. Geertz 1972). Thus, it is easy to see the way in which many archeologists at least implicitly employ style in their interpretations of prehistoric cultures: as an indicator of social boundaries. But what this discussion intended to do, as does the more recent work by Wobst (1977), is to view style not so much as an indicator of social boundaries but as a component in the process of boundary maintenance.

It is the point of this chapter to consider how these notions of art and style fit in with human biocultural evolution and, more specifically, with the evolution of human symbolic behavior and information transmission. In the ethnographic present we can observe cultural entities that are often internally integrated and externally differentiated from other cultural entities, at least partially, on the basis not only of their being conscious of their identity as a social group but also because of their participation in a style—whether art, clothing, speech, or the like. The maintenance of this style is related to the selective pressures favoring both internal integration within and external differentiation among identity conscious social groups. In the diachronic perspective on hominid behavior it is important to consider that the appearance of style or stylistic behavior is related to cognitive evolution. This cognitive evolution produced (a) self-consciousness, or a concept of self such that one can then be a viewer in relation to others and in relation to the environment; (b) groups that are conscious of their identity and can conceptualize themselves as distinct from others ("identity-conscious social groups"); and (c) conceptualizations that can be and are communicated within the social context within which the manufacture of material culture takes place. This communication, in turn, produces the degree of standardization or "family resemblances" characteristic of a style. In addition to these products of cognitive evolution are involved those selective pressures favoring internal cohesion and external differentiation. This differentiation, particularly under conditions of increasing social complexity, and with the increasing amount of information contained in evolving living systems (including human ones), tends to become a kind of preferential differentiation: "Thus, to the proposition that populations are partially open systems must be added the second proposition that populations are partially closed systems [Morris 1971:34]." That is, just as all populations may be genetically open or closed to hybridization with members of other populations, they are also behaviorally, ethologically, or culturally open or closed to hybridization. Margalef (1968) refers to the role of information in the evolution of living systems and suggests that there exist three different layers or subchannels of information:

> One is the genetic channel in replicable individual structures. Another is a truly ecological channel based on the interaction between different cohabiting species. . . . A third channel may be called "ethological". . . or "cultural"; it transmits what has been learned by individual activity or experience and is transmitted to future generations outside the genetic channel. Now, if we project the relative size of the channels back in time, the total channel is like a fan divided into three unequal parts: an ecological channel enlarging negligibly, a genetic channel enlarging considerably, and a cultural channel appearing later but enlarging explosively [pp. 97–100].

It is on the basis of information contained in and communicated by any system that successful hybridization, mixing, or interaction can take place. As the explosion of "cultural" or "ethological" information takes place with the evolution of the vertebrates, it is not surprising to find that it is "cultural" or "ethological" sorts of information that are superceding genetic sorts as isolating mechanisms among populations. This may be particularly true of populations (including hominids) in periglacial and north temperate zones during the Pleistocene wherein single polytypic species evolved, differentiating "ethologically" rather than genetically (cf. Geist 1971). And obviously style has the potential to operate as one of these cultural isolating mechanisms.

But the real question is how far back into the Pleistocene can we project the attributes that constitute a culturally bounded group in the sense of those existing in the ethnographic present? Does the archeological record of the PlioPleistocene hominids indicate behaviors characteristic of identity conscious social groups?

It is no wonder that in a symposium on the clarification of terminologies in African prehistory Kleindienst (1967:831) wanted to discard *culture* as a term of reference for archeological units, for certainly among the international Africanists there is no agreement as to what is meant by "culture," much less what its archeological indicators are. The "traditional paradigm" of the culture history school *does* project the existence of different "cultures," or identity conscious social groups, back into time with the hominids (cf. L. Binford 1972a). Recent analyses have challenged not only the anthropologically unsophisticated concept of culture that Kleindienst objects to but also the very existence of distinct "cultural entities" during most of the Pleistocene (L. Binford 1972a; Isaac 1969, 1972a,b,c). Binford's analysis of the Acheulean and related industries associated with the hominid populations of the Middle Pleistocene (usually *Homo erectus*) suggests that if cultural entities did obtain, their material culture does not indicate such entities to the point that he would argue that "cultures" (i.e., identity conscious social groups participating in an adaptive system of meanings embodied in symbols) did not exist. Isaac's work also suggests that if cultural entities did exist, the material culture *at hand* (i.e., the available sample) does not reflect their existence. A heuristic synthesis of these views might state that the data at hand do not reflect cultural entities as we know them for *Homo sapiens sapiens* populations, and that for presapiens populations "we cannot assume the same or even similar organization of adaptive behavior [L. Binford 1972a:288–290]." Furthermore, I would argue, the relative lack of data for earlier, presapiens populations cannot be attributed solely or mainly to sampling error. Throughout human biocultural evolution a number of trends can be noticed, one of which is the increasing size and density of artifact assemblages. As Isaac (1972a) points out, this may be in part due to increased sedentism and to the fact that tool-making behavior became a more habitual and important hominid activity. Certainly the manufacture of material culture is a more regular and systematic behavioral adaptation participated in by more hominids and increasingly passed on in a more regular and standardized way. Furthermore, it seems to be a characteristic of less mature systems (such as presapiens hominids) that less information is being transferred, even to the future, "in the form of structures and fossils [Margalef 1968:94]."

That our ideas on the duration and tempo of human biocultural evolution are constantly changing should be obvious even from popular press releases. We are finding that hominid remains, once dramatically dated to 1.8 million years ago at Olduvai Gorge, now extend back into the Pliocene to 5+ million years ago. We are finding that stone tool manufacture may be as old as 2.5 to 3 million years, that the earliest members of the genus *Homo* may exceed not just 1 but perhaps 2 million years, that early populations of *Homo sapiens* may have existed twice as early as previously thought, and that *Homo sapiens* more modernized in some respects than neanderthals may have existed in East Africa 100,000 years ago (Pilbeam 1971:186–187). But this impressive array of earlier and earlier dates is not the point. Rather, what most of these temporal extensions have done has been to elongate the development of biological and cultural phases prior to the appearance of anatomically modern humans, *Homo sapiens sapiens*, and their rich, dense material culture at about 35,000–40,000 years ago. Despite the Pliocene locus for the earliest hominids, it is not until the late Pleistocene that we can begin to discern "critical changes in the tempo of cultural evolution [Isaac 1972a:382]."

That we do not find clear and systematic differentiation among the material cultural systems of hominids until the Upper Pleistocene is contrary to what we would expect if cultural entities, ethnic groups, or the adaptive behavioral systems characteristic of *Homo sapiens* populations existed before that time (L. Binford 1972a:288–289). With the radiation over most of the Old World achieved by the early *Homo* populations and given the relatively low population density that would have existed even if we tripled the number of known sites, we would expect to find many localized cultural traditions. It is precisely for this time period of as much as 1 million years long that we can hardly admit from one to three.

The first major grouping of hominid material culture is referred to as the Olduwan industry. It is doubtful that this is evidence of much more than ad hoc tool manufacture that may differ from chimpanzee termine–twig manufacture only in the "empirical appreciation of the principles of conchoidal fracture [Isaac 1972a:397]," for even chimps select suitable twigs (cf. L. Binford 1972a:287–288). Even with the succeeding Acheulean and related industries, the establishment of meaningful typologies has been not only challenged (Bowman 1971) but seems to be more arbitrary and idiosyncratic than not (cf. Isaac 1972b,c). Before advancing any interpretative statements concerning the significance of the variability of material culture, the nature of the variability must be elucidated. Isaac's studies of Acheulean assemblages, especially from the African site of Olorgesaillie (1972b), suggest a lack of standardization; that is, idiosyncratic, perhaps stochastic, or at least unsystematic tool-making behavior. A lack of standardization implies that participation in a tool-making style or tradition is not taking place, and that a tradition or style that is passed on by means of precise modes of communication (other than observational learning) does not exist. It would be difficult to argue that other than personal concepts of the end product or of the means to achieve it existed (if even such concepts existed), or that much more than merely adapting a form to a function was taking place. That diversity exists in these early tool assemblages seems more attributable to idiosyncratic tool-making behavior that shows only a very limited amount of "progressive" change through time (Isaac 1969). "Cultural tool-making" (Tobias 1965) has yet to be demonstrated for these hominids. That there *is* a trend toward increasingly standardized tool assemblages culminating in the highly standardized blade tool industries associated with modern humans is of considerable concern. Standardization implies at least three aspects:

1. The achievement of a conceptualized end *via* a conceptualized means that is characteristic of more than a few individuals. That this involves the cognitive ability to objectify or conceptualize is clear, and perhaps the strongest candidate for the uppermost time

at which this ability existed is the Levallois technique of some Mousterian assemblages usually associated with Neanderthal humans.

2. In order that a similar end (and its means) is achieved by a population of tool makers, it would seem that a more precise means of communication, of information transmission and exchange, would be necessary than the observation–imitation sequence (cf. Hamburg 1969) characteristic of most primate learning behavior.

3. To the degree that this communication network has only a limited extent, more tightly bounded contexts of production and/or use are implied.

Archeologists are only just beginning to devise ways for measuring standardization (Conkey 1978; Isaac 1972b; Sackett 1966; Washburn 1974, 1977), but whether a relative presence or absence of standardization existed in the manufacture of material culture will be of great significance for interpreting the increasingly systematic variation that seems to exist in the Late Pleistocene. A statement concerning the presence and/or degree of standardization is a statement only on the *nature* of the variability.

In the case of Neanderthals and associated industries, the Mousterian, standardization of tool kits seems to exist to the point that both Bordes (1961) (by means of his cumulative graph of tool types) and Binfords (1966a, 1968) (by means of a factor analysis) recognize at least four major groupings, or "kinds," of Mousterian. The somewhat volatile debate as to the significance of this variability (Binford and Binford 1966a, 1968; Bordes and de Sonneville Bordes 1970; Mellars 1970) was succinctly summed up by S. R. Binford (1971) and L. Binford (1927b). It seems anthropologically sound to challenge, as the Binfords have done (1966a, 1968), Bordes's hypothesis that the four kinds of Mousterian represent four "tribes" (Bordes 1961; 1968:370) because his hypothesis assumes that "differences and similarities in lithic assemblages signify cultural (i.e., sociocultural–ethnic) affiliation [S. R. Binford 1971:199]." That the nature of these similarities and differences has not been established is the Binfords' main critique. Their assertion that the nature is functional predisposes the interpretation of the significance to be in terms of functional (i.e., activity) variations.

> Varying frequencies of functional classes of artifacts (points, scrapers, knives, etc.) can tell us nothing of the subspecific or ethnic affiliation of the Hominids who made the tools. Rather, we gain information on the racial and specific affiliation of past populations by the study of Hominid remains; information on sociocultural ethnic affiliation is derived from the *stylistic* attributes of material culture [S. R. Binford p. 200].

The Binfords argue that the four "types" of Mousterian are explicable in terms of activity sets being performed (Binford and Binford 1966a, 1968; S. R. Binford 1968a). Systematic variation in tool manufacture is shown to exist, but of a nature that involves more systematic adaptation of forms, and combinations of forms, to function.

It is with Neanderthals that we have evidence of the ability to form and communicate concepts for the manufacture of stone tools, as is manifest at least by the Levallois technique, and of the systematic (rather than somewhat haphazard) adaptation of forms to function just discussed. There is also evidence of what is interpreted as a manifestation of conceptualization of self and others: the burial of the dead. The many, often elaborate, and diverse forms of treatment of the dead have been widely documented and analyzed (cf. S. R. Binford 1968a,b; Howell 1965; Solecki 1971). Not only decoration of others at death (with flowers, artifacts, and possibly red ocher) but decoration of self may have been characteristic of some Neanderthals (cf. Clarke 1970), although there is no clear-cut evidence for the latter. Necklaces and bracelets, for example, are not known until the Upper Paleolithic. But one could argue that some degree of self-consciousness is a necessary, though not sufficient, basis for self-decoration. The adaptive value of self-decoration may be related to the necessity for identification and formalization of interpersonal relationships both within and between social groups and/or as part of the process of sexual selection (Clarke (1970). That the development of symbolic modes of behavior may be based on concepts of self and of one's body (cf. Douglas 1970; Turner 1966) suggests that for additional reasons the emergence of self-consciousness may have been a precondition for the appearance and elaboration of symbolic behavior.

The shift to anatomically modern forms is more critical a development in the appearance of human culture as we know it than I had previously thought. It is a well-established idea that the evolution of a cultural mode of adaptation was *not* an all-or-nothing phenomenon that was achieved with the crossing of a critical threshold (such as the "cerebral Rubicon" theory postulates) (e.g., Geertz 1962; Hallowell 1959, 1961). This has been particularly supported by the tool-making, food-sharing, hunting, and home base activities claimed for the australopithecines of at least 1.8 million years ago (cf. Isaac 1969). But this does not mean that the *organization* of such cultural and adaptive behavior "typical" for the ethnographic present has also existed since these australopithecines. The transition to modern humans, approximately 40,000 years ago, is perhaps the earliest that we can document such behavioral organization. The explanations of and for the appearance of *Homo sapiens sapiens* and the Upper

Paleolithic blade tool industries at this time have been many and varied (cf. Bricker 1976). We have gone far in superceding vitalistic kinds of "explanations" that claim the intellectual "superiority" effected the replacement or extinction of the Neanderthals and related "archaic" sapiens populations (cf. Isaac 1972a). Sally Binford (1968a) once suggested a plausible set of selective pressures that would account for the technological readaptation and perhaps even the social and demographic conditions that would have facilitated the relatively rapid phyletic transformation. She argues for an adaptive shift, which heuristically was labeled the "predatory revolution" (Binford and Binford 1966b), to the more systematic exploitation of a single or a few species of migratory herd animals. In this context both new tools for the new adaptive tasks and new patterns of social and demographic organization to effect the tasks are plausible. Isaac (1972a:398) suggests that, technologically, the invention of the punch technique may have been a critical threshold for the wide-spread manufacture of the characteristic Upper Paleolithic blade tools. These explanations are typical of archeological approaches to culture change, based on the more readily available technoecological information of the archeological record and/or on a more cultural–materialist view (cf. Trigger 1971:322, 325 ff.).

With the continuing attempts to document the evolution of human language, and in the context of a more cybernetic approach to evolution that reminds us of the critical role of information—particularly in the transformation toward more mature systems (Margalef 1968; Rivera 1973)—an additional, if not more powerful, explanatory variable must be considered—namely, the appearance of, if not an increasing dependence on, truly symbolic communication systems ranging from language to ritual to art. Whether it was *only* with the appearance of *Homo sapiens sapiens* (e.g., Lieberman, Crelin, and Klatt 1972), or before, that the lowered larynx and mobile tongue developed, allowing the production of the "primary vowel triangle" of (a), (i), (u), the effect of its appearance must have been the same. The production of these sounds are important not just in enhancing the range of basic phonological elements and subsequent structures that can be produced, but primarily because they enhance the predictability of human communication. The controversial interpretation of Lieberman *et al.* does not mean that Neanderthals or earlier *Homos* lacked a relatively precise and even phonologically based communication system. But at whatever point in human evolution the symbolic mode of communication we know as human language became established as a regular component of human behavior, the adaptive advantages that it conferred upon its users must have been significant.

The ability and the use of that ability to communicate anything that can be conceptualized—not only in the past or future but even things that are empirically not true—signals a critical threshold in the human means for storing and transmitting information. And the transformation of these conceptualizations into not only vocabularies but also material culture, such as engraved bones and antlers, enriches the amount and kind of information that can be and needs to be transmitted. Not only is it a plausible hypothesis that a cultural informational transformation contributed to the "replacement" of Neanderthals by fully sapiensized populations, but also it is easy to see how a communication advantage could have enhanced the learning of new adaptive tasks. One must consider that an informational transformation may be seen not just as corollary to but perhaps as more central than previous more materialistic explanations based on adaptive shifts (which are not held by all prehistorians, e.g., Klein 1969:224) and technological innovations. Systemically, that *all* of these transformations would have taken place is consistent with our expectations for the evolution of living systems: toward richer information, transforming more energy at a less net cost (Margalef 1968).

Essentially, I am suggesting that after 70,000 years ago—if not later, that is, after 40,000 years ago—an "explosion" of symbolic behavior took place, involving the development of style among and within human groups that enhanced the processes of sociocultural integration and differentiation. Given the many trends of human cognitive evolution noted in the previous discussion, such as increasing intelligence and ability to conceptualize, consciousness, concepts of self, capacities for and use of phonologically based linguistic communication, and given other sociosexual developments, such as the "loss" of estrus, the role of the individual was enhanced. One might predict that hominid evolution was characterized by an increasing tension between trends favoring the individual and the viability of a social way of life. Rappaport (1971) has already discussed the necessity for the evolution of sacred concepts as a way of reducing the ambiguity, the arbitrariness, and the potential chaos of a symbolically based way of life among a primate, and therefore social, group. As Rappaport points out, "Lies are the bastard offspring of symbols [p. 30]," and although a symbolic language system may have the advantage of and potential for transmitting qualitatively richer kinds and amounts of information while retaining great flexibility, it is also characterized by the potential for communicating deceit and lies. With the relative arbitrariness of symbols and the symbolic mode, selective pressures must have favored developments that reduced or restrained the potential chaos and randomness inherent in symbolic communication.

One such development, he argues, was the evolution of the concept of the sacred. When concepts, propositions, and relations are made "sacred," a "quality of unquestionable truthfulness [is] imputed by the faithful to unverifiable propositions [p. 29]." The establishment of the sacred is a way of establishing predictability: "The acceptance of messages as true whether they are true or not, contributes to orderliness, and may, in fact, make it possible [p. 30; cf. Bateson 1951]."

The symbolic mode of communication demands restraints, even in order to make it a possible mode, and the evolution of something at least functionally equivalent to culture, especially in its normative aspect (e.g., Isaac's [1972a] "cultural rule system"), is almost necessary. A general property of living systems was perhaps operative among evolving human behavioral systems, namely, that acquired information—in this case, symbolic communication—forms the basis for, and is "subsequently used to close the door to [,] a further inflow of information [Margalef 1968:29]." The evolution of the sacred, the reduction of the perhaps infinite forms of social organization possible to just a few alternatives, and the "explosion" of symbolic behavior that follows the appearance of true language can all be viewed in this perspective: as mechanisms for enhancing predictability yet transmitting great amounts of information. Human ritual behavior may be viewed as a cultural attempt at stereotyping, or at least insuring adequate redundancy. It is in this context that the "standardization" of concepts, of encoding and decoding strategies for the translation of these concepts into material and other behavioral form, could take place.

Between 70,000 and 100,000 years ago there were important hominid groups who were coping with the fluctuating climate of a periglacial and low-latitude tundra habitat associated with the onset of the Würm, or final, glaciation. These groups became located within the ecological circumscription of southwestern Europe, which was bounded by the Atlantic, the Mediterranean, a glacial front, and high mountain regions (which often experienced local high-altitude glaciations). Under such conditions, it may have become increasingly difficult for a total population to interact and mix without differentiation, if only in terms of their abilities to receive and process information.

Although we are far from demonstrating the increase in population size and density so frequently assumed for the Upper Paleolithic of southwestern Europe, and particularly for the Magdalenian (Bordes 1968; Butzer 1971; Campbell 1972; Smith 1973), it would be supportive of the argument being developed here to marshall evidence for population growth. The population growth notion would allow us to point out that there would have been increasingly more individuals and groups to be accounted for, in terms of the symbolic if not just the genetic or ethological classification process. Differentiation within this total population would allow for greater predictability in intergroup relations.[1]

However, there are additional processes that could lend credibility to the hypothesis that Late Pleistocene populations were successfully responding to adaptational stresses by increasing participation in certain classes of symbolic behaviors. Increasing adaptation to a local and microenvironmental resource base rather than a regional one (cf. Campbell 1972), population stress related to ecological and climactic change (Gonzales-Echegaray 1972–1973), shifts in subsistence strategies (Freeman 1973) and/or settlement patterns, and consideration of not only birth rates but also death rates,[2] as well as the ecological circumscription and local topographical features that may have enhanced or reduced

---

[1] The following discussion quoted from Wilden (1972:245–246) concerning anthropological, particularly Levi-Straussian, notions on the distinction between nature and culture is quite provocative when considering the Upper Paleolithic "explosion" of cultural behavior in the context of *sociocultural* differentiation:

> The passage from nature to culture as posited by Levi-Strauss, depends upon two simple principles: a) the introduction of what can be called the "law of the distinction of difference": the prohibition of incest, and b) the correlative introduction of the discrete, discontinuous, combinatory component into the nondiscrete continuum of nature. We have a Bororo myth interpreted by Levi-Strauss which explains this introduction of the discrete component, the passage of the continuous world of difference into the discontinuous world of distinction and oppostion. After a flood, the earth became so full of people that the sun decided to reduce their number. All perished by drowning in a river at his command, except Akaruio Bokodori (who, like Oedipus, limps). Those who were lost in the rapids had wavy hair; those who were lost in the pools had straight hair. Akaruio Bokodori then brought them all back to life, but accepted only those clans whose presents he liked. All others he killed with arrows.

> Levi-Strauss comments:
> It was necessary that men should become less numerous so that neighboring physical types could be clearly discerned. For if the existence of clans and peoples bearing INSIGNIFICANT or NON-SIGNIFYING gifts were permitted—that is to say, clans whose distinctive originality was as minimal as one could imagine—then there would be a risk that between two given clans or populations there might be interpolated an unlimited number of other clans or peoples who would differ so little from their immediate neighbors that all would end up by being confounded together. Now, in any domain whatsoever, it is only with the introduction of the discrete quantity that a system of significations can be constructed [Levis-Strauss 1964:58–63].

> (I shall not argue about the word "quantity" here, but read "component").

[2] Another provocative line of reasoning to explore might be the hypotheses set forth by Douglas (1970) concerning degree of ritual behavior as correlated with degree of cohesiveness of the social group, and individualistic parameters (degree of "group" and "grid," respectively). She suggests that social experience derived from well-defined or closed social groups would more likely result in a high level of ritual and symbolic activity:

> The most important determinant of ritualism is the experience of closed social groups. The man who has that experience associates boundaries with power and

potential communication among sites under certain conditions,[3] are all potentially relevant and knowable data that could contribute to a more specific reconstruction of the socioecological system within which humans were living. Reorganization and new integrative mechanisms, as well as the appearance or intensification of stylistic behaviors, could be responses to stress of a different nature from mere population growth.

In terms of sheer site numbers, information that is often used as evidence for population growth, for the late Upper Paleolithic in Cantabrian Spain, for example, we do not have noticeably more Magdalenian than Solutrean sites in Santander-Asturias. Further, with 28 Solutrean (Straus personal communication; see also Straus 1975) and 31 Magdalenian (Moure 1974) sites, 18 bear both Solutrean and Magdalenian deposits. These are not necessarily significant data, for they do not reflect intensity, duration, extent of occupation, or even contemporaneity. Nonetheless, they do not suggest population growth. However, there are data suggestive of a locational shift during Solutrean–Magdalenian times, which would support a hypothesis of a "reaggregation" that may be in part related to the gradually deteriorating climate of the Dryas Phases of the Würm IV. Not only were the general stresses of a fluctuating glacial period environment present, but specific ecological–climatological transformations can be documented for the Solutrean–Magdalenian transition, and throughout the Magdalenian as a whole (Gonzalez-Echegaray 1972–1973). It is noticeable that within broad ecological zones (as suggested by Straus 1973a,b, 1975), both Magdalenians and Solutreans

---

danger. The better defined and the more significant the social boundaries, the more the bias I would expect in favour of ritual. If the social groups are weakly structured and their membership weak and fluctuating, then I would expect low value to be set on symbolic performance [p. 14].

If increasingly circumscribed social groups were demonstrable for the Upper Paleolithic, then the high level of symbolic performance exhibited by material culture systems may be explicable, in part, by such social experience.

[3] It has been noted that some Neanderthal skeletal remains bear evidence of rickets and osteoarthritis (Campbell 1972), and some authors suggest these afflictions are responsible for Neanderthal morphology. Of interest is the possiblity that some Neanderthals did suffer and die from rickets. This disease may be related to their being among the first hominid populations to persist for some time in the northerly latitudes during a glacial phase, and perhaps being the first hominids to wear clothing. Such a low-insulation environment without much evidence for exploitation of such vitamin D sources as fish oils may well have contributed to the premature demise of many individuals. Campbell suggests that "shortage of this vitamin may indeed have been one of the factors that mitigated against their survival [p. 51]." Unfortunately, we don't know the extent of such a disease among these Neanderthals. But if the regular addition of fish to the diet, as evidenced among some Upper Paleolithic populations, contributed to their health and protection against premature death due to rickets, we may have at least one line of evidence pointing toward a decrease in the mortality rate during the Upper Paleolithic.

were primarily (> 50% of their sites) inhabiting, at least part of the year, the shore and coastal plain. But with the Magdalenian there seems to be a significant increase in sites located along the coastal ridge and river valley system up to 20 km from the sea and a corresponding decrease in interior sites. It may be of no small significance that despite a notable increase from the Solutrean through the Magdalenian in coastal ridge–river valley sites, a clear-cut majority of the wall art, though not portable art, sites are *outside* this zone, being either in the first range of interior hills (e.g., Castillo, Hornos de la Peña) or along the coastal plain (e.g., Altamira, Tito Bustillo). Unfortunately, for these analytical purposes, the chronology of cave art sites still remains subjective and, at best, relative. Although it would fit the hypothesis being put forth here, we cannot yet feel confident that, for example, the "more interesting" (e.g., Altamira) wall art sites correspond to the Magdalenian III and early Magdalenian IV (which are the beginning stages of the Magdalenian in the Cantabrian sequence) (Gonzalez-Echegaray 1972–1973:178). This would lend credibility to the hypothesis that adaptational stress was being resolved by new and/or increasing symbolic patterns.

Lewis Binford's (1972a) perceptive characterization of the Upper Paleolithic as a time of increasingly "complex social geography [p. 291]" avoids the reliance on the still undemonstrated causal factors, such as population growth, and yet conveys insight into the population dynamics that were most likely characteristic not only of hominids but also of other species in Late Pleistocene environments of temperate Europe. Although we are not sheep, Geist's discussion (1971) of mountain sheep adaptations during this same time period provides additional contributions toward a model for understanding the evolution of style and the "explosion" of human symbolic behavior. These mountain sheep evolved enlarged and more greatly differentiated characters of social significance, such as horns, which Geist views as new ways of dealing with companions while still retaining the unity and viability of the species in a precarious periglacial environment. It is plausible that hominids effected a similar process by participating in stylistic behavior, by informing certain classes of material culture with attributes that contribute to the definition and maintenance of group boundaries.[4] That hominids effected this primarily

[4]An additional factor to consider in assessing communication networks is potential dialectical variation. It would be interesting to speculate on the *rate* of linguistic variation among sociogeographically separate and/or proximal groups, whether this would be a barrier or facilitator in subsequent attempts at regional integration, and to what degree it would enhance local group differentiation. Especially *if* the Lieberman *et. al.* (1972) hypothesis on the appearance of "language-as-we-know-it" is tenable, it should be theoretically possible to simulate the rate and degree of differentiation of local dialects since the appearance of *Homo sapiens sapiens*, that is, during the Upper Paleolithic.

in terms of symbol systems instead of genetically based, especially secondary sex, characteristics would be testimony to the explosion of the *cultural* channel of information (see p. 68, and Margalef 1968:97–100). It is to be expected that style in the manufacture of stone tools, as well as style in the development of such symbol systems as art, would obtain for the Upper Paleolithic. Since this time and to the present, human evolution has been characterized not by species diversity but by pattern diversity, that is, cultural differentiation within a single polytypic species (cf. Pielou 1966).

With a shift to a new organizational level—an organization of adaptive behavior dependent on symbol systems—diversity within that level results. Paleolithic art may be viewed as a part of the resulting diversity of symbolic behavior, and Paleolithic art may be viewed as part of the attempt to reduce the arbitrariness of symbols, of the concepts derived from experience, into manageable categories (cf. Munn 1966). Further, stylistic variability in Paleolithic art can be viewed as one of the informational processes that favor behavioral redundancy and predictability such that a social group could effectively maintain order, as well as its identity/boundaries in relation to other groups, whether preferentially isolated or favored.

In general, we are still not yet at ease when thinking about style in Paleolithic assemblages. Sackett (1972), for example, clearly feels more comfortable in talking about style among twentieth-century hammers than among Paleolithic assemblages. And as Isaac (personal communication) has suggested, it's no wonder that the Mousterian is such a volatile topic of debate, for it seems that after 70,000 B. P. not only the tempo (Isaac 1972c), but, as I am arguing here, the mode of cultural change among hominid populations began to change. The Mousterian assemblages exhibit neither the stochasticity more typical of some Acheulean assemblages nor the seemingly more systematic patterns of some Upper Paleolithic material cultural systems. Archeologists' attempts to elucidate or define style among Paleolithic material cultural systems have been relatively unsuccessful for at least two reasons. One should be clear from the foregoing discussion, namely, that stylistic treatment of material culture was probably neither in existence nor systematic, especially at the level of an inclusive social group, during most of the Lower and even Middle Paleolithic. Second, archeologists have not adequately considered what kinds of material culture systems would most likely be the bearers of stylistic information, information that may be transmitted in the process of defining and maintaining the boundaries of social groups (cf. Wobst 1977). I would argue that the *art mobilier*, or portable art, would be more likely to be informed with stylistic messages than would either stone tools or wall art. Despite the fact that most engravings or treatments of bone–

antler implements and pieces of raw material are not visible even at relative proximity, their very portability and the fact that some are and some are *not* engraved enhance their role as potential informers on stylistic groups. As Wobst (1977) so succinctly points out, an artifact or material culture class loses its "signaling innocence," or neutrality, when even some members of that class are treated stylistically and become bearers of stylistic messages. That only *some* bone and antler implements are engraved—that is, the fact that some are engraved and some are not—in itself is significant, particularly if these are used or made in a culturally stipulated mode or as part of a culturally defined context. The loss of signaling neutrality in Wobst's theory of style predicts precisely the kind of behavioral phenomenon discussed here:

> It argues for the *sudden* appearance of stylistic form in material culture, instead of the gradual incremental evolution often anticipated: a state of no-stylistic-messaging should suddenly be replaced by a state in which stylistic form has pervaded at least one (or more) categories of material culture [p. 1977:326; italics mine].

A current analysis (Conkey 1978) of engraved treatments of bone–antler artifacts and fragments, carried out along some of the same analytic dimensions suggested by Redman (Chapter 8), constitutes one test of the predictions put forth in this discussion. But the purpose of this chapter has been primarily to work toward understanding why one should even *expect* stylistic variability to exist at all among certain Paleolithic assemblages. As an outgrowth of the Binfordian program of the early–mid 1960s, stylistic analysis has been viewed as *de rigueur* among ambitious "new" archeologists. Paleolithic archeologists have not, with rare exceptions (e.g., Isaac 1972a,b,c; Kleindienst and Keller 1976; Smith 1973), attacked this problem; most have done so indirectly and from the perspective of design "targets" among lithics (Isaac 1974; Kleindienst and Keller 1976). The present model (*sensu latu*) has been developed not only to build a case for stylistic behavior among certain Paleolithic populations and under certain socioecological conditions, but also to encourage archeologists to consider, theoretically, the potential *sources* of variability that can be employed as at least partial explanations for observed or expected variability in prehistoric material culture. Although demonstration of precise styles or "style zones" for the Upper Paleolithic has yet to be done, this chapter has been an attempt to lay the groundwork for why this is a most testable and urgent hypothesis.

REFERENCES

Adams, Marie Jeanne
   1973   Structural aspects of a village art. *American Anthropologist* 75:265–279.

Bateson, Gregory
  1951   Conventions of communication: Where validity depends upon belief. In *Communication: The social matrix of society*, edited by J. Ruesch, G. Bateson. New York: Norton. Pp. 212–227.
  1972   Style, grace and information in primitive art. In *Steps to an ecology of mind*, edited by G. Bateson. New York: Ballantine. Pp. 128–152.
Binford, Lewis
  1962   Archaeology as anthropology. *American Antiquity 28* (2):217–225.
  1965   Archeological systematics and the study of cultural process. *American Antiquity 31* (2, Part 1 [October]):203–210.
  1972a   Paradigms, model-building and the state of Paleolithic research. In *An archaeological perspective*. New York: Seminar Press. Pp. 252–294.
  1972b   Interassemblage variability—The Mousterian and the 'functional' argument. In *The explanation of culture change*, edited by Colin Renfrew. London: Duckworth.
Binford, Lewis, and Sally R. Binford
  1966a   A preliminary analysis of functional variability in the Mousterian of Levallois facies. *American Anthropologist* (Special issue: Paleoanthropology) *68*(2, Part 2):238–295.
  1968b   The predatory revolution: a consideration of the evidence for a new subsistence level. *American Anthropologist 68*(2, Part 2): 238–295.
  1968   Stone tools and human behavior. *Scientific American 220*:70–84.
Binford, Sally R.
  1968a   Variation and change in the Near Eastern Mousterian of Levallois faces. In *New Perspectives in Archeology*, edited by S. R. Binford and L. R. Binford. Chicago: Aldine. Pp. 49–60.
  1968b   A structural comparison of disposal of the dead in the Mousterian and Upper Paleolithic. *Southwest Journal of Anthropology 24*:139–154.
  1971   The significance of variability: A minority report. UNESCO Conference, "The Origins of Homo Sapiens" (*Ecology and Conservation 3*) Paris.
Bordes, François
  1961   Mousterian cultures in France. *Science 134*:803–810.
  1968   *The Old Stone Age*. London. World University Library.
Bordes, François, and Denise DeSonneville-Bordes
  1970   The significance of variability in Paleolithic assemblages. *World Archaeology 2* (1 [June]): 61–73.
Bowman, Daniel C.
  1971   Problems and methods in archaeological classification with special reference to studies of the Lower Paleolithic and earlier Stone Age. Unpublished Master's thesis, Department of Anthropology, Univ. of Chicago.
Bricker, Harvey
  1976   Upper Paleolithic archeology. *Annual Review of Anthropology 5*:133–148.
Butzer, Karl
  1971   *Environment and archaeology*. Chicago: Aldine.
Campbell, Bernard
  1972   Man for all seasons. In *Sexual selection and the descent of man*, edited by B. Campbell. Pp. 40–58.
Charbonnier, G.
  1969   *Conversations with Claude Levi-Strauss*. London: Jonathan Cape.
Child, Irvin L., and Leon Siroto
  1965   Bakwele and American aesthetic evaluations compared. *Ethnology 4*, (4 [October]): 349–360.

Clarke, Grahame
    1970   Aspects of prehistory. Berkeley and Los Angeles. Univ. of California Press.
Conkey, Margaret W.
    1973   Style and the evolution of symbolic behavior. Paper presented to Anthropology
            Board of Studies, Colloquium, University of California, Santa Cruz.
    1978   An analysis of design structure: variability among Magdalenian engraved bones
            from northcoastal Spain. Ph.D. dissertation, Department of Anthropology. Univ.
            of Chicago.
D' Aquili, Eugene
    1972   The biopsychological determinants of culture. Addison-Wesley McCaleb Modules
            in Anthropology.
Douglas, Mary
    1966   Purity and danger: An analysis of the concepts of pollution and taboo. New York:
            Praeger.
    1970   Natural symbols: Explorations in cosmology. London: Barrie and Rockcliffe.
Freeman, Leslie G.
    1973   The significance of mammalian faunas from Paleolithic occupations in Canta-
            brian Spain. American Antiquity 38 (1):3–44.
Friedrich, Margaret Hardin
    1970   Design structure and social interaction: Archaeological implications of an ethno-
            graphic analysis. American Antiquity (35):332–343.
Geertz, Clifford
    1962   The growth of culture and the evolution of mind. In Theories of the Mind, edited
            by J. M. Scher. New York: Free Press of Glencoe. Pp. 713–740.
    1966   Religion as a cultural system. In Association of Social Anthropologists, Monograph
            3: Anthropological approaches to the study of religion, edited by Michael Banton.
            London: Tavistock. Pp. 1–46.
    1972   Deep-play: Notes on the Balinese cockfight. Daedalus (Winter): 1–37.
Geist, Valerius
    1971   Mountain sheep, A study in behavior and evolution. Chicago: Univ. of Chicago
            Press.
Gombrich, E. H.
    1961   Art and illusion: A study in the psychology of visual representation. Bollingen
            Series XXXV, 5 (2d edition). New York: Pantheon.
Gonzalez-Echegaray, Joaquin
    1972–   Consideraciones climáticas y ecológicas sobre el Magdaleniense III en el norte de
    1973   España. Zephyrus XXIII–XXIV:167–187.
Hallowell, A. Irving
    1959   Behavioral evolution and the emergence of self. In Evolution and anthropology,
            A centennial appraisal, edited by B. Meggers. Anthropological Society of Wash-
            ington, D.C. Pp. 36–60.
    1961   The protocultural foundations of human adaptation. In Social life of early man,
            edited by S. L. Washington. Chicago: Aldine. Pp. 236–255.
Hamburg, David
    1969   Observations on mother–infant interactions in primate field studies. In Determi-
            nants of infant-behavior, edited by B. M. Foss. (Vol. IV). London: Methuen. Pp.
            3–14.
Howell, F. Clark
    1965   (and subsequent editions 1968, 1974) Early Man. New York: Time-Life.
Isaac, G. L.
    1969   Studies of early culture in East Africa. World Archaeology 1 (1 [June]): 1–28.
    1972a   Chronology and the tempo of cultural change during the Pleistocene. In Calibra-

tion of hominoid evolution, edited by W. W. Bishop and J. A. Miller. New York: Scottish Academic Press for the Wenner-Gren Foundation for Anthropological Research. Pp. 381–430.

1972b Some experiments in quantitative methods for characterizing assemblages of Acheulian artifacts. In *Congrès Panafricain de Préhistoire, Dakar 1967*, edited by H. Hugot. Paris: Imprimeries Chambery. Pp. 547–555.

1972c Identification of cultural entities in the Middle Pleistocene. In *Congrès Panafricain de Préhistoire, Dakar 1967*, edited by H. Hugot. Paris: Imprimeries Chambery. Pp. 556–562.

1974 Form and design: Aspects of rule systems in the Pleistocene. Paper presented at 73rd annual meeting, American Anthropological Association, Mexico City.

Klein, Richard G.

1969 *Man and culture in the Late Pleistocene*. San Francisco: Chandler.

Kleindienst, M. R.

1967 Questions of terminology in regard to the study of Stone Age industries in eastern Africa: Cultural stratigraphic units. In *Background to evolution in Africa*, edited by W. W. Bishop and J. D. Clarke. Chicago: Univ. of Chicago Press. Pp. 821–859.

Kleindienst, Maxine R., and C. Keller

1976 The elusive concept of style and stone artifacts. Paper presented at IXe Congrès, Union Internationale des Sciences Prehistoriques et Protohistoriques, Nice, France.

Kubler, George

1971 Commentary on "Early architecture and sculpture in Mesoamerica" by Tatiana Proskouriakoff. In *Observations on the emergence of civilization in Mesoamerica*, edited by Robert F. Heizer and John A. Graham. *Contributions of the University of California Archaeological Research Facility* No. 11 (April). University of California, Department of Anthropology, Berkeley.

Leach, Edmund

1966 Ritualization in man. In A discussion on ritualization in animals and man (organized by Sir Julian Huxley). *Philosophical Transactions of the Royal Society of London, Series B, Biological Sciences* Vol. 251 (No. 772): 29.

Lee, Richard, and Irven Devore (Editors)

1968 *Man the Hunter*. Chicago: Aldine.

Levi-Strauss, Claude

1963 The effectiveness of symbols. In *Structural Anthropology*. New York: Basic Books. Pp. 186–205.

1964 *Le cru et le cuit; mythologiques*. Paris: Plon.

Lieberman, P., E. S. Crelin, and D. Klatt

1972 Phonetic ability and related anatomy of the newborn and adult human, Neanderthal man and chimpanzee. *American Anthropologist* 74(3): 286–307.

Margalef, Ramon

1968 *Perspectives in ecological theory*. Chicago: Univ. of Chicago Press.

Mellars, Paul A.

1970 Some comments on the notion of "functional variability" in stone-tool assemblages. *World Archaeology* 2 (1 [June]): 74–89.

Morris, Laura Newell

1971 *Human populations, genetic variation and evolution*. San Francisco: Chandler Pub.

Moure, J. A.

1974 Magdaleniense superior y Aziliense en la region Cantabrica espanola. Unpublished Ph.D. dissertation, Facultad de Filosofia y Letras, Univ. Complutense de Madrid.

Munn, Nancy D.
  1966   Visual categories: An approach to the study of representational systems. *American Anthropologist* 68 (4):936–950.
  1969   The effectiveness of symbols in Murngin rite and myth. In *Forms of symbolic action*, edited by Robert Spencer. Seattle: American Ethnological Society, Univ. of Washington Press.
Pielou, E. C.
  1966   Species-diversity and pattern-diversity in the study of ecological succession. *Journal of Theoretical Biology* 10:370–383.
Pilbeam, David
  1971   *The Ascent of Man*. New York: Macmillan.
Rappaport, Roy
  1971   The sacred in human evolution. *Annual Review of Ecology and Systematics* 2: 23–42. Palo Alto, Calif.: Annual Reviews, Inc.
Rivera, Edwin S.
  1973   Changing paradigms in cultural evolutionary theory. Unpublished honors thesis, Department of Anthropology, San Jose State University, San Jose, California.
Sackett, James
  1966   Quantitative analysis of Upper Paleolithic stone tools. In *Recent studies in paleoanthropology*, edited by J. D. Clark and F. C. Howell. *American Anthropologist*. Special Publication 68(2, Part 2): 356–394.
  1972   Style, function and artifact variability in Paleolithic assemblages. In *The explanation of culture change*, edited by C. Renfrew. London: Duckworth. Pp. 317–328.
Simpson, G. G.
  1967   *The meaning of evolution*. New Haven: Yale Univ. Press.
Smith, Philip E. L.
  1973   Some thoughts on variations among certain Solutrean artifacts. *Estudios dedicados al Prof. Dr. Luis Pericot*. Barcelona. I:67–75.
Solecki, Ralph S.
  1971   Neanderthal is not an epithet, but a worthy ancestor. *Smithsonian I:* 20–26.
Straus, L. G.
  1973a   The Vasco-Cantabrian Solutrean: Site locations and faunal evidence. Unpublished manuscript, Department of Anthropology, Univ. of Chicago.
  1973b   A study of the Solutrean in Vasco-Cantabrian Spain. Ph.D. dissertation research proposal to the National Science Foundation.
  1975   A study of the Solutrean in Vasco-Cantabrian Spain. Unpublished Ph.D. dissertation, Department of Anthropology, Univ. of Chicago.
Tobias, P. V.
  1965   Early man in East Africa. *Science 149* (3679 [July 2]): 22–33.
Trigger, Bruce
  1971   Archaeology and ecology. *World Archaeology 2* (3 [February]): 321–336.
Turner, Victor
  1966   Ndembu color classification. In *Association of Social Anthropologists, Monograph 3: Anthropological approaches to the study of religion*, edited by M. Banton. London: Tavistock. Pp. 47–84.
Washburn, Dorothy Koster
  1974   Symmetry universals in primitive design. Paper presented to American Anthropological Association Annual Meeting, Mexico City.
  1978   A symmetry analysis of Upper Gila area ceramic design. *Papers of the Peabody Museum of Archaeology and Ethnology, Harvard University 68*.

White, Leslie
  1949   *The evolution of culture*. New York: McGraw-Hill.
Wilden, Anthony
  1972   *System and structure: Essays in communication and exchange*. London: Tavistock.
Wobst, H. Martin
  1977   Stylistic Behavior and Information Exchange. In *Papers for the Director: Research essays in honor of James B. Griffin*; edited by Charles E. Cleland. Anthropology Papers. *Museum of Anthropology. Univ. of Michigan* No. 61: 317–342.

chapter 5

Information Sources and the Development of Decision-Making Organizations

GREGORY A. JOHNSON

A number of recent studies have emphasized the potential explanatory importance of information transfer and processing, or decision making, in the investigation of the development of urbanism (T örnqvist 1968; Wright 1969), states (Johnson 1973; Wright and Johnson 1975), and societies in general (Naroll 1956; Flannery 1972). This chapter constitutes a more detailed consideration of a model suggested by Wright and Johnson (1975:285), which incorporates a principle of "requisite variety" and an assumption of cost–benefit optimization to examine variable relationships involved in increasing complexity of societal-level, decision-making or administrative organizations.

Decision-making hierarchies essentially allow the coordination of a larger number of activities and/or integration of a larger number of organizational units than would be possible in the absence of such hierarchies. Decision-making organizations increase in complexity through two basic processes: horizontal and vertical specialization (Simon 1944). Horizontal specialization increases the number of decision-making units at a given level of a decision hierarchy, whereas vertical specialization

Social Archeology:
Beyond Subsistence and Dating

increases the number of hierarchic arranged levels of such an organization.

The general relationship between a decision-making organization (regulatory mechanism) and the activities or units integrated by this mechanism may be considered to be a special case of the relationship described by a principle of requisite variety (Ashby 1968:135). This principle is one of the foundations of regulation theory, and states that given two interdependent sets, variety in one set can only be reduced by increment in variety in the other set. To phrase it in terms of the present case, variety in decisions required to integrate a set of units or activities in the absence of a specialized integrative mechanism can only be reduced by the development of such a mechanism. Further, independent increase in the variety of decisions required to integrate a system already regulated by a specialized decision-making organization can only be reduced by increment in the variety of decisions made by that organization. As will be shown in the following discussion, increment in decisions made selects for increment in the complexity of a decision-making organization.

An initial assumption of cost–benefit optimization is the second major factor in the present model. Given pressure for increase in the complexity of a decision-making or administrative organization, such increase might be accomplished in a variety of ways. Not all of these possible alternatives, however, will be equally efficient. A cost–benefit optimization assumption will be used to generate a baseline of most efficient increase in organizational complexity, aganist which the implications of specific deviations from efficiency maximazation may be evaluated.

A formal model for the development of decision-making organizations is presented in the following pages. Although this model is a simple one, its construction requires a rather tedious process of definition of variables, examination of assumptions, and numerical illustration of variable relationships. The reader may find it useful to refer to the summary flowchart for the model (Figure 5.5, p. 98) while considering this section. A variety of possible anthropological implications of the model are discussed in the latter portion of this chapter.

DEFINITIONS AND ASSUMPTIONS OF THE MODEL

The following definitions are required:

1. *Information*: "Information is defined, in general, as that which causes or logically validates representational activity—activity in

which a structure, purporting to represent something else, is produced or augmented [Mackay 1969:133]."

2. *Source*: The minimal organizational unit under consideration. Types of source units may include territorial units, population units, residence units, activity units, etc.

3. *Source channel*: An information transfer channel between two sources, or between a source and a vertical control unit.

4. *Source channel-monitoring work unit*: The work involved in monitoring one source channel.

5. *Source integration*: Activity integration between or among sources.

6. *Source integration work unit*: Work involved in integration of two sources.

7. *Vertical control unit*: An organizational unit specialized in providing integration among sources or lower-level vertical control units.

8. *Source–control integration*: Activity integration between sources and control unit(s).

9. *Source–control integration work unit*: Work involved in activity integration between one source and one control unit.

10. *Control channel*: An information transfer channel between two control units.

11. *Control channel-monitoring work unit*: Work involved in monitoring one control channel.

12. *Control unit integration*: Activity integration between or among control units.

13. *Control integration work unit*: Work involved in activity integration between two control units.

14. *Channel capacity*: Maximum amount of information that may be transferred in a single channel with minimal information loss.

15. *Administrative advantage*: The proportional relationship of work load savings due to increment in the complexity of a control mechanism to the total work load required to obtain those savings.

16. *Administrative efficiency*: Administrative advantage per unit work load required with increase in the number of sources being integrated by a control mechanism.

17. *Control mechanism*: An organization specialized in providing integration among sources.

The following assumptions are required:

Entire Model:

1. The number of information sources integrated increases at a uniform rate.
2. Complete source integration is maintained.
3. Individual information channel loads are maintained within channel capacity.
4. Organizational decisions are made so as to maximize administrative advantage or efficiency.

Stage I (horizontal integration):

5. Information sources produce equivalent information output.
6. Information sources involved equivalent channel-monitoring work.
7. A source integration work unit is equivalent to a source channel-monitoring work unit.

Stage II (vertical integration—one vertical control unit):

8. A source–control integration work unit is equivalent to a source integration work unit.

Stage III (vertical integration—multiple vertical control units):

9. Control units produce equivalent information output.
10. Control unit information channels involve equivalent channel-monitoring work.
11. A control channel-monitoring work unit is equivalent to a source integration work unit.

Stage IV (second-order vertical integration—one control unit):

No additional assumptions required.

Beyond efficiency maximization, three of the assumptions just cited require special comment. These are: (*a*) maintenance of channel loads within channel capacity, (*b*) equivalency of channel-monitoring and source and/or control unit integrative work, and (*c*) maintenance of complete integration. Given assumption (*a*) arbitrary values may be assigned to the types of work involved in assumption (*b*). In that I have no present way to evaluate relative work load involved in these two activities, I will assume that they are equivalent and set the value of a work unit of each type at 1.0. Finally, the assumption of maintenance of complete integration allows this variable to be treated as a constant.

A more sophisticated approach to the type of model presented here would involve systematic consideration of the implications of deviation from the model's basic assumptions. Only implications of deviation from efficiency maximization will be considered in the following discussion.

One additional point must be made here. Increasing organizational complexity is generated in the following model through continued increment in the number of information sources integrated. The model attempts to describe various organizational responses to system growth, not explain that growth.

THE MODEL

Given the definitions and assumptions just described, we may proceed to the model itself. The first issue to be considered involves the relationship between increase in number of information sources integrated and work load required to achieve that integration in the absence of a vertically specialized control mechanism. In this situation the number of one-to-one relationships among the activity or other units that constitute effective information sources will be equivalent to the number of one-to-one information channels linking those units. Figure 5.1 (see also Table 5.1) graphically presents the relationship between increase in number of sources and increase in work load required to integrate those sources. This relationship is clearly nonlinear. Increase in sources produces increase in work load per source required for integration. As discussed previously, this work load may be decreased by the development of a specialized vertical control mechanism. The question becomes one of at what point development of such a mechanism would become efficient.

Figure 5.2 plots administrative advantage of a single-unit vertical control mechanism against work load required for integration of increasing numbers of sources. It is evident that development of such a mechanism (first-order vertical specialization) first results in overall work load reduction when six information sources are integrated. Note that these savings are obtained by reduction of the number of information channels that must be monitored to achieve integration. Vertical specialization thus reduces work load involved in information transfer.

Although work load savings obtained by initial vertical specialization increase with increase in sources integrated, the rate of such increase declines rapidly. This decline constitutes increasing pressure for division of labor (horizontal specialization) within this single-unit vertical control mechanism. Again the question is one of at what point such specialization

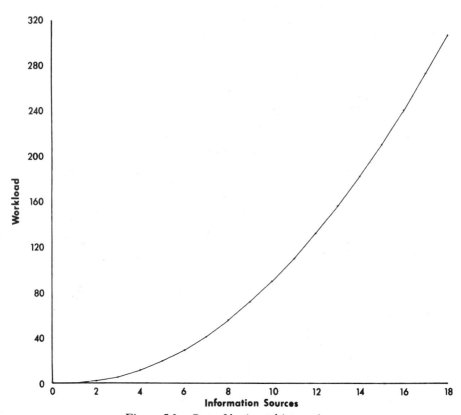

Figure 5.1. Cost of horizontal integration.

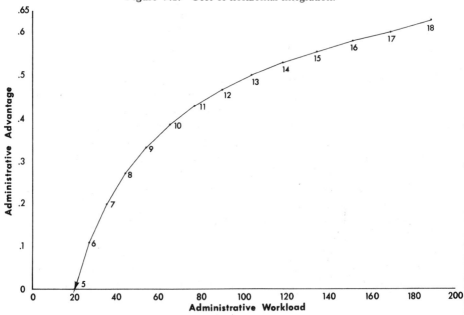

Figure 5.2. Administrative advantage of a first-order vertical control unit. n = information sources.

Table 5.1

WORKLOADS INVOLVED IN SYSTEM INTEGRATION: HORIZONTAL
AND FIRST-ORDER VERTICAL CONTROL UNITS

Horizontal control			
Sources	Source channels	Source integration	Total work
1	0	0	0
2	1	1	2
3	3	3	6
4	6	6	12
5	10	10	20
6	15	15	30
7	21	21	42
8	28	28	56
9	36	36	72
10	45	45	90
11	55	55	110
12	66	66	132
13	78	78	156
14	91	91	182
15	105	105	210
16	120	120	240
17	136	136	272
18	153	153	306
19	171	171	342
20	190	190	380

Vertical control						
Source channels	Source integration	Source–control integration	Total work	Work savings	Administrative advantage	Administrative efficiency ($\times 10^{-2}$)
1	0	1	2	−2	—	—
2	1	2	5	−3	—	—
3	3	3	9	−3	—	—
4	6	4	14	−2	—	—
5	10	5	20	0	0	0
6	15	6	27	3	.111	.412
7	21	7	35	7	.200	.571
8	28	8	44	12	.272	.618
9	36	9	54	18	.333	.616
10	45	10	65	25	.384	.590
11	55	11	77	33	.428	.555
12	66	12	90	42	.466	.517
13	78	13	104	52	.500	.480
14	91	14	119	63	.529	.444
15	105	15	135	75	.555	.411
16	120	16	152	88	.578	.380
17	136	17	170	102	.600	.352
18	153	18	189	119	.629	.332
19	171	19	209	133	.636	.304
20	190	20	230	150	.652	.283

would be expected to occur. This problem may be approached in two ways. Figure 5.3 presents a plot of administrative efficiency of a single-unit vertical control mechanism on number of information sources regulated. Note that efficiency peaks at integration of eight sources, and declines thereafter. Such diminishing returns in efficiency would provide one pressure for horizontal specialization.

A second approach to this problem is illustrated in Figure 5.4 (see also Table 5.2), which presents a plot of administrative advantage of horizontal specialization on work load associated with such specialization. Note that in terms of overall work loads, a two-unit, first-order, vertical control mechanism is more efficient than a single-unit mechanism when six sources are integrated. Thus initial development of a first-order control unit is associated with immediate selective pressure for horizontal specialization of that unit.

Figure 5.4 also plots efficient points for subsequent horizontal specialization of a first-order, vertical control mechanism to a maximum of six units. Work load savings are obtained by reduction of the number of source relationships that must be considered and decisions that must be made to achieve source integration. Horizontal specialization thus reduces work load involved in information processing.

Figure 5.4 also illustrates that absolute gains in administrative advantage obtained by horizontal specialization decrease as such specialization continues. These diminishing returns of horizontal specialization constitute effective selective pressure for second-order vertical specialization. As in the case of first-order vertical specialization, second-order specialization becomes efficient when six sources must be integrated. In this case, the six information sources involved are the six horizontally specialized units of a first-order, vertical control mechanism.

Figure 5.5 presents a flowchart of variables, variable relationships, and transformation formulae necessary to generate a second-order, vertical control unit. Note the three primary negative feedback loops incorporated in this information. Initial vertical specialization reduces the number of source channels that must be monitored in order to achieve system integration. Horizontal specialization of a first-order control unit reduces work load involved in explicit source integration. Second-order vertical specialization reduces the number of control channels that must be monitored to achieve system integration.

Two positive feedback loops are of interest. Both vertical specialization and horizontal specialization of a vertical control unit *permit*, in general, some degree of subsequent increment in number of sources integrated without further elaboration of the control mechanism. This is

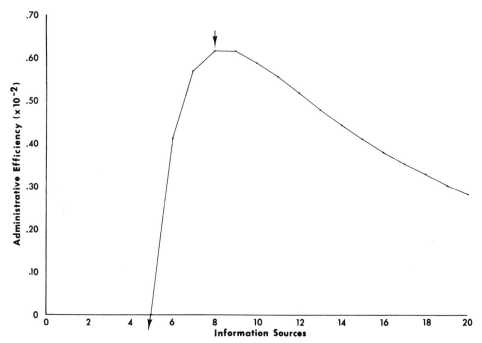

Figure 5.3. Administrative efficiency of a first-order vertical control unit.

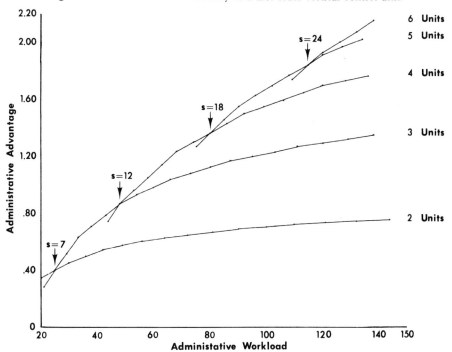

Figure 5.4. Horizontal specialization of first-order control unit. s = information sources.

Table 5.2

WORK LOADS INVOLVED IN HORIZONTAL SPECIALIZATION OF A
FIRST-ORDER VERTICAL CONTROL UNIT

Vertical control	
Sources	Total work
6	27
7	35
8	44
9	54
10	65
11	77
12	90
13	104
14	119
15	135
16	152
17	170
18	189
19	209
20	230

Horizontal specialization of vertical control (two units)							
Source channels	Source integration	Source–control integration	Control channels	Control integration	Total work	Savings	Administrative advantage
6	6	6	1	1	20	7	.350
7	9	7	1	1	25	10	.400
8	12	8	1	1	30	14	.460
9	16	9	1	1	36	18	.500
10	20	10	1	1	42	23	.547
11	25	11	1	1	49	28	.571
12	30	12	1	1	56	34	.607
13	36	13	1	1	64	40	.625
14	42	14	1	1	72	47	.652
15	49	15	1	1	81	54	.666
16	56	16	1	1	90	62	.688
17	64	17	1	1	100	70	.700
18	72	18	1	1	110	79	.718
19	81	19	1	1	121	88	.727
20	90	20	1	1	132	98	.742

an enabling relationship. Neither type of specialization generates increase in basic information sources. As stated previously, such increase is
related to variables not included in the present model.

The efficient development of a decision-making organization is ex-

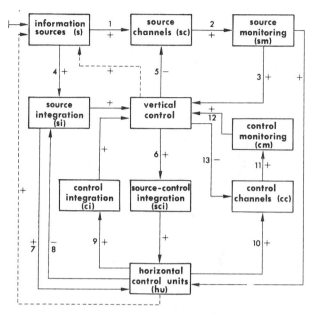

Figure 5.5. Development of second-order vertical control unit—flowchart. Notes: 1: $sc = (s^2 - s)/2$ (Dubin 1959); 2: $sm = sc$; 3: when $s \geq 6$; $si = (s^2 - s)/2$; 5: $sc = s$; 6: $sci = s$; 7: when $s \geq 6$; 8: $si = [(s^2/hu) - s]/2$; 9: $ci = (hu^2 - hu)/2$; 10: $cc = (hu^2 - hu)/2$; 11: $cm = cc$; 12: when $s \geq 24$; 13: $cc = hu$.

tended to the point of third-order vertical specialization in Figure 5.6. Here administrative work load is plotted against complexity of decision-making organization. Prior to initial vertical specialization, this complexity is measured simply as the number of horizontal units integrated in the system. With initial vertical specialization, complexity is measured by the number of units involved in a most efficiently organized control mechanism.

Figure 5.6 illustrates that efficient increase in complexity of a control mechanism is associated with effective step functions in administrative efficiency. Vertical and immediately subsequent horizontal specialization of such a control mechanism results in absolute decrease in work load involved in the integration of an increasing number of sources. I would suggest that the presence of such step functions has important implications for the investigation of the evolution of social systems. Not only do these step functions indicate points of critical evolutionary change, but they also allow partitioning of a continuum of such change into theoretically justifiable analytical units.

The model as developed thus far, has relied on an assumption of cost–benefit optimization. One of the most interesting aspects, however,

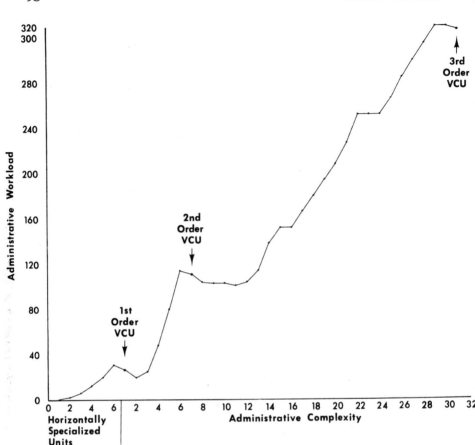

Figure 5.6. Development of efficient administrative organization. *VCU* = vertical control unit.

of any maximization model is the implications of deviation from maximizing assumptions. Figure 5.7 presents plots of administrative work load on number of information sources integrated, given a baseline efficiency maximization and two types of deviation from this assumption. Plot A illustrates the effects of suppression of first-order vertical specialization, whereas plots B and C illustrate the effects of suppression of horizontal specialization of first- and second-order vertical control units. In all three cases, deviation from a maximizing assumption involves marked increases in work load required for source integration.

If work loads may be directly related to effective costs, the increasing costs of deviation from efficiency in system integration may be related to an increasing probability of system failure. Identification of social processes that facilitate and those that inhibit cost–benefit optimization in

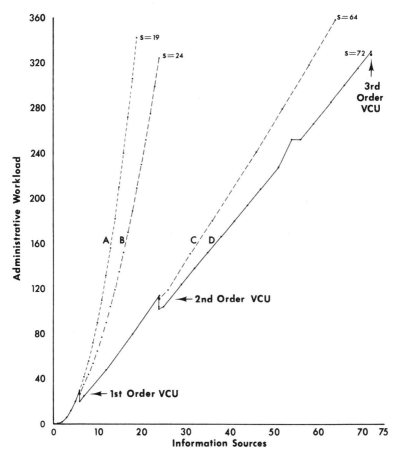

Figure 5.7. Deviations from efficient administrative development. s = information sources; VCU = vertical control unit. A: First-order vertical specialization suppressed. B: Horizontal specialization of first-order VCU suppressed. C: Horizontal specialization of second-order VCU suppressed. D: Efficient development of administrative organization.

the organization of societal-level control mechanisms should provide one source of explanation for the continued development, or breakdown and failure, of social systems.

Before continuing with a more detailed consideration of various implications of the present model, it might be well to summarize the basic observations made thus far.

1. Increase in the number of information sources integrated in a system selects for increase in the complexity of the system's control mechanism.

2. Vertical specialization in administrative organizations reduces work load involved in channel monitoring (information transfer).
3. Horizontal specialization in administrative organizations reduces work load involved in explicit source integration. Since such integration directly involves decision making, the work load reduction involved is in information processing.
4. Efficient increase in administrative complexity produces step functions in administrative efficiency.
5. Suppression of vertical and/or horizontal specialization in administrative organizations produces marked increase in work loads and costs involved in system integration.

IMPLICATIONS OF THE MODEL

A model of the sort presented here would be of little anthropological interest if it could not be more directly related to specific behavioral problems. In the following sections, an attempt is made to discuss specific social, organizational, and spatial implications of this model.

Suppression of first-order vertical specialization has been shown to involve major increments in information transfer and processing costs. At the societal level such specialization is presumably inhibited or facilitated by explicitly social factors. It is possible that selective pressure for initial vertical specialization of a societal-level, decision-making organization also selects for the development of ascribed status differentials and regularized status inheritance rules (ranking systems) as one possible social strategy for the solution of problems inherent in the operation of a vertically specialized organization.

These problems may be divided into two categories: those involved in decision making and those involved in decision implementation. Decision-making problems would seem to include recruitment and training of personnel, and general maintenance or organizational continuity. Decision implementation requires that the general population of a society acquiesce to and carry out operational aspects of decisions made by vertically specialized personnel.

Decision implementation has received considerable anthropological attention in discussion of such topics as influence, authority, law, and power. Here influence will be defined as the ability of one individual or organization unit to initiate, modify, or terminate specific behavior or types of behavior of another individual or unit. Use of social status differences to structure or supplement differential influence in decision-making organizations has been frequently noted (Sutherland 1975:290; Udy 1970:48; Wallace 1971:5). Simply stated, if differences in social status are positively related to differences in influence, then incorporation of individuals of differentially higher status in a decision-making hierarchy should increase the probability of decision implementation.

In evolutionary terms, I would expect a high degree of association among initial vertical specialization of decision-making systems, development of ascribed social status differences, and increment in effective influence. Thus in Fried's (1967:110 ff.) discussion of the evolution of political society, ranked societies are differentiated from egalitarian ones partially by the development of: (a) specialized leadership; (b) ascribed social status differences; and (c) increase in authority.

Decision implementation, however, is of little importance if decisions are not made. As mentioned previously, decision making in a vertically specialized system may involve problems of personnel recruitment and training, and of organizational continuity. Specialized decision making involves nongeneral knowledge and skills acquired during a training period. Decision-making positions may be highly valued because of their social and/or material rewards. A regularized recruitment system may serve to reduce potentially disruptive competition and dissension in selection of individuals to occupy such positions, although succession conflicts may still be common in hereditary systems (Burling 1974:13 ff.). Finally, lack of organizational continuity may involve changes in operating procedure that inhibit organizational efficiency.

If status differences function to increase the probability of decision implementation, then the development of regular status inheritance rules may reduce problems of recruitment, training, and continuity. Such inheritance systems would function to designate probable individuals to eventually occupy decision-making positions. A high-status child living in close proximity to a high-status decision maker would be afforded the opportunity of training by example for future decision-making activity. A system in which decision-making positions are effectively inherited would also provide an increased probability of organizational continuity.

Sahlins's (1963) distinction between "big-man" societies and "petty" chiefdoms in Melanesia and Polynesia would seem to reflect these predicted social responses to problems related to initial vertical specialization of a decision-making system. Although functioning with specialized leaders, big-man systems lack regularized provision for recruitment, training, and continuity, as well as the real or potential increase in effective influence characteristic of petty chiefdoms.

The hypotheses I have just suggested are summarized in Figure 5.8 and suggest that development of ranking systems may be associated with

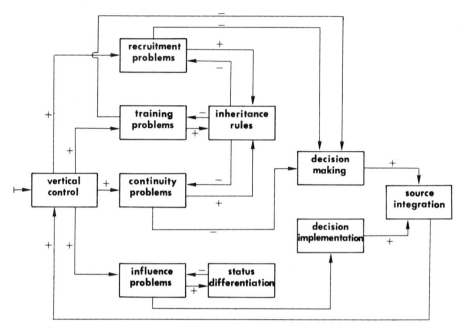

Figure 5.8. Function of inheritance rules and status differentiation in integration of information sources—flowchart.

increment in the number of information sources integrated on a societal level. Fried (1967:183) suggests five processes as being among those potentially leading to the development of ranking systems.

1. "Maintaining connections between parent settlements and those that have budded off; . . ."
2. "Diversifying the consuming sector of the economy by maintaining regular trade relations with communities exploiting somewhat different resources; . . ."
3. "Better handling of food supply by organizing special labor forces for simple irrigation tasks; . . ."
4. "Rationalization of a sequence of habitation in which original settlers are joined, albeit peaceably, by subsequent settlers; . . ."
5. "Formalization, as Service has pointed out, of trans-settlement sodalities, often as a means of enlarging the area of relative peace."

Note that processes 1, 4, and 5 involve increment in residence and/or population units as information sources, whereas processes 2 and 3 involve increment in residence and/or activity units as information sources.

Simple population increase within a context of limited resources has also been cited by Carneiro (1970:736) and Burling (1974:18) as generating status differences in order to reinforce leadership in intergroup conflict. It would seem that each of these suggested processes may be considered to be a special case of a more general organization model.

One would expect that the more complex the decision-making organization, the more serious the problems just discussed might be. To the extent that these problems can be resolved in the context of social organization, increment in information sources integrated and associated increment in the complexity of a decision-making organization should select for increasing social status differentiation and increasing regularity of status inheritance. Thus, primogeniture, which provides very specific designation of status inheritance and long training periods as well as considerable continuity, is apparently characteristic of complex kin-based societies (Service 1975:74). It seems that many of these societies are also characterized by marked social stratification (Sahlins 1958).

Sahlins's work on social stratification in Polynesia is of particular interest here in that "it was suggested, therefore, that stratification is directly related to productivity, [and] productivity was measured by the number of people embraced in the largest redistributive network of food and how frequently this overall network was utilized [Sahlins 1958:249]." The Polynesian cases examined by Sahlins would seem to reflect an expected high correlation between degree of social stratification and number of population units as information sources integrated.

I do not mean to imply that this organization model can account for the origin and development of status differentiation and status inheritance rules in general. I would suggest, however, that such developments constitute one viable social alternative to the resolution of critical problems generated by initial vertical specialization in societal-level, decision-making organizations. Whatever the specific mechanisms involved, it is clear that the increasing costs of failure to resolve such problems have grave implications for the future of a society.

Suppression of first-order vertical specialization is, however, only the first of the two major evolutionary problems I have defined. The second was suppression of horizontal specialization of a highest-order control unit. Recall from Figure 5.7 that in terms of increasing costs, suppression of horizontal specialization of this sort is much more cost intensive in a system with a first-order than in one with a second-order, vertical control mechanism. This might suggests that in evolutionary terms this problem of horizontal specialization decreases in significance with increasing complexity of a system. Further considerations, however, suggest that this view would be incorrect.

Here it might be suggested that despite selective pressure for administrative efficiency, one major factor leading to suppression of horizontal specialization is probably the resistance of individuals holding positions in such a vertical control unit to the effective division of administrative influence or power that such specialization would entail. Differently phrased, nonadministrative considerations may produce attempts to maintain effective concentration of political power.

This problem has recently been considered in some detail by Burling (1974). He concludes that power sharing of this sort is relatively rare and often beset when present by disagreement among coequal leaders and breakdown in the coordination of their activities (Burling 1974:255). In that there seems to be a high positive correlation between vertical complexity of an administrative organization and the amount of political power involved in such a system (Wirsing 1973:153), resistance to horizontal specialization (power sharing) may be positively correlated with overall administrative complexity. In contradiction to this expectation, Burling (1974:153) suggests that such power sharing is more common in complex than in simpler societies.

The problem is not one that will be resolved here. I suspect, however, that much of the ethnographic record fails to distinguish between ostensible administrative role and actual administrative function. A king may reign, but a council of ministers may rule. The proportionally high incidence of power sharing in complex, not to say modern, societies cited by Burling may simply reflect a decline in the ability to disguise effective coequal leadership with a variety of social fictions.

ORGANIZATIONAL AND SPATIAL
IMPLICATIONS OF THE MODEL

In the following pages, specific numerical implications of the present model are examined with ethnographic, geographic, and archeological data. Such examination is undertaken with considerable trepidation. There is no a priori reason to believe that such a simple model, based on such restrictive assumptions, should provide an accurate description of real-world processes. As will be seen in the following discussion, however, there is a rather remarkable fit between various model predictions and various classes of field data. This fit is best intepreted as indicative of the potential utility of an organization theory approach, rather than of the predictive power of the present formulation.

One of the more interesting parallels between present model predictions and field data is in the area of the organization of administrative hierarchies. In the context of a much more general cross-cultural study of the organization of work in nonindustrial societies, Stanley Udy (1959, 1970) attempts to predict the number of levels of management hierarchy appropriate to coordination of a given number of activities. Such prediction involves estimation of the maximum number of activities that any given administrator can effectively coordinate. Udy (1959:38) cites a number of studies in experimental psychology indicating that the maximum number of items to which an individual can give simultaneous attention ranges between three and seven, with a mode of five. Udy's (1970:50) own data suggest that in activity coordination, this number is probably four.

Tables 5.3a and 5.3b present administrative organizations of various degrees of complexity as predicted by the present information model. The figures in Table 5.3a were generated with an efficiency maximization assumption, whereas those in Table 5.3b reflect the results of suppression of horizontal specialization of a second-order, vertical control unit.

The numbers of administered units at various levels of a given administrative hierarchy are not even multiples of a base number but exhibit considerable variability from one organization to the next. Across the whole organizational range considered, however, the mean number of organizational units integrated by an immediate superior unit in an administrative hierarchy generated on an assumption of efficiency maximization is 3.66, with a range of 2.33 to 6.00. This mean of 3.66 is a reasonable approximation of Udy's figure of 4.0, and the range of 2.33 to 6.00 is remarkable close to that of 3.0 to 7.0 reported in the psychological literature.

The figures in Table 5.3b are of additional interest. Given suppression of horizontal specialization of a second-order, vertical control unit, the average number of organizational units integrated by an immediately superior unit is increased to 7.25, with a range of 3.0 to 15.0. It would seem that this particular form of deviation from efficiency considerations not only results in marked increase in work loads as shown previously but also produces a work load that may severely tax individual or unit capacities.

Evolutionary problems of power sharing were discussed in an earlier section of this chapter. Given present considerations, we might predict that systems in which a single highest-order control unit attempts to integrate a number of immediately subordinate units markedly in excess of six or seven is under considerable selective pressure for horizontal specialization of that highest-order unit. In societal-level systems, such

Table 5.3a
UNITS OF ADMINISTRATIVE ORGANIZATION—EFFICIENT DEVELOPMENT [a]

Levels of hierarchy

	1	2	3	4	5	6		1	2	3	4	5	6
3													1
2	6							6					6
1	6					4		4					4
0	1-5	3-3.5	2.33-4	3-4.5	3.6-4.8				3-3.5	2.33-4	3-4.5	3.6-4.8	3
									4-3.43	2.92-3.43	2.92-3		
Sources	1-5	6-7	7-12	12-18	18-24	24		24	24	24-35	35-54	54-72	72

[a] Average number of administered units = 3.66.

Table 5.3b
UNITS OF ADMINISTRATIVE ORGANIZATION—HORIZONTAL SPECIALIZATION OF SECOND-ORDER VERTICAL CONTROL UNIT SUPPRESSED [a]

Levels of hierarchy

	1	1	1	1	1	1	1	1	1
3									1
2									6
1									4
0	6-7	7-8	8-9	9-10	10-11	11-12	12-13	13-14	3
	4-3.71	3.71-3.88	3.88-4	4-4.6	4.6-4.73	4.73-4.83	4.83-4.92	4.92-5	14-15
									5-5.66
Sources	24-26	26-31	31-36	36-46	46-52	52-58	58-64	64-70	70-85
									72

[a] Average number of administered units = 7.25.

pressure should be reflected minimally by high administrative costs, and often by the attempts of lower-level administrators or even the general population of the society to induce such specialization.

For example, prior to 1901 the Ashanti state of West Africa was composed of nine originally autonomous chiefdoms and a number of subsequently incorporated communities (Fortes 1969:140). Thus the central Ashanti administrative organization was attempting to integrate in excess of nine subordinate units. This situation suggests high administrative costs and possible lower-level pressure for horizontal specialization of the central organization. In fact the Ashanti state was subject to attempts at secession and was maintained largely by the military power of the central Kumasi chiefdom (Fortes 1969:140).

A similar situation seems to have characterized the Bulamogi state of East Africa. In one period prior to British domination, the state consisted of nine territories administered by client–chiefs of the king and three princely areas over which the king exercised administrative control (Fallers 1965:134). Thus some twelve units were integrated, presumably at rather high cost. Again, as our model would predict, there were apparently frequent princely revolts (p. 136), which, interestingly enough, were often attributed to excessive tribute demands by the king (p. 143).

In an archeological example, Richard Blanton (personal communication, 1976) suggests that just prior to its collapse in about A.D. 900, the central administrative organization of Monte Alban in the valley of Oaxaca, Mexico, integrated some thirteen major territorial units within the city itself. Administrative control of areas outside the city may have increased this number. Blanton further suggests that the marked population increase noted in this period was related to increased labor demands in response to increasing taxation. Heavy taxation and eventual collapse of the system might then be related to the increasing costs of integration of an inefficiently large number of administrative units.

In contrast to these examples of system stress, the nineteenth-century Yoruba state of West Africa seems to have suffered from relatively little internal dissension. Administration of the state under the king was territorially divided among the capital and five provinces (Bascom 1969:29). Recall that the present model predicts that administration of six immediately subordinate sources is relatively cost efficient.

One should keep in mind that while integration of a large number of subordinate units by a single-unit, highest-order, vertical control mechanism may also simply indicate a rather low level of integration. Heavy tribute or taxation and attempts at revolt may be among the attributes useful in making a distinction between a high level of integration at high cost and a low level of integration of a larger than expected number of information sources.

The organization model presented here may be used to generate spatial as well as social and explicitly organizational predictions. One such spatial prediction deals with the territorial organization of societies without vertically specialized decision-making organizations. Most such ethnographically known societies are of hunters and gatherers.

Wilmsen (1973) and Wobst (1974) have considered various aspects of hunting-and-gathering group size and territorial organization. They both consider a hexagonal distribution of band territories to be most efficient in maximization of use of available resources and minimization of travel and boundary maintenance costs.

The number of band territories bordering on the territory of an individual band (contact number) may be taken as a rough index of territory shape. Thus if maximization of resource utilization and minimization of movement are primary determinants of hunting-and-gathering spatial organization, the average contact number for individual bands should be six.

Considerations of interband interaction may alter this expectation. One of the most theoretically important forms of interband interaction involves the operation of mating systems (Wobst 1974). If bands tend to be hexagonally distributed, individuals within a given band consider mate availability and a series of additional ecological variables in at least six surrounding band territories.

The organization model just presented suggests that integration of six sources is more efficiently undertaken through a specialized control mechanism of a sort that most hunters and gatherers lack. In the absence of such a control mechanism, there may be some selective pressure to maintain the number of sources monitored within efficient limits. Phrased in terms of the present case, there may be some selective pressure to minimize the average number of adjacent band territories.

Actual spatial distributions should reflect responses to major operative selective pressures. As just seen, resource utilization and movement considerations suggest that the mean band contact number should approximate six, with a range of variability on either side of this value. Integration considerations, on the other hand, suggest that mean band contact number should be less than six—the lower, the better. An optimizing response to these contradictory pressures might then involve maintenance of mean contact number at close to, but less than, six.

Wilmsen (1973:11) gives a mean contact number for 22 Northern Paiute bands of 5.4 and for 15 Southern Paiute bands of 5.5. Birdsell (1958:196–199) provides a mean contact number of 5.5 for 100 Australian tribes. Wobst (1974:154) cites a mean contact number of 5.67 for 31 groups of Eastern Sub-Arctic hunters. Note that in all of these cases, the mean values are less than but close to six, suggesting that pressures involved in source integration operate in conjunction with those involved in resource utilization and movement minimization in the determination of the spatial organization of hunters and gatherers.

If there is pressure for maintenance of territorial contact number at a value of less than six in societies without specialized vertical control mechanisms, then we would expect the absence of such pressure in societies having such mechanisms. Consideration of minimization of movement and boundary costs might then select for a spatial distribution such that territorial contact numbers may more closely approximate 6.0. Few such contact numbers are available in the literature. Haggett's (1965:52) value of 6.21 for 100 Brazilian counties is most frequently cited. Two small groups of Chinese market areas illustrated by Skinner (1964:22,25) have mean contact numbers for completely bounded areas of 6.20 and 6.67 respectively. Smith (1972:6–7) cites a mean contact value of 5.93 for 127 Guatemalan townships.

Although the figures presented here are by no means conclusive, they do suggest systematic differences in territorial organization between societies lacking and societies having specialized vertical control mechanisms. The present model suggests that the cause for such differences may reside in selection for efficiency in monitoring and integration of organizational units that function as basic information sources.

PROBLEMS FOR FURTHER WORK

I hope that the latter portion of this chapter has indicated something of the variety of problems to which organization models might be applicable. Although the actual model just presented is crude in the extreme, it is an attempt to more rigorously examine critical information variable relationships in the development of decision-making organizations. Thus it has been possible to lend additional support to statements such as the following: "A new institution will appear only after some critical threshold in need for information-processing is reached; thus, evolution appears steplike [Flannery 1972:423]."

Further work along present lines should consider the implications of deviation from a number of assumptions made here. For example, it was assumed in this chapter that all sources generate equivalent information output and involve equivalent channel monitoring costs. There is every reason to believe, however, that sources produce differential information output both synchronically and diachronically. Further, even sources of equivalent output may involve information transfer over different distances, and thus differential monitoring costs. The principle of requisite variety suggests that additional system variability related to these factors will also select for increment in the complexity of societal-level, decision-making organizations.

Other factors that should be examined include the following: What are the implications of monitoring information sources that are critical to system decision making but do not constitute organizational units integrated within the system? Increment in such sources would primarily result in increment in channel-monitoring work and thus differentially select for vertical specialization in decision-making organizations. Such differential selection would alter details of the sequence of most efficient increase in organizational complexity projected in this chapter. Such alteration would probably directly involve problems of channel capacity not considered in the present model.

Irrespective of the merits of the present formulation, I would suggest that organization models have a sufficient generality of applicability to contribute to the integration of a large number of more special purpose models. Such integration is essential to the development of general theory in anthropology, without which the probability of success in the description and explanation of the operation of cultural systems is low indeed.

ACKNOWLEDGMENTS

This chapter was originally prepared for the Conference on Social Differentiation and Interaction sponsored by the Anthropology Graduate Organization of the State University of New York at Binghamton, and held in Binghamton April 2–3, 1976. In addition to the other participants in that conference, I would like to thank Robert McC. Adams, Daniel G. Bates, Richard E. Blanton, Gary Feinman, Stephen Kowalewski, Susan H. Lees, Burton Pasternak, John Pfeiffer, John D. Speth, and H. Martin Wobst for their helpful comments on various drafts of this chapter.

REFERENCES

Ashby, Ross W.
    1968   Variety, constraint, and the law of requisite variety. In *Modern systems research for the behavioral scientist*, edited by Walter Buckley. Chicago: Aldine. Pp. 129–136.
Bascom, William
    1969   *The Yoruba of southwestern Nigeria*. New York: Holt, Rinehart & Winston.
Birdsell, Joseph
    1958   On population structure in generalized hunting and collecting populations. *Evolution* 12: 189–205.

Burling, Robbins
  1974   *The passage of power: Studies in political succession*. New York: Academic.
Carneiro, Robert L.
  1970   A theory of the origin of the state. *Science* 169:733–738.
Dubin, Robert
  1959   Stability of human organizations. In *Modern organization theory*, edited by Mason Haine. New York, London. Wiley. Pp. 218–253.
Fallers, Lloyd A.
  1965   *Bantu bureaucracy: A century of political evolution among the Basoga of Uganda*. Chicago: Univ. of Chicago Press.
Flannery, Kent V.
  1972   The cultural evolution of civilizations. *Annual Review of Ecology and Systematics* 3:399–426.
Fortes, Meyer
  1969   *Kinship and the social order: The legacy of Lewis Henry Morgan*. Chicago: Aldine.
Fried, Morton H.
  1967   *The evolution of political society: An essay in political anthropology*. New York: Random House.
Haggett, Peter
  1965   *Locational analysis in human geography*. New York: St. Martin Press.
Johnson, Gregory A.
  1973   *Local exchange and early state development in southwestern Iran. The University of Michigan Museum of Anthropology, Anthropological Papers* No. 51.
Mackay, Donald M.
  1969   *Information, mechanism and meaning*. Cambridge: M.I.T. Press.
Naroll, Raoul
  1956   A preliminary index of social development. *American Anthropologist* 58 (4): 687–715.
Sahlins, Marshall D.
  1958   *Social stratification in Polynesia*. Seattle. Univ. of Washington Press.
  1963   Poor man, rich man, big-man, chief: Political types in Melanesia and Polynesia. *Comparative Studies in Society and History* 5 (3): 285–303.
Service, Elman R.
  1975   *Origins of the state and civilization: The process of cultural evolution*. New York: Norton.
Simon, Herbert A.
  1944   Decision-making and administrative organization. *Public Administration Review* 4: 16–30.
Skinner, G. William
  1964   Marketing and social structure in rural China. *Journal of Asian Studies* 24 (1): 3–43.
Smith, Carol Ann
  1972   The domestic marketing system in western Guatemala: An economic, locational, and cultural analysis. Ph.D. dissertation, Stanford Univ.
Sutherland, John W.
  1975   *Systems: analysis, administration, and architecture*. New York: Van Nostrand Reinhold.
Törnqvist, Gunnar
  1968   Flows of information and the location of economic activities. *Geografiska Annaler* 50B (1): 99–107.

Udy, Stanley H., Jr.
1959   *Organization of work: A comparative analysis of production among nonindustrial peoples*. New Haven, Conn.: HRAF Press.
1970   *Work in traditional and modern society*. Englewood Cliffs, N.J.: Prentice-Hall.
Wilmsen, Edwin N.
1973   Interaction, spacing behavior, and the organization of hunting bands. *Journal of Anthropological Research* 29 (1): 1–31.
Wirsing, Rolf
1973   Political power and information: A cross-cultural study. *American Anthropologist* 75 (1): 153–170.
Wobst, H. Martin
1974   Boundary conditions for Paleolithic social systems: A simulation approach. *American Antiquity* 39 (2, Part 1): 147–178.
Wright, Henry T.
1969   *The administration of rural production in an early Mesopotamian town. The University of Michigan Museum of Anthropology, Anthropological Papers* No. 38.
Wright, Henry T., and Gregory A. Johnson
1975   Population, exchange and early state formation in southwestern Iran. *American Anthropologist* 77 (2): 267–289.

chapter **6**

Early Craft Specialization: An Example from the Balkan Chalcolithic

ROBERT K. EVANS

Recent research on the part of several individuals and the appearance of useful syntheses (e.g., Tringham 1971) have provided the basic framework for the Neolithic–Chalcolithic development in the Balkan Peninsula. Thus, it is possible to pose specific types of questions of the existing data and to use these data to test propositions related to general theory. A specific example of the development of craft specialization is presented here and is related to the phenomena of prehistoric sociocultural growth and differentiation.

The area considered here is what may be called the eastern portion of the Balkan Peninsula. It is centered in the Maritsa Valley of central Bulgaria and includes northern Bulgaria and southern Romania to the north, southern Bulgaria and northeastern Greece to the south, and a small portion of eastern Yugoslavia to the west. This is essentially the area of the Boian–Gumelniţa, or Karanovo V–VI, culture of the Balkan Chalcolithic. This period is now dated (in the light of radiocarbon dating and calibration) to ca. 5000–3500 B.C. (Gimbutas 1973). It is no longer to be considered as a short, transitional period but as a distinct period for

113

Social Archeology:
Beyond Subsistence and Dating

classification and analysis, and as important for investigating questions of sociocultural development.

THE EAST BALKAN CHALCOLITHIC

One of the important features of this period is that it lies between the period of the establishment of the early village agriculture and the period characterized by the appearance of bronze metallurgy. As the term *chalcolithic* (or *Eneolithic*) indicates, the period is defined by the presence of copper metallurgy.

The sites of the eastern Balkan Chalcolithic are generally mound or tell sites representing a long-term sedentary population of agriculturalists. Remains of houses from several sites indicate solidly built structures. Construction was of posts and clay, and there were often two or three rooms. Houses have clay floors, hearths, and often decorated walls. In those sites where large areas have been exposed, it is clear that the houses were often arranged in rows along narrow streets. Subsistence was based on agricultural products, such as wheat, barley, and lentils, and domesticated animals, such as cattle, sheep, goat, and pig. The material equipment includes various pottery wares and the basic flint, stone, bone, horn, and antler tools common to the Neolithic and Chalcolithic cultures. In addition to these materials there is an increasing frequency of copper tools and ornaments. There are also numbers of both anthropomorphic and zoomorphic figurines in clay, bone, stone, and gold (Berciu 1967; Childe 1957; V. Dumitrescu 1965a,b; Gaul 1948; Georgiev 1961, 1963; Gimbutas 1974; Renfrew 1970).

My investigation of the development of craft specialization and related phenomena in this area and time period began with the results of experiments conducted on the production of graphite-decorated pottery, which characterizes this period (Evans 1973). In short, these experiments indicated a complexity of the craft that suggested the possibility of craft specialization. This phenomenon was also suggested by recent research on the development of copper metallurgy (Jovanović 1971a,b; Renfrew 1970). A few additional crafts were listed as possibilities, and finally, I investigated the possibility of craft specialization in pottery production, copper metallurgy, gold metallurgy, flint working, figurine manufacture, shell bracelet manufacture, and weaving.

CRAFT SPECIALIZATION

Craft specialization, as a particular phenomenon, may be present in almost any culture. Certainly there are possible examples from the

Neolithic and even the Paleolithic–Mesolithic. However, the Chalcolithic is a period during which we may expect this phenomenon to become an especially important feature of the sociocultural system.

In order to investigate the phenomenon of craft specialization, it is necessary to define it. Numerous definitions have been offered, for example:

> In my mind, a specialist is an individual who holds a position or vocation because he controls a set of skills that most of his communal fellows do not control. It is obvious that this definition depends on the societal or communal context [Rodgers 1966:410].

Considering this and other definitions, I utilized the following points (Evans 1973) in my definition of craft specialization:

1. The manufacture of certain craft products is limited to a small percentage of the total number of individuals in any given community.
2. These individuals devote some of their productive time to the manufacture of these craft products.
3. Consequently, they must withdraw themselves from some or all of the basic subsistence activities.
4. Thus, they must obtain some or all of their subsistence goods through some kind of exchange system for their craft products [p. 55].

Next, a series of general hypotheses were listed that involve the interrelationships of the phenomenon of craft specialization with population size, technological complexity, efficiency, spatial differentiation of work space, and functional differentiation of tools. And, finally, a list of expected phenomena was made, which indicated the types of finds that should be present if craft specialization was present. These expectations included:

1. *Workshops:* specialized areas for craft activities.
2. *Tool kits:* specialized tools for craft activities.
3. *Storage facilities and/or hoards:* delimited locations for storing completed craft products.
4. *Resource exploitation:* regular exploitation of particular resources.
5. *Exchange and trade:* distribution of resources or craft products.
6. *Differential distributions.*

In addition to these specific expectations for craft specialization, a complex of four related expectations was formulated. This complex relates directly to the proposed explanation of the development of craft specialization, or why craft specialization should be important in this Chalcolithic context. This complex includes population growth, subsistence, role and status differentiation, and competition.

INDICATIONS OF CRAFT SPECIALIZATION IN THE EASTERN BALKAN CHALCOLITHIC

Pottery Production

One existing view of the possibility of craft specialists in pottery is that of Mikov (1966), who divides the pottery of the eastern Balkan Chalcolithic into a class of domestic wares and a class of artistic wares. His view is that the domestic wares were made by amateur, domestic potters, whom he identifies as women, and the artistic wares were made by artisans with much experience, whom he identifies as men. The question of this proposed sexual division of labor for pottery production will not be considered here; however, this type of division of labor could well be valid for this period. The important point here is that Mikov has recognized the possibility of pottery specialists for such artistic wares as the graphite-decorated pottery.

Although the experiments with graphite-decorated pottery initiated my research, this particular fabric could not be investigated in isolation from the other pottery fabrics. Thus, pottery production in general was investigated for the possibility of craft specialization. The most important features expected for this craft are workshops (including kilns) and storage facilities for completed pottery vessels.

The best example of a pottery workshop was reported from the site of Rašev by Father Jérôme (1901). Gaul (1948) argued that the materials and features that Jérôme had interpreted as a pottery workshop were more likely the remains of a shrine. However, I believe that Jérôme's description of the finds supports his original interpretation much more than Gaul's. I find that the following features support the workshop interpretation: materials for the craft, storage facility, tool kit, and spatial delimitation.

Jérôme reported "mounds of kneaded clay" and a large vase filled with prepared clay "bearing the finger impressions of the potter [pp. 331–332]." This certainly appears to be the raw material (i.e., clay) for pottery manufacture. In addition, there was a pot containing caramine for red color and cakes of white material. Both of these could be utilized for decorating pottery.

The identification of potters' tool kits is somewhat difficult. It could be argued that potters' tool kits are rather simple, and for handmade pottery the most important tools are the potter's hands. However, within the context of the workshop at Rašev, a few tools may be tentatively identified as those of the potter. Jérôme identified some pebbles as those used for burnishing the pots. Several tools of bone and antler were found in the area and may be tools of the potter. Three tines of antler were worked to a bevel at the widest part of the tine. Two of these were perforated. Jérôme suggests, for the unperforated one, that it is a tool we can visualize in the hands of a potter. He does not comment on the possible use of the other two.

A large piece of antler from Rašev weighs about .5 kg. This is perforated and could be used as a pickaxe according to Jérôme. This is the type of tool that I would expect was utilized in obtaining the clay by the potter and/or in processing the clay (i.e., breaking up the lumps). The remaining pieces of bone found in this workshop area are a well-worked piece of bone shaped like a knife with perforations and a slightly curved "blade" of bone. It is not clear what use these may have had for a potter.

This workshop area at Rašev also has probably the best indication of a storage area for completed pots. Jérôme reported a two-tier storage and/or display facility made of pisé. It was exposed to a length of about 3 m and stood about 1 m high. In his catalogue of finds Jérôme indicated 14 pottery vessels and a zoomorphic (bull) vessel that came from this facility. This is not really an impressive number of pots for a storage facility; however, the manner in which they were apparently arranged is most important in terms of the expectation concerning storage facilities. According to Jérôme, the finest wares were placed on the upper shelf and the larger, heavier vessels were placed on the lower level. In addition, some of the vessels were set inside others.

One of the major expectations for the craft of pottery production has been the presence of kilns for firing. A few examples of kilns have been identified in the literature (Georgiev and Angelov 1957; Mikov 1966); however, the frequency is rather low. Perhaps this can be explained by Georgiev and Angelov's statement that kilns were destroyed after each firing.

Nevertheless, one good example of a kiln from the Chalcolithic period has been reported. This kiln is from the site of Gălăbovtsi, near Sofia, Bulgaria. It has internal dimensions of ca. 1.6 m by 2.5 m and is oval in shape. It contained 26 pottery vessels, a clay "phallus," an "incenser," a spindle whorl, and a pottery lid. The pottery vessels include at least two graphite-decorated pots (Petkov 1964).

In addition to the storage facility at Rašev just described, other pottery storage facilities are known. A good example is a structure at the site of Karanovo, which contained more than 100 pottery vessels. "In a habitation-workplace at Karanovo were found more than 100 pottery vessels. It is clear that they were not produced for the individual household necessities, but to supply the needs of the entire settlement (Georgiev 1961:78)." This certainly conforms to my criterion of a quantity more than would be expected to be used by a single household. Other structures reported with large numbers of pottery vessels are from the site of Hotnitsa (N. Angelov, personal communication, October 23, 1970). Here one structure contained about 60 pots and another about 40. Finally, a "depot" for pottery vessels has been reported from the site of Căscioarele. This is described as a surface of several square meters covered with pottery (V. Dumitrescu, 1965b; Dumitrescu and Banațeanu 1965).

Copper Metallurgy

The technological development of copper metallurgy in the Balkan Chalcolithic has recently been well documented by Borislav Jovanović (1971a,b) and Colin Renfrew (1970). In addition, various studies have been carried out on specific types of copper artifacts, for example: spiral-headed pins (Comşa 1965) and copper axes (Vulpe 1964). The combination of these various studies provides a good picture of the level of development of this copper metallurgy. With the addition of the other artifacts of copper (awls, needles, chisels, rings, pins, blades, etc.), we have a good idea of the extent and degree of this craft activity. The most important expectations for this craft are workshops, tool kits, and the exploitation of appropriate raw material.

A structure that I have interpreted as a copper workshop has been described from the site of Karanovo. The description is brief, and the structure is identified only as from the Karanovo V–VI period (Georgiev 1958). My interpretation of this structure as a workshop for copper metallurgy is based on the finds of two small cylindrical vessels (crucibles) within the structure, and several more of these vessels in embankments around the structure where they were thrown with other rubbish. According to the report (Georgiev 1958), traces of copper were found in at least some of these vessels; and, one of the small cylindrical vessels in the structure contained clean, ground powder of malachite ore (50% copper). This structure and surrounding area thus show the criteria of tool kit, raw material, and (apparently) spatial delimitation.

Of special interest here are those vessels that have been interpreted as crucibles. They are the best examples we have to represent the tool kits of copper metallurgists. It has been assumed, and in several cases demonstrated, that these vessels were used for melting and/or smelting copper or copper ore. The cases where this has been demonstrated are those where copper ore, slag, or traces of copper have been found inside these vessels. In addition to the Karanovo example just discussed, there are vessels of this type on display in the Ruse Museum with pieces of copper ore in them. Also, many small pottery vessels for working copper, some containing pieces of azurite ore, were found in the excavation of the site of Azmak (Mincho Dimitrov, personal communication, October 13, 1970).

If we turn to the question of the exploitation of the appropriate raw materials for copper metallurgy, it is clear that these early metallurgists had numerous sources of native copper available. One might conclude that the copper that was utilized in the eastern Balkan Chalcolithic was obtained from surface finds of pieces of nearly pure copper, most likely obtained from near the particular prehistoric settlement. In fact, this has been the generally accepted view, for example: "Copper ore, mainly malachite and azurite, was gotten on the surface of the ground. Inhabitants of the Karanovo site collected malachite ore in the neighborhood or further environs [Georgiev 1958:384]." This statement is quite accurate; however, recent evidence indicates the possibility of much more extensive exploitation of copper ore deposits. This is very important for the question of the amount of copper metallurgy being done and the possibility of specialist metallurgists.

The recent discovery is that of Chalcolithic copper mines at Rudnik–Knevni kop at Rudna Glava, Yugoslavia. These mines demonstrate two points: (a) that the quantity of copper extracted by the Chalcolithic population was much greater than previously assumed; and (b) that oxide ores of copper were exploited. The finds that have been published consist of several shafts with access platforms. These shafts were uncovered by modern mining operations and have been dated to the Chalcolithic by finds of Vinča pottery in them (Jovanović 1971a,b).

Of course, these mines are just outside the area of direct consideration here, and the question remains as to whether or not such evidences of copper ore exploitation can be expected to be found in the eastern Balkan area. These mines are certainly the kind of phenomenon I had in mind when I included the expectation of resource exploitation in the series of expectations. In fact, these mines are evidence of a much greater degree of resource exploitation than I had expected. I would not be surprised if similar exploitation had occurred in the eastern Balkan area.

Gold Metallurgy

The second type of metallurgy investigated was that of gold. Artifacts of gold ("pendants," rings, and bracelets) are not nearly as common in the eastern Balkan Chalcolithic as those of copper; however, they are distributed throughout the area (M. Dumitrescu 1961; Renfrew 1970) and may have been the products of craft specialists.

The most spectacular find of gold objects in this area and time period is the group of 44 gold objects from Hotnitsa. This "treasure" consists of 40 gold wire bracelets and 4 concave–convex pendants or medallions (Angelov 1959:Figures 19–24). The total weight of these gold objects is 312 g. They were found in Structure 4 on the site (Angelov 1959; Venedikov 1965).

> This treasure was found in one of the ruined structures, which differed from the remaining ones. It was not only smaller, but was uninhabited, as is apparent from the fact that there was no hearth in it. This led the excavators to consider that they had come upon a shrine of Aeneolithic man. That is why the treasure itself is considered a ritual one, i.e. connected with the religion of that distant age. The rings found here, which it is thought, probably ornamented the figures of large Aeneolithic idols favour this supposition [Venedikov 1965:9].

Angelov (1959; personal communication, October 23, 1970) reports that this was the smallest of the 22 structures on the site. It was located in the center of the site and was surrounded by a plaza. Angelov (personal communication, October 23, 1970) said that, other than the gold objects, only two or three pottery vessels were found in this structure. The interpretation of this structure as a shrine would seem to be acceptable. Its location, size, features, and inventory all combine to set it apart from the other structures of the site, and, so far, to set it apart from other structures of this period at other sites.

Flint Knapping

Flint knapping, of course, is one of the oldest of man's craft activities. By the Chalcolithic period in the eastern Balkans there had been several thousand years of development in the practice of flint knapping. Nevertheless, if certain individuals were specializing in the craft activity of flint knapping, it is expected that significant development took place during this period. The important expectations related to this craft are workshops, exploitation, and trade.

The best example of a workshop for flint knapping is from the site of Căsicoarele in Romania. This workshop is from the Gumelniţa B period and was found in Structure 2 at the site (V. Dumitrescu 1965a,b).

> Among the flint tools and weapons we note massive axes specific to the Gumelniţa culture, blades, scrapers, etc., and beautifully finished triangular arrowheads. Even a flint workshop was discovered in one of the dwellings—the first of its kind in a Neolithic settlement in Roumania [V. Dumitrescu 1965a:38].

This structure has been interpreted as a workshop for flint on the basis of the flint materials found within it—14 axes, 13 cores, and more than 60 large pieces of flint. There were also 4 hammerstones (V. Dumitrescu 1965b). Thus, the structure contained completed artifacts, tools for their manufacture, and the raw materials—exactly the features expected for workshops.

Other flint "work-stations" have been discussed in the literature, especially the site of Madara in northeastern Bulgaria.

> In several settlements, in whose environs occur high-grade types of stone and flint, there exist such work-stations for stone tools and weapons. One such work-station for flint implements, especially arrow points, projectile points, and other tools, existed in the settlement below the cliffs of Madara, Kolarovgrad district. It derives from the Eneolithic and not, as earlier thought, from the Neolithic [Georgiev 1958:386].

This Madara location is also well known as a source of high-quality flint, and various authors have discussed the so-called "Madara flint." Gaul (1948) noted the possibility of the exploitation of flint at this site: "Peoples of the Mound Culture had settled here at 'Pod-Grada' quite possibly to work the flint lodes found in the cliffs. But the occupation was not intense [p. 139]." It is apparent that Gaul recognized the temporary (or sparse) occupation of the site. Test excavations also indicate a light or brief occupation as compared with the mound settlements. The Chalcolithic deposit is only 1 m in depth (Georgiev 1959). These indications, plus the location of the site in and around a cave, differerentiate this site from the common Chalcolithic sites. This is again exactly the differentiation expected for sites occupied by persons exploiting a limited resource, that is, mining flint.

References to trade in flint have been made by many authors, especially referring to the "Madara flint." It has been assumed that this good-quality flint was traded over a wide area of the eastern Balkans. If this is the case, it would fit the trade expectation very nicely; however, there are no data (in the sense of physical or chemical tests) that can be used to verify the numerous identifications as "Madara flint."

Figurine Manufacture

A large number of anthropomorphic (and zoomorphic) figurines have been found in the sites of the eastern Balkan Chalcolithic. These figurines (of clay, bone, or marble) have generally been considered as unique items and have been studied for their possible information on the religious beliefs of the prehistoric population, as well as for their symbolic importance (e.g., Gimbutas 1974). Little has been done concerning their manufacture and the related technological development. It is possible that they were made by specialists. The major expectation for figurines is workshops.

A good example of the workshop of a craftsman of flat, bone figurines is known from the site of Hotnitsa. This workshop was found in Structure 8 on the site. From the plan of the structure (Angelov 1961), it appears to have been a dwelling as well as a workshop. The workshop aspect is indicated by "unfinished bone figurines" and bone figurines "in their final phase of manufacture [Angelov 1961:35–37]." The two pieces of bone in Angelov's Figure 4, which are identified as "unfinished bone figurines," might be more realistically identified as refuse from the figurine manufacture. Also, four pieces ("flakes") of bone in Angelov'a Figure 5 may be refuse, or even raw materials. In the same structure is a set of tools that have been identified as a tool kit (Angelov 1961, personal communication, October 23, 1970; Renfrew 1970). These tools include the four bone "tools" in Angelov's Figure 5, a small stone axe, two "plaques of gritstone," and six "points of flint."

Another interesting example of an accumulation of figurines is the group of 15 (8 bone, 6 clay, 1 marble) from House 1 at the site of Pietrele (Berciu 1956). This quantity is about large enough to suggest a storage facility; however, other features of the house (e.g., "horns of consecration" with red ocher, a "scepter" of polished bone, "powder boxes" of clay, deposits of red ocher, etc.) suggest that this structure contains the ritual paraphernalia of a religious specialist and/or chief.

Spondylus Shell Bracelets

The shell of *Spondylus gaederopus* was used throughout the Balkans during prehistoric times to make a variety of ornaments. During the Chalcolithic the *Spondylus* shell bracelets were most common and are included here as possible craft specialist products. The important expectations for this craft are workshops, the exploitation of the raw material, and trade.

In Structure 5 at the site of Hirşova (Gumelniţa I level) were found the material remains of what may be interpreted as the workshop of a *Spondylus* bracelet manufacturer and/or the storage facility of such a craftsman (Galbenu 1962). The finds include a pottery vessel that contained "several" completed *Spondylus* bracelets and several other pieces of *Spondylus* shell, which are reported to be partially drilled for beads. One could take these materials to represent a workshop and/or storage facility. In addition, there were 10 completed artifacts of copper in this structure. Thus, it is also possible that this whole inventory represents that of a craftsman in *Spondylus* and in copper.

The question of resource exploitation for the *Spondylus* shell has recently been given a tentative conclusion. For many years authors have discussed whether this shell came from the Black Sea or the Aegean Sea, or both. Oxygen isotope analysis, based on the ratio of $^{18}O{:}^{16}O$, however, indicates that samples of *Spondylus gaederopus* from four widespread sites of the Balkan Chalcolithic all derive from the Aegean (Shackleton and Renfrew 1970). This obviously indicates that *Spondylus* shell was being exploited as a resource from the Aegean and was being rather widely traded and exchanged. These early results very nicely fit the expectations concerning resource exploitation and trade.

Weaving

The craft of weaving was investigated for the possibility of craft specialization due to the frequency of finds of weaving equipment—especially loom weights and spindle whorls—and the apparent complexity of operation of the warp-weighted loom (Hoffmann 1964). Weaving and weaving equipment of the eastern Balkan Chalcolithic have been discussed by Petkov (1965) and by Comşa (1954), who states that weaving was the natural preoccupation of women.

If specialization were occurring in weaving, I expected this would be indicated by groups of loom weights, and perhaps other weaving tools, in a limited number of structures—that is, workshop areas. The available data do not present this pattern. Groups of about 10 loom weights have **been found** *in situ* in various sites but apparently, as reported for Căscioarele (V. Dumitrescu 1965b), these groups (each apparently representing a loom) have been found in most of the structures of a settlement. This then indicates that weaving was a household craft, not a specialized one.

One large quantity of clay weights have been reported from the site of Căscioarele. This is a deposit of "more than 100 clay loom weights and fish-net weights" found alongside a hearth in Structure 4 (V. Dumitrescu 1965a:36). The large number of weights here would not seem to represent a loom but, perhaps, the deposit of a clay weight manufacturer. The same may be the case for a deposit of 28 loom weights from a structure at the site of Salcuţa (Berciu 1961).

Differential Distributions

One of the keys to analyzing the types of phenomena I have been discussing is the knowledge of differential distributions of artifacts and features in the prehistoric sites or between sites. Obviously, the data I have discussed are of this type, or I have assumed that they are. Also, it should be obvious that these data are rather limited.

Actually, good published data of this type are available from only two sites in the eastern Balkan Chalcolithic. I will very briefly summarize those sites here in order to indicate what might be done with more available data.

Perhaps the most clear-cut pattern of differential distributions is from the site of Hotnitsa in Bulgaria. I have already discussed the structure with the 44 gold objects and the structure with the equipment of the bone figurine craftsman. The inventories of the other 20 structures are not available, so I will assume that they are quite similar and represent the households of the villagers. Thus, it is possible to suggest that the site of Hotnitsa exhibits differentiation in the technological subsystem (i.e., the bone figurine craftsman) and the ritual subsystem (i.e., the "shrine" indicated by the deposit of gold objects).

The second site is that of Căscioarele in southern Romania. Seventeen structures have been described for this site, and it is possible to indicate certain aspects of differentiation (V. Dumitrescu 1965a,b). Differentiation in the technological subsystem is indicated by Structure 2 (the flint workshop) and structure 4 (with the more than 100 clay weights). Structure 1 may relate to this, with its domed oven and lack of a hearth. Differentiation in the ritual subsystem may be indicated by Structure 3 (with various "cult" items) and Structure 16 (small size and located near an open space).

RELATED EXPECTATIONS

The complex of related expectations are important for the discussion of the conclusions that follow. That is, they help to construct the sociocultural system of the period. I will only briefly summarize the relevant data here.

Population Growth

The major related expectation is that the overall system is growing—that is, there is an increase in the number of individuals and communities. Various types of data indicate that population growth was occurring during the Neolithic–Chalcolithic. The best data are the maps and site lists of Comşa (1962).

Subsistence

With population growth I also expected to find indications of development in the basic agricultural subsistence pattern, such as the addition of new crops or domesticated animals, greater control over crops and breeding, etc. Certain data support these expectations and certain data do not. Apparently the basic agriculture remains fairly constant during the period. The data, however, do suggest possible increased efficiency in agricultural techniques, such as the apparent use of flint, bone, and antler hoes (Kunčev 1967) and the possible appearance of the antler plow (Dumitrescu and Banaţeanu 1965; Mikov 1959).

Role and Status Differentiation

I also expected that as the system grows, there would be increasing indications of role and status differentiation. These data unfortunately are not abundant and give little support to the expectations. Data from burial populations are quite rare. Comşa (1960) reviewed these data and concluded that the Chalcolithic society was egalitarian. However, the largest burial population in the area, that from the cemetery of Cernica, which just preceeds the Chalcolithic, does indicate patterns of differentiation (Cantacuzino 1969). I expect that these continue into the Chalcolithic.

Competition

Finally, I expected competition to increase also as the sociocultural system grows. This is supported by the appearance of a variety of fortifications (Morintz 1962). It may also be supported by the appearance of triangular arrowheads in the later Chalcolithic (Păunescu 1970).

CONCLUSIONS

I suggest that craft specialization was developing during the Chalcolithic period of the eastern Balkan Peninsula. The particular crafts that are indicated are pottery manufacture, copper metallurgy, and flint knapping. Certain indications are present for the crafts of gold metallurgy, figurine manufacture, and shell bracelet manufacture; however, the data are insufficient to form a conclusion. And, the craft of weaving appears to be a more generalized (household) craft activity.

I would also suggest that the degree of craft specialization at this time was not great. Certainly the available data show only a low frequency of the types of phenomena listed in the expectations. I would suggest that the craftsmen of the Chalcolithic were not spending a large percentage of their productive time in these craft activities.

Obviously, a strong, definitive conclusion cannot be stated at this time. The suggestions offered are tempting; however, the phenomenon of craft specialization has by no means been measured. This will require a detailed research design and the collection of a good deal more data. Nevertheless, I believe that the tentative conclusion is significant in terms of our beginning to understand the technological subsystem and the total sociocultural sytem of the Chalcolithic period. Future research and data collection may be conducted with this particular question in mind.

Why Craft Specialization?

In attempting to explain the development of craft specialization and why it should be important in the Chalcolithic period, I have utilized various concepts from general systems theory (e.g., Miller 1965). In this sense, differentiation in general and craft specialization in particular are seen as phenomena of growing systems and/or complex systems.

I view craft specialization as one particular aspect of a growing or complex sociocultural system. With a greater number of individuals in the system, there is a concomitant increase in the number of roles and role combinations available. Each individual has a wider selection of roles or role combinations from which to choose, or to be ascribed. Actually, certain individuals begin to experiment with different possibilities of utilizing their productive time. As these experiments develop, the sociocultural system selects for the successful experiments and against the unsuccessful experiments (Evans 1973; Rodgers 1966).

The particular selective advantage of specialization in the technological subsystem is efficiency. Specialists are more efficient in the long run in a multitude of activities. This has been demonstrated in modern farming, business, industry, science, etc. The same principle of efficiency applies to the technological subsystems of prehistoric societies (Adams 1966; Evans 1973; Reynolds 1967; Rodgers 1966, 1971). It seems that the Chalcolithic of the Balkan Peninsula is an excellent situation in which to test these concepts.

ACKNOWLEDGMENTS

I would like to thank Colin Renfrew and Marija Gimbutas, who gave me the opportunities to conduct this research and the encouragement to carry it through. I would also like to thank numerous individuals in Bulgaria and Romania, especially Georgi Georgiev and Alexandru Vulpe.

REFERENCES

Adams, Robert M.
1966   The evolution of urban society: Early Mesopotamia and prehispanic Mexico. Chicago: Aldine.
Angelov, N.
1959   Zlatnoto sukroviše ot Hotnitsa. Arkheologiia 1: 38–46.
1961   Rabotilnitsa za ploski kosteni idoli v selištnata mogila pri s. Hotnitsa, Turnovsko. Arkheologiia 3: 34–38.
Berciu, Dumitru
1956   Săpăturile de la Pietrele, Raionul Giurgio—1943 şi 1948. Materiale şi Cercetari Arheologice II: 503–544.
1961   Contribuţii la problemele Neoliticului in Rominia in Lumina Noilor Cercetări. Bucharest: Institutul de Arheologie al Academiei R. P. R. Editura Academiei Republicii Populare Romine.
1967   Romania before Burebista. In Ancient Peoples and Places, edited by Glyn Daniel. (Vol. 57). London: Thames and Hudson.
Cantacuzino, G.
1969   The prehistoric necropolis of Cernica and its place in the Neolithic cultures of Romania and of Europe in the light of recent discoveries. Dacia (Nouvelle Serie) XIII: 45–59.
Childe, V. Gordon
1957   The dawn of European civilization (6th ed.). London: Routledge & Kegan Paul.
Comşa, Eugen
1954   Considerţii cu privire la evoluţia culturii Boian. Studii şi Cercetări de Istorie Veche V (3–4): 361–398.
1960   Considerations sur le rite funeraire de la civilisation de Gumelniţa. Dacia (Nouvelle Serie) IV: 5–30.
1962   K voprosu ob otnositel'noj hronologii i o razvitii neoliticeskih kul'tur na Jugo-vostoke Rum'inskof Respubliki i na vostoke nr Bolgarii. Dacia (Nouvelle Serie) VI: 53–85.
1965   Quelques données sur les aiguilles de cuivre découvertes dans l'aire de la civilisa-tion de Gumelniţa." Dacia (Nouvelle Serie) IX: 361–371.
Dumitrescu, H.
1961   Connections between the Cucuteni–Tripolie cultural complex and the neighbor-ing eneolithic cultures in the light of the utilization of golden pendants. Dacia (Nouvelle Serie) V: 69–93.
Dumitrescu, V.
1965a   Căscioarele, a late Neolithic settlement on the lower Danube. Archaeology 18 (1): 34–40.
1965b   Principalele rezultate ale primelor două campanii de săpături din asezarea neolitica tîrzie de la Căsioarelle. Studii şi Cercetari de Istorie Veche XVI (2): 215–237.
Dumitrescu, V., and T. Banaţeanu
1965   A propos d'un soc de charrue primitive, en bois de cerf, découvert dans la station néolithique de Căscioarele. Dacia (Noubelle Serie) IX: 59–67.
Evans, Robert K.
1973   Craft specialization in the Chalcolithic period of the eastern portion of the Balkan Peninsula. Ph.D. Dissertation. Univ. of California, Los Angeles.
Galbenu, Doina
1962   Aşezarea neolitică de la Hîrşova. Studii şi Cercetări de Istorie Veche XIII (2): 285–306.

Gaul, James Harvey
    1948   The Neolithic period in Bulgaria. Peabody Museum of Archaeology and Ethnol-
            ogy, Bulletin 16, Harvard University, American School of Prehistoric Research.
Georgiev, Georgi I.
    1958   Za njakoi orudiia za proizvodstvo ot neolita i eneolita v Bulgariia. In Izsledvanija v
            Čest na Akad. D. Dečev, edited by Veselin Beshevlieve. Sofia: Bŭgarska Akademiia
            na Naukite. 369–387.
    1959   Otnosno Datuvaneto na Purvobitnoto Seliste pri Madara, Kolarovgradsko. Izves-
            tiia na Arheologičeskiia Institut. Bŭlgarska Akademiia na Naukite, Series 2.
            (Kniga XXII). 29–39.
    1961   Kulturgruppen der Jungstein—und der Kupferzeit in der Ebene von Thrazien
            (Sudbulgarien). In L'Europe à la fin de l'âge de la pierre, edited by Jaroslav Böhm
            and Sigfried J. DeLaet. Praha: Académie tchécoslovaque des Sciences. Pp. 45–
            100.
    1963   Glavni Rezultati ot Razkopkite na Azmaskata Selistna Mogila prez 1961 g. Izves-
            tiia na Arheologiceskiia Institut, Bŭlgarska Akademiia na Naukite (Kniga XXVI:
            157–176.
Georgiev, G., and N. Angelov
    1957   Razkopki na Selištnata Mogila do Ruse prez 1950–1953 godina. Izvestiia na
            Arheologičeskiia Institut, Bulgarska Akademiia na Naukite (Kniga XXI): 41–127.
Gimbutas, Marija
    1973   Old Europe c. 7000–3500 B.C.: The earliest European civilization before the
            infiltration of the Indo-European peoples. The Journal of Indo-European Studies 1
            (1:) 1–20.
    1974   Gods and goddesses of old Europe. Berkeley, Calif.: Univ. of California Press.
Hoffmann, Marta
    1964   The warp-weighted loom: Studies in the history and technology of an ancient
            implement. Studia Norvegica No. 14. Universitetsforlaget.
Jérôme, Father
    1901   L'époque néolithique dans la vallée du Tonsus. Revue Archeologique, 3me Serie
            XXXIX: 328–349.
Jovanović, Borislav
    1971a   Early copper metallurgy of the central Balkans. Actes du VIIIᵉ Congrès Interna-
            tional des Sciences Prehistoriques et Protohistoriques, Tome Premier, Rapports
            Generaux. Comite National d'Organisation, Belgrade. Pp. 131–140.
    1971b   Metalurgija Eneolitskog Perioda Jugoslavije. Arheoloski Institut. Posebna Iz-
            danja. Kniga 9. Belgrade.
Kunčev, Kunčo
    1967   Zemedelski Orudiia ot Neolita i Eneolita v Bulgarsikte Zemi. Arheologiia IX
            (Kniga 3): 50–64.
Mikov, Vasil
    1959   The prehistoric mound of Karanovo. Archaeology. 12 (2): 88–97.
    1966   Tehnika na Keramičnoto Proizovodstvo prez Praistoričeskata Epoha Bulgariia.
            Izvestiia na Arheologičeskiia Institut, Bŭlgarska Akademiia na Naukite (Kniga
            XXIX): 165–210.
Miller, James G.
    1965   Living systems: Basic concepts. Behavioral Science 10 (3): 193–237. Living systems:
            Structure and process. Living systems: Cross-level hypotheses. Behavioral Science
            10 (4): 337–411.
Morintz, Sebastian
    1962   Tipuri de asezari şi sisteme de fortificaţie şi imprejmuire in cultura Gumelniţa.
            Studii şi Cercetări de Istorie Veche XIII (2): 273–284.

Păunescu, Al.
  1970   Evoluţia uneltelor şi armelor de piatră cioplită descoperite pe teritoriul României.
          Biblioteca de Arheologice XV. Bucharest. Editura Academiei Republicii
          Socialiste România.
Petkov, N.
  1964   Grunčarska Pešt ot Eneolitnoto Selište pri s. Gǎlǎbovtsi, Sofiisko. Arheologiia VI
          (Kniga1): 48–59.
  1965   Praistorieski Pletki i Tukani ot Sofiiskoto Pole i Blizkite mu Okolnostič.
          Arheologiia VII (Kniga 1): 45–57.
Renfrew, Colin
  1970   The autonomy of the south-east European copper age. Proceedings of the Prehis-
          toric Society for 1969 XXXV: 12–47.
Reynolds, Barrie
  1967   An ethnographic study of the Kwandu people, south-western Barotseland, with
          particular reference to the role of craftsmen in the society. Ph.D. Dissertation,
          Linacre College, Oxford University.
Rodgers, William B.
  1966   Development and specialization: A case from the Bahamas. Ethnology V (4):
          409–414.
  1971   Incipient development and vocational evolution in Dominica. Human Organiza-
          tion 30 (3): 239–254.
Shackleton, Nicholas, and Colin Renfrew
  1970   Neolithic trade routes re-aligned by oxygen isotope analysis. Nature 228 (5276):
          1062–1065.
Tringham, Ruth
  1971   Hunters, fishers and farmers of eastern Europe: 6000–3000 B.C. London: Hutchin-
          son Univ. Library.
Venedikov, Ivan
  1965   Bulgaria's treasures from the past. Sofia: Foreign Language Press.
Vulpe, Alexandru
  1964   Cu privire la chronologia topareolo de armă cu bratle "în cruce." Studii şi Cer-
          cetări de Istorie Veche XV (3): 457–466.

chapter 7

Architectural Differentiation in Some Near Eastern Communities, Prehistoric and Contemporary

PATTY JO WATSON

It is undeniably true that archeologists potentially control immense quantities of data pertinent to the solution of problems of cultural and social evolution and systemic change. But to realize that potential and contribute to solution of those problems, archeologists must utilize knowledge of the existing behavioral correlates of archeological or material remains. That is, they must use knowledge of proven or possible interrelationships among cultural phenomena, so that on the basis of past *material* traits or trait complexes revealed by archeological techniques, various *behavioral* traits or trait complexes can be imputed—at least as testable hypotheses (Watson in press b)—to the extinct societies being investigated.

Archeologists are especially concerned with such interrelationships as those between population density or forms or levels of social organization on the one hand, and archeologically determinable settlement patterns (size and distribution of dwellings within a single settlement and of whole settlements) on the other, or between various social units and the patterning of artifactual material characteristic of them. This sort of data

131

is not usually provided in any comprehensive way in ethnographic accounts. Hence, it is up to archeologists to obtain it themselves, and many are doing just that (e.g., David and Hennig 1972; Gould 1968, 1971; Kramer 1976, in press; Stanislawski 1969a, b; Watson 1966, in press a).

Part I of this chapter concerns ethnoarcheological research I carried out in Iran in 1959–1960, and the discussion centers on spatial organization. In Part II, comparative attention is given to the wide variety of spatial organization present in some prehistoric Mesopotamian and Anatolian communities.

The contemporary Iranian village is a place I call Hasanabad, located in the Zagros Mountains of western Iran not far from the city of Kermansha. At the time of my study, the village population was about 193 peasants (I was able to obtain architectural and domestic details for only 181 of these villagers) and 12 to 14 gendarmes. The village covers approximately 2.4 ha (this is a maximum figure and includes the ash and dung midden areas that lie immediately adjacent to the village walls and nearly ring the community). The peasants live in puddled adobe (*chineh* in Farsi; *tauf* in Iraqi Arabic) houses arranged in household complexes as shown in Figure 7.1. There are 41 such household residence units, most of which are occupied by nuclear families, although a few contain some form of virilocal extended family. The average family comprises 4.4 members.

PART I. HASANABAD: ECONOMIC STRATIFICATION

Although everyone in Hasanabad was poor in 1960—all were landless, sharecropping agriculturalists—some were poorer than others, and there was in fact a perceptible microcosmic economic hierarchy, which I will discuss briefly as an example of how economic organization is reflected materially in a contemporary Near Eastern community. I have split the hierarchy, as I perceived it, into four groups, with the better-off households in Group I and the poorest families in Group IV.

A family's position in this village economic hierarchy is defined or marked by a long series of discrete and continuous attributes, but those that could be conceived to be archeologically relevant are emphasized here.

Discrete Attributes

1. More than one living room. The extra living room functions as a guest room or parlor and hence is a luxury, representing considerable expense in construction materials.

Figure 7.1. Hasanabad village plan (June 1960).

2. Two-story construction versus one-story construction.
3. Sheet metal stove versus open fire pit or hearth for winter heating.
4. Kerosene lantern versus tin can lamp.
5. Carpets versus felt mats and homemade *gilims*.
6. Mirror (presence or absence).
7. Glass windowpanes (presence or absence).
8. Kinds of animals owned. Goats are less high class than sheep; horses are luxury items, as are milk cows.

Continuous Attributes

1. Furnishing and condition of living room.
2. Condition and furnishings of rest of household complex and of the outer walls and roof.
3. Amount of bedding available to the family (blankets, bolsters, rugs).
4. Quantity of pots, pans, and dishes.
5. Amount of clothing (members of the poorest families have only the outfits they are wearing).
6. Number of animals owned: quantity of sheep or goats (more than 8 to 10 each is a mark of relative affluence), donkeys or oxen (more than 1 is indicative of wealth).
7. Number and kinds of storerooms.

Another variable is size and variety of rooms per household, but this is somewhat ambiguous for two reasons:

1. The size and number of rooms (apart from presence–absence of a spare living room or parlor) is probably more directly related to size of resident family than to wealth or poverty per se of that family.
2. Size and number of rooms and of surface stables may reflect conditions one or even two generations in the past.

The most sensitive indicator of family size and relative wealth or poverty is the size, condition, and furnishings of the living room. Some data on these matters are provided in Tables 7.1–7.3, which are self-explanatory. It might be noted here, however, that the average Hasanabad complex includes about 37 m² of roofed living space.

Although they will not be considered here, hierarchies other than economic ones probably exist in most contemporary villages. For instance, Sterling (1965) notes for the Anatolian community of Sakaltutan:

Table 7.1

HASANABAD ROOM AREAS[a]

Room type	Average area (in m²)	Maximum (in m²)	Minimum (in m²)
Living room (n = 25)	18.20	34.70 (5)	9.25 (36)
Aywan (n = 5)	6.85	9.70 (13)	5.0 (8)
Surface stable (n = 14)	11.85	27.50 (13)	3.15 (19)
Utility (n = 3)	13.05	17.50 (19)	7.55 (23)
Storeroom (n = 13)	12.35	30.80 (20)	5.90 (36)

[a] Numbers in parentheses under the maximum and minimum area figures are the numbers of specific households in Hasanabad. See Table 7.3 for size of the family designated, and see Figure 7.1 for location of household.

Household (36) has two living rooms, the second one is 21.25 m². Household (13) has two surface stables, the second is 13.75 m². Household (19) has two surface stables, the second is 3.15 m². Household (20) has two storerooms, the second is 16.2 m².

Table 7.2

HASANABAD OWNERSHIP OF MULTIPLE ROOMS

Living rooms		Surface stables		Storerooms	
Household number	Number of rooms	Household number	Number of rooms	Household number	Number of rooms
(3)	3	(7)	2	(7)	2
(9)	3	(13)	2	(12)	3
(11)	2	(20)	2	(18)	3
(17)	2	(23)	2	(32)	2
(20)	2	(31)	2	(1)	2
(27)	2	(42)	2	(6)	1½
(32)	2			(11)	3
(34)	2			(15)	2
(35)	3			(20)	2
(36)	2			(22)	2
(37)	2			(28)	2
(38)	2			(30)	3
(39)	2			(38)	2
				(42)	2

Table 7.3

SOME SPECIFICS ON HOUSEHOLDS APPEARING IN TABLES 7.1 AND 7.2

Household number	Size of household	Economic stratum[a]
(1)	4	IV
(3)	7	II
(4)	7	II
(5)	3	I
(6)	8	III ?
(7)	4	III
(8)	5	III
(9)	6	III
(11)	4	III ?
(12)	4	III
(13)	4	IV
(15)	4	IV
(17)	3	III ?
(18)	7	II
(19)	2	III
(20)	6	I
(22)	1	?
(23)	5	IV
(27)	6	II
(28)	2	I
(30)	6	?
(31)	3	III
(32)	7	III
(33)	5	II
(34)	6	IV
(35)	1	?
(36)	5	I
(37)	8	III
(38)	7	I
(39)	5	III
(42)	3	I

[a] I is the highest economic stratum; IV is the lowest.

intravillage ranking based on secular criteria such as age (among the male population only); position in household and in lineage (men only); wealth (the most important single factor in village ranking); skill and occupation of nonfarmers (carpenter or smith or mason versus unskilled laborers); and religious ranking based on religious knowledge and piety, morality, and honor (conduct, behavior in socially defined situations).

A little comparative information is available from other ethnographic accounts. For instance, at the Turkish village of Yassıhöyük (Middle East

Technical University 1965) there are said to be four major income groups (probably corresponding to modern tax brackets), and the attributes characterizing the higher versus the lower groups are reminiscent of those noted for Hasanabad. The population of Yassıhöyük is 355 (75 families, average family size 4.67).

Discrete Attributes Defining Economic Status in Yassıhöyük

1. Houses (two story versus one story).
2. Separate kitchen and food storage arrangements versus food processing and cooking going on in the room that is also the family living room and bedroom.
3. Guest room (presence or absence).
4. Inside toilet versus outside toilet.
5. Wood fuel plus dung versus dung only.
6. Fancy, heavy metal stove versus cheap thin sheet metal stove.
7. Pressure lamp versus kerosene lamp.

Continuous Attributes Defining Economic Status in Yassıhöyük

1. Quality of maintenance of houses.
2. Quality and abundance of clothing of family members.
3. Quality of house furnishings (expensive rugs, steel-framed beds instead of straw mats on the floor, upholstered chairs, and radios are indicative of affluence).
4. Quantity and size of glass windowpanes.

Space and People

There are 41 household complexes in Hasanabad comprising unroofed space in the form of walled courtyards as well as three kinds of roofed spaces: living rooms, stables, and storage or utility rooms. In addition, several households include a passageway or entry chamber called an *aywan*.

Average roofed dwelling area per person in Hasanabad is 7.3 m^2 (LeBlanc 1971), although the variability masked by that average figure is fairly high (SD 4.1 m^2). The average number of rooms per family is 4.5 if underground stables are included in the room total, or 4.1 if they are excluded. The ratio of rooms to people is 1:1 if the subterranean stables are included and is .9 : 1.0 (or 1.1 person per room) if they are excluded.

The relevance of data of this sort—which are now beginning to accumulate for the Near East (Kramer 1976, in press; Watson 1977)—to a multitude of questions about prehistoric demography is obvious. The more secure our estimates of population based on size and distribution of architectural remains, the better our grasp of prehistoric population sizes, distributions, and fluctuations.

Relationships between Agricultural and Pastoral Patterns and Village Population

Agriculture

With respect to early food producers, we are particularly interested in the cultivational practices pertaining to unirrigated wheat and barley. The available Hasanabad data indicate that a family of five (father, mother, three children) annually sows 150 *mann* (450 kg) of wheat and barley (100 *mann* wheat, 50 *mann* barley) plus a few other crops, such as chick-peas, onions, tomatoes, melons, and leguminous cattle fodder. The family requires about 500 *mann* (1500 kg) of wheat that will be ground to flour to provide the year's supply of bread.[1] (They do not eat barley, except as a starvation food, but rather use it for animal fodder or as a cash crop.) This means the total 41 households at Hasanabad must require a minimum of 120 to 125 ha for dry-farmed wheat and barley (1 ha per family for wheat, .5 ha per family for barley, making a total of 1.5 ha; but this must be fallowed every other year so the family actually requires at least 3 ha of wheat–barley land that will yield tenfold).

Information on crop yields in unirrigated situations is highly relevant to propositions about grain yields for prehistoric nonirrigation cultivation of small grains. In turn, these propositions can be of great assistance in refining and evaluating models concerning population pressure and the practice of early agriculture.

[1] Details of the calculations are as follows: 100 *mann* of wheat sown in the fall will yield, if all goes well, 1000 *mann* of wheat at the spring harvest. One-third of this total must go to the landlord, which leaves some 666 *mann* for the sharecropper. From his share, the peasant subtracts seed grain for the next year, leaving 566 *mann* of wheat to be ground into flour, just about enough to feed a family of five for a year. (An 80% extraction rate is assumed—i.e., 100 *mann* of wheat yields 80 *mann* of flour—and a consumption rate of 1.5 kg of flour per day.)

Pastoralism

Nearly 1000 head of livestock were owned by Hasanabad villagers during the fall and winter of 1959. By June 1960, the number had increased to almost 1400 because of the birth of kids and lambs. Average numbers of animals owned per family are as follows:

	Average number of animals per family	
Kind of animal	Winter	Spring
Adult		
goats	7.70	6.30
sheep	13.30	13.90
oxen	1.00	.98
cows	.60	.73
donkeys	.80	.85
horses	.23	.20
Kids		4.80
Lambs		6.80
Calves		.40

Sheep and goats far outnumber all other mammalian livestock, and sheep are preferred to goats. The village was in a state of economic depression at the time I was there, as is most strikingly indicated by the figures for oxen: The average number per household is slightly less than 1 in spite of the fact that a yoke of oxen is essential for agricultural work. Similarly, numbers of cows, donkeys, and horses are very low.

Quantitative information on livestock patterns can be tied in with agricultural figures in building or assessing the models just referred to that describe various aspects of early food production and the possible effects of population pressure.

Domestic Activity Patterns

Average dimensions of the measured examples of Hasanabad room types are summarized in Table 7.1. Figures like these on room sizes and on the composition and sizes of household complexes where the human occupants are known (i.e., where we know how many people occupy a given residence unit and what their relationships are) are necessary if archeologists are to make valid inferences about population size and social organization from numbers and sizes of rooms and houses they excavate.

As would be expected, or at least hoped, the significance and functions of the various rooms are indicated by their sizes and by the nature and distribution of architectural features and artifacts characteristically found in them. For example, the family living room—actually a combination kitchen, dining room, dormitory bedroom, and, for poorer households, parlor or guest room as well—is the largest roofed space. Living rooms always have a stone-lined hearth, wall niches or wall pegs for storage of various household equipment, furniture of various kinds, the family bedding, and an array of vessels and utensils for the preparation and serving of food. Storerooms and stables lack all these (unless they are reused living rooms). Storerooms are essentially featureless but may contain unused agricultural or other equipment. Stables are usually furnished with adobe mangers.

Part II of this chapter is devoted to a summary account of architectural remains at a series of prehistoric Near Eastern sites. My objective is to demonstrate the wide variety in physical layout that characterized prehistoric Near Eastern communities and to indicate how the ethnographically derived Hasanabad data can help elucidate the archeologically known settlements.

PART II. THE PREHISTORIC COMMUNITIES

Nine sites will be briefly discussed, seven in Mesopotamia and two in Anatolia. The Mesopotamian ones are in northern and eastern Iraq. The Anatolian ones are Hacılar and Çatal Hüyük in southwestern and south central Anatolia respectively.

Çatal Hüyük   Umm Dabaghiyah   Hassuna I–II   Yarim Tepe I   Hassuna III–IV   Matarrah   Sawwan   Hacılar   Choga Mami   Yarim Tepe II

6200 B.C. ←————————————————————————→ 4500 B.C.

Approximate Chronological Relationships of Sites Discussed

These sites were chosen according to the nature of the published information and to what was obtainable in the research time available. What follows, then, is by no means an exhaustive accounting of relevant architectural data from Near Eastern prehistory but rather an illustrative account of one interesting period, the sixth millennium B.C.

Intracommunity variation of the sort discussed for Hasanabad is, of course, not analogous to that in these modern communities where the economy is a cash-based one. But relationships among number of people, their organization, and the size and shape of living quarters must be similar in prehistoric communities to that in appropriate modern ones. In addition, architectural remains comprise one of the few categories that is usually fully and accurately described in available reports on Near Eastern sites. Hence, I consider only architecture in this chapter.

Hassuna

This site in northern Iraq is a mound about 200 × 150 m in area and 7 m in height. The basic pattern revealed by the 1940s excavations is of households architecturally much like Hasanabad ones: a series of rooms of different functions (living rooms and storerooms are distinguishable) grouped around an open court. Except for one round house (5.25 m in diameter, and therefore 21.6 m² in area), the 45 measurable rooms are all rectangular and only one (area of 19.5 m²) is comparable in size to the *average* Hasanabad living room (18 m² area). All the others are much smaller than the Hasanabad average (Tables 7.1, 7.4), nor is there much evidence of significant intracommunity variation.

Matarrah

This mound is about 150 m × 100 m in area and 4 m in height. Portions of three or four *tauf* (puddled adobe) houses were found in Operation IX, Levels 1 and 2. These houses were made up of several small rooms (the average area of the 17 measurable rooms is less than 4.0 m², the biggest rooms being 8.4 m² and 7.0 m² [see Table 7.5]); the general pattern is apparently very similar to that of Hassuna and Hasanabad in that each household consisted of a series of rooms fronting or adjoining a court or open space. In the largest room of one of the houses was an oven, but in general very few features were preserved.

Table 7.4

HASSUNA ROOM MEASUREMENTS[a]

		Linear dimensions (in m)	Area (in m²)	
Level IV:	(1)	1.75 × 1.60 =	2.8	⎫ Probably part of the same house; total 15.73 m²
	(20)	4.00 × 2.75 =	11.00	
	(—)	1.75 × 1.10 =	1.93	⎭
	(3)	3.50 × 1.10 =	3.85	⎫
	(4)	3.75 × 1.10 =	4.13	
	(5)	3.00 × 1.75 =	5.25	Probably a single house; total 17.73 m²
	(6)	1.80 × 1.00 =	1.80	
	(15)	1.80 × 1.50 =	2.70	⎭
	(10)	2.50 × 2.50 =	6.25	⎫ Probably a single house; total 15.25 m²
	(11)	4.50 × 2.00 =	9.00	⎭
Level V:	(1)	4.50 × 2.50 =	11.25	⎫
	(2)	6.70 × 3.20 =	21.44	
	(3)	5.60 × 2.80 =	15.68	Probably a single house; total 67.12 m²
	(18)	4.50 × 3.00 =	13.50	
	(19)	3.00 × 1.75 =	5.25	⎭
	(6)	2.50 × 1.20 =	3.00	⎫
	(7)	2.30 × 1.50 =	3.45	
	(8)	1.75 × 1.60 =	2.80	Probably a single house; total 29.27 m²
	(9)	1.60 × 1.50 =	2.40	
	(13)/(14)	4.60 × 2.20 =	10.12	
	(—)	3.00 × 2.50 =	7.50	⎭

Totals: 5 houses; 21 rooms; 145.10 m², presumably roofed living space.

[a] Lloyd and Safar (1945: Figures 31–32). These maps are published at such a small scale that errors of measurement up to 50 cm are easily possible; hence the figures in this table are approximate.

[b] The excavators indicate this house may have had one more room; see grid squares A2 and A3 of Figure 31 (Lloyd and Safar 1945).

Yarim Tepe I

Excavations are still in progress here, so the data available are sketchy and undoubtedly somewhat out of date. The mound is about 100 m in diameter and 4.5 m high. In Level IV several kilns were excavated as well as two rectilinear houses, each comprising several small square rooms plus one larger room with an oven. In the same level was a round house 9 m in diameter. The largest rooms (presumably living rooms) in

Table 7.5

MATARRAH ROOM MEASUREMENTS[a]

	Linear dimensions (in m)	Area (in m²)	
Operation IX			
Level 1:	2.00 × 1.20 = 2.40		⎫
	4.20 × 2.00 = 8.40		⎬ Probably a single house; total
	1.75 × 1.50 = 2.55		⎭ 13.35 m²
	2.25 × 1.20 = 2.70		⎫
	1.75 × 1.50 = 2.63		⎪ Probably a single house; total
	2.00 × 2.00 = 4.00		⎪ 11.08 m²
	1.75 × 1.00 = 1.75		⎭
	2.00 × 2.00 = 4.00		⎫
	2.00 × 2.00 = 4.00		⎪
	4.50 × 1.10 = 4.95		⎬ Probably a single house; total
	1.50 × 1.00 = 1.50		⎪ 18.20 m²
	1.25 × 1.00 = 1.25		⎪
	2.00 × 1.25 = 2.50		⎭
Level 2:	3.50 × 2.00 = 7.00		⎫
	2.10 × 1.00 = 2.10		⎪ Probably a single house; total
	2.00 × 2.00 = 4.00		⎬ 16.60 m²
	3.50 × 1.00 = 3.50		⎭

Totals: 4 houses; 17 rooms; 59.23 m², presumably roofed living space.

[a] Braidwood, Braidwood, Smith and Leslie (1952: Figure 3). These maps are published at such a small scale that errors of measurement up to 50 cm are easily possible; hence the figures in this table are approximate.

the rectilinear houses of this level and of the underlying Level V are 4 m², 5.5 m², and 8.75 m², respectively. Again, these are appreciably smaller than Hasanabad living rooms but comparable to the larger Hassuna and Matarrah rooms.

In Level V remains of the same kinds of houses were found, but there were also buildings without domestic debris or features that are interpreted as storehouses. These are made up of batteries or magazines of 2 × 2 m or slightly larger cubicles in a double row (one of the better preserved of these buildings is said to have contained 14 such cubicles).

At Yarim Tepe I, then, there *is* some basic intracommunity variation: pottery kilns, domestic structures of two quite different plans (round, and rectilinear roughly similar to Hasanabad), and separate banks of possibly communal storage chambers. Once again the houses are composed of smaller rooms than are the Hasanabad ones.

Umm Dabaghiyah

This small mound (100 × 85 m in area and 4 m in height) is interpreted as being different from the more or less autonomous communities so far noted. It lies in a very marginal area of dry steppe, and the excavator believes it may have been some sort of trading outpost or satellite to a larger, unknown community.

Intrasite patterning consists of a central open space with a few houses on one side. These are rectilinear structures with small rooms (see Table 7.6), the largest rooms being 9–10 m² in area and the smallest 1–2 m². On the other three sides of the square or plaza are storerooms, somewhat smaller than those of Yarim Tepe I (1.45–1.75 m on a side or 2–3 m² in area). In one level there are over 70 of these little rooms laid out in rows with "a precision that would not disgrace a Roman barracks [Kirkbride

Table 7.6

UMM DABAGHIYAH ROOM MEASUREMENTS[a]

	Linear dimensions (in m)	Area (in m²)	
Level II:	3.50 × 1.50 =	5.25	
	3.00 × 1.50 =	4.50	
	1.00 × 1.00 =	1.00	
	1.50 × 1.50 =	2.25	
	4.00 × 2.00 =	8.00	Probably a single house; total 55.50 m²
	6.00 × 1.50 =	9.00	
	6.00 × 1.75 =	10.50	
	3.00 × 2.50 =	7.50	
	3.00 × 2.50 =	7.50	
	6.25 × 1.50 =	9.38	
	3.00 × 2.80 =	8.40	Probably a single house; total 23.78 m²
	1.50 × 1.50 =	2.25	
	2.50 × 1.50 =	3.75	

Totals: 2 houses; 13 rooms; 79.28 m², presumably roofed living space.

[a] Kirkbride (1973: Plate LXXVIII). These maps are published at such a small scale that errors of measurement up to 50 cm are easily possible; hence the figures in this table are approximate.

1973]." Most of the cubicles were empty when excavated, but one had hundreds of sling missiles in it.

As at Yarim Tepe I, there is internal differentiation in functional areas, with an emphasis on storage.

Tell es-Sawwan

This mound is 230 × 110 m in area and 3.5 m in height. The bottom level contains two large, multiroomed buildings (15–20 rooms each). The better preserved of these contains rooms ranging from 35.75 to 3.6 m², with the average being 11.4 m² (see Table 7.7). Many burials occurred beneath these buildings, but there is no detail available on the nature of debris or features (if any) within these structures.

Level III is the best known architecturally, and is quite different from the basal horizon just referred to. At the period of Level III the site was surrounded on three sides by a ditch 3 m deep and 2.5 m wide cut in bedrock and backed by a mud brick wall. On the fourth side, the site was protected by the river.

Within the wall were the remains of at least seven, 10- to 12-room houses of a fairly uniform overall "T-shaped" plan. These are made of mud brick with gypsum paving. There are also some large structures interpreted as granaries.

The Sawwan houses differ from the Hasanabad–Hassuna–Matarrah type in that they were not built around courtyards and were detached from one another, most being freestanding individual structures.

The Sawwan community was then characterized by an impressive defense system (unique in Mesopotamia at this time level but reminiscent of PPN Jericho), detached houses, and nondomestic architecture (perhaps storage structures).

Choga Mami

The mound is 350 × 100 m in area and 2 to 5 m in height. So far only three house plans have been published, but these also reveal separate or detached structures like the Sawwan ones. They comprise many very small rooms (the average room sizes are 2.5 to 3 m² [see Table 7.8]). Possible storage structures were also found, consisting of rows of small cubicles.

Once again there is some indication of basic intrasite architectural differentiation with respect to function (storage versus residence) and the possibility of communal storage.

Table 7.7

TELL ES-SAWWAN ROOM MEASUREMENTS

	Linear dimensions (in mn)	Area (in m²)	
Level I			
Building 2:	7.20 × 3.50	= 25.20	
	5.50 × 1.50	= 8.25	
	3.50 × 2.50	= 8.75	
	3.50 × 1.80	= 6.30	
	4.00 × 3.00	= 12.00	
	4.00 × 1.75	= 7.00	
	3.80 × 3.00	= 11.40	
	5.75 × 2.50	= 14.38	
	5.50 × 2.50	= 13.75	Perhaps a public building; total 206.07 m²
	3.50 × 1.80	= 6.30	
	3.80 × 1.80	= 6.84	
	2.00 × 1.80	= 3.60	
	5.00 × 1.50	= 7.50	
	3.10 × 2.00	= 6.20	
	5.00 × 3.00	= 15.00	
	2.50 × 3.00	= 7.50	
	4.00 × 2.50	= 12.00	
	4.00 × 2.50	= 12.00	
	3.00 × 1.50	= 4.50	
	8.80 × 2.00	= 17.60	
Level III A			
Building 2:	(349) 3.00 × 2.75	= 8.25	
	(350) 2.75 × 1.50	= 4.13	
	(351) 4.80 × 1.10	= 5.28	
	(352) 4.75 × 1.10	= 4.75	
	(353) 4.75 × 0.75	= 3.56	
	(354) 2.00 × 1.75	= 3.50	"T-shaped house;" total 55.01 m²
	(355) 1.80 × 1.10	= 1.98	
	(356) 2.00 × 1.60	= 3.20	
	(345) 3.00 × 2.00	= 6.00	
	(346) 2.80 × 1.20	= 3.40	
	(348) 2.75 × 1.60	= 4.40	
	(347) 3.75 × 1.75	= 6.56	
Building 4:	(534) 4.00 × 0.80	= 3.20	
	(384) 5.00 × 1.25	= 6.25	
	(383) 5.20 × 1.00	= 5.20	
	(370) 2.50 × 1.25	= 3.13	
	(372) 3.25 × 2.50	= 8.13	"T-shaped house;" total 45.71 m²
	(371) 3.25 × 3.10	= 10.08	
	(368) 1.50 × 1.25	= 1.88	
	(382) 1.75 × 1.50	= 2.63	
	(380) 1.50 × 1.20	= 1.80	
	(381) 3.10 × 1.10	= 3.41	

	Linear dimensions (in m)	Area (in m²)

Level III A
  Building 6:

(375) 3.50 × 0.80 =	2.80
(377) 3.50 × 0.90 =	3.15
(378) 3.50 × 0.80 =	2.80
(379) 2.50 × 2.20 =	5.50
(392) 2.10 × 0.80 =	1.68
(394) 2.80 × 2.75 =	7.70
(396) 3.00 × 1.00 =	3.00
(—) 1.50 × 1.20 =	1.80
(—) 1.25 × 1.20 =	1.50
(—) 1.25 × 1.00 =	1.25

"T-shaped house"; total 31.18 m²

  Building 7:

(385) 3.00 × 1.20 =	3.60
(386) 3.00 × 2.25 =	6.75
(389) 2.70 × 2.70 =	7.29
(405) 5.75 × 1.00 =	5.75
(413) 1.00 × 0.80 =	0.80
(390) 2.75 × 1.00 =	2.75
(397) 2.50 × 1.10 =	2.75
(404) 2.50 × 1.00 =	2.50
(388) 1.30 × 1.10 =	1.43
(387) 1.10 × 1.00 =	1.10
(412) 1.25 × 1.10 =	1.38

"T-shaped house"; total 36.10 m²

  Building 8:

(407) 2.50 × 1.20 =	3.00
(402) 2.80 × 2.60 =	7.28
(411) 4.20 × 1.00 =	4.20
(415) 1.50 × 1.20 =	1.80
(408) 1.20 × 0.80 =	0.96
(410) 2.50 × 1.20 =	3.00
(409) 2.60 × 0.75 =	1.95
(417) 1.50 × 1.50 =	2.25
(422) 1.40 × 1.10 =	1.54
(423) 1.30 × 1.00 =	1.30
(418) 3.00 × 3.00 =	9.00
(424) 3.00 × 1.10 =	3.30

"T-shaped house"; total 39.58 m²

  Building 10:

(484) 2.60 × 1.30 =	3.38
(375) 3.50 × 1.00 =	3.50
(488) 5.10 × 1.20 =	6.12
(487) 5.10 × 1.00 =	5.10
(485) 3.10 × 1.50 =	4.65
(483) 3.00 × 1.50 =	4.50
(486) 3.00 × 1.10 =	3.30
(490) 3.75 × 3.75 =	14.06
(491) 1.75 × 1.25 =	2.19
(494) 1.60 × 1.50 =	2.40
(495) 1.50 × 0.75 =	1.13
(492) 3.75 × 1.10 =	4.13

"T-shaped house"; total 54.46 m²

Table 7.7 (*Continued*)

	Linear dimensions (in m)	Area (in m²)	
Level III A			
Building 13:	(444) 1.20 × 1.00 =	1.20	
	(445) 2.60 × 1.20 =	3.12	
	(446) 3.10 × 1.10 =	3.41	
	(447) 3.10 × 3.00 =	9.30	
	(449) 3.10 × 1.00 =	3.10	
	(453) 3.10 × 1.50 =	4.65	"T-shaped house"; total 50.54 m²
	(454) 3.20 × 1.00 =	3.20	
	(455) 1.60 × 1.50 =	2.40	
	(456) 3.90 × 2.90 =	11.31	
	(457) 1.60 × 1.50 =	2.40	
	(458) 1.50 × 1.40 =	2.10	
	(459) 2.90 × 1.50 =	4.35	

Totals: 7 houses; 79 rooms; 312.58 m², presumably roofed living space.

[a] Al-Wailly and es-Soof (1965: Figure 24) and Yasin (1970: Plate I).

Yarim Tepe II

Nearly all the buildings are round mud brick houses 3 to 5 m in diameter (7 m² to 19 m² in area). Some have rectangular annexes, and a few rectangular buildings also occurred (available dimensions are: 3.5 m × 3.5 m = 12.25 m² area, and 3 m × 2 m = 6 m²), including a possibly monumental one (badly preserved).

Hacılar

This site is 26 km southwest of Burdur in southwestern Anatolia. The mound is about 5 m high and 135 m in diameter. The sequence runs from Chalcolithic (fifth millennium B.C.) to Late Neolithic (mid to late sixth millennium B.C.), then—after a break in the stratigraphy—to Aceramic. The latter is not sufficiently exposed to yield much architectural information.

The buildings in Level VI (which was burned) are the simplest to work with. Eight whole houses were excavated, and pieces of 12 more were cleared. The houses consist of rooms built around a large central court. Walls are of 50 cm square mud brick and are 1 m thick or more; walls and floors are plastered. The typical plan comprises a large oblong

Table 7.8

CHOGA MAMI ROOM MEASUREMENTS[a]

	Linear dimensions (in m)	Area (in m²)	
011-12:	(1) 1.60 × 1.50 = 2.40		
	(2) 2.00 × 1.50 = 3.00		
	(3) 1.50 × 1.50 = 2.25		
	(4) 1.50 × 1.50 = 2.25		
	(5) 1.75 × 1.50 = 2.63		Probably a single house (rooms 6 and 10
	(6) 1.75 × 1.60 = 2.80		might have been combined into a
	(7) 1.60 × 1.60 = 2.56		single room, and 5 and 9 may have
	(8) 1.60 × 1.60 = 2.56		been a single room); total 30.05 m²
	(9) 1.60 × 1.50 = 2.40		
	(10) 1.50 × 1.50 = 2.25		
	(11) 1.50 × 1.30 = 1.95		
	(12) 2.00 × 1.50 = 3.00		
H8:	(58) 1.75 × 1.50 = 2.63		
	(59) 1.80 × 1.30 = 2.34		
	(60) 1.60 × 1.25 = 2.00		
	(61) 2.00 × 1.50 = 3.00		Probably a single house (63 and 58
	(62) 2.00 × 1.75 = 3.50		might have been combined into a
	(63) 2.00 × 1.75 = 3.50		sinlge room); total 22.74 m²
	(64) 1.75 × 1.25 = 2.19		
	(65) 1.75 × 1.10 = 1.93		
	(66) 1.50 × 1.10 = 1.65		
H9:	(50) 1.75 × 1.60 = 2.80		
	(51) 1.75 × 1.60 = 2.80		
	(52) 1.75 × 1.60 = 2.80		
	(53) 1.75 × 1.60 = 2.80		Probably a single house; total
	(54) 1.60 × 1.50 = 2.40		20.76 m²
	(55) 1.75 × 1.50 = 2.63		
	(56) 1.75 × 1.50 = 2.63		
	(57) 1.25 × 1.50 = 1.90		

Totals: 3 houses; 29 rooms; 73.55 m², presumably roofed living space.

[a] Oates (1969: Plate XXIV).

room, 5.5 × 8.5–10.5 m long (see Table 7.9), with a wide doorway in one long side.

Opposite the door is an oven with a raised hearth in front of it. Sometimes benches or platforms were found near the hearth. "Screen walls" are thought to have been used to divide up the large rooms. These partitions were apparently built of plastered stakes that did not quite reach

Table 7.9

ROOM MEASUREMENTS FOR HACILAR VI[a]

	Linear dimensions (in m)	Area (in m²)	
Q (1)/(4):	3.60 × 2.00	7.20 ⎫	Probably a single house;
	3.50 × 2.50	8.75 ⎬	total 53.15 m²
	6.20 × 6.00	37.20 ⎭	
Q(2):	8.50 × 5.00	42.50	Probably a single house
R (5)A:	10.20 × 5.10	52.05 ⎫	Probably a single house
(5)B:	3.10 × 2.10	6.51 ⎭	
P (1):	9.00 × 4.90	44.10	Probably a single house
P(2):	7.50 × 5.50	41.25	Probably a single house

Totals: 5 houses; 8 rooms; 239.53 m², presumably roofed living space.

[a] Mellaart (1970. Vol. II:58–59, Figure 7).

the room ceiling. Most of the artifacts in these rooms are said to have been found clustered in screened-off corners. Grain was stored in sacks on the floor or in adobe bins built against the wall. Traces of a "domestic cult" were noted in some houses: stelae with schematized faces on them.

The main roof beam of one of these large rooms was supported by a row of four posts. The outer posts in the row were set against the walls to take the ends of the beam. Remains of posts found in room corners are thought to have been supports for an upper story.

Each house has a number of cubicles used for kitchens, food preparation and processing, etc., on either side of the entrance. Inside are plastered platforms, grinding platforms with milling stones, and an oven and hearth. Sometimes there is also a raised table with a rounded kerb in the kitchen or living room. The excavator believes that many of these houses consisted of two stories, the upper story perhaps like the modern Turkish *sofa*, or veranda, overlooking the court, and that there were originally about 50 such houses.

The basic pattern at Hacilar is more like Hassuna–Matarrah–Hasanabad than Sawwan–Choga Mami but differs in the way the roofed space is subdivided. At Hacilar a house consisted of one big room containing as much space as a whole household complex at Hasanabad, but cut up by relatively flimsy partitions.

Çatal Hüyük

This is probably the single most famous prehistoric site in the Near East. It is also the largest (32 acres, or about 13 ha, so the population was probably well over 1000 if the whole area was occupied simultaneously). The mound is 450 × 275 m in area and 17.5 m in height; the deposit continues to at least 4 m below the plain. Several levels of architectural remains were exposed in Horizons II to VII (a total of 10 so far investigated), with the great bulk of the material dating to the sixth millennium B.C.

The basic settlement plan in all levels was apparently that of a U.S. Southwestern pueblo. The houses are well built and well laid out but rather monotonously uniform throughout the sequence (see Table 7.10 for room dimensions). All are constructed of adobe bricks and were entered through the roof by means of a wooden ladder, usually placed against the south wall of the living room. Also on the south wall (presumably so smoke could escape through the roof hatch) are the hearth and oven plus a deep wall niche, probably for fuel. The kitchen area takes up about one-third of the space in the living room.

Lining the walls in the rest of the room are raised platforms often in a standardized arrangement: a small square one on the northeast, a much larger one at the south end against the east wall and framed between two wooden posts, one or more against the north wall, and one in the southwest corner near the oven. These platforms would have been covered with matting, rugs, blankets, cushions, etc., and used for lounging, working, and sleeping surfaces. The dead were also sometimes buried beneath them. Mellaart (1967) says there is a correlation between the burials and their locations: The northeastern platform seems to have been a male area and the southern platform a female area. The skeletons of children were found under various of the platforms with the exception of the northeastern one (interpreted by Mellaart as specific to the male household head). No single house had sleeping space for more than eight people and there was usually less. No house has more than five platforms and only one has as few as one.

This is fascinating domestic detail even without the artifacts which are spectacular (especially those with the burials), but Çatal Hüyük's real claim to fame is the shrines. These are elaborate, exotic, and abundant. Although the decoration *is* striking, still the shrine rooms are equipped with platforms like those in the ordinary living rooms, and they also have hearths and ovens. Burials occur beneath the platforms in most of them. The criterion for designating a room a shrine was that it be decorated; decoration comprises wall paintings with "obvious ritual significance[;]

Table 7.10

ROOM MEASUREMENTS FOR CATAL HÜYÜK[a]

	Linear dimensions (in m)	Area (in m²)	
Level IV:	(2) 6.00 × 3.00 =	18.00	Probably a single house
	(3) 5.00 × 4.60 = 23.00 3.00 × 1.00 = 3.00 }		Probably a single house; total 26.00 m²
	(6) 4.50 × 4.10 =	18.45	Probably a single house
	(7) 5.00 × 3.50 = 17.50 6.00 × 1.25 = 7.50 }		Probably a single house; total 25.00 m²
	(9) 3.50 × 2.50 = 8.75 2.50 × 2.00 = 5.00 }		Probably a single house; total 13.75 m²
	(10) 4.00 × 4.00 = 16.00 3.50 × 1.25 = 4.40 }		Probably a single house; total 20.40 m²
	(11) 7.00 × 4.00 = 28.00 7.00 × 1.00 = 7.00 }		Probably a single house; total 35.00 m²
	(12) 4.10 × 4.10 =	16.80	Probably a single house
	(14) 6.25 × 5.00 =	31.25	Probably a single house
Level V:	(9) 6.00 × 5.00 =	30.00	Probably a single house
	(10) 6.00 × 4.10 =	24.60	Probably a single house
	(11) 4.75 × 3.50 =	16.60	Probably a single house
	(15) 4.00 × 3.00 =	12.00	Probably a single house
	(17) 6.50 × 4.00 = 26.00 2.00 × 1.00 = 2.00 3.75 × 1.00 = 3.75 }		Probably a single house; total 31.75 m²
	(61) 6.00 × 3.50 =	21.00	Probably a single house
	(—) 6.00 × 4.80 =	28.80	Probably a single house
Level VIA:	(1) 4.10 × 4.00 = 16.40 1.00 × 1.00 = 1.00 3.00 × 1.00 = 3.00 }		Probably a single house; total 20.40 m²
	(2) 3.50 × 3.00 =	10.50	Probably a single house
	(3) 3.50 × 3.10 =	10.85	Probably a single house
	(4) 5.00 × 4.00 = 20.00 4.10 × 1.00 = 4.10 }		Probably a single house; total 24.10 m²
	(5) 4.00 × 4.00 = 16.00 4.00 × 1.50 = 6.00 }		Probably a single house; total 22.00 m²
	(18) 3.80 × 3.50 =	13.30	Probably a single house

	Linear dimensions (in m)	Area (in m²)	
	(24) $4.50 \times 2.50 = 11.25$		Probably a single house
	(26) $3.75 \times 3.50 = 13.13$		Probably a single house
	(27) $4.00 \times 4.00 = 16.00$		Probably a single house
	(46) $4.25 \times 3.50 = 14.88$		Probably a single house
	(51) $4.10 \times 4.00 = 16.40$		Probably a single house
	(63) $4.00 \times 2.00 = 8.00$ $3.00 \times 2.00 = 6.00$ $3.00 \times 3.00 = 9.00$		Probably a single house; total 23.00 m²
	(67) $3.25 \times 3.10 = 10.08$		Probably a single house
Level VIB:	(3) $3.25 \times 3.00 = 9.75$		Probably a single house
	(4) $4.00 \times 3.50 = 14.00$ $4.00 \times 1.00 = 4.00$ $4.00 \times 1.00 = 4.00$		Probably a single house; total 22.00 m²
	(9) $3.50 \times 2.50 = 8.75$ $2.10 \times 1.00 = 2.10$		Probably a single house; total 10.85 m²
	(18) $3.50 \times 3.25 = 11.38$		Probably a single house
	(23) $5.00 \times 3.50 = 17.50$ $3.10 \times 0.60 = 18.60$		Probably a single house; total 36.10 m²
	(25) $5.00 \times 3.75 = 18.75$		Probably a single house
	(25)ᵇ $6.50 \times 3.50 = 22.75$		Probably a single house
	(27) $4.00 \times 3.60 = 14.40$		Probably a single house
	(28) $4.00 \times 3.75 = 15.00$ $4.00 \times 0.60 = 2.40$		Probably a single house; total 17.40 m²
	(34) $5.50 \times 5.00 = 27.50$ $4.00 \times 1.75 = 7.00$ $1.00 \times 1.00 = 1.00$		Probably a single house; total 35.50 m²
	(53) $4.20 \times 3.00 = 12.60$ (56) $4.00 \times 1.00 = 4.00$		Probably a single house; total 16.60 m²
	(54) $4.50 \times 3.50 = 15.75$ $4.50 \times 0.75 = 3.38$		Probably a single house; total 19.13 m²
	(63) $6.50 \times 2.60 = 16.90$ $2.00 \times 1.00 = 2.00$		Probably a single house; total 18.90 m²
	(65) $4.50 \times 4.00 = 18.00$		Probably a single house

Table 7.10 (*Continued*)

	Linear dimensions (in m)	Area (in m²)	
Level VII:	(4) 3.80 × 3.50 =	13.30	
	1.20 × 1.00 =	1.20	
	3.00 × 2.00 =	6.00	Probably a single house; total 26.38 m²
	4.20 × 1.00 =	4.20	
	2.10 × 0.80 =	1.68	
	(6) 3.50 × 2.50 =	8.75	Probably a single house
	(7) 4.10 × 4.00 =	16.40	Probably a single house
	(17) 5.50 × 3.00 =	16.50	Probably a single house
	(18) 4.00 × 3.00 =	12.00	Probably a single house; total 14.80 m²
	3.50 × 0.80 =	2.80	
	(19) 4.75 × 4.00 =	19.00	Probably a single house; total 32.50 m²
	2.00 × 1.75 =	3.50	
	(20) 4.80 × 4.25 =	20.40	Probably a single house; total 21.70 m²
	1.30 × 1.00 =	1.30	
	(24) 5.20 × 3.50 =	18.20	Probably a single house
	(25) 6.50 × 3.00 =	19.50	Probably a single house; total 26.50 m²
	7.00 × 1.00 =	7.00	
	(39) 5.30 × 4.50 =	23.85	Probably a single house

Totals: 53 houses; 84 rooms; 1042.38 m², presumably roofed living space.

[a] Mellaart (1967: Figures 6–10).
[b] *Sic.*

. . . plaster reliefs showing deities, animals, or animal heads; horns of cattle set into benches; rows of bucrania and groups of cult statues; "ex-voto figures" stuck in the walls; "human skulls set up on platforms, etc." [Mellaart 1967: 78].

The proportion of ordinary living rooms to shrine rooms is very high, ranging in different occupation horizons from a maximum of 5 or 6 to 1 to 2 to 1.

CONCLUSION

There is demonstrable basic functional differentiation within some of these sites: pottery manufacturing areas, residence areas, storage areas are present in several, defense system in one, possible public buildings in two.

Although intrasite social differentiation of the sort described for Hasanabad—where an economic hierarchy is clearly perceptible—is not demonstrable from the present architectural evidence for these sites, there are clear-cut differences in the layout of residence units within and between sites (round versus rectangular plans, detached versus attached or contiguous). There is also marked variation in the organization of roofed living space. At one end of the spectrum provided by the nine sites is Hacılar, with very large rooms, each one comparable in area to an entire Hasanabad house complex. At the other end is Choga Mami, with rather small houses cut up into *very* small rooms.

Another interesting contrast is provided by Sawwan and Hacılar with closely comparable house sizes of around 45 m² but with strikingly different patterns in subdivision of that space (see Table 7.11): many small rooms at Sawwan versus one or two large rooms at Hacılar (the large rooms possibly subdivided by partitions but also possibly with a second story). Çatal Hüyük and Hacılar (and Hasanabad) have the largest average

Table 7.11

SUMMARY TABLE OF HOUSE AND ROOM SIZES FOR VARIOUS PREHISTORIC SITES PLUS HASANABAD

Community	Number of houses	Mean area of houses (in m²)	Average number of rooms per house	Average room size (in m²)
Hassuna	5	29.02	4.20	6.90
Matarrah	4	14.80	4.25	3.48
Umm Dabaghiyah	2	39.64	6.50	6.10
Sawwan	7	44.65	11.29	3.97
Choga Mami	3	24.52	9.67	2.54
Hacılar VI	5	47.90	1.60	29.94
Çatal Hüyük	53	19.67	1.58	12.40
Hasanabad	—[a]	50.45[b]	3.80[b]	12.60[b]
		62.30[c]	4.70[c]	12.46[c]

[a] The figures for mean area of houses and for average room size for Hasanabad are based on the dimensions of 60 rooms I was able to measure on the ground in the village (see Table 7.1). There are 41 households containing 193 rooms (counting surface stables; 156 rooms if stables are not included), so my sample of measured rooms is about 31% of the total number of rooms in Hasanabad. The figures for average number of rooms per house, however, are based on counts made from the village plan (Figure 7.1 is a reduced version of that plan). Room sizes derived from this plan are much less accurate than the figures for the 60 rooms just mentioned, hence the latter are presented here.

[b] Excluding surface stables; see note c.

[c] Including surface stables; subterranean stables are not included in any of the Hasanabad figures, although several are present in the village.

room sizes, but the Hacılar rooms are 2½ times the size of those at Çatal Hüyük and over 1½ times as large as the average Hasanabad living room.

There are similarly striking contrasts in the overall nature of the dwelling complexes in these communities. At Hassuna, Matarrah, Hacılar, and Hasanabad the rooms making up a household are agglomerated around courts; at Sawwan and Choga Mami houses are separate or detached. Çatal Hüyük is unique in its pueblo-like architecture, with houses being entered via the roof. Umm Dabaghiyah is also unusual because the houses appear to be semidetached and—according to Mellaart (1975: 136)—some of them may have been entered via the roof.

The round houses of Yarim Tepe II (and of other Halafian sites), of course, contrast strongly with the rectilinear construction at the Hassunan and Samarran sites, although the excavators of Yarim Tepe II believe a combination of round and rectangular rooms was one of the standard house plans there (Merpert and Munchaev 1973: 110).

In spite of rather extreme variation in the categories discussed (overall settlement plan, area of houses, area of rooms), it nevertheless seems clear from examination of the published plans for all these communities that the basic residential unit in each settlement was probably the same: a nuclear family (see also Flannery 1972:42). Even the very large Hacılar living rooms contain only one hearth and do not appear to be multifamily dwellings. Thus, the residence unit exemplified at Hasanabad (man, woman, and offspring) apparently represents an old pattern in the Zagros area, and in a portion at least of Anatolia as well. In these two regions—as represented in the sites considered in this chapter—intravillage social organization based on the nuclear family as primary residence unit, and presumably primary economic unit as well, was expressed in a wide variety of domestic arrangements as early as the sixth millennium B.C.

ACKNOWLEDGMENTS

This chapter comprises revised portions of two different papers. One was originally presented at the 74th Annual Meeting of the American Anthropological Association in San Francisco (in a symposium organized by Charles Redman and entitled "Archeology in Anthropology: Broadening Subject Matter"), and the other was first presented at a Conference on Social Differentiation and Interaction, sponsored by the Anthropology Graduate Organization of the State University of New York at Binghamton. The American Anthropological Association Meeting paper was read December 5, 1975, and was entitled "Archeological Ethnography in Western Iran." The Binghamton paper was read April 3, 1976, and was entitled "Social Differentiation in Some Near Eastern Communities: Prehistoric and Contemporary."

REFERENCES

Braidwood, R. J., L. Braidwood, J. Smith, and C. Leslie
1952   Matarrah. *Journal of Near Eastern Studies* XI:2–75.
David, N., and H. Hennig
1972   The ethnography of pottery: A Fulani case seen in archaeological perspective. *Addison-Wesley Modular Publications 21*.
Flannery, Kent V.
1972   The village as a settlement type in MesoAmerica and the Near East: A comparative study. In *Man, settlement and urbanism*, edited by P. Ucko, R. Tringham, and G. Dimbleby. London: Duckworth. Pp. 23–53.
Gould, R. A.
1968   Living archaeology: The Ngatatjara of western Australia. *Southwestern Journal of Anthropology* 24:101–122.
1971   The archaeologist as ethnographer: A case from the western desert of Australia. *World Archaeology* 3:143–177.
Kirkbride, Diana
1973   Umm Dabaghiyah 1973: A third preliminary report. *Iraq* XXXV:205–209.
Kramer, Carol
1976   An archaeological view of a contemporary Kurdish village. Paper presented in the symposium "Ethnoarchaeology: Implications of Ethnography for Archaeology," organized by Carol Kramer for the 75th annual meeting of the American Anthropological Association, Washington, D.C., November 17–21, 1976.
in   An archaeological view of a contemporary Kurdish village. In *Ethnoarchaeology:*
press   *Implications of ethnography for archaeology*, edited by C. Kramer. New York: Columbia Univ. Press.
Le Blanc, Steven
1971   An addition to Naroll's suggested floor area and settlement population relationship. *American Antiquity* 36:210–211.
Lloyd, Seton, and F. Safar
1945   Tell Hassuna. *Journal of Near Eastern Studies* IV:255–289.
Mellaart, J.
1967   *Çatal Hüyük. A Neolithic town in Anatolia*. London: Thames and Hudson.
1970   *Excavations at Hacılar*. Edinburgh: Univ. of Edinburgh Press.
1975   *The Neolithic of the Near East*. London: Thames and Hudson.
Merpert, N. Y., and R. M. Munchaev
1973   Early agricultural settlements in the Sinjar Plain, northern Iraq. *Iraq* XXXV:93–113.
Middle East Technical University
1965   *Yassıhöyük: A village study*. Ankara: Middle East Technical University.
Oates, Joan
1969   Choga Mami, 1967–68: A preliminary report. *Iraq* XXXI:115–152.
Stanislawski, M. B.
1969a   What good is a broken pot? An experiment in Hopi-Tewa ethnoarchaeology. *Southwestern Lore* 35:11–18.
1969b   The ethno-archaeology of Hopi pottery making. *Plateau* 42:27–33.
Sterling, Paul
1965   *Turkish village*. London:Weidenfeld and Nicolson.

Watson, Patty Jo
    1977   Ethnoarchaeology in the Near East. Paper presented in the symposium· "The
            Development of Ethnoarchaeology: A World-Wide Perspective," organized by
            M. B. Stanislawski for the 42nd annual meeting of the Society for American
            Archaeology, New Orleans, La. April 28–30, 1977.
    in   Archeological ethnography in western Iran. *Viking Fund Publications in An-*
    press–a *thropology.* Tucson: Univ. of Tucson Press.
    in   The idea of ethnoarchaeology: Notes and comments. In *Ethnoarchaeology: im-*
    press–b *plications of ethnography for archaeology,* edited by C. Kramer. New York: Co-
            lumbia Univ. Press.
    1965   The excavations at Tell es-Sawwan. First preliminary report. *Sumer XXI*:17–32.
Yasin, Walid
    1970   Excavation at Tell es-Sawwan, 1969. Report on the 6th season's excavations.
            Sumer XXVI:3-20.

chapter 8

Multivariate Artifact Analysis: A Basis for Multidimensional Interpretations

CHARLES L. REDMAN

The conjunctive approach . . . aims at drawing the completest possible picture of past human life in terms of its human and geographic environment. It is chiefly interested in the relation of item to item, trait to trait, complex to complex *within* the culture-unit represented and only subsequently in the taxonomic relation of these phenomena to similar ones outside of it [Taylor 1967:93–94]

In 1948 Walter Taylor suggested that archeologists concern themselves with the processual functioning of societies rather than with the distinctions among societies. "New" or "processual" archeologists emerged during this period and have made various approaches to the explanation of the functioning and changes in past societies their primary goal, rather than the elucidation of cultural histories. Following is an approach to artifact analysis that I believe provides a practical method for delineating organizational subdivisions within complex societies that can be used in social archeological studies.

Despite the shifting goals and associated renovations in interpretive perspectives, substantive advances by processual archeologists have been

159

Social Archeology:
Beyond Subsistence and Dating

limited by outdated means of classifying and analyzing archeological data. Whereas interpretive theory, quantitative techniques, and field methods have advanced rapidly, classificatory schemes have lagged behind. The use of traditional artifact types or type–variety systems alone reflects a partitive, genetic concept of culture and not the holistic, multivariate view that theoreticians such as Taylor and Lewis Binford advocate. At the same time, this should not be construed as a rationale for introducing naive attribute approaches that overlook important empirical patterning and are difficult to operationalize. Although these problems exist throughout archeology, the situation is most critical in the study of complex societies where the interpretive patterns being sought are complex and the data base is enormous.

Classification and analysis of artifacts is at the heart of most archeological research and has been the center of considerable theoretical controversy (Doran and Hodson 1975, Hill and Evans 1972, Read 1974, Whallon 1972). Unfortunately, simple solutions have not been forthcoming, as is demonstrated by the many research projects that are frustrated despite the enormity of their data base.

The essential nature of the type–variety approach to classification is to summarize the variability in the data, often relating it to a single cause: chronological change. Hence, many micropatterns of variation are obscured and lost to the investigator. Even in regions such as the southwestern United States, where the typological system is well developed, it has been documented that widely accepted types, such as St. John's Polychrome and Heshota Polychrome, are only normative constructs, and in some collections over half the sherds are not classifiable into either type (LeBlanc 1975:24–25). The problem with material analyzed in the normal type–variety manner is twofold: First, the artifacts discovered do not exhibit the total expected constellation of attributes, and second, most of the recovered sherds are so small that only a few of the attributes used to define the types are present on any one sherd. I believe that these problems are characteristic of typological systems and archeological remains in all parts of the world. If we, as archeologists, are to derive the maximum amount of information from the recovered artifacts, then basic approaches to classification and analysis must be reevaluated and overhauled. By this I do not mean to diminish the importance of artifact types—the basic analytical unit of archeology—which have provided much of what we know about world prehistory. Rather, I believe that the derivation of types must be better understood and that various forms of attribute analysis be integrated with the typological approach.

The recent literature of new archeology suggests a dichotomy in the manner with which archeologists approach artifact classification. This situation is lucidly described by Hill and Evans (1972), who characterize the differing stances as "empiricists" and "positivist." The recognition of these positions has raised some crucial questions concerning artifact classification and interpretation. The two central questions are

1. Is there a natural typological system inherent in the artifact collection, composed of types with historical integrity, that can be discovered?
2. Is it possible for the researcher to determine deductively the precise attributes that are relevant to a proposed study in order to make them the focus of the analytical system?

Empiricists would answer yes to the first question while positivists would say yes to the second question, and each would then organize their procedures in accordance with these assumptions. What I have recognized in my own research is that there has been a significant disjuncture between what I *believe*, in a theoretical sense, is the appropriate strategy for formulating an artifact analytical system, and what I have *actually done* to create recording systems for two artifactual inventories. Hence, although I answer no to the first question and yes to the second in a theoretical sense, my own experience shows that I come out straddling both issues.

The two analytical systems that are the focus of this study were created for the Cibola Archeological Research Project and the Qsar es-Seghir Project, which have distinct artifactual inventories, excavation strategies, and substantive goals. Although the discussion of the details of each classificatory scheme is applicable only to the material in question, I believe that the organizational strategy and the principles behind these schemes are applicable to a wide range of investigations. Several especially significant aspects of this approach are emphasized.

1. A multivariate perspective is integral to stages of artifact analysis as well as to the interpretive results.
2. The nature of attribute selection and typological analysis must be systematized.
3. Distributional analysis of artifact variability across a site or region should combine examination of the patterning of individual attributes, artifact types, and microvariability within artifact types.

To illustrate the suggested methodological points, some examples are given, but this chapter is not meant to be a cookbook description of techniques that can immediately be applied to other inventories. The analyses of material from both of these projects are currently in progress, so the results presented are not intended to offer definitive interpretations about the cultures concerned.

ARTIFACT CLASSIFICATION AND VARIABILITY

To interpret or communicate about the world around is, it is necessary to categorize it according to some agreed-upon referents. In the same manner, to describe or explain the archeological record, we must categorize it into classes in order to recognize the empirical patterns that are reflections of past behavior. Categorization is a complex process that is influenced by a variety of learned and physiological factors. Any attempt to propose simple procedures or solutions to the problems of archeological classification is unrealistic and destined to be inadequate.

Classification is a broad term referring to the general process of ordering material or concepts by placing them in groups or classes. The overall working principle is that there are greater similarities among the entities within each class than between different classes. For archeologists, classification is the procedure for deriving information about the past cultural system. Because inferences are based on the observed patterning in the data through space and time, it should be the goal of a classificatory system to maximize the available information. Although most archeologists believe that the classification they employ is designed to enhance the patterning in the artifactual inventory, in many cases the systems seem to render much of it unobservable.

A *typology* results from a more specific process whereby empirically verifiable units—types—are derived, which are basic to future analysis. The existence of types is due to a variety of factors, but a common belief of archeologists is that shared knowledge of the ancient artifact makers concerning appropriate behavior is largely responsible for the existence of distinct types. Although types are often derived implicitly, the basic assumption is that the type is a set of similar artifacts often recognizable through the nonrandom clustering of their observable attributes.

Attributes are the basic, observable components of artifacts or of any phenomena. Each entity under study has a potentially limitless number of measurable attributes. Although the potential number of attributes of an object is theoretically infinite, in practice this number is limited by methods of measurement, interests of the researcher, and available effort for defining and recording the attributes. Measurable values for each attribute may be either discontinuous (i.e., discrete, qualitative categories), continuous (i.e., quantitative categories in a continuum), or separated into intervals (i.e., quantitative categories broken down into discrete but ordered categories). Separate attribute observations can often be organized into a set of dimensions, or classes of attributes, such as color (hue and chroma), size (length, width, and thickness), or raw material (smoothness, chemical composition, and hardness).

Attribute recognition and selection is the most crucial step in the analysis of archeological material. It is at this juncture that the archeologist is required to incorporate all available knowledge of similar artifacts, previous classificatory systems, insights on the relevance of particular attributes, and initial observations of the patterning of potential attributes. Atrribute recognition is not an automatic process, and the decisions made directly affect the outcome of any subsequent analysis. "Attribute recognition . . . is a well blended compound of implicit functionalism, typological insight, and intuition based on experience. It is this area of attribute recognition that is the heart of archeological expertise [Spaulding 1960:62]."

Artifact variability in a general sense is the ultimate source of all archeological knowledge. Formal and spatial patterns of variability in the archeological record are the source of all inferences and the data with which hypotheses can be tested. Hence, it is a primary goal of archeologists to discover and explain the observable variability in the archeological record. The basic physical components of the archeological record are artifacts. Although it is artifacts and their context that are described, the properties that are actually observed are attributes selected by the archeologist because they are believed to have cultural meaning.

The following discussion of analytical procedures utilizes a modified form of David Clarke's (1968:71) proposition that although it is desirable initially to treat all attributes as if they were of equal importance for interpretive analysis, it is useful to separate attributes into three kinds on the basis of their empirical behavior. *Inessential attributes* are those that do not vary significantly in the collection under study. Since variability either over space, temporal divisions, or in differing contexts is the source of archeological knowledge, inessential attributes carry little perceptible information for the particular study. Consequently, their role in the current analysis is minimal. *Essential attributes* are those whose values are found to vary with respect to at least one interpretive dimension of the assemblage. Essential attributes form the basic elements of subsequent typological and distributional analyses. *Key attributes* are groups of two or more essential attributes that are found to covary within the assemblage being investigated. Hence, according to Clarke, it is the goal of the archeologist to discover and explain the observable patterns of essential and key attributes.

Several critical issues are raised by these definitions and approach to artifact analysis. A method must be formulated that utilizes the information and structuring provided by archeological types yet includes the insights into microvariation and nontypological variability available only through attribute analysis. To adequately deal with this issue, the archeologist must answer the theoretical question of whether types are "attribute clusters [Spaulding 1960]" or "item clusters [Doran and Hodson 1975]." The crucial stage of attribute selection relies on the ability of the researcher to delineate significant variability, a problem that is both enormous and complex for most artifact assemblages. The approach suggested here is an attempt to grapple with these issues in an explicit and systematic fashion.

THE NATURAL LABORATORIES

The Cibola and Qsar es-Seghir projects are particularly well suited for organizational studies in the following ways:

1. The chronologies can be determined largely on evidence independent of the ceramic analysis.
2. Both societies were densely populated and generated complex organizational mechanisms.
3. The material inventories in each case are complex and abundant.

A summary of the nature of the remains, the strategies for fieldwork, and substantive questions being pursued by each project will aid in the understanding of the analytical systems as they developed.

Cibola Archeological Research Project

During the summer of 1972 and 1973 the Cibola Archeological Research Project, directed by Patty Jo Watson, Steven A. LeBlanc, and myself, gathered data on the cultural adaptations and behavior of thirteenth century A.D. inhabitants of the El Morro Valley in west-central New Mexico (Watson, LeBlanc, and Redman n.d.). Through an intensive program of surface survey and excavation, about 200 sites were recorded and preliminarily investigated, and 12 sites were partially excavated (Figure 8.1). We discovered that this area has great potential as an archeological laboratory for testing hypotheses on certain types of prehistoric behavioral processes. This is due to the fact that during a relatively short period of time there was a great increase in the valley's population,

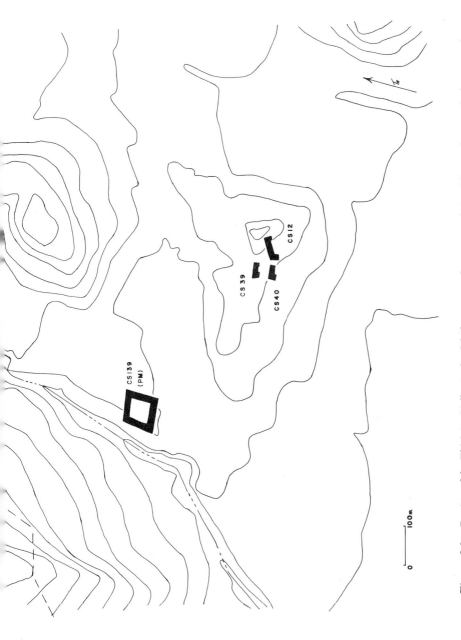

Figure 8.1. Portion of the El Morro Valley in the Cibola region of west-central New Mexico showing the location of Pueblos de los Muertos (CS 139) and the Scribe S site (CS 12, CS 39, and CS 40).

which was soon followed, within 50 or 75 years, by almost total abandonment.

An accurate and detailed chronology is derived from the previous descriptions of pottery similar to that found in the El Morro Valley (Carlson 1970), ceramic seriation analyses carried out by members of this project that subdivide the existing typologically based chronology (Le-Blanc 1975; Marquardt 1974), and the relative abundance of dendrochronological dates from the excavations (ca. 300).

The analysis of the Cibola survey and excavations is still at a preliminary stage, but it is possible to outline some results that have influenced the analytical program. About 25% of the 50-square-mile valley was intensively covered by the survey. Of the approximately 200 sites located, about 50% had traces of masonry architecture. Of the sites that are easily dated, 90% are from a limited range of time, ca. A.D. 1240–1320. The estimated maximum population during this period of intensive occupation could have reached 5000 people. During this relatively short span of dense occupation in the El Morro Valley, there was an apparent consolidation of numerous medium-size sites (10 to 60 rooms) into a few larger, probably more defensible sites (up to 500 rooms). This appears to be the case with the 20 medium-size room blocks that we have named the Scribe S site (including CS 12, CS 39, and CS 40) from an early period that may have agglomerated into the later large-room block of Pueblo de los Muertos (CS 139). One of the goals of the ceramic analysis described here is to provide information on the patterns of integration of groups of people within the valley and to determine whether the large sites, such as CS 139 (ca. 500 rooms), are composed of the descendants of the occupants of nearby earlier sites, among others CS 12, CS 39, and CS 40.

Project Qsar es-Seghir

During the summers of 1974 and 1975 and the spring of 1977, I have been directing an interdisciplinary project centering on the medieval port–fortress of Qsar es-Seghir. In addition to questions of culture history and cultural inventory characteristically addressed by archeologists, we have proposed a series of investigations that involve the various mechanisms of organization within the settlement and how they related to the external societal matrix. To achieve these substantive objectives, the development of effective methods for the archeological investigation of settlements in an urban society is an essential task. Our methodological efforts have focused on two major aspects of research: first, the ongoing evaluation and reformulation of research strategies (cf. Redman 1975), and second, the development of flexible, yet uniform methods of fieldwork and analysis that are commensurate with the nature of the data.

Qsar es-Seghir is situated midway between Tangier and Sebta on the Moroccan coast of the Strait of Gibraltar, at the mouth of a permanent stream that empties into a sheltered bay. The location of the site implies an effort to dominate access from the interior via the stream valley while controlling one of the few natural harbors on the Moroccan coast of the strait. Only 23 km from Spain, this is one of the narrowest parts of the strait. Although the population of Qsar es-Seghir never grew to urban proportions, it was an important military stronghold through the Muslim occupation of Andalusia (especially twelfth to fifteenth centuries A.D.).

The Islamic remains of Qsar es-Seghir comprise a roughly circular enclosure wall 200 m in diameter, a dense distribution of stone-and-brick-constructed buildings within the enclosure, and two major gate complexes (Figure 8.2). During the fiteenth- and sixteenth-century Portuguese occupation, additions were made to the fortifications, including a citadel that dominates the site today, and the nature of domestic architecture was drastically altered.

During the first two seasons of excavations, over 2000 m² have been excavated within the enclosure walls of Qsar es-Seghir in addition to approximately 50 small-scale architectural soundings along the fortification system and in the two gate complexes. Excavation efforts are divided between a stratified systematic unaligned sample of 10-x 10-m squares (8% of the enclosure) and excavation units selected by judgment. So far, 12-sample squares and 13-judgment squares have been excavated at least to the uppermost period of occupation. The judgment squares have primarily been selected in an effort to clear a few broad exposure revealing the contiguous layout of buildings or to excavate the two public buildings discovered; a church, formerly a mosque, and a *hammam* ('public bath'), subsequently used as a military structure. Altogether 7.2% of the area within the enclosure wall has been excavated during the first two seasons. The total exposure after four seasons of excavation is projected to be between 20 and 25% of the enclosure.

The abundance of architecture uncovered provides a meaningful framework for the recording and analysis of artifactual finds. Individual houses can be identified, as well as differing types of rooms within them. The superposition of walls and floors produces a stratigraphic sequence for relative intrasite dating of the materials.

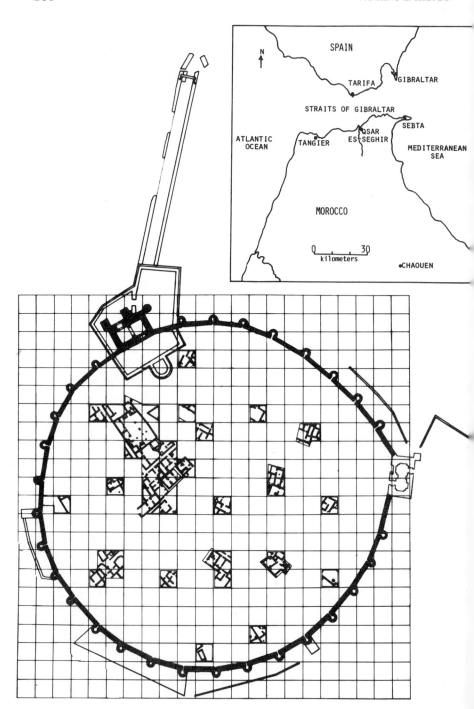

MULTIVARIATE, NESTED APPROACH TO ARTIFACT ANALYSIS

The following is a description of the methods of artifact classification and analysis used to process the material from the Cibola and Qsar es-Seghir projects. The proposed analytical system is presented in four sections: principles, attribute selection, typological analysis, and distributional analysis.

Principles

Seven general principles have guided the formulation of this approach to artifact analysis.

1. For any system of analysis that is aimed at making detailed inferences and handling archeological data in a complex fashion, the analysis must be based on material recovered with excavation controls at least as precise as the desired detail of final interpretations.

2. Systems of recording and analysis must be flexible in order to adapt to the diverse nature of archeological evidence. First, it must be remembered that differing categories of materials may have relevance to the same interpretive problems. Second, recording in the field and laboratory must be set up so that excavation unit-by-unit data can be integrated with individual artifact item-by-item attribute information in certain analyses. Third—particularly crucial problem of ceramic analysis—a recording system must be devised that will combine the detailed, yet scarce, information from complete vessels with the more abundant, but less detailed, data on fragmentary sherds.

3. The state of the archeological record is caused by a complex series of cultural factors and currently exists in a form that can be recorded according to numerous semi-independent attributes. Differing patterns of behavior related to such variables as administrative group, precincts, subsistence, or wealth affect the form, composition, and distribution of material in the archeological record. In order to maintain the maximum usable diversity of information, an optimal approach combines the study of artifact types with investigations of the patterning of individual attribute modalities.

4. Wherever feasible, the attribute values for any category of variability should be organized into a nested or hierarchical system (e.g., Figure 8.6). This has two advantages over a single-level, nominal category

---

Figure 8.2. Map of the defensive walls and excavated units (1974, 1975, and 1977 seasons) at Qsar es-Seghir, the architecture represented is from the Portuguese occupation.

classification: First, fragmentary examples can be recorded at a more general level, thus increasing the sample size for general analyses; second, the levels of the hierarchy can sometimes be structured to be comparable, allowing for different "degrees" or "kinds" of variability to be assessed.

5. In order to guide the typological process and discover significant variability, it is necessary to determine attributes of primary importance. These are used in a stepwise fashion to facilitate the discovery of attribute modalities and to examine them against the basic patterning of the artifact assemblages.

6. The formulation of *tentative interpretive frameworks* also facilitates typological and substantive analyses. These frameworks may include the chronological intercorrelation of widely separated excavation units or the identification of the nature of various rooms or spaces found during excavations. The analysis of materials recovered from any site can proceed in one of two possible orders: Either one can analyze all of the material in detail, concluding with the suggestion of one or more interpretive frameworks to account for the regularities observed, or one can begin by suggesting several tentative frameworks on the basis of initial observations of data external to the ceramic analysis. I strongly recommend the second alternative. These tentative frameworks are used to structure subsequent analyses and are themselves refined by additional interpretive results. In addition to their use in typological analysis for determining which attributes are of interpretive value, these frameworks facilitate the identification of the relationship between the observed empirical patterning of the artifacts and more readily identifiable cultural patterns.

7. Typological and interpretive analyses should be structured in a reiterative multistage manner so that results of initial seasons can give guidance to subsequent fieldwork, refine the classificatory system, and provide interpretive results at varying levels of detail.

Attribute Selection

The heart of the empiricist–positivist debate over the nature of classification revolves around the appropriate method for selecting attributes. The procedures outlined in the following discussion and summarized in Figure 8.3 represent my attempt at reconciling the two somewhat conflicting viewpoints to which I, and probably many others, adhere. Although much of what goes on in the formulation of an analytical system is difficult to describe, the following is a suggested series of interrelated steps that I believe are both realistic and theoretically supportable. There are three sets of procedures that comprise the total

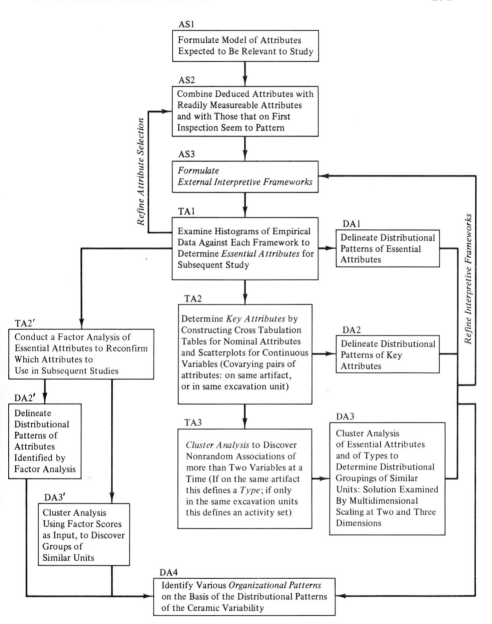

Figure 8.3. Flow chart of the steps involved in a multivariate, nested approach to artifact analysis (attribute selection, typological analysis, and distributional analyses).

analytical system: *attribute selection* (AS1, AS2, and AS3), *typological analysis* TA1, TA2, and TA3), and *distributional analysis* (DA1, DA2, DA3, and DA4).

The system begins by deriving a list of attributes to record on the basis of logic and patterns initially observed in the collection. Defining a few attributes that are believed to be of primary significance allows for the determination of basic types and the examination of microvariability of certain covarying attributes. The formulation of tentative interpretive frameworks provides a means of recognizing attributes that are directly useful and facilitates the cultural identification of their patterning. The recognition of artifact types is pursued both stepwise and through multivariate approaches in order to define both similar artifacts and excavation units that contain similar sets of attribute values. At each stage of analysis it is productive to examine the distribution of attribute values or artifact types across the site. In this manner several overlapping, yet differing, patterns of variability can be discerned that I believe provide a basis for multidimensional behavioral interpretations.

AS1. Formulate Model of Attributes Expected to be Relevant to Study

The initial step in any classificatory system is to select the attributes to be recorded. This procedure begins with a thorough investigation of the substantive problems being pursued and the insights that can be gained from ethnographic, historical, or other archeological interpretations dealing with similar societies and questions. From these diverse sources of data the researcher is able to gain a sense of relevant categories of attributes that are sensitive to questions being pursued. Although I believe it is possible to "deduce" attributes expected to be generally relevant to organizational hypotheses, such as decorative elements, I do not believe that this deduced list is usually complete or adequately defined for operationalizing in the laboratory.

General ideas drawn from ethnographic studies and past archeological work contribute to the selection of attributes for the Cibola analysis, while historical sources have been most valuable in proposing attributes for the Qsar es-Seghir analysis. In both cases, attributes related to technology of manufacture and function are included in order to maintain controls over stylistic variability, but the major focus of recording is decorative elements.

Painted designs, the foci of the Cibola ceramic analysis, were applied to ceramic bowls and jars by prehistoric potters of the Cibola region for a variety of reasons. To the extent that pottery was produced, used, and deposited in the locale of the group that produced it, the distribution of shared decorative elements reflects patterns of interaction within and between communities. Although the identification of the actual nature of the social segments that are represented is difficult and not attempted here, it is possible to delineate various hierarchical systems of grouping of localities that are assumed to represent differing networks of interaction or learning transmission (Redman 1977).

The context of production, use, and deposition of ceramic vessels at Qsar es-Seghir is significantly different from that in the prehistoric Southwest (cf. Rubertone 1976). Historical accounts of the late medieval period indicate that production was likely carried on by workshops of specialists and then commercially distributed, or made by villagers in the region and periodically marketed to the inhabitants of the town. Hence, two separate sets of activities and individuals are responsible for the ultimate form and deposition of the ceramics: patterns related to producers (variety generation) and patterns related to consumers (variety selection).

AS2. Combine Deduced Attributes, Readily Measurable Attributes, and Those That Appear to Pattern on First Inspection

This stage of analysis is a complex procedure that relies on both general propositions and the empirical nature of the artifacts being analyzed. Utilizing the ideas of production and use of artifacts derived from external sources, the researcher must examine the artifacts themselves in an attempt to operationalize the more general notions on the actual material. At this point the attributes found useful by other researchers, initial impressions of attribute variability noticed in the assemblage, and the pragmatics of defining easily measurable attributes all must be taken into account. The result is usually a long list of attributes that are expected to be meaningful for the proposed hypotheses and can be unambiguously measured on the assembled artifacts. One of the major purposes of subsequent steps in the analysis is to determine which of these attributes actually are meaningful (i.e., provide useful information).

On the basis of what is known of prehistoric pottery manufacturing, it is possible to suggest attributes related to three general cultural factors for the Cibola analysis (Figure 8.4): technology of production, function of vessel, and appearance. The form and size of vessels were highly standardized in the Cibola assemblages. Although each of the three basic vessel forms may have served more than one purpose, it is likely that jars were most closely associated with food storage, bowls with food prepara-

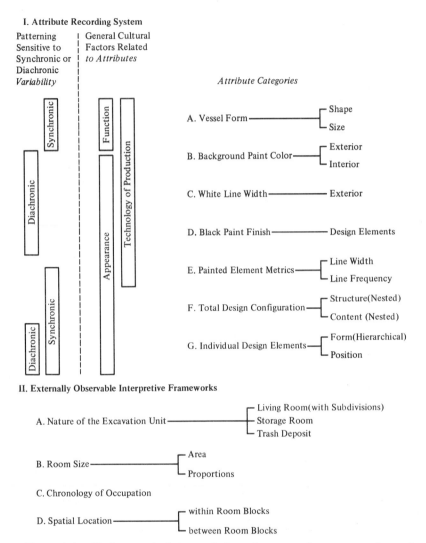

Figure 8.4. Cibola ceramic design analysis attribute recording system and tentative interpretive frameworks.

tion and serving, and ladles with food serving. Several other formal characteristics are recorded that are involved with the methods of producing and decorating the pots. Included are background paint color of the vessel, the width of white lines painted on the exterior of bowls, the finish of the black paint used in painting designs, and the width and frequency of lines in the painted designs. These are related to decisions about the composition of the paint, firing conditions, and the nature of brushes. These characteristics might reflect both unconscious learning patterns and explicit decisions made about the appearance of the pot. Previous studies (Carlson 1970; LeBlanc 1975; Marquardt 1974), have found vessel color, white line width, and black paint finish to be sensitive to change over time. The present study confirms the temporal variability in these factors but also observes cooccurring synchronic variability. The fourth class of attributes, line metrics, might be related to the motor skills of individuals or teaching patterns of small groups and might be sensitive to synchronic variability reflecting small social segments.

Aspects of decoration are hypothesized to be directly related to patterns of interaction and organization. The core of the Cibola analysis is the coding of individual design elements or portions of elements. This is done according to a master chart of 203 possible elements developed by detailed examination of the pottery to be analyzed. The design elements are hypothesized to be basic units in the repertoire of the potter, with transmission of elements being related to contact between individuals or groups. The actual list of elements is defined in terms of geometric possibilities and is arranged in a hierarchical format. Each level of the hierarchy can be examined separately during analysis in order to determine at what level of design certain cultural patterning is reflected most clearly (and with the largest sample of sherds). It could be the basic motifs (e.g., hatching, lines, solids), the bounded shape (e.g., bands, triangles, steps), or even the orientation of the hatching within the shapes that encodes the most interesting data. Patterning of different details of execution comprising generally similar overall designs is hypothesized to be a reflection of specific learning groups and is a key to understanding the interactional networks of the prehistoric occupants.

The selection of attributes for the Qsar es-Seghir analysis did not have previous work of a similar nature to rely upon or any ubiquitous decorative elements similar to the Cibola painted designs. However, there is greater variability in vessel form, surface finish, and presence of morphological parts (e.g., handles, rims, bases), all of which reflect functional as well as other kinds of diversity (Figure 8.5). The differing patterns of production employed by the potters of that period relate to the factors just mentioned, the nature of the ware, and the implements used for making tactile designs. The appearance of the vessel, which is hypothesized to be a reflection of patterns of user selection, is affected by a series of attributes consisting of surface finish, morphological parts, tactile designs, and painted designs. The most detailed aspect of recording involves the microvariation in morphological parts (Figure 8.6). The subdivisions are based on geometric differences hypothesized to form distinct patterns

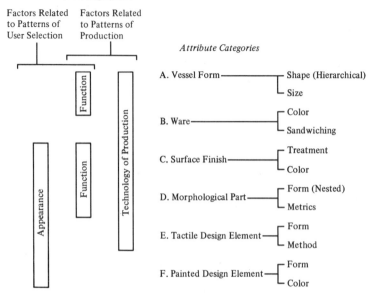

I. Attribute Recording System

Factors Related   Factors Related
to Patterns of   to Patterns of
User Selection   Production

Attribute Categories

A. Vessel Form ──────── ┬ Shape (Hierarchical)
                        └ Size

B. Ware ──────── ┬ Color
                 └ Sandwiching

C. Surface Finish ──────── ┬ Treatment
                           └ Color

D. Morphological Part ──────── ┬ Form (Nested)
                               └ Metrics

E. Tactile Design Element ──────── ┬ Form
                                   └ Method

F. Painted Design Element ──────── ┬ Form
                                   └ Color

II. Externally Observable Interpretive Frameworks

A. Nature of Excavation Unit ──────── ┬ Street/Plaza
                                      ├ Living Room(with Subdivisions)
                                      └ Courtyard

B. Chronology of Occupation

C. Spatial Location within Community

Figure 8.5. Qsar es-Seghir generalized ceramic analysis; attribute recording system and tentative interpretive frameworks.

that can be arranged into a hierarchy. Bases (36 categories), handles (22 categories), and rims (57 categories) are the most important elements.

AS3. Formulate External Interpretive Frameworks

The next stage in analysis is to formulate a series of interpretive frameworks on the basis of evidence external to the proposed ceramic

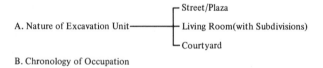

Figure 8.6. Nested, hierarchical chart of attribute categories for recording microvariation in morphological parts for the Qsar es-Seghir ceramics.

QSAR ES-SEGHIR CERAMIC MORPHOLOGY HIERARCHY

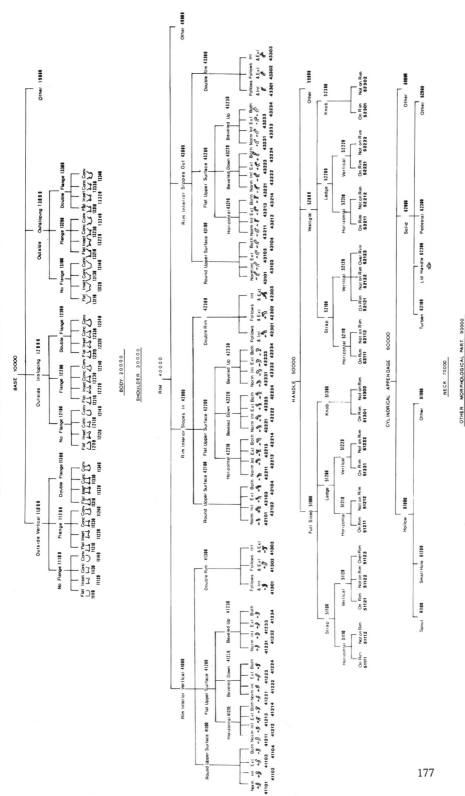

analysis. For the Cibola project a number of frameworks are being utilized (Figure 8.4). The nature of the excavation unit, size of the room, and spatial location of the room are important factors related to the social context within which the post was used. The chronology of occupation is important in determining what variability is primarily related to changes in learning patterns affected by the passage of time. Tree ring dates and a microseriation of pottery types provide the basis for this chronology.

Similar frameworks have been proposed for the Qsar es-Seghir material. There has been an initial chronological division into four phases of occupation of the site. Stratigraphic levels from each excavation unit are ordered into this temporal framework on the basis of superposition of buildings, relative elevations, and similarities of construction techniques. The second interpretive framework is intrasite location. It is expected that divisions in the composition and organization of the town's inhabitants will be related to the location of their residence. The third framework is the locus type. Identification is based on the presence of architectural features and the layout of excavated rooms, courtyards, houses, and streets. By studying the materials in reference to these locus types, it should be possible to associate artifacts or attributes with expected activities for the locus.

Typological Analysis

TA1. Examine Empirical Data against Each Framework in Order to Determine Essential Attributes for Subsequent Study

The first step of the typological analysis is, in effect, the final step in the process of attribute selection. At this stage the attributes that have just been defined and recorded are examined to see if they exhibit variability or maintain a constant value within the assemblage. As defined previously, those attributes that empirically are found to vary are considered *essential attributes* for typological and distributional analyses, whereas those attributes that remain constant are termed *inessential attributes* and are not pursued further. In addition to limiting the number of attributes to be examined in later stages of analysis, the definition of essential attributes can be used to restructure the initial data recording of artifacts for future field seasons.

Checking for variability takes several forms. First, continuous and interval attribute values can be examined in a histogram of the entire assemblage while multimodalities are looked for. This would imply distinct patterns of behavior and allow interpretative divisions to be made according to that single attribute. However, it is most often the case that attribute values in an entire collection produce a complex histogram, or at least one that is not readily interpretable. That is why tentative interpretive frameworks are necessary, forming the basis for the second form of examination. Histograms of the distribution of each continuous or interval value attribute are constructed as they vary against each interpretive framework. For nominal variables patterning can be examined by the construction of a cross-tabulation table of interpretive framework alternatives versus attribute values. To the extent that these frameworks parallel the substantive interests of the researcher, attributes that fail to vary when viewed against them carry little or no information for these particular investigations.

The examination of variability is facilitated by the tentative selection of primary variables, such as vessel form or surface finish, against which the variability of other attributes can be checked. Similarly, obvious and easily defined ceramic types (based on one or combinations of two primary attributes) may exist in an inventory and should be utilized as the basis of microvariational studies of other attributes. If the structure provided by these primary attribute categories is not used, the computational problems of "checking" variability are enormous, and there is a greater likelihood that many of the statistical patterns observed may be spurious or that culturally meaningful differences may remain unobservable. To a certain extent, this step is equivalent to what many experts do according to "intuition" or their "experience with the material." Rather, than denying the crucial importance of this type of expertise, I suggest that it is possible to conduct this stage in the analysis in a more systematic manner by explicitly outlining criteria of judgment.

TA2. Determine Key Attributes by Constructing Cross-tabulation Tables for Nominal Attributes and Scatterplots for Continuous Variables

The second step of the typological analysis is for the researcher to identify *key attributes* by seeking pairs of essential attributes that covary. These attributes will probably be the most effective unit for interpretive studies. Covariation of essential attributes measured on a continuous scale is sought by the construction of scatterplots of the values. When many attributes are examined, a correlation matrix should be calculated in order to suggest which of the larger number of possible scatterplots to investigate. For nominal variables, or continuous variables split into intervals, cross-tabulations are the method of investigation. Table 8.1 is a

Table 8.1

TWO-WAY CROSS-TABULATION TABLE OF ATTRIBUTES OF VESSEL BACK-
GROUND COLOR AND VESSEL FORM FOR THE ENTIRE CIBOLA COLLECTION

	Color		
Form	Red	Yellow-Red	White
Bowl	167	→ 1601	136
row %	9%	84%	7%
Jar	73	344	→ 351
row %	10%	45%	46%
Ladle	3	11	→ 15
row %	10%	38%	52%

cross-tabulation for two general attributes of the Cibola ceramics, form
and background paint color. Although color red does not appear to
associate with any particular form, unexpectedly high proportions of
yellow red (YR) bowls, white jars, and white ladles exist in the total
collection. In addition to seeking the nonrandom covariation of attributes
in the entire collection, it is useful to examine cross-tabulation charts for
each division of each interpretive framework in order to determine if the
pattern exists in only one particular period, location, or section of the site.

Two types of covariation exist, and they must be treated differently.
The first, covarying pairs of attributes that occur on the same pieces, is
the initial step in defining artifact types. The second, pairs of attributes
that cooccur in the same excavation units but not on the same pieces,
probably reflects the components of activity sets or tool kits that are
functionally or behaviorally related. If all of the recording were tallies
done on an excavation unit-by-unit basis (e.g., proportions of different
glaze colors found in a room), it would not be possible to differentiate
between these two types of covariation.

Individual artifact item-by-item recording, even of only a portion of
the total material, allows for the testing of whether attributes are cooccurring on the same piece or not, and the investigation of whether dependent relationships exist among various attribute categories. By examining
Table 8.2, one can make the inference that in the area under study the
ratio of white ware to red ware decreases over time. Although this pattern
is confirmed by overall trends in the Southwest, there is reason to believe
that within the short time span of the El Morro Valley occupation other
variables may have been responsible for causing this change. Table 8.1 is
a cross-tabulation of vessel form and color, showing that white ware
largely occurs in the form of jars, and red ware as bowls. Table 8.2 also

Table 8.2

VALUES FOR TECHNOLOGICALLY RELATED ATTRIBUTES OF THE CIBOLA
CERAMICS HYPOTHESIZED TO HAVE TEMPORAL SIGNIFICANCE

Excavation unit	rooms(n)	Occupational phase	Whiteware (%)	Shiny glaze (%)	X White line width (in mm)
Scribe S site					
CS 12 3	50	1	20	1.5	5.5
CS 12 8		1	20	0.0	6.5
CS 12 11		1	22	8.0	5.3
CS 12 13		1	24	2.7	5.0
CS 12 14		1	32	4.3	6.7
CS 40 61	30	1	24	12.0	6.0
CS 40 62		1	42	1.3	5.2
CS 39 65	24	1	29	1.4	4.9
CS 39 66		1	21	7.1	5.0
Pueblo de los Muertos					
CS 139 5617/9	500	1	14	5.0	5.9
CS 139 5617/3		2	7	10.7	3.8
CS 139 304		2	13	11.4	3.6
CS 139 20		2	6	19.1	2.8
CS 139 108		3	6	34.0	3.0
CS 139 418		3	9	19.4	3.2

includes the relative percentage of bowls in each excavation unit from the
Cibola project. The percentages are internally consistent for each site
(except room 62, which was a storage room) and show a distinct increase
between the Scribe S site and the later CS 139. In addition, the percentage of bowls seems to increase directly with the size of the site. Both of
these factors are related to a changing ratio of bowls to jars and may have
been more important in causing the changing proportion of white ware
than the color itself.

Another example of the utility of item-by-item analysis is its ability to
determine whether design elements are associated with vessel form in a
nonrandom manner. Various design element studies (e.g., Hill 1970;
Longacre 1970), have assumed that this was not the cause. In the Cibola
region, at CS 139, at least the major motifs (hatching, lines, and solids)
seem to occur equally on bowls and jars. However, at the three earlier
room blocks there is a significant perference for solids on jars and hatching on bowls. Hence, the ratio of bowls to jars deposited in a room, which
is related to the functional nature of the room, has an impact on the
distribution of design elements.

TA3. Conduct a Cluster Analysis in Order to
Discover Nonrandom Associations of More
Than Two Variables at a Time

One can carry the typological analysis to its conclusion by seeking higher order pairings of covarying attributes. Groups of three, four, or more attributes that covary may be identified either by a stepwise procedure of two-at-a-time cross-tabulations or directly by a multivariate cluster program to discover groupings of similar artifacts followed by a discriminant analysis to identify the key attributes responsible for these clusters. If the attributes cooccur on the same artifacts, then the cluster program will identify statistically verifiable types as defined by Spaulding (1960). If the attributes occur in the same unit but not on the same pieces, then the clusters define some sort of behaviorally related activity set.

TA2'. Conduct a Factor or Principal
Components Analysis of Essential Attributes
in Order to Reconfirm Which Attributes to
Use in Subsequent Studies

A second strategy, in addition to examining histograms (TA1 and TA2), can be pursued for determining the attributes relevant for study. By conducting a factor or principal components analysis using the already defined essential attributes or even the entire selection of attributes from step AS2, one can learn which attributes pattern most distinctly over the units of study (cf. LeBlanc 1975; Marquardt 1974). As with all multivariate techniques, the results are immediate and often usable but sometimes difficult to interpret or understand how they emerged. I recommend using this approach as a supplement to the more direct, time-consuming study of individual histograms and cross tabulations.

Distributional Analyses

DA1, DA2, and DA3. Delineate Distributional
Patterns of Essential Attributes, Key Attributes,
and Artifact Types in Order to Represent Ceramic
Variability as the Data Base for Discovering
Organizational Patterns

Although the major portion of most research efforts is devoted to attribute selection and typological analysis, neither of these procedures, in themselves, produces information about the past societies. Rather, they yield units to be used in distributional analyses, which are the basic elements of interpretive studies. It is the results of these analyses and their interpretation by archeologists that determines whether the entire analytical system has been effectively designed. The overall objective of the artifact system described here is to delineate interpretable patterns of variability at different levels (i.e., single attributes, covarying attribute pairs, artifact types, and microvariation within types) and numerous patterns at any one level. By examining these diverse distributional patterns against the hypothesized interpretive frameworks, one can interpret the distribution of many of the essential attributes and types.

The crucial element in an analysis based on the proposed multivariate, nested system is that although one framework, such as chronology, may be important in the explanation of much of the observed variability, there are patterns that crosscut time periods or spatial units. *The refinements in this analytical approach are not designed to improve the precision of one dimension of variability, time, but to enable the investigation of other patterns of variability, especially those that are organizational.*

Following are a few examples of different types of distributional analyses that are currently under way with the data from the Cibola and Qsar es-Seghir projects. In order to examine in a graphic manner some of the distributional patterns of selected essential attributes, I have constructed a topological map of the 4 room blocks under study from the Cibola project with the relative placements of the 12 rooms and 3 trash trenches excavated (Figure 8.7). This map portrays the relative positions of rooms within sites and each of the sites to one another, but not to scale. This is a mechanism to facilitate interpretation and delineation of associations that crosscut room blocks or time periods.

Figure 8.7 is a map showing the relative percentage of bowls in each of the excavation units (number in upper right-hand corner of each unit). Two patterns are clear: first, the internal consistency of values for Sites CS 12 and CS 139; and second, the relative increase in percentage of bowls at sites of increasing size. The distribution of this one attribute implies a close connection between Room 61 and the rooms of CS 12, with the value for Trench 5617-09 being the lowest for CS 139. These patterns are reconfirmed by other distributions.

Analysis of the individual painted design elements on the Cibola ceramics is only beginning yet promises to provide data on groupings based on a variety of attributes. For each of the attributes studied so far, the difference between units of the two major time periods (CS 139 versus the Scribe S room blocks) is a primary determinant, yet additional pat-

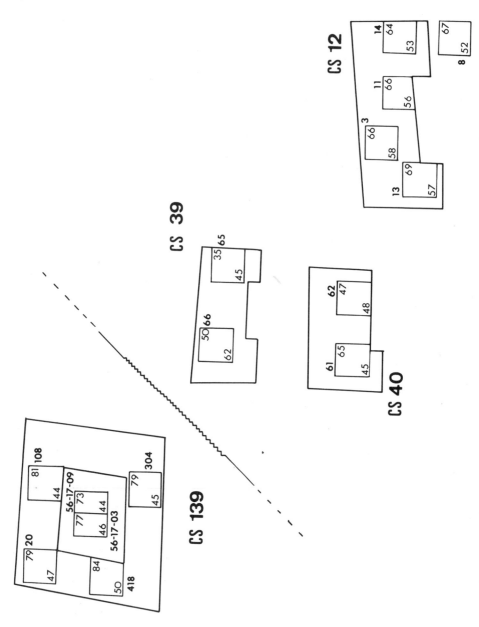

Figure 8.7. Topological map of four room blocks examined in Cibola ceramic study, values for the percentage of bowls in

terns can be perceived that are operating within single periods and across the two periods.

Figure 8.7 also contains the percentage of designs that are solid in the lower left-hand corner of each unit. For the percentage of solids, CS 139 and CS 12 have internal consistency and are quite different from each other, while CS 39 and CS 40 provide mixed values. Other less "obvious" measures of design variability are probably related to unconscious learning patterns and yield more complex groupings of units that crosscut each of the sites. The pattern that seems to be emerging from the initial examination of a selected series of attributes involves more standardized choices being made by the potters of CS 139 than by those of the Scribe S site, although the population of CS 139 was probably five times that represented by the three Scribe S room blocks and the actual ground area covered by CS 139 is even greater than the three separate room blocks of CS12, CS39, and CS40. It is also likely, although difficult to document at this point, that the span of occupation represented by the six units from CS 139 is greater than that represented by the nine units of the Scribe S site. Each of these factors might suggest that there should be less standardization at CS 139, but this appears not to be the case.

Two alternative explanations might be suggested for further testing:

1. With the formation of the large site of CS 139, the production of pottery no longer was conducted in each individual household but was carried out by fewer and more specialized craftswomen, leading to increasing standardization of choices and products.

2. The number of individual pottery-producing social segments remained large, but the intensity of interaction among these groups increased significantly.

These alternate hypotheses are amenable to testing with a variety of data. So far only one line of additional evidence is utilized: measurements on the execution of painted lines. If a situation of specialized potters had emerged at CS 139, one would expect to find increasing skill of execution in technical aspects of the design. According to the values for mean line width and mean line frequency for painted designs, the opposite pattern exists. Individual line widths are greater at CS 139 and drawn farther apart. On the basis of these measurements and qualitative impressions from complete vessels, technical competence in drawing is significantly higher at the Scribe S site.

Two approaches to distributional analyses with higher-order associations of attribute values can be pursued. Individual attributes can be clustered into artifact types and the distribution of types delineated, or a series of patterns produced by individual attribute distributions can be compared and amalgamated. I have experimented with the second approach, using eight ceramic attributes not initially assumed to have chronological significance. Ultimately a much larger number of attributes will be utilized as input for a cluster analysis of excavation units that should yield groupings of units with similar contents, which would not be immediately apparent from examining one attribute at a time.

Table 8.3 is a summary of the values for the eight attributes investigated. A rough measure of the similarity of units can be computed for each pair of units. Figure 8.8 is a two-dimensional summary of the similarity coefficients calculated from the attributes in Table 8.3. High numbers (7, 6, or 5) imply similar values, whereas low numbers imply lack of similarity according to these eight attributes. Three groupings are clearly portrayed: Rooms 62 and 65; Rooms 11, 13, 14, and 61; and all of the rooms at CS 139. In addition units 3, 8, and 66 in the Scribe S site exhibit weak linkages with other Scribe S units as well as with units from CS 139. Some insight into the nature of each group is possible. Rooms 11, 13, 14, and 61 are large living rooms in Scribe S with a diversity of cultural material. Rooms 62 and 65 are smaller and may represent a more limited

Table 8.3

EIGHT ATTRIBUTE VALUES FROM 15 EXCAVATION UNITS IN THE CIBOLA DESIGN ELEMENT STUDY (INPUT FOR SIMILARITY DIAGRAM)

Excavation unit	Bowls (%)	Lines (%)	Hatching (%)	Hatched triangles	Solids (%)	Solid triangles	Line width (in mm)	Line frequency
Scribe S site								
CS 12 3	66	19	19	5.5	58	11.8	3.1	3.0
CS 12 8	67	23	23	2.3	52	4.5	2.1	3.5
CS 12 11	66	12	29	9.4	56	20.1	2.3	3.1
Cs 12 13	69	12	28	9.1	57	5.9	2.3	4.0
CS 12 14	64	16	28	8.6	53	12.0	2.4	3.7
CS 40 61	65	23	29	8.1	45	10.1	2.5	3.7
CS 40 62	47	17	28	9.8	48	10.8	2.7	3.5
CS 39 65	35	18	32	11.0	46	12.8	2.9	3.9
CS 39 66	50	23	15	3.0	62	1.5	3.4	3.5
Pueblo de los Muertos								
CS 139 5617/9	72	38	17	5.3	44	6.7	2.7	3.3
CS 139 5617/3	77	50	2	.9	46	3.5	3.4	3.0
CS 139 304	79	45	6	1.8	45	4.2	3.0	3.0
CS 139 20	79	46	2	0.0	47	9.6	3.1	3.0
CS 139 108	81	50	2	.2	44	5.0	3.2	2.5
CS 139 418	84	43	3	0.0	50	6.0	3.8	2.8

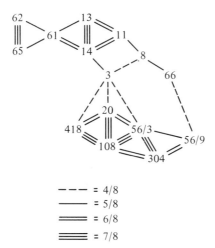

```
--- = 4/8
——— = 5/8
=== = 6/8
≡≡≡ = 7/8
```

Figure 8.8. Cluster diagram of similarities of Cibola study units based on shared values of eight attributes on a pair by pair basis.

range of activities or a different type of social segment. Rooms 3 and 66 appear to be aberrant units for their respective room blocks according to a number of activities. It is possible that they each belonged to social segments not represented in the other excavated rooms, and they exhibit attributes similar to those found at CS 139. Their position in the northwest quadrant of their respective room blocks (direction toward CS 139) may be relevant.

The overall impression of this "similarity" graph parallels the observation made on several of the individual attributes: There was closer association among the units of CS 139 than among the three room blocks of the Scribe S site.

By investigating different aspects of the total system of analysis, the researcher can gain interpretive pictures of different detail. For example, classical types or design symmetry would group all the Cibola sites together or perhaps differentiate between CS 139 and the Scribe S; analysis of technologically related attributes (Table 8.2) involves the subdivision of the sites into three chronological phases (Marquardt 1974); examination of even the general information on the design elements involves the subdivision of phase 1 (Scribe S) into two or three organizationally related groups. In addition, by examining a large number of different attributes individually and then grouping the distributional patterns, the researcher can produce several different distributional groupings all at the same level of detail, but presumably reflecting different combinations of cultural or organizational factors.

The distributional analysis of the Qsar es-Seghir data generated by the analysis of its ceramics has so far been primarily oriented toward testing the effectiveness of the analytical system itself. One overall interpretive goal of this project involves the definition of components of the organizational structure of the community at one point in time, and ultimately their changing nature over time. As part of the preliminary analysis, the ceramics were divided into 158 units based on their stratigraphic and horizontal provenience. These units were grouped into 26 larger units according to excavation square and occupation phase in order to increase the sample size of individual units and to simplify the initial results. A cluster analysis to discover groups of similar excavation units (step DA3) was performed, utilizing nine attributes of surface finish selected on the basis of variability in their chronologically divided histograms. These attributes were the input for a minimum overall variance hierarchical cluster program. The solution for this analysis is portrayed in Figures 8.9 and 8.10. Figure 8.9 is a dendrogram that represents the levels

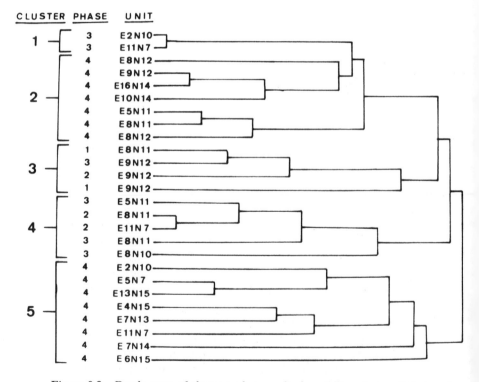

Figure 8.9. Dendrogram of cluster analysis results from tallies of nine attributes of ceramic surface finish in 26 units from Qsar es-Seghir.

QSAR ES-SEGHIR

SITE DISTRIBUTIONAL DATA , 1974-75

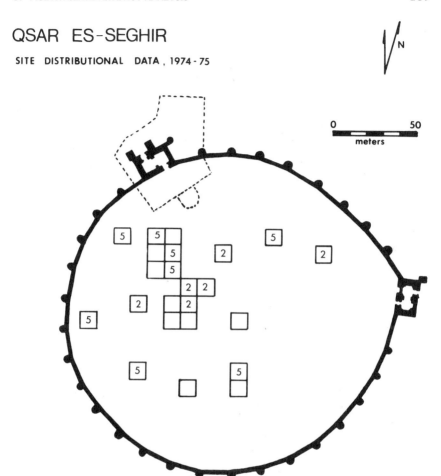

Figure 8.10. Spatial distribution of results of cluster analysis shown in Figure 8.9; Cluster 2 is interpreted as military and residential areas, while Cluster 5 is the church and residential areas.

of "similarity" at which members were joined together into pairs or attached to existing groups. The excavation unit occupation and designation is portrayed on the figure. Two patterns emerge from this cluster analysis. First, the major clusters of the units are grouped according to chronological phases, especially differentiating between phase 4 (clusters 2 and 5) and all that preceeds it. Second, within one phase the clusters seem to delineate spatially meaningful groupings of units.

Figure 8.10 represents the location of units that comprise the two clusters of phase 4 units. Cluster 2 contains three excavation units that are components of a military building (prison or arsenal) and two additional residential units (one with substantial military equipment). Cluster 5 contains five residential units spread around the periphery of the site and three units from the church area. Although the attributes used in this analysis are not those expected to be especially sensitive to subtle organizational patterns, they have outlined what may be the two major residential- occupational divisions in the Portuguese community: military and nonmilitary personnel. Similar cluster analyses performed on other attributes will be executed to examine whether this pattern is maintained, replaced, or subdivided further. It is also expected that more than one pattern of organization (reflected by similarity of attribute distribution) will exist at any one time in the community. The distribution shown in Figure 8.10 is related to differences in occupation that probably parallel differences in status. Subdivisions within these two major groups may emerge, such as the crosscutting of divisions according to regional derivation of the inhabitants or occupational specializations.

The Qsar es-Seghir classificatory system does not have an attribute category as diverse or as previously well-tested as painted design elements in the Cibola system. However, preliminary inspection of the data suggests that rather than one major category, the categories of vessel form, surface finish, morphological part, tactile design, and painted design will each provide significant distributional data. This diverse data base will enhance the multivariate nature of the results from the Qsar es-Seghir analysis, enabling the investigation of organizational patterns within this complex society.

CONCLUSIONS

The ultimate effectiveness of the artifact classificatory and analytical system described in this chapter does not rest in its theoretical justification, but in the reliable interpretations it generates and documents. Although the analysis remains incomplete, detailed examination of the distribution of attribute values for the Cibola ceramics suggest several organizational groupings that crosscut room blocks and even time periods. In addition to this, there is the hypothesized processual change in relative interaction among the social segments in the two major periods under study, with the inhabitants of CS 139 being more tightly integrated than their predecessors. The Qsar es-Seghir organizational inferences are given meaning by the presence of readily identifiable central buildings, such as the church and military structure. With this information it is possible to identify organizational patterns that are shared by central buildings and residential structures that may have housed people who were associated with the central buildings.

The procedures described in this chapter are drawn from a variety of previously employed artifact systems and in many ways represent only a subtle change from what has gone before. The emphasis of this entire approach is on creating a multidimensional set of data that will allow the archeologist to document more than one pattern of variability at a time. Quantitative studies have too long focused on chronology alone or some other single variable. Culture is a complex, multidimensional phenomenon, and its material products are the archeologist's embodiment of this information. For an analytical system to take the incredibly complex data of ceramic variability and simply represent it along a single axis of variation does not do justice to our potential for documenting complex organizational patterns. Accepting this position, the real challenge becomes the development of methods for both maintaining this complexity of information and deriving understandable behavioral patterns from it. The tendency I have observed is for the researcher to become mired in the enormous amount of information and be able neither to complete a detailed analysis nor to come up with satisfying interpretive results. It is toward the elimination of these problems that I have attempted to systematize the procedures and the directions that I and others are currently pursuing.

ACKNOWLEDGMENTS

The formulation of the approach to artifact analysis described in this chapter has been carried out in the context of two archeological expeditions, with staff members contributing their energies and ideas at various points. The Cibola Archeological Research Project, directed by Patty Jo Watson, Steven LeBlanc, and myself, was supported by National Science Foundation grant number 32987. Patty Jo Watson and Keith Kintigh were instrumental in the formulation of the Cibola system and continue to participate in its development. The Qsar es-Seghir project is sponsored by Smithsonian Institution Foreign Currency grant SF3-00091 and the State University of New York at Binghamton. The Qsar es-Seghir ceramic system was developed through the cooperative efforts of Keith Kintigh, Renata Holod, Judith Rasson, and Patricia Rubertone.

REFERENCES

Carlson, R. L.
  1970   White Mountain redware. *Anthropological Papers of the University of Arizona* No. 19.

Clarke, D. L.
    1968   *Analytical archaeology*. London: Methuen.
Doran, J. E., and F. R. Hodson
    1975   *Mathematics and computers in archaeology*. Cambridge, Mass.: Harvard Univ.
            Press.
Hill, J. N.
    1970   Broken-K pueblo: Prehistoric social organization in the American Southwest.
            Anthropological Papers of the University of Arizona No. 18.
Hill, J. N., and R. K. Evans
    1972   A model for classification and typology. In *Models in archaeology*, edited by D. L.
            Clarke. London: Methuen. Pp. 231–273.
LeBlanc, S. A.
    1975   Micro-seriation: A method for fine chronological differentiation. *American An-
            tiquity* 40:22–38.
Longacre, W. A.
    1970   Archaeology as anthropology: A case study. *Anthropological Papers of the Univer-
            sity of Arizona* No. 17.
Marquardt, W. H.
    1974   A temporal perspective on late prehistoric societies in the eastern Cibola area.
            Unpublished Ph.D. thesis, Dept. of Anthropology, Washington Univ., St.
            Louis.
Read, D.
    1974   Some comments on typologies in archaeology and an outline of a methodology.
            American Antiquity 39:216–242.
Redman, C. L.
    1975   Qsar es-Seghir: Preliminary report on the 1975 excavations. Annual report to
            Smithsonian Institution.
    1977   The "analytical individual" and prehistoric style variability. In *The individual in
            prehistory*, edited by J. Hill and J. Gunn. New York: Academic.
Rubertone, P. E.
    1976   Explanation of ceramic variability: A multidimensional model of interaction.
            Abstracts of 41st annual meeting of the Society for American Archaeology.
Spaulding, A. C.
    1960   Statistical description and comparison of artifact assemblages. In *The application
            of quantitative methods in archaeology*, edited by R. Heizer and S. Cook.
            Chicago: Quadrangle. Pp. 60–92.
Taylor, W. W.
    1967   A study of archaeology. *American Anthropological Association, Memoirs* No. 69.
Watson, P. J., S. A. LeBlanc, and C. L. Redman
    n. d.   Aspects of Zuni prehistory.
Whallon, R. C.
    1972   A new approach to pottery typology. *American Antiquity* 37:13–33.

PART II

Interpretation

Interpretation is an inextricable component of the investigative process. It is operative during the formulation of the hypothesis as well as in its testing and explanation. In the following section, interpretation is represented at each one of these junctures. Every chapter included here required a certain amount of interpretive insight in the construction of models, tests, and explanations. The entries of Sanders and Webster, Redman and Sterud are models that require further testing. The chapters of Wright, King, Plog, Morris, and Rathje are examples of work in which interpretation occurred upon conclusion of the analysis of data.

The interpretations put forth in these chapters reflect the approaches that archeology has adopted from other disciplines. Systems and ecological principles applied in a hypothetical–deductive manner are the most viable and recurring of these. In addition, the following chapters reflect the focus of contemporary archeology to describe and explain the emergence and functioning of social and political systems. What differentiates the chapters in the following section from many previous studies is the use of explicitly formulated and logically derived models.

This section begins with the separate demonstrations of Gary Wright (Chapter 9) and Thomas King (Chapter 10) that prehistoric data can provide insights of which there are no historical or contemporary examples. Their individual studies—Wright's on a Natufian burial population and King's on a late prehistoric–early historic Californian group—suggest that the typological construct that has directed our conceptualization of hunting and gathering societies and ultimately the evolution of the state needs to be reexamined. Both investigators demonstrate, with a logical set of assumptions and arguments, that societies practicing a hunting and gathering economy need not be organized according to an egalitarian system, as the type concept indicates. Their evidence reveals that hunters and gatherers can be and were organized in a ranked manner. The authors argue that typologies based on the mode of production and a constellation of traits related to it should be reconstructed. Both authors suggest that the maintenance of exchange brings about and supports a ranked system of organization. According to them, societies do not have to progress through trajectories consisting of band–tribe–chiefdom, egalitarian-ranked, stratified stages in order to achieve statehood. The authors assert that the order of the stages through which a society passes does not have to conform to this model. For example, a society does not have to pass through both ranked (chiefdom) and stratified stages in the course of evolution. In addition, the tempo at which a society enters a new level of complexity varies from one area to the next.

Unilineal schemes ignore the primary determinants of evolutionary change. These are: environmental risk, environmental diversity, environmental size, and environmental productivity. In Chapter 11, Sanders and Webster propose that it is these factors in the environment that determine population size, exchange, competition, and other phenomena that have in the past been viewed as causative agents of increasing complexity. Although Sanders and Webster acknowledge the operation of these factors in the evolution of society, they feel that they are originally determined by the variables characterizing the environment. These variables and certain combinations of them produce various trajectories and are responsible for the processes characterizing evolutionary development. For example, a high-risk environment engenders centralization, whereas high-diversity areas encourage specialization. Sanders and Webster trace the trajectories and paces at which these developments took place for the Olmec, Valley of Oaxaca, Basin of Mexico, and the lowland Maya from the perspective of the causal powers of risk, diversity, productivity , and size of the respective environments.

In Chapter 12, William Isbell, employing concepts presented to us in the previous chapters, explains the origin of the Andean state. Highland Peru is environmentally diverse. It is also a high-risk environment characterized by severe energy perturbations. Since energy is not constant, a social system, in order not to overstep its average carrying capacity, must employ several strategies to return the system to its equilibrium state. In an attempt to deal with their energy fluctuations, the Inca and the groups preceding their hegemony, practiced two kinds of energy-averaging strategies. These represent their responses to and effective solutions in dealing with the uncertainty of their environment. The strategies are spatial averaging and temporal averaging. Spatial averaging refers to the process of expanding or combining resource bases through centralization. Temporal averaging "involves redistribution of energy through time, storing and transferring surplus production of the past to future times of shortage."

As a result of the long-term success of these strategies in keeping Andean societies within the limits of their average carrying capacity and in buffering them against environmental perturbations, there was a population increase previous to the emergence of the state. This in turn necessitated the development of even more efficient means of administering spatial and temporal energy-averaging strategies. The appearance of centralized ceremonial centers (spatial averaging) followed by the construction of public storage facilities (temporal averaging) at these loci characterized the emergence of the Inca state.

Craig Morris in Chapter 13 discusses the function of reciprocity and redistribution in the maintenance of the Inca state. These modes of exchange, operative both on the community and state levels, are derived from archeological and ethnohistorical models. Where models or data for such models are lacking, Morris proposes a series of ways in which to formulate and derive them. It may be a great surprise to many, Morris notes, that as expansive and complex a state system as that of the Inca engaged in exchange behavior normally associated with simpler societies. Reciprocity and redistribution functioned successfully, Morris reasons, because economic transactions were embedded in political, symbolic, and religious relations. Exchange reaffirmed those ties between the rulers and the ruled. On one level the state provided food, beer, shelter, and pottery in exchange for labor, which the populace supplied for the construction of state buildings, movement of state goods, or manufacture of state items. On the other hand, these reciprocal and redistributive arrangements represented a means of maintaining order and ensuring the people's cooperation in the running of the state. In the systemic terms employed by Redman, these exchange mechanisms would function as negative feedback mechanisms, whereas Isbell would see such exchange activities related to energy-averaging strategies.

In Chapter 14 by Redman, the usefulness and clarity of employing ecological concepts with systems theory for understanding and explaining evolution of urban society is demonstrated. Beginning with its preurban occupation, Redman traces the events leading up to and characterizing the evolution of urbanism in lowland Mesopotamia. Mesopotamian society is treated, in its pre-urban and urban stages, as alternate states of a system. Through the interaction of complex sets of relationships of the components of the system with one another and with the environment, and through the generative and stabilizing behavior of positive and negative feedback mechanisms, Mesopotamian society's emergence as a class-stratified society is described. Although he views environmental stimuli as bringing about system changes, Redman acknowledges the causative powers of political institutions, symbolic informational systems, and individual behavior.

In Chapter 15, Fred Plog accounts for the variability of contemporary and prehistoric Puebloan social structure by examining the interrelationships of environment, subsistence, and social organization. He argues that it is not enough to acknowledge the operation of selective pressures of the environment in evolutionary change and in the functioning of societies. The nature of environmental variability must be expressed in terms of risk and diversity.

In the first part of his chapter, Plog explains why Pueblo Indians do not share the same social structure. Differences in social structure reflect dissimilar land-use–subsistence patterns. These in turn represent adaptations to the elements of risk and diversity in each society's local habitat. The Western Pueblo live in a high-risk, low-diversity environment and practice a farming strategy designed to accommodate these factors. To operate successfully, the resulting land-use patterns require a social organization based on lineages. The Eastern Pueblo, on the other hand, occupy a low-risk, high-diversity environment and engage in irrigation agriculture. Their affairs are handled by a variety of specialized organizations and offices that are conducive to that land-use pattern.

In the second half of his chapter, Plog discusses the interplay of environment, subsistence strategies, and social organization as they are expressed in the archeological record. From the time they began employing it in their subsistence repertoire, Plog argues that southwestern groups have experimented with agriculture. By A.D. 1100 they were practicing an irrigation strategy similar to the one currently practiced by the Eastern Pueblo. Approximately 200 years later a new strategy, similar to the one of today's Western Pueblo, appeared in eastern Arizona and western New Mexico. Irrigation was retained in the Rio Grande area, however; Plog attributes the change in the strategies to the failure of irrigation in a high-risk, low-diversity environment. Its survival in the Rio Grande area is due to the low-risk, high-diversity aspects of its environment. Similarly, Plog suggests that the diversity observed in settlement patterns (which are reflections of organizational variability), represent experiments in organization, as societies continued to develop ways to exploit the variability of their environments.

William Rathje (Chapter 16) reveals how the study of contemporary refuse and the practices associated with its discard enables us to test further behavioral patterns. In his study, Rathje found that the nationwide beef shortage and high prices associated with it affected the eating and discard patterns of contemporary Americans. As prices went up, people began buying large quantities of meat as well as previously untried cuts. Waste increased dramatically. As people grew accustomed to the prices, however, waste decreased. These observations enabled Rathje to develop a "food discard equation," which states, "The amount of regularity in purchase consumption behavior varies inversely with the percentage of food input that is discarded." Rathje's study is an example of how a society does not always come to accept or integrate innovation strategies (as expressed by altered purchasing habits during times of stress) into its behavioral regime. The reasons for the failure of such experimentation must be explored further, as they were in Plog's chapter. Rathje's study reveals how the methodolqgy employed by archeology and the data derived in such a manner can be employed by other disciplines in the planning of resource management.

In the final chapter of this section Eugene Sterud (Chapter 17) deals with the practice of transhumance in a pre-urban context. He proposed that during the earliest stages of food production in the Dinaric and other high-risk environments of Mediterranean Europe, societies engaged in seasonal transhumance as an alternative to farming. Transhumance is viewed as a risk-reducing strategy in areas where agricultural productivity was limited. During the middle Neolithic, Sterud notes that societies practicing transhumance, an extensive mode of exploitation, start practicing an intensive pattern. Sterud presents several hypotheses regarding this shift. These hypotheses consider both environmental and social factors. Sterud's ideas shed new and previously unexplored insight into the role of transhumance in the adoption of agriculture in Mediterranean Europe.

chapter 9

Social Differentiation in the Early Natufian

GARY A. WRIGHT

INTRODUCTION

Recently, there has been a resurgence of interest among archeologists in mortuary practices. Although descriptions of burials in reference to their chronology, the demographic structure, and their osteological characteristics are common in site reports or areal syntheses, it is only of late that attention has been redirected back to the theoretical study of the social dimensions of interment (Brown 1971). If we assume that variations of interment mode within the group are indicative of internal differentiation of individual group members—whether by age, sex, and/or social position—and that pattern variations among groups reflect differences in structural complexity, then archcologists have at their disposal a powerful tool through which they may understand certain aspects of the organizational properties of extinct social systems (Binford 1971).

Intentional interment of the dead apparently first appeared during the Mousterian. The custom of including grave furniture was still weakly

201

Social Archeology:
Beyond Subsistence and Dating

developed, however. This phenomenon increased during the succeeding Upper Paleolithic. Cemeteries are first seen in abundance during the early post-Pleistocene and are known, for example, from the European Mesolithic and the eastern North American Archaic periods. A third area in which cemeteries are found at this date is the Levant of southwestern Asia.

Neanderthal burials in the Levant (e.g., Skhul, Qafzeh, and Amud) seem to be late in the Mousterian sequence and to include only a few with possible grave goods. The reported grave furniture consists of animal parts and/or red ocher, and the graves generally appear to lack associated tools, weapons, and ornaments. Interestingly, during the Upper Paleolithic in the Levant, unlike in Europe, human remains are rare. In contrast, during the early post-Pleistocene Natufian, burials reappear—this time in large numbers and in cemeteries, and with differing amounts and kinds of grave furniture with different individuals.

I will begin this chapter with a brief synopsis of the Natufian. The remainder of the chapter will be concerned with four matters. First, using the burials from el-Wad, I will attempt to demonstrate that social differentiation was present in the Natufian there. Second, I will attempt to show that it had occurred by the earliest stages of the Natufian at this site. Third, I will consider to what extent the same degree of social differentiation is found on other early Natufian sites. Finally, we must ask what causative factors may have been involved in the evolution of social differentiation among the Natufian.

THE NATUFIAN

The Natufian takes its name from the Wadi en-Natuf in western Judea. It was first excavated *in situ* by Garrod (1942) at the cave of Shuqbah in this wadi in 1928. The earliest synthesis of the Natufian was attempted by Neuville (1934), the most recent by Henry (1973). Its lithic industry has a large component of distinctive microliths, and bone tools are now common. It is preceramic in age, stratigraphically overlying terminal Pleistocene industries, such as the Atlitian at el-Wad and the Kebaran at Kebara. However, early Natufian is contemporaneous with Geometric Kebaran B; the latter is replaced by the Natufian around 9000 B.C. in the Sinai and Negev (Bar-Yosef 1975). The Natufian underlies the Pre-Pottery Neolithic A (PPNA) at Jericho and the Pre-Pottery Neolithic B (PPNB) at Beidha. There are 10 carbon 14 dates available for the Natufian from four sites. They suggest a temporal span from ca. 10,000 to 8000 B.C. radiocarbon years (Henry 1973).

Natufian sites are known from caves, cave terraces, and in the open (Garrod 1957; Perrot 1968). We see the appearance of architecture in the construction of houses at sites such as Jericho, Beidha, Nahal Oren, Rosh Zin, and Ain Mallaha, indicating permanent settlements. Perrot (1968: 371) has suggested a population of 200–300 contemporaneous inhabitants at Mallaha. Alteration of cave terraces is seen—for example, at el-Wad, where storage basins were cut into the limestone bedrock and a tightly packed stone pavement and a stone wall were built (Garrod and Bate 1937), and in the construction of houses at Nahal Oren (Stekelis and Yizraely 1963). Stone pavements are known in the open at Rosh Zin (Henry 1973) and at Mallaha (Perrot 1966) and inside caves, such as at Erq el-Ahmar (Neuville 1951).

Because of the presence of permanent architecture, sickles and handles, and mortars and pestles, a number of authors have suggested that the Natufians were agriculturalists. However, this contention has been disputed (Henry 1973; Perrot 1966, 1968; Wright 1971). The earliest domesticated plants are not known in Palestine until the Pre-Pottery Neolithic: emmer and hulled two-row barley in the PPNA at Jericho, the addition of einkorn to the diet in the PPNB at Jericho, and the addition of naked two-row barley in the PPNB at Beidha (Renfrew 1969). The earliest domesticated animal in Palestine is the goat, which is found at el Khiam, Beidha, and Jericho at ca. 7000 B.C. (Wright 1971).

Using stylistic variables in the stone tool industry, Henry (1973) was able to seriate 20 Natufian sites. His seriation was then checked against the radiocarbon dates and found to be valid. Early Natufian was restricted to the Mediterranean biotic zone. Around 9000 B.C. there was an expansion into the Irano-Turanian zone. The Natufian expansion occurred during a climatic interval that was wetter than the present (Henry 1973: 188). Palynological data seems to confirm the observation of Bar-Yosef and Tchernov (1970), Marks (1971), and Wright (1971) that Natufian sites are distributed within the biotic zones containing the wild prototypes of the later domesticated emmer wheat and barley and that the expansion followed the distribution of these wild cereals (Henry 1973: 189).

Wright (1971) has pointed out that a new technological complex evolved early in the Natufian (cf. Henry 1973). It included sickles, mortars and pestles, and stone pavements (often found in association with roasting hearths and storage pits). It appears to have been directed toward the harvesting, preparation, and storage of these wild grains. Fishing, as attested by gorges and fishhooks, became important for the first time, and hunting of game such as gazelle continued (Henry 1975).

In conjunction with the technological innovations, we also see a major change in settlement patterns in comparison with the preceding

Kebaran (Bar-Yosef 1975; Henry 1973). The Kebaran adaptive strategy required several seasonal movements. In contrast, with the Natufian we find permanent base camps with several satellite transitory work camps. Natufian base camps are generally over 100 m² in size and have burials, architecture, and ground stone for the first time. Transitory camps are less than 200 m² and lack architecture and burials.

The evidence indicates that the Natufian population was larger than that of the preceding Upper Paleolithic hunters, and that the new economy of wild grain harvesting, coupled with hunting and fishing, permitted greater food collection and storage (Bar-Yosef 1975; Henry 1973; Wright 1971). One result was the appearance of permanent nonagricultural villages, such as Mallaha and Beidha. Second, it has been proposed that the evolution of agriculture in this area resulted from subsequent pressures on wild cereal resources (Wright 1971). There is clear evidence of a population expansion around 9000 B.C., well prior to the appearance of domesticated plants (Bar-Yosef 1975: 373; Henry 1973). Demographically, the Natufian population is different from contemporary Mesolithic populations in Europe (Henry 1973). Henry (1973: 194) concludes that it was population pressure that caused the initial expansion.

There were also further elaborations in the Natufian way of life. As Bar-Yosef and Tchernov (1970) have noted: "This improved economic position was to have its social effect: it was now possible for larger numbers of people to live together by sharing food surpluses. We now encounter collective burials, storage facilities for food and artistic efforts which indicate communal activities [p. 148]." I believe that this burial analysis will indicate the presence of social differentiation within the local groups.

Thus, it is within this new adaptive pattern that large numbers of burials and cemeteries first appeared. More than 200 Natufian skeletons have been excavated from el-Wad, Hayonium, Mallaha, Nahal Oren, Kebara, Shuqbah, and Erq el-Ahmar. The largest numbers are from Mallaha (82), el-Wad (62) and Nahal Oren (ca. 50). They include both group and individual burials, with and without grave goods, and in caves, on the cave terraces, and within and outside of houses. Unfortunately, much of the skeletal material remains unpublished, but some data are available (e.g., Ferembach 1961; McCown 1939; Vallois 1936).

THE EL-WAD BURIAL DATA

There are a number of problems in dealing with the published burial data from el-Wad. There were 62 burials recovered in the excavations.

Unfortunately, only 44 were described in the final report (Garrod and Bate 1937). The additional 18 burials were "not scattered or isolated bones, but the remains of badly preserved burials too fragmentary to describe [p. 19]." Lacking descriptions entirely are nine single burials placed just to the east of the Natufian stone wall on the terrace and numbered H-33-35, H-42, and H-44-48 (Figure 9.1; Garrod and Bate 1937: Plate 3). Nine other individual burials from the terrace are also not discussed in the final monograph. Included in these latter nine are H-38, H-51, and H-61, which were described by McCown (1939) in his Ph.D. thesis on the relatively complete Natufian crania from el-Wad. Thus, although "too fragmentary to describe" as burials, these three crania were intact enough for McCown to record 40 or more measurements on each. Further, among the 44 described burials, some lack notation of certain variables in which I was interested. For example, head orientation and age (adult, child, or infant) were not reported for a few burials (Tables 9.1–9.3). I have combined both Garrod's and McCown's data.

A second problem arises in the discrepancies between preliminary reports and the final monograph. For example, a group burial (my Group 1) was found in Chamber 1 of the cave (Figure 9.1). In an earlier paper, Garrod (1931: 7) noted that the group included 11 individuals: 4 adults and 7 children. In the final report, the number of individuals in this group is 10: 4 adults, 2 children, and 4 infants (Garrod and Bate 1937: 14–15). McCown (1939: 15) commented that the group burial in Chamber 1 "comprises at least ten individuals." I have used 10 for my sample. A second example of this problem is that two H-13's are described. A careful reading of the papers, however, shows that one of them dates to the Early Bronze Age or later, the other to the Natufian.

Finally, the preservation of the skeletal material was poor. McCown (1939) had only 11 relatively complete crania with which to deal, thus making aging and sexing difficult. I also have little confidence in the sex data contained in the final site monograph, since there are differences of opinion between that report and McCown's work. For example, Garrod labeled H-2 a male and H-3 a female; McCown sexed them as a female and a male, respectively. For these reasons, I felt unconfident of Garrod's sex data and did not use them.

These problems notwithstanding, there appeared to be sufficient data to warrant a preliminary attempt to search for regularities in interment at el-Wad. The variables utilized were those most completely reported for each burial (Table 9.1). One set of the variables includes various characteristics of the individual or the mode of interment: (a) flexed or extended (F, E), (b) head orientation (see Tables 9.2 and 9.3), (c) group or single (G, S), (d) age (adult, child, or infant [A, C, I]); (e) location (within the cave,

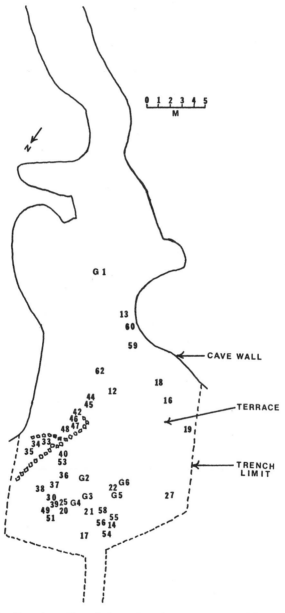

Figure 9.1. Location of burials from el-Wad excavations (modified after Garrod and Bate 1937: Plate 3).

cave mouth, or terrace [W, M, T]); and (f) date (Lower Natufian, Upper Natufian, or unspecified Natufian [LN, UN, N]).

Burials were placed in two positions, either flexed or extended. They are found in three locations: the terrace, the mouth of the cave, or within the cave. All primary terrace burials were flexed; all burials within the cave were extended. Burials at the mouth of the cave included both flexed and extended.

Both group and individual burials occurred. There are six group burials—five on the terrace, one in the cave, and none at the cave mouth. Both group and single burials are found on the terrace, only single burials at the mouth, and only group burials within the cave.

The cave group burial differs from the terrace groups in several respects. One of these is that the cave group was reopened at least twice to admit more bodies. The lowest level contained one child (H-10). The second level had three adults (H-2-4), one child (H-5), and three infants (H-6, 7, 9). The upper level held one adult (H-1) and one infant (H-8). All were primary burials. In contrast, there is no evidence that the terrace groups were reopened, suggesting that all the members were buried at one time. However, all of the members of group burials on the terrace, with the exception of one in each group, were fragmentary. I suggest that the terrace groups contain one primary burial and one or more secondary burials, a pattern we will observe in other Natufian sites.

For aging, I used only adult, child, and infant. No infant burials were reported from the terrace, only adults and children. All three are found within the cave and at the mouth. Orientation is provided for only 27 of the 44 described burials and will be discussed later.

The second set of variables includes the presence or absence of different types of grave furniture and is recorded by P or A in Table 9.1: (a) limestone blocks or slabs; (b) mortars and pestles; (c) dentalium shell; (d) twin bone pendants; (e) bird bone pendants; (f) bone tools; (g) hearths[1]; and (h) flint.

Inspection of Table 9.1 shows that there are major differences in the way grave furniture was handled by the Natufians at el-Wad. For example, dentalium shells are found only in the group burials on the terrace. The single burials on the terrace, the cave group, and the cave mouth burials lack this item entirely. Further, only one member in each terrace group—the primary burial—received a dentalium shell headdress or necklace. Also this member of the group is the only one to receive any grave goods; all others in the terrace groups have no grave furniture. In

---

[1] For convenience I have included hearths under grave furniture.

Table 9.1

EL-WAD BURIAL DATA[a]

Number	F/E	G/S	Age	Location	Date	Lime-stone	Mortars	Denta-lium	Twin bone pendant	Bird bone pendant	Bone tool	Hearths	Flint	Type	Comments
1	E	G1a	A	W	LN	P	P	A	A	A	P	P	A	I	Carved bone sickle handle
8	E	G1a	I	W	LN	P	A	A	A	A	A	P	A	I	
2	E	G1b	A	W	LN	P	A	A	A	A	A	P	P	I	2 and 3 facing each other
3	E	G1b	A	W	LN	P	A	A	A	A	A	P	A	I	Turtle carapace with flint knife
4	E	G1b	A	W	LN	P	A	A	A	A	A	P	P	I	
9	E	G1b	I	W	LN	P	A	A	A	A	A	P	A	I	
5	E	G1b	C	W	LN	P	A	A	A	A	P	P	A	I	Bone points, Dama antler lissier
7	E	G1b	I	W	LN	P	P	A	A	A	A	P	A	I	
6	E	G1b	I	W	LN	P	A	A	A	A	A	P	A	I	
10	E	G1c	C	W	LN	P	A	A	A	A	A	P	A	I	Also calcite human head
41	F	G2	A	T	LN	A	A	P	A	P	A	A	A	II	Both below undisturbed limestone pavement
43	F	G2	A	T	LN	A	A	A	A	A	A	A	A	II	
23	F	G3	A	T	LN	A	A	P	P	A	A	A	A	II	
23a	F	G3	A	T	LN	A	A	A	A	A	A	A	A	II	
23b	F	G3	C	T	LN	A	A	A	A	A	A	A	A	II	
25	F	G4	A	T	LN	A	A	P	A	A	A	A	A	II	

25a	F	G4	A	T	LN	A	A	A	A	A	A	A	II
25b	F	G4	A	T	LN	A	A	A	A	A	A	A	II
25c	F	G4	A	T	LN	A	A	A	A	A	A	A	II
26	F	G4	A	T	LN	A	A	A	A	A	A	A	II
28	F	G5	C	T	LN	A	A	P	A	A	A	A	II
28a	F	G5	A	T	LN	A	A	A	A	A	A	A	II
28b	F	G5	A	T	LN	A	A	A	A	A	A	A	II
28c	F	G5	A	T	LN	A	A	A	A	A	A	A	II
28d	F	G5	A	T	LN	A	A	A	A	A	A	A	II
57a	F	G6	A?	T	LN	A	P	P	P	A	A	A	II
57b	F	G6	A	T	LN	A	A	A	A	A	A	A	II
57c	F	G6	A	T	LN	A	A	A	A	A	A	A	II
57d	F	G6	A	T	LN	A	A	A	A	A	A	A	II
57e	F	G6	A	T	LN	A	A	A	A	A	A	A	II
57f	F	G6	A	T	LN	A	A	A	A	A	A	A	II
57g	F	G6	A	T	LN	A	A	A	A	A	A	A	II
56	F	S	A	T	LN	A	A	A	A	A	A	A	III
19	F	S	A	T	N	A	A	A	A	A	A	A	III
27	F	S	A	T	UN	A	A	P	A	A	A	A	III
17	F	S	A	T	UN	A	A	A	A	A	A	A	III
21	F	S	A	T	UN	A	A	A	P	A	A	A	III
15	F	S	A	T	UN	A	A	A	A	A	A	A	III
13	E	S	I	M	N	A	A	A	A	A	A	A	IV
59	E	S	C	M	N	A	A	A	A	A	A	A	IV
60	E	S	A	M	N	P	A	A	A	A	A	A	IV
12	F	S	A	M	LN	P	A	A	A	A	P	A	V
18	F	S	A	M	LN	P	A	A	A	A	P	A	V
62	F	S	A	M	LN	P	A	A	A	A	P	A	V

Note (at rows 57 a–d): 57 a-d encircling one mortar

a See text for explanation of symbols.

209

contrast, each member of the cave group has grave goods, if only lime-stone blocks covering the cranium.

ANALYSIS

The problems inherent in the burial data become readily apparent when one wishes to perform statistical analyses. Full counts could not be obtained on any burial good. Thus, I could only note the presence or absence of an item. Lacking continuous variables, I was unable to utilize such statistical tests as correlation coefficients. Using the presence or absence of goods, I can suggest some preliminary distinctions, but it is difficult to test them statistically. For reasons mentioned earlier, we cannot have full confidence in the data and this should be kept in mind. I shall now proceed as if there were no problems.

As I noted earlier, there were some very evident distinctions among the burials—for example, cave burials were extended and terrace burials were flexed. Also, group as opposed to single burials appeared to be an important distinction on the terrace in that dentalium was found only with the group burials. Because the distinctions seemed clearest here, I employed as a base these three variables—flexed–extended; location; and group–single—against which to examine some of the other variables.

In some burial analyses, orientation has been found to be a key variable (e.g., Gruber 1971). For el-Wad, McCown (1939:17) commented that "no consistent plan appears to have been followed with respect to orienting the body." Combining data from Garrod and Bate (1937) and McCown (1939), I was able to obtain orientations for only 27 burials (Tables 9.2 and 9.3). Fourteen have their heads toward the southeast and northwest. This is the longitudinal axis of the cave, with the entrance facing northwest. However, the 10 cave burials exhibit five different orientations, none of which are northwest (Table 9.3). Unfortunately, the

Table 9.2

ORIENTATION OF EXTENDED, AS OPPOSED TO FLEXED, BURIALS AT EL-WAD

	W	SW	S	SE	E	NE	N	NW	
Extended	1	2	2	4	0	1	0	2	
Flexed	0	0	0	4	1	4	0	6	
Total									27

Table 9.3

ORIENTATION AND LOCATION OF BURIALS AT EL-WAD

	W	SW	S	SE	E	NE	N	NW	
Cave	1	2	1	4	0	1	0	0	
Mouth	0	0	1	1	1	1	0	2	
Terrace	0	0	0	3	0	3	0	6	
Total									27

sample size is too small, and there are too many cells with fewer than five cases for meaningful χ^2 analyses to be performed.

Using the full sample, I can first make some preliminary distinctions by dividing the burials by location and group or single:

I. Cave–Group ($n = 10$). These are extended burials, have hearths (usually below the body), and the crania and/or trunks covered by limestone blocks or slabs, or by broken or whole mortars. Infants were present. Dentalium shell, bird bone pendants, and twin bone pendants were absent. Bone and flint tools were present, but not with all members. One burial, H-10, had a carved calcite head. The grave was reopened twice, and all the members seem to be primary burials.

II. Terrace–Group ($n = 22$). There are five groups ($n = 2, 3, 5, 5,$ and 7), and all primary burials are flexed. Graves show no evidence of having been reopened, and secondary burials were present. Only one individual in each group had grave goods, always including dentalium shell. These burials lacked hearths, limestone (though four members of Group 6 were arranged around one mortar), bone and flint tools. Bone pendants were found, but not in each group grave.

III. Terrace–Individual ($n = 6$). Many additional burials probably fit here, but they were not described. The impression we have from the series of reports is that all were adults and were flexed. No dentalium shell was recorded. Burials H-17 and H-21 had a twin bone pendant and a bird bone pendant, respectively.

The six described burials at the cave mouth are all single interments, but there the similarity ends. The three adults on the terrace side (outside) of the mouth (H-12, 18, and 62) were flexed like terrace burials but had hearths and limestone-like cave burials. The three on the inside of the cave mouth (H-13, 59, and 60) were extended like cave burials and included one adult, one child, and one infant. However, they lacked hearths, and only one, H-60, had limestone. I suggest two different modes of interment may be present.

For el-Wad, then, I suggest the following interment patterns:

Type I. Cave–Group: Extended, hearths, grave reopened, limestone, and no dentalium shells but grave furniture with each burial.[2]

Type II. Terrace–Group: Flexed, one primary and one or more secondary interments, no hearths, no limestone, no reopening, and the presence of dentalium with only one member of the group.

Type III. Terrace–Individual: Flexed, no hearths, no limestone, and no dentalium shell.

Type IV. Inside of cave mouth–Individual: Extended, no hearths, no limestone, and no dentalium shell.

Type V. Outside of Cave Mouth: Flexed, hearths, limestone (?), and no dentalium shell.

I am not entirely happy with the latter three types. However, I will argue in the following discussion that in the context of this chapter they are irrelevant because individual burials are late in the Natufian sequence.

DISCUSSION

In the past there have been few studies that have dealt specifically with the social dimensions of mortuary practices. Works that have appeared have generally taken one of two forms: The first of these is exemplified by Bendann's (1930) *Death Customs: An Analytical Study of Burial Rites*, which is not an analytical study at all but is more a listing of exotic mortuary practices from various areas of the world. It shows little attempt to correlate particular features of burial rites with other aspects of culture. The second type of study has been one that has suggested, without any rigorous statistical testing, that such correlations do not exist (e.g., Kroeber 1927; Ucko 1969). In contrast, one recent paper has dealt with this problem and has concluded that the search for these kinds of correlations is indeed fruitful.

Binford (1971), in his ethnographic review of mortuary practices, found that there are six dimensional distinctions that may be symbolized. These are (a) condition of death; (b) location of death; (c) age; (d) sex; (e) social position of the deceased in terms of relative rank and distinctiveness within the social unit; and (f) "the affiliation of the deceased with respect to membership segments of the broader social unit, or in the case of intersocietal symbolism, the form appropriate to the society itself [p.

---

[2] Because the grave was reopened twice, I view this one group burial as actually consisting of three groups of the same type, in the same manner that Type II consists of five separate group burials.

17, Table 2]." His ethnographic survey found that statistically there were no differences among hunters and gatherers, shifting agriculturalists, and pastoralists in the mean value of dimensions utilized. However, settled agriculturalists employed more dimensional distinctions. He relates this to a direct correlation between the structural complexity of mortuary rituals and status systems (p. 18).

Second, Binford investigated the proposition that the structure of the mortuary ritual is related to status differentiation (p. 20). That is, age and sex should serve as the primary bases for mortuary distinctions within egalitarian systems, whereas social position and subgroup affiliation, varying independently of age and sex, should play this role among ranked systems. His sample, although not fully representative, tended to confirm this hypothesis and should now be further tested.

Finally, Binford looked at the rituals themselves. He employed three categories: (a) preparation, treatment, and disposition of the body; (b) form, orientation, and location of the facility into which the body was interred; and (c) form and/or quantity of grave furniture. A number of interesting associations were recorded.

There are two that are relevant to this study.

First, in terms of location of the grave, a criterion I believe is important at el-Wad, Binford discovered that in 7 examples (out of 33) age was the determining factor. Children and infants may be differentiated by burial away from adults at the edge of the settlement or under houses, with adults being interred in cemeteries. This seems to occur when social position is not inherited. In 8 cases location was determined by social position, and in 15 by subgroup affiliation (e.g., clan, sodality). Thus, burial locations that show adults, children, and infants interred together might then indicate that some type of ranking and subgroup affiliation was present and that status is inherited.

Second, in terms of the form of grave furniture, sex was the important variable in 16 of 21 cases, whereas social position made up the remainder. Form was related to sex where the particular types of artifacts symbolized the male–female division of labor. Where ranking is present, it may be so in the form of particular symbols of office, and additionally through accompaniment of large quantities of grave goods.

These provisional correlations may be summarized as follows:

1. Children and infants buried away from adults suggest that social position was not inherited.
2. Children, infants, and adults buried in the same location suggest that ranking and subgroup affiliation were present.
3. Grave goods relating to male–female division of labor suggest an egalitarian society.

4. Grave furniture that crosscuts sex lines suggest a ranked society.
5. The reappearance of the same type of artifact (or symbol) in some burials, while all others lack the artifact, might suggest a specific ranked position in the society.

With these preliminary hypotheses in mind, we may now look at the el-Wad burial types. It is clear that some kinds of distinctions were made among types and among members within some types. In assessing the social structure significance of this differentiation, we must ask: How many of the interment patterns were contemporaneous? The Natufian itself spanned at least 2 millennia. We must derive an internal chronology of the burial types.

The Natufian occupation at el-Wad was divided into two stratigraphic levels by Garrod: B-1 and B-2 (Garrod and Bate 1937). Henry's (1973) restudy of the tools confirmed Garrod's analysis, and it is again supported by three ^{14}C dates from the site. Unit B-2 has two dates: 9970 ± 660 B.C. and 9525 ± 650 B.C.; unit B-1 has a single date of 7845 ± 650 B.C. (Henry 1973). The 9970 B.C. date derives from one of the skeletons in the cave group burial.

The stratigraphy at this site suggested to Garrod (Garrod and Bate 1937) that individual burials were later in time than the group burials. Thus, Types I and II burials would be the earliest on this site and, I suggest, should be dated early within the Natufian phase itself. Recall that one cave burial dates to 9970 B.C. Garrod also believed that H-12, 18, and 62 (Type V) were Lower Natufian in age but were later than the group burials. They share characteristics with both Types I and II. Like Type I burials, they have hearths and limestone, and they are flexed like Type II burials. The individuals comprising our Type IV were dated merely as Natufian by Garrod. But they also share characteristics with Types I and II—for example, they are extended and include an infant. The Type III burials are dated as Upper Natufian. McCown (1939: 19) specifically dated the individual burials H-17, 21, and 27 to the upper Natufian.

Stratigraphically, I suggest that the group burials at el-Wad are the earliest on the site and are contemporaneous, Types IV and V are slightly later, and Type II is late in the sequence. This proposition may be tested by ^{14}C dates. Other Natufian sites with group burials, such as Kebara (Turville-Petre 1932: 270), Hayonim (Henry 1973) and Erq el-Ahmar (Neuville 1951; Vallois 1936), date along with el-Wad B-2 as earliest within Henry's (1973) seriation. Nahal Oren (Stekelis and Yizraely 1963), with only one group of two individuals, shows predominantly single interments (ca. 50) and is late in the Natufian sequence according to Henry (1973). I shall return to the comparative data in the following discussion.

Since I am concerned only with the appearance of social differentiation, I shall now ignore the individual burials.

There are clear distinctions between the two types of group burials at el-Wad. These two types differ in all attributes, except multiple interments. Type I burials contain adults, children, and infants, whereas Type II burials had adults and children. Using the burial location hypotheses, we would expect that ranking was present and that we are dealing with two subgroups whose membership was symbolized through interment on different parts of the site. The idea of ranking is further strengthened, I feel, by the presence of burial goods with both children and infants in Type I burials, and with the child in Group 5 of Type II. This child is the primary burial in the group and is wearing a dentalium shell headdress. This suggests that the particular social and/or economic role in the society being symbolized by the grave goods, particularly as shown in the case of Type II burials, is one that was *ascribed* rather than achieved.

In terms of the forms of grave goods, the two affiliations are different. Dentalium shell only appears with Type II. Seemingly, since only one member in each group burial received this item, it is also directly related to a *specific* status position with the subgroup. The forms of grave goods in Type I burials are all different from those in Type II burials. Yet, no one individual stands apart so dramatically in either form or quantity of grave furniture. Thus, if the subgroup members in Type I were internally ranked, we cannot arbitrarily select one symbol—for example, the calcite head or the turtle shell—and relate it to an important status position. Finally, the presence of the dentalium shell in only Type II as the single reoccurring grave good on the site that marks status might also suggest that the highest ranked position in the local group, or that particular role in the society, was restricted to this one subgroup.[3]

Because of the numerous problems in the el-Wad data, to which I have frequently alluded, I am reluctant to carry this exercise any farther with respect to the remaining burials at the site. Let me state again that my purpose was only to demonstrate that social differentiation was present here and in the earliest stage of the Natufian. I think that much is clear. I wish now to consider other early Natufian sites for comparison.

For the most part here, I will restrict myself to those Natufian sites that are believed, either by Henry's seriation or by the ^{14}C dates, to be

---

[3] It is worthwhile to point out here that for a population of Sudanese hunters and gatherers contemporaneous with the Natufian Saxe's (1971: 52) burial analysis found that "status differences between individuals reflect sex, age, and some personally achieved chacteristics . . . the sum indicates participation in an egalitarian status system in life." They are a complete contrast to the Natufian, both economically and socially.

early in the sequence. One of these sites is Kebara, Level B. The site is located 8 miles south of el-Wad and has a ^{14}C date of 9200 ± 400 B.C. (Henry 1973). Here, Turville-Petre (1932: 270) recovered a Natufian group burial consisting of adults and infants. He reported no grave goods but noted that the grave was packed with stones. The bodies were oriented in several different directions like el-Wad.

There was a group burial at Erq el-Ahmar in the Judean Desert south of Jerusalem (Neuville 1951; Vallois 1936). The grave was hollowed out to a depth of 55 cm below a flagstone pavement. It consisted of four adults and three children. Only one of the adults had its head in direct associa-tion with the postcranial skeleton. Each adult head at least one horse molar with it, and the complete skeleton had a necklace of dentalium shells and gazelle phalanges. Thus, like Type II at el-Wad, there appears to be secondary interment correlating with the use of dentalium shell.

Henry (1973: 81) has briefly noted some of the attributes of the burials from Hayonim Cave, which is situated to the northeast of el-Wad. Briefly, he reported that seven group burials were present. Like el-Wad, both reopening of graves and secondary burials occurred. Many burials were associated with limestone slabs, and dentalium shells were recovered with some individuals. All of these elements are known from el-Wad, and I suggest that at least two interment patterns are present. Henry's seriation places Hayonim Cave in the early Natufian.

At Mallaha, in the Jordon Valley near extinct Lake Huleh, also early Natufian according to Henry (1973), Perrot (1966) recovered 82 Natufian burials. He has provisionally divided them into two types:

A. Secondary disarticulated group burials in shallow graves. Parts of the skeletons are generally missing, and the number of individuals in each grave is determined only by the number of crania present—for example, Graves 25, 28, and 64 have five, six, and three crania, respectively. Often, these burial pits were covered by large stones and human bones are stained by red ocher. In Grave 25, there were three gazelle horn pins.

B. Primary burials, usually flexed or occasionally semiflexed (e.g., H-80–82). Perrot believes there is no consistent orientation to this type. Perrot describes one group burial from Grave 3, House 1. Seven skeletons were buried, then the grave was reopened and H-15 was interred, disturb-ing the previously buried bodies. H-15 was laid on its back, face to the northeast, and the head was wedged by stones. H-19 was placed near H-15, on its back also but with the limbs arranged differently. A dentalium shell headdress accompanied H-19. A stone pavement, surrounded by a low stone wall, was then constructed. Several large stones were laid off-center on the pavement and were surrounded by a stone circle. Then the grave was recovered.

Grave goods seem to be rare at Mallaha (Perrot 1966: 465). In addition to the bone pins with Grave 25 and the dentalium shell headdress with H-19, only three other burials are specifically mentioned with grave furniture. There was a flint dagger near the cranium of H-82. Burial H-23 had a necklace of dentalim shell and gazelle phalanges. An infant with a dentalium shell necklace of three rows of shell was found below the floor of the lowest level of Abri 26 (Perrot 1966: Plate 5).

Briefly, then, sites dated to early in the Natufian sequence appear to show a predominance of group burials. The attributes isolated in two types of group burials proposed for el-Wad are also reported at these additional sites. Note that at Hayonium and Mallaha at least two types are present and dentalium is always rare. I would suggest that the best manner to test the validity of the hypothesized societal partioning at el-Wad would be through a statistical analysis of the burials from Hayonim Cave and Mallaha, since they are the most recently, and presumably the best, excavated sites.

By way of contrast, the cave of Shuqbah was dated as Upper Natufian by Garrod (1942). This was confirmed by Henry (1973). At least 45 individual burials are known from the site (Keith 1931), but they are very poorly described. There was, in addition, one group burial consisting of an adult and two children.

Nahal Oren (Wadi Fallah) is located just to the north of el-Wad. There are two Natufian levels on the terrace in front of the cave, with architecture (Stekelis and Yizraely 1963). Most of the ca. 50 excavated burials were single interments. One group burial is mentioned, however, consisting of an adult and a child. Burials were flexed, covered with red ocher, and generally oriented toward the north. Most burial pits had limestone mortars or blocks, often placed above the burials in a manner such that the authors refer to them as possible "tombstones." Note that the site, again considered to be late by Henry (1973), had predominantly single interments and an attempt at consistent orientation of the burials.

Assuming that I have demonstrated my first three points, it is now necessary to seek some causative factors. Before doing this, let me reiterate several facts about the Natufian:

1. A major change in adaptive strategy had taken place. It included a permanent base camp occupied year around.
2. Local group size had increased.

3. Wild cereal grain had become important in the diet for the first time, and settlements may be correlated with the distribution of these resources. Later population expansion was into areas where the cereals were growing.

Let me add a final comment. Henry (1973: 189) has noted that recent dental attrition studies of Natufian burials suggest an increasing importance of stone ground foods over time. Dependency on wild cereals enlarged.

The causative factors for the appearance of social differentiation may be divided into two categories: internal and external. Let me begin with the former. The first point is simply the maintenance of order within the local group as it increases in size. Harris (1975) writes that "as an egalitarian population expands it becomes increasingly difficult to act by consensus [p. 372]." One role of status positions and their attendant authority is to integrate the society—to coordinate activities and to prevent hostile factionalization. One finds in the ethnographic literature on mobile egalitarian hunters and gatherers a tendency for offended members of the group to move away, to join other bands. But with the appearance of settled communities it becomes increasingly difficult to do so because you now have a stake in the community.

If you build a substantial house or even cut mortars or storage basins into the bedrock, you have expended considerable energy. In the Natufian the stake was compounded by the nature of the resource base. Harlan (1967) estimated that a family could collect nearly a ton of wild grain in less than a month. Sedentation is forced upon one, and leaving because of a real or fancied insult is no longer a viable alternative. Also, the important wild grain resources are not evenly distributed across the landscape. Being localized, it is necessary to reside where they are adequate. Hence the maintenance of internal order within the local group demanded new solutions.

Local group activities must be coordinated. One is again struck by the fact that redistribution is a major organizing principle in nonstate societies. Work parties must be organized and the redistribution of the production controlled. Redistribution also functions as a reward, thus further increasing the integration of the local group.

Externally problems can arise. With population growth, local groups began to fission. What the critical population maximum for a Natufian group was is unknown. It is generally assumed that splits of this type are caused by pressure on the available food resources, but this may not always be the case. Olsen (1976) found that the Hutterites, who had a redistributional economy, had a critical mass of about 166 people. However fissioning occurred not because of resource pressure but because of social problems, such as those revolving around the elevation of younger members to high status positions.

Whatever the reasons for the Natufian expansion, it did take place. Yet, even with these splits, I suggest that alliances would still be maintained. I suggest, further, that there was at least one good ecological reason for these alliances beyond that of simply staying in contact with close kinsmen. Wilmsen (1973) found that hunters and gatherers generally delineate their exploitative territories on the basis of the distribution of the plant resources most vital to them rather than on game. How predictable from year to year is a wild cereal such as emmer wheat? Many wild food crops are subject to both good years and bad years. Alliances may function to promote peaceful incursions over territorial boundaries in order to share resources.

I propose that the dentalium shell trade inland from the Mediterranean and Red seas (Henry 1973; Wright 1974) was a method by which alliances could be reinforced. Archeologically, dentalium shells are recovered in what I have interpreted to be high status burials. At el-Wad I suggested they symbolized a particular status role that was inherited within one sub group affiliation. Alliances then would have linked high status individuals in different local groups, which in turn would have promoted peaceful intergroup relationships.

CONCLUSION

I have attempted to do four things. First, I outlined five types of burials at el-Wad. Second, based on the ^{14}C dates and the site stratigraphy, I suggested that the two types of group burials were contemporaneous, were earliest on the site, and dated early within the Natufian sequence in the Levant. I further suggested that they represented two subgroup affiliations. I proposed that the dentalium shell symbolized a particular status position that was inherited within one of these affiliations. Dentalium shell is found in a similar, but perhaps not identical arrangement, at three additional early Natufian sites. Two of them, Hayonim and Mallaha, also exhibit multiple interment patterns. I then discussed several internal and external problems that would have arisen under the conditions of the new Natufian adaptive system that might have selected for the evolution of social differentiation. The overall result was a social structure very much like that of settled agricultural communities, but the early Natufian depended upon wild resources.

POSTSYMPOSIUM REFLECTIONS

The test of this chapter was originally a paper I delivered at the Symposium on Social Differentiation and Interaction. Two of the other papers in the symposium, in addition to the discussion that followed mine, raised some points that should be elaborated upon. First, Thomas King (see Chapter 10) and I are in complete agreement concerning the proposition that many groups of hunters and gatherers in the past were more complex than is generally thought. Now that we have some idea of what to look for, cases similar to those presented by us will be "discovered." Unfortunately, however, King did not approach the topic of causation in relation to the California sample.

In terms of Gregory Johnson's paper (see Chapter 5), what I am discussing for the Natufian is his initial vertical control unit. The appearance of status differentiation functioned to solve the various problems faced by the new adaptive system. As Johnson pointed out, regular inheritance rules for high-status positions lessened potential problems of recruitment, continuity, and training. I interpret the children with dentalium shell headdresses as evidence of ascribed status. I cannot believe that at their young age they had already achieved high status in their local groups, they must have been recruited for a particular ranked position.

In the text of the paper, I suggested that the alliances linked the Natufian groups, at least in part, to allow sharing of resources. In the subsequent discussion I elaborated more. Such alliances would have been particularly important in terms of linking coastal groups to those farther inland. From an ecological standpoint, I would predict that the wild grain resources on the coast would have been less viable than those of the Jordan Valley. Not only less dense, with their brittle rachises and natural reseeding mechanism, they were probably more subject to local catastrophes from high winds off the Mediterranean and unseasonal rains during the crucial few days of harvesting. These alliances would have been highly selective for the coastal groups, and their direct access to dentalium shell, which was the status marker, provided a means to cement these relationships.

Perhaps the most interesting question was posed by Johnson. He inquired why it appeared that variation in mortuary patterning seems to have been less in the late Natufian compared with that described for the early Natufian. In looking at the data once more, I am not sure that is the case. I think that a case may be made that social differentiation was still present and that Nahal Oren, when the burials are fully published, will be the best test. At el-Wad two of the individual burials contained bone pendants (see Table 9.1).

There are two facets to this question. In addition to local status differentiation, there remains the alliances. There does by now seem to be no symbol linking the groups. I suspect, and here I am referring only to the Mediterranean zone in the north, that the alliances proposed for the early Natufian were no longer functioning by the later period. Why might this be so?

I suggested that for ecological reasons these alliances linked the more marginal coastal groups with those inland. If the subsistence system had undergone a change, then greater surpluses or a more predictable food supply would have reduced the ecological problem. One possibility is the manipulation of the wild grain resources through planting—that is, agriculture. This would date the evolution of agriculture earlier than the PPNA, where it is already well attested. This still well fits the hypothesis suggested elsewhere (see Wright 1971).

Alliances still, however, might have been extremely important to the groups migrating out of the Mediterranean zone after 9000 B.C. into the Irano-Tauranian zone. I would predict that this alliance symbol— dentalium shell—might have persisted within the latter biotic zone until much later and would have linked the fissioning populations to one another as they moved throughout this new habitat. Here alliances would have remained functional.

There is no a priori reason to expect a monolithic Natufian culture. The term was defined on the basis of stone tools. We should expect variations in local economic and social systems. Perrot (1968) suggested that in the Jordan Valley agriculture did not appear until the fifth millennium B.C., several millennia after we see it in adjacent areas. When we have a clearer picture of the Natufian, I believe we will find important variations in the Mediterranean zone (coast versus inland), and these will again contrast to the Irano-Tauranian zone.

ACKNOWLEDGMENTS

I wish to thank Professor F. Clark Howell, Department of Anthropology, University of California, Berkeley, for providing me with a copy of Theodore McCown's unpublished doctoral dissertation.

REFERENCES

Bar-Yosef, O.
  1975   The Epipaleolithic in Palestine and Syria. In *Problems in prehistory: North Africa and the Levant*, edited by F. Wendorf and T. Marks. Dallas: SMU Press. Pp. 363–378.

Bar-Yosef, O., and E. Tchernov
1970   The Natufian bone industry of ha-Yonim Cave. *Israel Exploration Journal 20* (3–4): 140–150.
Bendann, Effie
1930   *Death customs: An analytical study of burial rites.* London: Kegan Paul, Trench, Truber.
Binford, Lewis R.
1971   Mortuary practices: Their study and their potential. In *Approaches to the social dimensions of mortuary practices,* edited by James A. Brown, *Memoirs of the Society for American Archaeology* No. 25: 6–29.
Brown, James A.
1971   Introduction. In *Approaches to social dimensions of mortuary practices,* edited by James A. Brown. *Memoirs of the Society for American Archaeology* No. 25: 1–5.
Ferembach, D.
1961   Squelettes du Natoufien d'Israel: Etude anthropologique. *L'Anthropologie 65:* 46–66.
Garrod, D. A. E.
1931   Excavations in the caves of the Wady el Mughara, 129–130. *Bulletin of the American School of Prehistoric Research 7:* 5–11.
1942   Excavations at the Cave of Shuqbah, Palestine, 1928. *Proceedings of the Prehistoric Society 8:* 1–20.
1957   The Natufian culture: The life and economy of a Mesolithic people in the Near East. *Proceedings of the British Academy 43:* 211–227.
Garrod, D. A. E., and D. M. A. Bate
1937   *The Stone Age of Mount Carmel* (Vol. I). Oxford: Clarendon Press.
Gruber, Jacob
1971   Patterning in Death in a late prehistoric village in Pennsylvania. *American Antiquity 36:* 64–76.
Harlan, J.
1967   A wild wheat harvest in Turkey. *Archaeology 20:* 197–201.
Harris, M.
1975   *Culture, people, nature: An introduction to general anthropology* (2nd edition). New York: Crowell.
Henry, D. O.
1973   The Natufian culture of Palestine: Its material culture and ecology. Ph.D. dissertation, Southern Methodist Univ.
1975   Fauna in Near Eastern archaeological deposits. In *Problems in prehistory: North Africa and the Levant,* edited by F. Wendorf and T. Marks. Dallas: SMU Press. Pp. 379–385.
Keith, Sir Arthur
1931   New discoveries relating to the antiquity of mankind. London: Williams & Norgate.
Kroeber, A. L.
1927   Disposal of the dead. *American Anthropologist 29:* 308–315.
McCown, Theodore D.
1939   The Natufian crania from Mount Carmel, Palestine, and their inter-relationships. Unpublished Ph.D. thesis, Univ. of California, Berkeley.
Marks, Anthony E.
1971   Settlement patterns and intrasite variability in the central Negev, Israel. *American Anthropoligist 73:* 1237–1245.

Neuville, Rene
  1934   Le prehistorique de Palestine. *Revue Biblique* 43: 237–259.
  1951   Le Paleolithique et le Mesolithique de desert de Judée. *Archives de l'Institue de Paleontologie Humaine* 24: 1–270.
Olsen, C. L.
  1976   The population dynamics of new colony formation in a human isolate: Analysis and history. Ph.D. Dissertation, Univ. of Michigan.
Perrot, Jean
  1966   Le gisement Natoufien de Mallaha (Eynan) Israel. *L'Anthropologie* 70: 437–483.
  1968   La prehistoire Palestinienne. In *Supplement au dictionnaire de la Bible* 8: 286–446. Paris: Letouzey and Ane.
Renfrew, J. M.
  1969   The archaeological evidence for the domestication of plants. In *The domestication and exploitation of plants and animals*, edited by P. J. Ucko and G. W. Dimblebey. Chicago: Aldine. Pp. 149–172.
Saxe, Arthur
  1971   Social dimensions of mortuary practices in a Mesolithic population from Wadi Halfa, Sudan. In *Approaches to the social dimensions of mortuary practices*, edited by James A. Brown. *Memoirs of the Society for American Archaeology* No. 25: 39–57.
Stekelis, M., and T. Yizraely
  1963   Excavations at Nahal Oren: A preliminary report. *Israel Exploration Journal* 13: 1–12.
Turville-Petri, F.
  1932   Excavations in the Mugharet el-Kebarah. *Journal of the Royal Anthropological Institute* 62: 270–279.
Ucko, Peter
  1969   Ethnography and archaeological interpretations of funerary remains. *World Archaeology* 1: 262–280.
Vallois, Henri
  1936   Les ossements natoufiens d'Erq el-Ahmar (Palestine). *L'Anthropologie* 46: 529–539.
Wilmsen, E. N.
  1973   Interaction, spacing behavior and the organization of hunting bands. *Journal of Anthropological Research* 29: 1–31.
Wright, Gary A.
  1974   Archaeology and trade. Reading: Addison-Wesley.
  1971   Origins of food production in southwestern Asia: A survey of ideas. *Current Anthropology* 12: 447–478.

chapter **10**

Don't That Beat the Band? Nonegalitarian Political Organization in Prehistoric Central California

THOMAS F. KING

My research has been focused on hunter–gatherers in California (T. F. King 1976). To state my basic bias at the beginning: I think that, if we are interested in explaining the evolution of complex forms of political organization, we may go astray by taxonomizing societies on the basis of distinctions in their modes of production. It is my impression that—even *since* the Man the Hunter Symposium (Lee and DeVore 1968)—most anthropologists have continued to assign all hunter–gatherers doggedly to the "band" level of political organization, bending the level like the most pragmatic of archeological field technicians to allow for peculiar sociopolitical humps and hollows. Sendentary village life, nonegalitarian status organization, class differentiation, craft specialization—these are the assigned characteristics of "chiefdoms" (Service 1962) or "rank societies" (Fried 1967), which are by definition composed of agriculturalists. The "Neolithic Revolution," as a guiding evolutionary concept, is alive and well and living in academia, and I think it is blinding us to some important processes that we should be observing.

If one assumes that hunter–gatherers always march in bands, one

225

Social Archeology:
Beyond Subsistence and Dating

does have to put up with some sticky ethnographic wickets. The best known is the Northwest coast, where the nonagricultural Tlinget, Haida, Kwakiutl, and their neighbors maintained substantial ruling groups, kept slaves, ran an elaborate interaction system, supported specialists, and so on. The Northwest coasters have typically been dismissed by evolutionary taxonomists because they had such unusually neat goodies to hunt and gather: whales, salmon, acorns, and such. During the last decade, however, people like Suttles (1968) and Piddocke (1969) have put forth detailed discussions of the Northwest coasters that make the resources available to them look not unlike those available to a lot of other hunter–gatherers. Though elements of the Suttles–Piddocke portrayal have been attacked by Drucker and Heizer (1967), who say the Northwest coasters seldom starved, and by Orans (1975), who feels that the potlatch is not satisfactorily explained, the general picture seems to hold firm; the Northwest coasters do not seem to have been the happy reapers of an unending fishy bounty, but to have been faced with scheduling problems much like other hunter–gatherers. Admittedly, one is likely to have much less trouble scheduling one's procurement on the Northwest coast than in the Great Basin or the Kalihari Desert, but in preagricultural times only a minority of hunter–gatherers lived in the Great Basin or Kalihari. It hardly seems necessary to assume—just because most surviving hunter–gatherers live in scruffy environments and are organized accordingly—that those who in the past lived in fairly nice places like the Mediterranean shore, the Tigris–Euphrates basin, California, or even the eastern woodlands other than Buffalo must have been similarly organized.

Archeological evidence has been accumulating to suggest that a lot of hunter–gatherers may have been more Kwakiutlesque than Paiute-like; Gary Wright's Natufian data (Chapter 9 of this volume) point in this direction. California is another place where the evidence is pretty good for village sedentation and complex political organization among hunter–gatherers.

The older ethnographic literature on California contains allusions to inheritance of chieftainship, chiefly control of redistribution, residential specificity of chiefly families, large-scale trade, and occupational specialization. Here, for example, is a comment from the early twentieth century by C. Hart Merriam (1967):

> Among the Mewuk are two classes of villages: (1) those in which the 'Royal Families' or families of the chiefs reside; and (2) those inhabited solely by the common people. Several or many of the latter are tributary to each of the former.
>
> The head chief or chiefs of the villages of the first class are called Hi-ah-po and belong to the Hi-am-po-ko or royal families and are men of high standing,

power, and influence in the tribe, and are recognized as head chiefs by the tributary villages.

The position of head chief is hereditary and may descend from either the father's or the mother's side, and may rest on either a man or a woman [p. 340].

This sort of information was incorporated with little comment into the massive ethnographic compilations put together under the leadership of A. L. Kroeber at the University of California and tends to be rather difficult to glean. Lately, research has focused on the primary notes of J. Peabody Harrington, who studied California groups in the first two decades of the twentieth century.

Chester King and Thomas Blackburn have drawn on Harrington's data and on other ethnographic and archeological information to analyze the socioeconomic systems of the Chumash Indians and their neighbors (C. D. King 1971; Blackburn 1974). The Chumash lived on both sides of the Santa Barbara Channel, northwest of Los Angeles. During the seventeenth to nineteenth centuries, the entire Chumash language group was organized into ranked blood groups, with supreme chiefs and village chiefs drawn from the highest-ranking group, which was relieved of manual labor. Each chief maintained community storehouses stocked with food obtained through donations to fiestas. Close cooperation between chiefs and religious practitioners provided the sanctions necessary to ensure orderly chiefly succession, validate the social order, and centralize the accumulation and distribution of economic goods. Canoe owners belonged to a special class of wealthy persons, who seldom actually operated canoes but instead employed others to engage in fishing operations. Many occupational specialists existed among the Chumash; these people were usually members of occupational guilds that regulated activities of members in many different communities.

The most direct test of the ethnographic data through archeology was provided by Linda King at the Medea Creek Cemetery. At this protohistoric cemetery near Los Angeles, some 450 burials were disinterred in 1966 during a volunteer salvage program, constituting virtually the total population of the site. Predicting that the general form of social organization—and perhaps some of the specific statuses—described by Harrington should be reflected in the structure of the cemetery, King looked at the association of sociotechnic, ideotechnic, and technomic artifact classes with various spatial burial clusters and types of burials. In an analysis of a few key variables, it was possible to distinguish subareas, or *lobes*, within the cemetery that could be interpreted as family burial plots. These plots showed evidence of ranking relative to one another in that the western lobe was by far the richest and was characterized by the presence of nonutilitarian objects and caches of wealth, with both adults and children. Caches and richly endowed burials tended to cluster in the center of the western lobe, suggesting internal ranking of the chiefly lineage; this lobe also contained burials with canoe planks and religious paraphernalia, suggesting that canoe owners and religious personnel were members of the high-ranked group, consistent with Harrington's data. The less rich lobes of the cemetery contained burials with evidence of various achieved statuses but with little suggestion of heritable rank (L. B. King 1969).

Medea Creek can be compared with the Rincon site, near Santa Barbara, reported by E. G. Stickel (1968). In this site, about 3700 years old, burials were almost maximally dispersed and nonutilitarian artifacts were almost totally lacking; the only associational distinction among burials was that some individuals were buried with more utilitarian items than were others. Using analytic procedures quite compatible with King's, Stickel concluded that Rincon society, presumably representing a population ancestral to the Chumash, was essentially egalitarian, or band like.

At Mrn-27, a small 2000-year-old occupation site on the Tiburon Peninsula in San Francisco Bay, D. A. Fredrickson and I supervised the salvage of a cemetery in 1967. The cemetery was small but highly structured, consisting of a central cremation area containing very large quantities of nonutilitarian artifacts, an encircling group of male burials without associations, and a loose outer cluster of males and females with few artifacts, plus a few anomalies. The rich central area contained almost equal numbers of males, females, and children. Using an interpretive system identical to those in use in southern California, I concluded that here again there was strong evidence for social ranking (T. F. King 1970, 1974).

It can thus be argued that in late prehistoric and early historical times much of California was occupied by hunter–gatherers living under the administration of fairly powerful chiefs who each stood at the apex of an hereditary hierarchy. Economic systems utilizing shell bead currencies and validated by ritual exchange obligations facilitated sharing of subsistence resources over broad areas while maintaining ruling lineages in positions of authority. Rulers were often fed and housed by the ruled and in turn might support specialists in various nonsubsistence trades. In terms of the general models generated by writers like Service (1962) and Fried (1967), then, California societies largely approximate "chiefdoms" or "rank societies" rather than "bands." There is tenuous but arguable evidence for at least 2000 years of time depth for such forms of organization in some areas, and for the development of such forms out of simpler systems over the last 3000–4000 years.

The problems with the archeological data on California political organization are many, however. Most of the data have been grubbed out of emergency salvage excavations, and the best data pertain to the protohistoric period, when the native Californians were being impacted by European society. Thus there has been a need for a thought-out test of the proposition that well before the time of contact with Europeans, California Indian populations were, in some instances, characterized by nonegalitarian forms of political organization.

In 1971, I found myself faced with an unusual opportunity to test such a proposition, at Buchanan Reservoir in central California. Figure 10.1 shows Buchanan Reservoir's location, and Figure 10.2 portrays

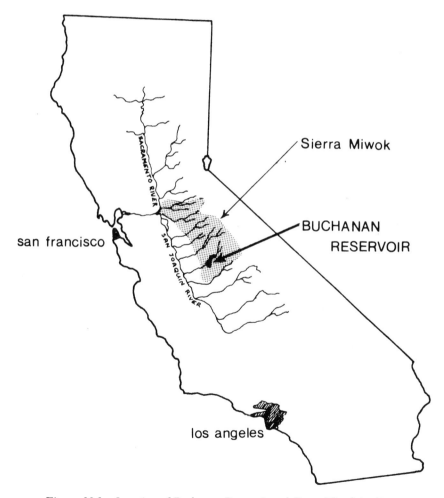

Figure 10.1. Location of Buchanan Reservoir and Sierra Miwok territory.

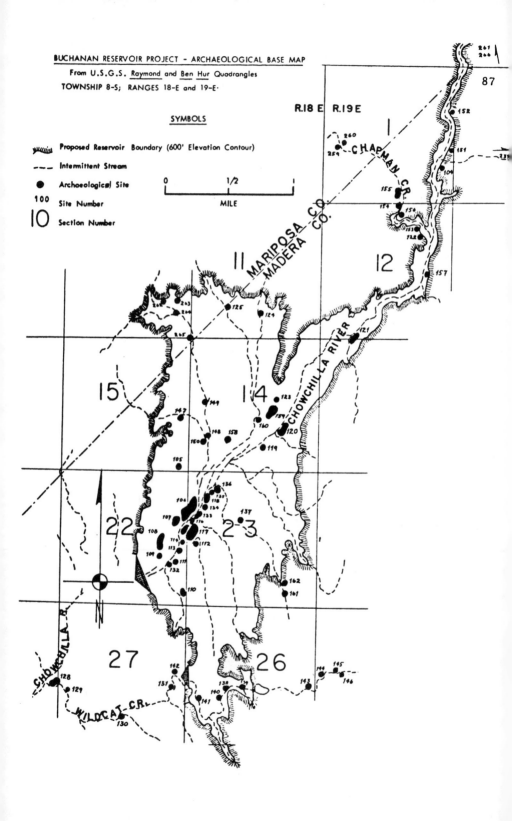

BUCHANAN RESERVOIR PROJECT - ARCHAEOLOGICAL BASE MAP

From U.S.G.S. Raymond and Ben Hur Quadrangles

TOWNSHIP 8-S; RANGES 18-E and 19-E·

SYMBOLS

Proposed Reservoir Boundary (600' Elevation Contour)

Intermittent Stream

Archaeological Site

100 Site Number

10 Section Number

0   1/2

MILE

Buchanan Reservoir. The area was a broad, oak woodland valley containing some 64 prehistoric sites. The largest sites are Mad-106 (Dancing Cow), Mad-117 (Schwabacher), and Mad-159 (Jones). I had initiated salvage operations in the reservoir area—proposed for construction by the Corps of Engineers—in 1967, together with Michael Moratto. After I left San Francisco State University, which held the salvage contract, Moratto continued the work and used it for his dissertation research (Moratto 1972). Substantial cemeteries were encountered and partially excavated at the three big sites. Moratto worked up a chronological sequence based in part on mortuary data, and for various sorts of reasons, whose details we need not go into here, I disagreed with it. Moratto basically accounted for variability in mortuary custom as an unexplained feature of passing time: During the early Chowchilla Phase people tended to be buried in an extended position with lots of goodies; during the later Raymond Phase they were flexed, with fewer goodies but—significantly—fewer of the *same kinds* of goodies as those possessed by the Chowchilla folk. The late prehistoric was represented by the Madera Phase, with cremation. Reading Moratto's dissertation, I concluded that something else was going on—that in essence, the fancy extensions of the Chowchilla Phase and the scruffy flexes of the Raymond Phase might be contemporaries, representing different sets of social statuses within the same population. Dating of the cemeteries was terrible; the rather strained salvage budget had not allowed for many ^{14}C determinations, and there hadn't been much charcoal found anyway. In 1967–1968 we didn't know about things like age determination on bone collagen. So, the extant data would support either Morrato's interpretation or mine; the contrast can be seen in Table 10.1.

Testing Moratto's thesis would not be too difficult; it simply involved making some good chronometric and stratigraphic studies. Simply to demonstrate that the two burial types were or were not coincident, however, wouldn't tell me much about what kinds of political organization they might represent. For this, I turned to Binford's (1971) paper and to Arthur Saxe's (1970) dissertation, cross-cultural studies of mortuary behavior. The following test implications could be adduced from the hypothesis that Chowchilla–Raymond Phase political organization was nonegalitarian, using Binford's and Saxe's documented observations about how social dimensions interlock with mortuary customs:

Test implication A: Distinctions in mortuary treatment should crosscut the dimensions "age" and "sex."

Test implication B: Children should not be distinguished from adults in burial location, and distinction between male and female in terms of

Figure 10.2. Buchanan Reservoir (after Moratto 1972:Map 2).

Table 10.1

SIMPLIFIED HISTORY OF BUCHANAN MORTUARY CUSTOMS
ACCORDING TO MORATTO AND KING

	Moratto's interpretation	King's interpretation
Madera Phase	At least some high-status individuals are cremated; disposal of others uncertain though possibly interred under houses in flexed position.	Some high-status individuals are cremated; some of lower status are interred under houses.
Raymond Phase	Flexed burial predominates with few grave goods, mostly utilitarian, in association.	Some individuals are certainly interred in flexed positions, and evidence of status differentiation appears slight.
Chow-chilla Phase	Extended burials predominate, with many nonutilitarian grave goods associated. Flexed burials begin to appear late in the phase, transitional into Raymond Phase.	High-status *personae* are associated with interment in extended positions, whereas those of lower status tend to be flexed in burial.

Time (vertical axis, arrow pointing up)

associated goods should be low. Location of interment may reflect membership in lineage or class; thus burial cluster composition should be random in terms of age and sex but associated with distinctive markers of rank or role. Orientation may be highly correlated with location and thus with sodality in this regard, and there should be much distinction among burial clusters in terms of kind and quantity of mortuary offerings.

Test implication C: Burials with few components identifiable as associated with rank should show greater individual variability in disposal mode, associations, etc., than should those with many such components. In other words, burials without markers of high status should collectively demonstrate greater variability in position, orientation, location, and associations than those with such markers.

Test implication D: The key structure of the mortuary customs exhibited should tend to be treelike rather than paradigmatic (Figure 10.3).

Test implication E: There should be evidence of formal disposal areas (i.e., cemeteries) for groups of higher status. In other words, burials with markers of high status should be clustered together in a definable space.

Paradigm: A perfect paradigm is represented by a key in which a given dimension occurs in only one column of the diagram and any given column contains only one dimension. A perfect paradigm, which almost never occurs in nature, is diagrammed below.

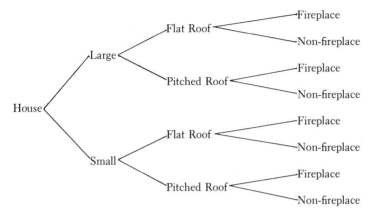

Tree: In a perfect tree, for any dimension, there is a unique node at which it is applied. Perfect trees also almost never occur in nature, but one is diagrammed below.

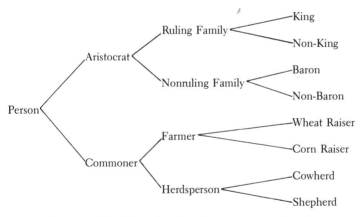

Figure 10.3. Examples of perfect paradigm and perfect tree.

To test such predictions required that I work with relatively complete mortuary assemblages. Although it would presumably be possible to sample a universe of burials in such a way as to control all significant variability, in practice it is difficult to imagine how this could be reliably done. In any event, at Buchanan Reservoir our samples of cemeteries were not the result of any rigorous attempt to treat mortuary diversity statistically, and they could not be counted on as typical of actual

local mortuary behavior. In every case the cemeteries had been encountered essentially by accident, and excavation merely proceeded until
terminated by the press of time or lack of funds. In no case could we
reliably define the boundaries of the burial area or establish what portion
of the mortuary universe we had sampled. To correct this situation and
provide complete samples against which to test my proposition, I under-
took further fieldwork in March 1972.

The Corps of Engineers was preparing to initiate construction at the
Buchanan damsite, thus presumably destroying the major sites in short
order. I had very little money to spend, much of it out of my own pocket,
but the corps could and did provide me with a bulldozer. About 50 very
dedicated volunteers did the rest. We bulldozed each site down to the
level at which burials began to appear, then prospected around the edges
until the boundaries of the cemeteries were approximately defined, then
excavated by hand to pedestal each burial. The burials were located by
transit and recorded on film, magnetic tape, and burial cards (King 1977).
At two sites, Schwabacher (Figure 10.4) and Jones (Figure 10.5), we
exposed excellent, essentially complete cemeteries; at the third site,
Dancing Cow (Figure 10.6), we failed to get the whole thing.

Most of my analysis was resultingly done on the Schwabacher and
Jones sites, from which I had, altogether, about 222 burials, in varying
stages of disrepair. I should mention that before undertaking this ravish-
ment, I sent out a notification of it that hopefully reached all the Native
American groups in the state so that if anyone wished to protest, he or
she could. I should also mention that at the time we understood that the
corps was going to destroy utterly all three sites, and in 1972 the modern
procedures for the protection of archeological resources were not yet in
effect. As it turned out, however, the sites were not totally destroyed, the
corps was eventually challenged for failing to comply with the procedures
of the Advisory Council on Historic Preservation, and there is now the
distinct possibility that much more work will have to be done to "mitigate
the project's impact," even though the dam is now built. I probably
shouldn't have done the bulldozing, but that's the way hindsight works.

In any event, I ended up with a fair amount of burial data, though not
as much as I'd hoped for. My testing of Moratto's proposed chronological
sequence involved doing detailed chronometric and stratigraphic studies:
fifteen ^{14}C determinations on bone collagen, studies of the types and sizes
of time sensitive shell beads associated with different kinds of burials, and
observations of overlapping, intercutting, and multiple burials provided
my answers here. My test implications on the central hypothesis demanded two kinds of analysis. First, I needed to see what elements tended

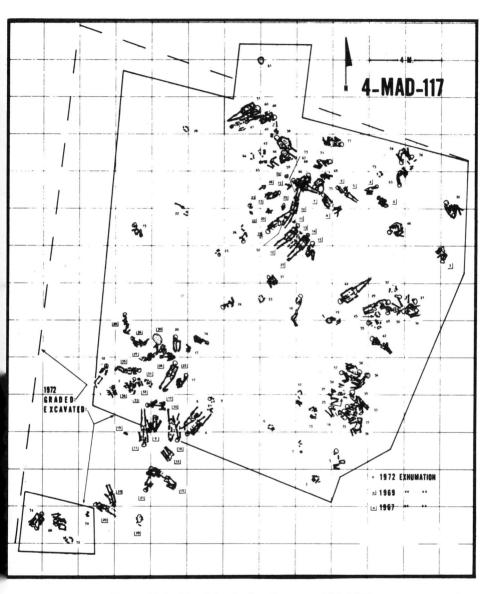

Figure 10.4. The Schwabacher Cemetery, 4-Mad-117.

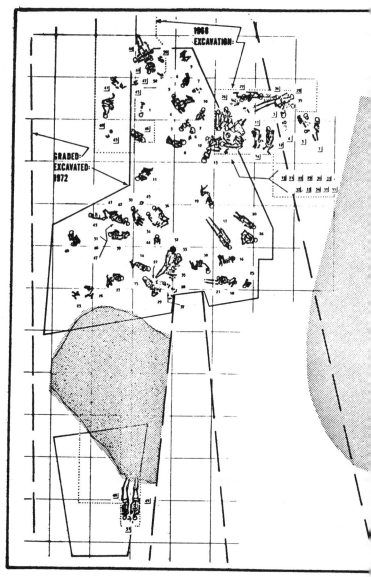

Figure 10.5. The Jones Cemetery, 4-Mad-159.

to structure the domain of mortuary practice, and particularly to see how these elements were associated with such characteristics as age and sex. Second, I wanted to see what the key structures of the cemeteries looked like as abstract phenomena: Were they relatively treelike or paradigmatic?

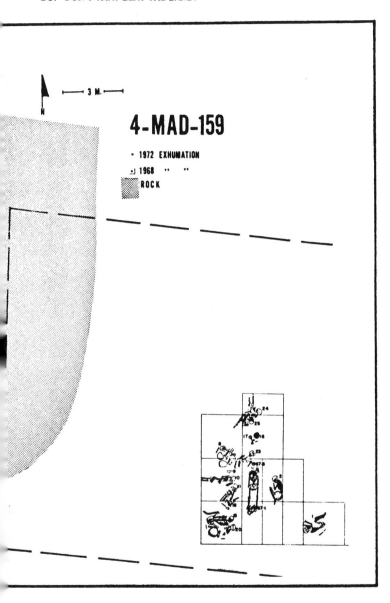

Through the good offices of Joseph Tainter, another member of the mortuary analysis siblinghood then finishing his dissertation at Northwestern on Woodland cemeteries in Illinois (Tainter 1975), I was able to utilize CLUSTAN 1A, a program for monthetic divisive analysis using the information statistic.

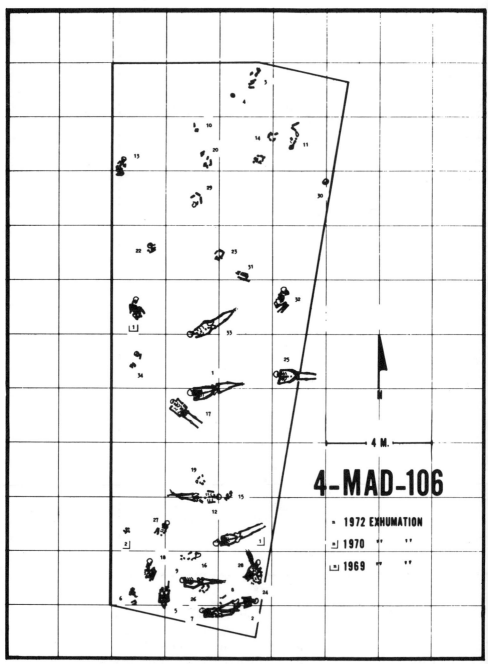

Figure 10.6. The Dancing Cow Cemetery, 4-Mad-106.

I will not discuss statistics in detail, since I am incompetent to do so, but essentially the information statistic, when applied to a set of binary variables in a 2 × 2 table, will select that variable upon which division should occur in order maximally to reduce the disorder expressed by that set of variables. CLUSTAN 1A applies the statistic to each possible combination of binary measures in a population of unordered data and then continues to do so to each possible combination given its previous divisions, producing a key in which each terminal subgroup is maximally homogeneous and maximally distinct from all other subgroups.

The keys for Schwabacher and Jones, and for both cemeteries combined, are shown in Figures 10.7, 10.8, and 10.9. We come out at the end of each key with eight or nine subgroups, which I called *clustats* for convenience. Now what I could do, and did, was cross-tabulate the clustats—which should approximate representations of social personae—against age, sex, and other characteristics suggested by the test implications. I won't try to detail my conclusions at this point, but I will summarize: First, there was no support for Moratto's chronological ordering. Flexed burials occurred before, during, and after the time when extended burials were being emplanted—which was about A.D. 200 to 800.

With regard to the test implications, the following was the case: Test implication A, that distinctions in mortuary treatment should crosscut the dimensions "age" and "sex" was largely met by the data as analyzed; by and large, age and sex did not appear to be highly associated with dimensions of the mortuary domain.

The expectations of test implication B, that children should not be distinguished from adults in location, that distinctions between male and female in terms of grave goods should be low, that lobe and sublobe composition should tend toward randomness in terms of age and sex but toward association with markers of rank and role, that orientation should be associated with location, and that there should be much distinction among burial clusters in terms of mortuary offerings, were partially met by the analyzed data. Children occurred in low frequency in those areas where nonutilitarian artifacts also were seldom found but occurred in normal frequencies in those areas with high status–wealth indicator frequencies. Distinctions between males and females in terms of associations were indeed low. Both sexes were normally represented in the west lobes; an overabundance of females was apparent in the east lobe at Mad-117, possibly reflecting a tendency toward the interment of nonlocal affines in this lobe. There was a marked tendency for apparent indicators of rank and

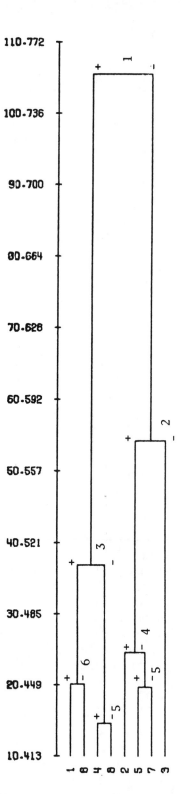

Figure 10.7. Keys of Buchanan cemeteries. Monothetic division of Mad-11 burial data using information statistic. Divisive attributes: 1 = flexed; 2 = high integrity; 3 = west lobe; 4 = high-energy beads predominant; 5 = grinding tools; 6 = cairn.

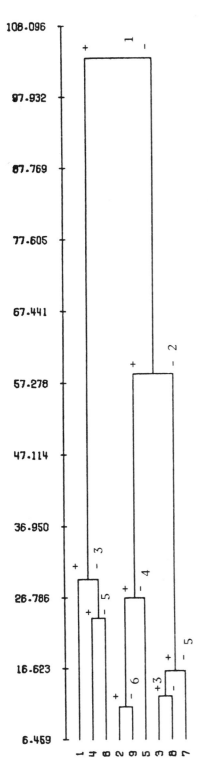

Figure 10.8. Keys of Buchanan cemeteries. Monothetic division of Mad-159 burial data using information statistic. Divisive attributes: 1 = flexed; 2 = high integrity; 3 = high-energy beads predominant; 4 = obsidian; 5 = west lobe; 6 = paint.

241

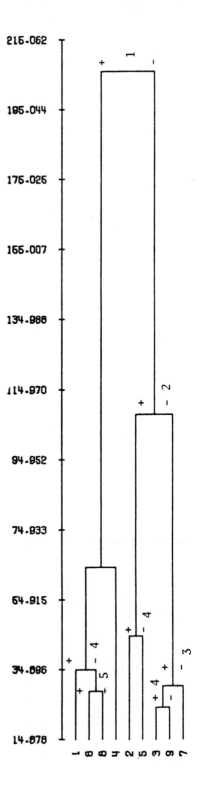

Figure 10.9. Keys of Buchanan cemeteries. Monothetic division of Mad-117 and Mad-159 burial data using information statistic. Divisive attributes: 1 = flexed; 2 = high integrity; 3 = west lobe; 4 = high-energy beads predominant; 5 = cairn.

role to cluster in particular lobes; clustats partly defined by such indicators were largely associated with west lobes at both sites. Orientation was not particularly correlated with anything but extended burials with high-quality beads predominant and/or obsidian (almost all of which are in the west lobes) tended to be consistently oriented north–south. There was some distinction among lobes and sublobes in terms of mortuary associations: Nonutilitarian offerings clustered in the west lobes, and some classes of offerings were significantly associated with particular sublobes.

Test implication C suggests that if the hypothesis holds, burials without markers of high status will be more variable along several dimensions than will those with such markers. The evidence indicated that extended burials and burials with a predominance of high energy beads tended to be spatially concentrated and—to some extent—consistently oriented, whereas burials not characterized by these attributes were highly variable in terms of location, orientation, and associations.

Test implication D holds that the key structure of the mortuary customs reflected in the cemeteries should be treelike or maximally redundant. Saxe (1970) has provided a statistic to be used in measuring redundancy of a key. Using it, I found that the keys of the Buchanan cemeteries have objectively high redundancy values, and are high relative to the ethnographic societies whose mortuary customs were keyed by Saxe. Thus the hypothesis appears to derive substantial support here, but in fact, since we have no scale based on a range of archeological cemeteries against which keys produced by methods like mine can be compared, it is not possible to say to what extent the hypothesis is actually supported.

Test implication E indicates that if the hypothesis holds, burials with indicators of high status should be spatially clustered. This test implication was met by the association of extended burials with the west lobes, by an association of high-quality beads with the west lobes, and by associations of large bead lots and shell ornaments with particular sublobes.

In no instance were the data unequivocal or clear-cut. On the whole, however, I take them to support the hypothesis that at Buchanan Reservoir between about A.D. 200 and 800, a nonegalitarian form of political organization existed that featured hereditary rank and a hierarchical authority structure.

So, in general, my data tend to support the contention that at least some California hunter–gatherer populations, by about 1500 years ago, were characterized by nonegalitarian political organization. How can we best account for this?

Let's first look at what Morton Fried (1967) says about the factors that could logically lead to political differentiation:

> What would lead to the narrowing and institutionalization of positions of rank? Undoubtedly there are many circumstances involved: problems of maintaining connections between parent settlements and those that have budded off; possibilities of diversifying the consuming sector of the economy by maintaining regular trade relations with communities exploiting somewhat different resources; the possibility of better handling of food supply by organizing special labor forces for simple irrigation tasks; rationalization of a sequence of habitation in which original settlers are joined, albeit peaceably, by subsequent settlers; the formalization, as Service has pointed out, of transsettlement sodalities, often as a means of enlarging the area of relative peace. These are but a few of the more obvious and probably most widespread stimuli to the emergence of ranking.
>
> If I had to select the two most significant factors, I would choose ecological demography and the emergence of redistribution . . . stem from an underlying revolution in the relations between the man and environment, expanding and stabilizing subsistence. Once accomplished, rank society is quite durable but as we already know and now must investigate, there are circumstances under which further developments occur which introduce a much more fundamental kind of inequality. This is the stratified society [pp. 183–184].

Fried does not, however, discuss in detail how any of these elements might operate to "narrow and institutionalize positions of rank." I think, though, that a picture of this process can be constructed that makes sense in terms of California societies, by the application of propositions advanced by Robert Carneiro and others. Carneiro (1970) suggests that hierarchical forms of social organization result from the subordination of conquered groups in a physically or socially circumscribed universe characterized by intense competition. His notion converges on that of Gearing (1962), who showed how a state could come into being—without subjugating other groups and incorporating them as lower classes—under pressure of war. Gearing pointed out, however, that there are factors other than war that can motivate similar internal changes in a society; I think this modification can save Carneiro's proposition from being too narrow and simplistic. In the case of aboriginal California, Carneiro's notion may well apply if intensive economic interaction is substituted for war as the prime mover in structural change.

California natural environments are highly variable, both spatially and seasonally. There are many areas where sufficient food resources would be available in varying seasonal configurations to allow a population with the proper technology and scheduling to become entirely seden-

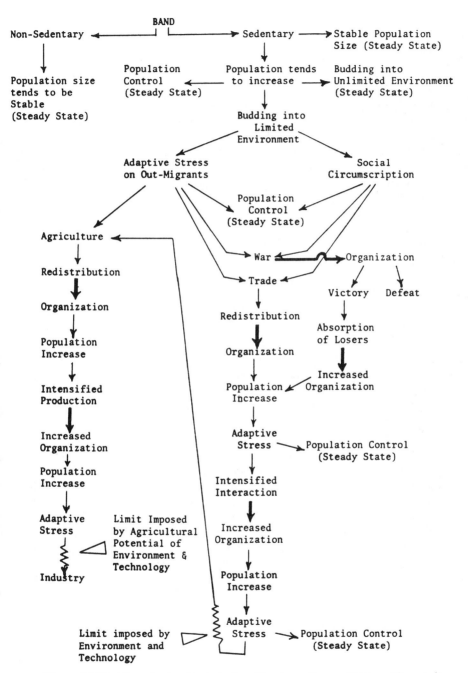

Figure 10.10. Organizational trajectories of hunter–gatherers (thickened lines indicate tendency toward increased political differentiation).

tary. Joseph Birdsell (1968) and Robert Sussman (1972) have told us that a
sedentary population is likely to increase in size until it begins to feel
subsistence stress, whereupon budding off or lineage fission will occur. In
California this budding would have two important effects. First, new
populations would be moving out into less varied environments, where
the danger of famine and the concomitant need for "banking" institutions
would be great. Second, each community would gradually become circumscribed by others, all potentially competing for the same resources.
The first condition, as Binford (1968) and Flannery (1970) have suggested,
would place strong adaptive value on the development of new forms of
subsistence among which intervillage trade as a means of resource banking would be an efficient strategy (cf. Vayda 1967; Bettinger and King
1971). Such trade requires entrepreneurial systems that typically involve
centralized redistribution. The second condition provides the state of
social circumscription described by Carneiro (1970) as conducive to
organized warfare resulting—through conquest and enslavement or
through the internal strains described by Gearing (1962)—in systems of
hierarchical rank. Intercommunity exchange and redistribution have
long been recognized as an alternative to warfare, and like warfare, they
require stable organizational systems that are often hierarchical in form.

   The adaptive stresses operating on hunter–gatherer communities in
California environments, then, can be seen generating internal strains
impelling the development of hierarchical ranking and complex economic systems for their alleviation. Figure 10.10 shows some possible
trajectories that such communities might follow toward greater organizational differentiation.

   There are some important zones in this trajectory—if a trajectory can
be said to have zones—that require some investigation. For example, way
up at the top, not all sedentary populations increase in size. The Ainu, for
example, had permanent villages with quite small, stable populations. My
current research, such as it is, is an investigation of some attributes that
are associated cross-culturally with such a situation. In general, though, I
think this trajectory provides a fair springboard—if trajectories can do
that either—for further thinking about the causes of political complexity
among hunter–gatherers. The most important thing to do at the outset,
though, is just to get the !Kung out of our eyes and recognize that
hunter–gatherers could and most likely did regularly possess nonegalitarian social institutions; from this we can begin to speculate about a lot of
evolutionary possibilities that are not available if we continue to respect
what Jane Jacobs (1969) has called the "myth of agricultural primacy."

ACKNOWLEDGMENTS

This chapter is essentially an abstract of my Ph.D. dissertation, prepared under the supervision of Alan R. Beals, Martin Orans, and Margaret Lyneis. Fieldwork at Buchanan Reservoir was supported by the National Park Service, the U.S. Army Corps of Engineers, the Archeological Research Unit at the University of California, Riverside and a dedicated crew of volunteers. It was conducted, during the final season, under terms of Antiquities Act Permit #WSC-71-CA-001.

REFERENCES

Bettinger, R. L., and T. F. King
    1971   Interaction and political organization: A theoretical framework for archeology in Owens Valley, California. *UCLA Archeological Survey Annual Report 13.*

Binford, L. R.
    1968   Post-Pleistocene adaptations. In *New perspectives in archeology,* edited by S. R. Binford and L. R. Binford, Chicago: Aldine.
    1971   Mortuary practices: Their study and their potential. In *Approaches to the social dimensions of mortuary practices,* edited by J. A. Brown. Memoirs of the Society for American Archaeology 25.

Birdsell, J. B.
    1968   Some predictions for the Pleistocene based on equilibrium systems among recent hunter–gatherers. In *Man the hunter,* edited by R. Lee and I. DeVore. Chicago: Aldine.

Blackburn, T.
    1974   Ceremonial integration and social interaction in aboriginal California. In *Antap: California Indian political and economic organization,* edited by L. J. Bean and T. F. King. Ramona, Calif.: Ballena.

Carneiro, R. L.
    1970   A theory of the origin of the state. *Science 169:733.*

Drucker, P., and R. F. Heizer
    1967   *To make my name good.* Berkeley and Los Angeles: Univ. of California Press.

Flannery, K. V.
    1970   Origins and ecological effects of early domestication in Iran and the Near East. In *The domestication and exploitation of plants and animals,* edited by P. J. Ucko and C. W. Dimbleby. London: Methuen.

Fried, M.
    1967   *The evolution of political society: An essay in political anthropology.* New York. Random House.

Gearing, F.
    1962   Priests and warriors: Social structures for Cherokee politics in the 18th century. *American Anthropologist 62:5, Part 2.*

Jacobs, J.
    1969   *The economy of cities.* New York: Random House.

King, C. D.
    1971   Chumash intervillage economic exchange. *Indian Historian 4:1.*

King, L. B.
1969   The Medea Creek cemetery: An investigation of social organization from mortuary practices. *UCLA Archeological Survey Annual Report 11.*
King, T. F.
1970   The dead at Tiburon. *Northwestern California Archeological Society, Occasional Paper 2.*
1974   The evolution of status ascription around San Francisco Bay. In *Antap: California Indian political and economic organization*, edited by L. J. Bean and T. F. King. Ramona, Calif.: Ballena.
1976   Political differentiation among hunter–gatherers: An archeological test. Ph.D. dissertation, Univ. of California, Riverside.
1977   An efficient method for exposing cemeteries and other complex cultural features. *Journal of Field Archaeology* 4:369–372.
Lee, R. B., and I. DeVore
1968   *Man the hunter.* Chicago: Aldine.
Merriam, C. H.
1967   Ethnographic notes on California Indian tribes. *University of California, Berkeley, Archeological Survey Reports 68.*
Moratto, M. J.
1972   A study of prehistory in the southern Sierra Nevada foothills, California. Ph.D. dissertation, Univ. of Oregon.
Orans, M.
1975   Domesticating the functional dragon: An analysis of Piddocke's potlatch. *American Anthropologist* 77:312–329.
Piddocke, S.
1969   The Potlatch system of the southern Kwakiutl: A new perspective. In *Environment and cultural behavior*, edited by A. P. Vayda. Garden City, N.Y.: Natural History Press.
Saxe, A. A.
1970   Social dimensions of mortuary practices. Ph.D. dissertation, Univ. of Michigan.
Service, E. R.
1962   *Primitive social organization.* New York: Random House.
Stickel, E. G.
1968   Status differentiation at the Rincon site. *UCLA Archeological Survey Annual Report 10.*
Sussman, R.
1972   Child transport, family size, and increase in human population during the Neolithic. *Current Anthropology* 13:258–259.
Suttles, W.
1968   Variation in habitat and culture on the Northwest coast. In *Man in adaptation*, edited by Y. Cohen. Chicago: Aldine. Pp. 93–105.
Tainter, J.
1975   The archeological study of social change: Woodland systems in west-central Illinois. Ph.D. dissertation, Northwestern University.
Vayda, A. P.
1967   Pomo trade feasts. In *Tribal and peasant economies*, edited by G. Dalton. Garden City, N.Y.: Natural History Press.

chapter 11

Unilinealism, Multilinealism, and the Evolution of Complex Societies

WILLIAM T. SANDERS AND DAVID WEBSTER

INTRODUCTION

A major recent focus of American archeology has been the evolution of complex societies. Investigation of this problem has primarily been concerned with elucidating basic processes that account for general similarities in independent sequences of cultural evolution. Several traditional evolutionary paradigms, particularly those of Fried (1967), Service (1962), Steward (1955), and White (1949), have been widely accepted as providing frameworks to which such processes may be applied. We recognize that all these authors later modified their views to some degree since formulating their basic evolutionary paradigms. Our main concern, however, is with their original arguments, since these have been most widely accepted by anthropologists and particularly by archeologists.

As detailed and reliable archeological evidence has accumulated, it has become evident that this emphasis on general processes and general unilineal evolution is increasingly inadequate in explaining the obvious variability present in specific sequences of complex social evolution. Al-

249

Social Archeology:
Beyond Subsistence and Dating

though we recognize the value of a comparative approach that seeks to identify and apply universal systemic evolutionary processes, variation cannot be explained by appealing to processes that are, in fact, universal. Variation must be explained in terms of factors that are variable and that themselves condition the general processes in variable ways.

We propose a modified multilineal paradigm in which different evolutionary trajectories relate to variations in the natural environment, such as degree of agricultural risk, diversity, productivity (as measured by energetic efficiency, yield per unit of cultivable land, and total area defined for the ecological community), and size and character of the environment. Among these we distinguish as first-order factors degree of agricultural risk and diversity, with productivity, and size, character, and location as second-order factors. We attempt to show through substantive archeological examples that various permutations of these factors result in different specific evolutionary sequences, different rates of development, and different limits to development. Our examples are drawn from Mesoamerican archeology for a variety of reasons. Primary considerations are that the authors are most familiar with this area, and Mesoamerica has produced, to date, the most consistent, abundant, and reliable body of data available pertaining to the problem of the evolution of complex societies. Furthermore, the region is a cultural unit in which major patterns were (and are) widely shared over the entire region, including such traits of critical significance in our paradigm as the complex of cultigens and level of production technology. On the other hand, it is a region of extraordinary geographic diversity, and this diversity must have had highly significant effects on the specific patterns of ecological adaptation and cultural evolution.

THE PROBLEM

In his paper, the "Cultural Evolution of Civilization" (1972), Kent Flannery provides us with a series of very useful and productive leads in the design of a research strategy to resolve the question of the evolution of complex societies.

Flannery distinguishes among environmental stimuli, processes, and mechanisms. He recognizes, as Leslie White (1949) did, that innovations are implemented by individuals operating within a specific set of historical circumstances. By circumstances we mean the knowledge of the innovator, his (or their) position within the social system, and the state of the social system at the time of the innovation. Instead of treating innovation as a unique and specific event, however (as historians traditionally would do), one can derive low-level generalizations about such implementations. These are referred to by Flannery as *mechanisms*. For example, various agencies of a central administration may take control of functions, such as irrigation systems or education, that were formerly the responsibilities of local communities. The mechanism here is *linearization*—the expropriation of the functions of a lower-order social institution by a higher one. Another such mechanism is *promotion*, whereby a lower-level office or institution with very limited and specific functions is promoted to a higher position in the system and at the same time its functions are expanded and generalized. Cited as an example by Flannery is the promotion of the office of *lugal* from war leader to secular ruler in predynastic Mesopotamia.

By *process* he refers to those broad, dynamic, repetitive patterns of culture that are universal or nearly universal in the evolution and functioning of all cultures. Examples would be cooperation, competition, segregation, and centralization. In his model mechanisms are seen as the agents by which the intensity of such processes is increased or decreased. The mechanisms of linearization and promotion, for example, are means by which the process of centralization is accelerated.

Flannery argues that the history of social evolution is essentially one of increasing *segregation* and *centralization*, two processes that are closely and functionally related. By segregation he refers to a process of differentiation within the social system into unlike but interdependent segments, based on economic specialization, professionalization of political and/or religious power, and differences in wealth, privilege, and life-style. By centralization is meant increasingly overt control by a dominant subgroup or subgroups of the social order and the regulation of the interaction among these subgroups. Flannery sees mechanisms and the processes they generate as the causes of cultural evolution, and he relegates such explanations of cultural evolution as warfare, population growth, and hydraulic agriculture to the status of environmental *stimuli*, which provided the proper climate and setting within which the mechanisms and processes function.

We see a serious semantic problem in this analysis of cultural evolution. Both Flannery's mechanisms and processes, as he himself states, are universal. If they are universal, we are faced with the paradox of explaining *variability* in culture by factors that are, by definition, *nonvarying*. The one component of his methodological scheme that does vary is the environmental stimuli, and we see these as basic causes of cultural evolution.

In summary we do not disagree with the basic structure for research as suggested in Flannery's paper. Neither do we deny the necessity of going beyond the identification of environmental stimuli in order to provide an adequate explanation. The difficulty with many earlier attempts to analyze cultural evolution was not so much that they selected the wrong causal factors (i.e., environment, as Flannery argues), but rather that they did not go much further than identifying the environmental simuli. What is needed, as he himself suggests, is analysis of the way in which such stimuli provide a setting for the mechanisms and processes of cultural dynamics to operate. What mechanisms, for example, does population growth trigger to accentuate the process of segregation?

DEFINITION AND MEASUREMENT OF ENVIRONMENTAL VARIABLES

Among the environmental variables we consider agricultural risk and diversity as first-order factors, with productivity, size, character, and location as second-order factors. Each of these is defined in the following discussion, and methods of measurement are suggested. Population size and density are not discussed in detail, since our utilization of these concepts is commonly understood. Nor will we closely examine the variables of *nature of the productive system* (by which we mean the major energy sources and technology utilized), since these can essentially be regarded as constants in the evolving Mesoamerican cultural sequences to which we apply the model.

It is important to emphasize that these environmental variables are not mutually exclusive but are functions of one another. Obviously various aspects of productivity, for example, are functions of agricultural risk, size and character of the environment, and technology. Even more important, the variables are not simply environmental "givens" but may be conditioned by transformations in the sociocultural system itself. Thus, on the one hand, high agricultural risk may be inherent in the environment as a result of natural constraints (e.g., insufficient or erratic rainfall, frosts), but agricultural innovations may change the environment to a low-risk one. On the other hand, population growth in an environment generally free from natural risks may ultimately produce risk by enforcing dependence upon increasingly marginal or degraded resources or by reducing the size of land holdings. Similarly, population growth may stimulate colonization of new productive areas where different subsistence resources are produced, consequently creating an agricultural heterogeneity not previously present. This same process may promote specialization in nonsubsistence resources, providing that raw materials are highly localized.

Risk

Theoretically the risk factor is closely related to the aspects of diversity and productivity. By risk we mean any essential environmental parameters essential to production of energy (e.g., moisture, temperature) with wide, relatively frequent, and unpredictable variations. Insofar as the risk factor differentially affects local areas, productive diversity is produced. For example, in the Teotihuacán Valley it is possible for one village to experience a very poor harvest because of erratic rainfall patterns, whereas another only a few kilometers away has a bumper crop. If, as is often the case, there are segments of the productive landscape that have a small risk factor, or none at all, the productive diversity of the total landscape is increased.

The risk factor operates primarily on the process of centralization. Again using the Teotihuacán Valley as an example, we find sharply contrasting local niches—for example, closely juxtaposed areas of differential frost, and most importantly, irrigable versus nonirrigable land. Minimally, the effects of such variable niches are to encourage differential settlement histories and patterns, and, in the case of irrigable land, to stimulate the emergence of patron–client relationships between those with access to irrigation resources and those without. Social stratification, in Fried's (1967) sense, is thus established. By a series of complex feedback relationships, however, this social situation frequently evolves into a much more highly centralized kind of power, in which the patrons create political institutions (the state), which, among other things, serve to reduce the risk factor by complex redistribution and/or the creation and management of large-scale water control projects.

The risk factor is fairly easy to measure if environmental conditions and the mode of production are known or can be reconstructed. We suggest that an index be established, based upon a 10- or 20-year period (in order to capture short-term cycles of significant variables like moisture, frost, disease, pests), and that values be attached to years of maximum productivity, moderate productivity, low productivity, and complete failure.

Diversity

By diversity we mean the closeness and pattern of spacing of contrasting environmental conditions significant in terms of human exploitation. Such diversity may involve subsistence or nonsubsistence resources; the role of diversity in the subsistence sense is more fundamental in the development of complex cultures and is our primary concern, although nonsubsistence diversity has considerable impact on ecological and evolutionary processes as well. A major concern here is that measures of diversity be closely related to human needs, not to diversity in some general sense. For example, diversity in soils in a region occupied by cultivators should be expressed in a typology emphasizing factors that influence agricultural fertility rather than type of parent material, etc. Variability in soil fertility may itself be of little significance in terms of one specific crop staple and be of considerable significance in the case of another—cereals, for example, are much more demanding of soil fertility than are root crops. Although the factor is easily understood and described in qualitative terms, what is needed is a means of quantification of the concept if it is to be used effectively as a predictive model. In the absence of a quantitative scale we are using qualitative terms such as low, moderate, and high diversity. To illustrate the meaning of this scale, we offer the following case examples:

We have selected four areas of comparable size (12,000 km², Figures 11.1–11.8) to illustrate differences in diversity of two factors that strongly influence agricultural production, temperature, and rainfall. The selection was based on the fact that the four cover the range of Mesoamerican environments very well and were the same areas selected for detailed analysis of their cultural histories in the final section of this chapter. For two of the areas we have comparable soil maps, which provide a further indication of differences in degree of heterogeneity. The Basin of Mexico and the adjacent area of the state of Morelos are located in the Central Plateau, the location of several major Mesoamerican sites such as Teotihuacán, Tenochtitlán, and Xochicalco. A second area includes the Valley of Guatemala and adjacent sections of the Motagua Valley and Pacific coastal plain and piedmont. A third area is the northeastern Petén, which was the demographic heartland of Classic Maya civilization. The fourth area is the Valley of Oaxaca and adjacent highland zones along with the Pacific escarpment. We would generally characterize the Petén as a low-risk environment with moderate to low diversity; the highlands and coast of Guatemala as a low-risk, high-diversity area; the Central Plateau and Oaxacan highlands as high-risk, high-diversity areas. We have also included a map (Figure 11.9) of highland Mesoamerica showing major patterns of topography and subsistence and nonsubsistence diversity.

It should be noted that the maps only illustrate in a gross way major patterns of diversity over very large areas and do not take into account the highly significant microdiversity particularly found in highland areas. The patterning of the larger units of analysis, however, almost certainly reflects differences in the microdiversity *within* the respective units as well.

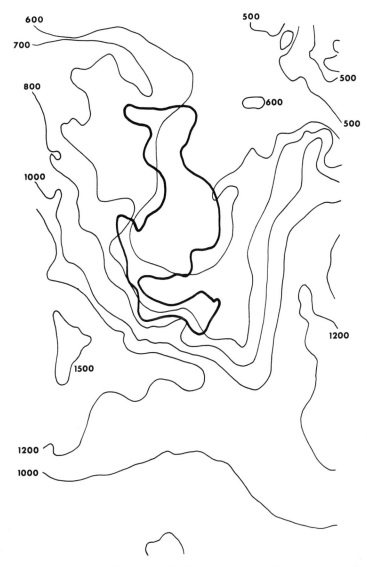

Figure 11.1. Basin of Mexico and adjacent portions of Morelos and Puebla. Mean annual precipitation (mm).

Figure 11.2. Basin of Mexico and adjacent portions of Morelos and Puebla. Mean annual temperature (°C).

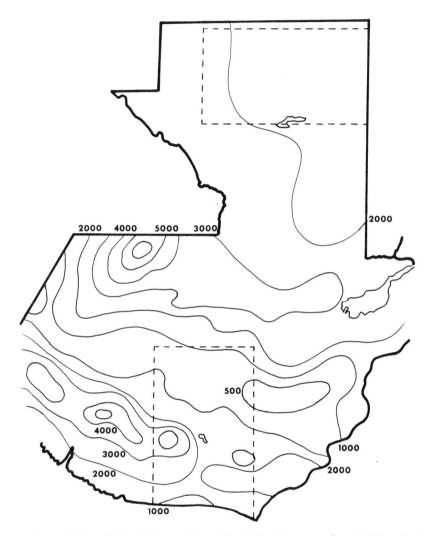

Figure 11.3. Highland Guatemala and the Petén. Mean annual precipitation (mm). Outlined areas are shown on accompanying soil maps (Figures 11.7 and 11.8).

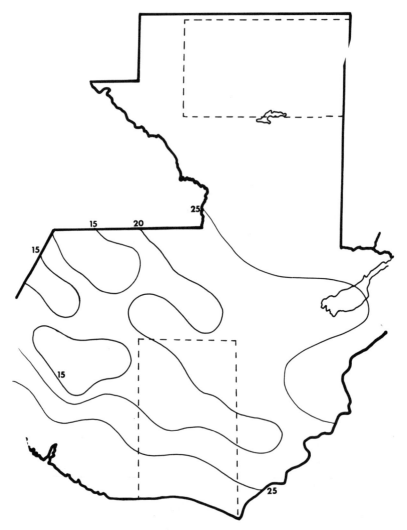

Figure 11.4. Highland Guatemala and the Petén. Mean annual temperatures (°C). Outlined areas are shown on accompanying soil maps (Figures 11.7 and 11.8).

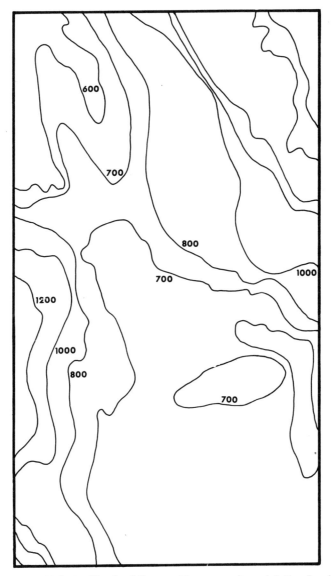

Figure 11.5   Highlands of Oaxaca. Mean annual precipitation (mm).

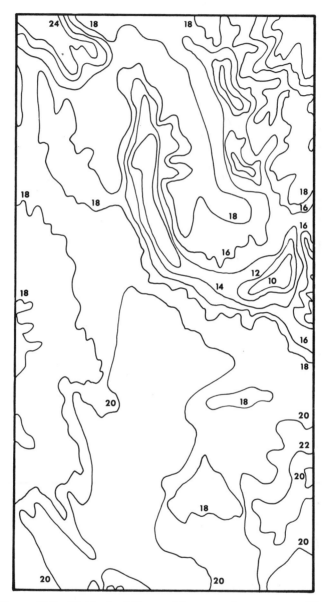

Figure 11.6. Highlands of Oaxaca. Mean annual temperatures (°C).

The microdiversity is significant in the patterning not only of subsistence but of nonsubsistence resources.

Productivity

By productivity we mean the potential of the landscape to produce energy in the form of subsistence products for the support of human populations. Although productivity may be absolutely constrained by environmental factors, we recognize that it is intimately linked to such cultural factors as levels of technology and organization, energy sources available, and variety of information. As with diversity, productivity affects all of the evolutionary processes. The problem with productivity is not so much how to measure it, but rather which of several alternative measures is most useful for assessing various kinds of evolutionary change:

1. *Input–output ratios.* Here we mean the ratio between energy expenditure and energy return characteristic of a given exploitative strategy. This measure offers insights into patterns of colonization and settlement distribution, into decision making about alternative forms of subsistence strategies through time, and, most important, into the ability to generate surpluses to counteract risk or to invest in socially complex organization, such as hierarchical political structure (centralization) or occupational specialization (segregation).

2. *Carrying capacity.* Biologists use this term to mean the maximum population of plants or animals that an area can sustain without long-range deleterious effects on the environment. This concept is of only minor utility in studies of human adaptation, since humans have the capacity, through cultural means, to adapt to such effects and can arrest or at least reduce the pace of such processes. William Allan, in his book *The African Husbandman* (1965), uses three factors to calculate carrying capacity. The first is the cultivable land factor, that percentage of the landscape that can be cultivated in terms of the technology of the sample population. The second factor is the cultivation factor, the amount of land needed in production in any one year in order to sustain a person. This is an empirical measure based on the specific economic system being analyzed. For example, in economies where economic specialization and social stratification are absent, such as in the case of many Neolithic societies, then the amount of land needed is that sufficient for the food production for the individual family, the basic production consumption unit. In the case of more complex social and economic organization, this calculation must include the surplus for trade or taxation. The final

measure is the land-use factor—that is, how many units of cultivated land (the cultivation factor) are needed to maintain year-after-year production. In a long fallow swidden system this figure may be as high as 10 or 12; in an annual cropping system it would be only 1. The formula for calculating carrying capacity could be written as follows: $cl/(lu \times cf)$. All of these variables are of course subject to change by cultural innovation, so carrying capacity is in reality a kind of constantly shifting scale.

Combining these two measures, we see four basic models or types. Type A productivity is one in which intensification results in an increase in the input–output ratio and demographic capacity. This kind of productivity occurs primarily in arid or semiarid regions where intensification involves major technological innovations that have a striking effect on yield and crop security. As a result, the increase in the productivity of planted fields more than makes up for the increased costs of work input. Type B is one where intensification leads to a decline in the input–output ratio but results in a greater demographic capacity. The decrease in the input–output ratio may be caused by an increase in labor input as related to crop yield, or the situation may be even worse in that the increased labor input is accompanied by a decrease of yield. This productive regime is most characteristic of humid regions where soil fertility presents a major problem and where agricultural innovation has little effect on crop security. Under some circumstances, in the case of type B, this process of steady decline in input–output ratio may actually reach the point where agriculture can no longer be sustained in a given area. This we would refer to as type C economy. In other cases the profile of productivity may involve an initial increase in the input–output ratio followed by very rapid decline. Examples of this would be situations in desert regions, where irrigation introduced at some time during the process of population growth would result in an initial increase in the input–output ratio, but then further intensification of the system would produce a process of salinization of the soils and a rapid collapse. We can call this productivity type D.

In summary, the most fundamental role of agricultural productivity is simply to provide adequate energy potential so that sufficiently large and dense populations necessary for the evolution and maintenance of complex societies may be supported. Local or regional variations in productivity (an aspect of diversity) encourage different settlement histories, different rates of population growth, and different demographic patterns,

Figure 11.7. Soil variation in the highlands of Guatemala (for location see Figure 11.4).

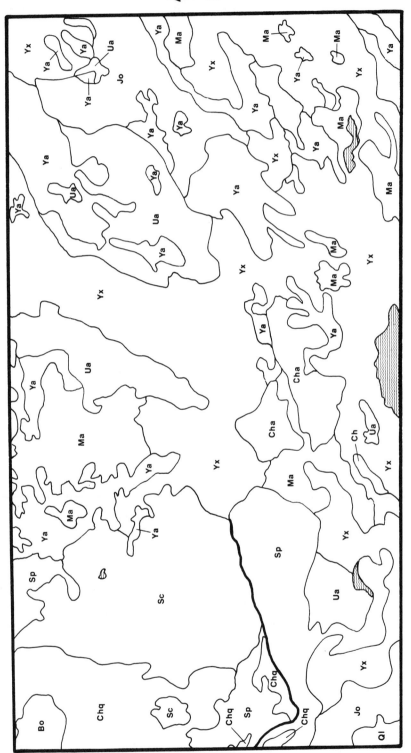

all of which affect the evolutionary processes, especially that of competition. Productivity is assumed to result from the dynamic interplay between natural conditions and subsistence technology and strategy. Of particular importance is the production of large gross surpluses above the subsistence level so that hierarchical centralization and nonsubsistence segregation may reach complex levels and proportions. Another essential productivity factor is the degree to which various opportunities for agricultural intensification are permitted or constrained by environmental conditions.

Size, Character, and Location

The major effect of the category of spatial size is on the two demographic parameters of population size and density. Most anthropologists would agree that, as a society increases in size, it must change its structure in order to continue to function as a social system. The unilineal stages proposed by Fried (1967), and Service (1962) as generalized kinds of social systems, can in essence be considered as stages in societal size. In band and tribal societies the interaction between individuals and households is basically egalitarian, both in terms of exercise of authority and control of basic resources. With chiefdoms or states interpersonal relationships become imbalanced or, as Service puts it, there is negative reciprocity. In the case of chiefdoms this imbalance is less marked, and the ideological basis of the system is phrased in terms of kinship, a persistence of tribal principles of organization in the social structure. With highly evolved states, however, kin-based organization disappears, atrophies, or, minimally, takes on a different set of functions. Access to basic resources by elites is more direct and social disequilibrium more pronounced, particularly in access to political power. Each of these levels or types permits the integration of larger numbers of people.

The major question is why social systems evolve at all, most particularly why individual households should agree to abide by a social contract in which their surplus time is put to work or appropriated by other households. One explanation has been in terms of rising population density. Included in this argument is the idea that social integration is closely related to the technology of communication and transportation. Each technological level of communication–transportation imposes a practical limit to effective social integration in terms of the size of the territory integrated; hence the only way more people can be incorporated

Figure 11.8. Soil variation in the Petén (for location see Figure 11.4).

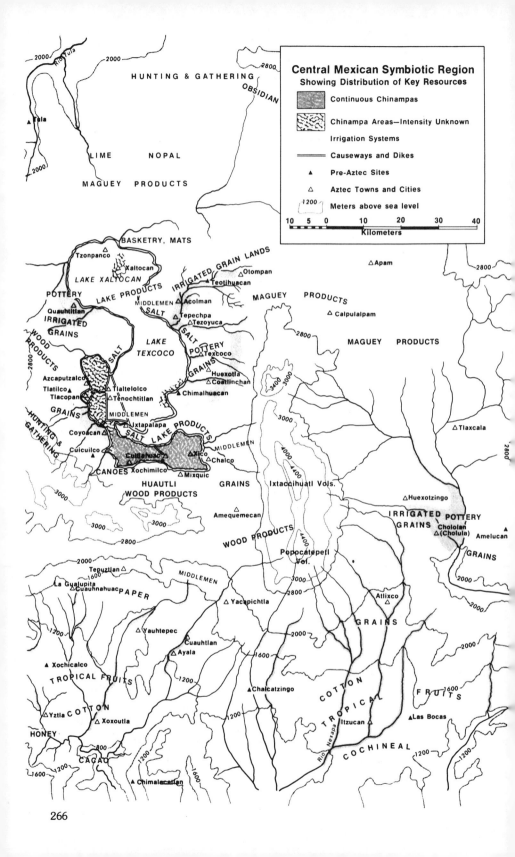

Central Mexican Symbiotic Region
Showing Distribution of Key Resources

Continuous Chinampas

Chinampa Areas—Intensity Unknown

Irrigation Systems

Causeways and Dikes

▲ Pre-Aztec Sites

△ Aztec Towns and Cities

1200 Meters above sea level

10 5 0 10 20 30 40
Kilometers

into a social unit is by increasing the number of people per square mile. This, however, leaves unexplained the question of why, as population per unit of space increases, we do not simply have social fission; that is, why not more units of the same size rather than larger social systems.

It is primarily through the processes of competition and cooperation that population density functions to stimulate social integration rather than social fission, as Carneiro (1970), Netting (1972), and others have argued. In Carneiro's view warfare under conditions of environmental and/or social circumscription and high population density results in economic and political subordination of defeated groups. Netting has emphasized that population growth under conditions of high density would raise the probability of many sorts of conflict—not necessarily over key resources—and the costs of feuding may act as a stimulus to voluntary submission of autonomy, in other words, increased cooperation.

The size of the environment affects the processes of cooperation and conflict by determining the size, density, and distribution of population on the landscape. The long-range effect of a large, productive environment is that it allows sustained increases in absolute population size and density. On the other hand, a spatial unit may be so small and so isolated that complex social organization is unnecessary or unworkable. A Pacific atoll with a maximum carrying capacity of five hundred people would be an extreme case, but isolating factors such as high ranges or desert zones may operate in even continental areas such as the far south coast of Peru. In cases where the spatial unit is sufficiently large to permit complex societies to evolve, differences in size would have a significant effect on the tempo of such evolution. Very large homogeneous regions, without significant internal barriers, would require much longer periods of time to fill in with the requisite population density levels than would small heterogeneous environments with internal barriers.

Character of the environment includes various factors, mainly topographical, which, like those just alluded to, serve to control isolation, to facilitate or discourage communication and transportation, or to determine overall cultural patterning on the landscape. For example, centers of population may be strung out along a river system, which creates not only the productive agricultural landscape but a linear settlement pattern and easy communication as well.

We include the locational factor because it is potentially important if we use Fried's (1967) pristine–secondary dichotomy, since the spatial relationships of complex societies in an extensive culture area would be a consideration in the dynamics of culture contact and culture change.

Figure 11.9. Central Mexican symbiotic region (showing distribution of key resources). From William T. Sanders and Barbara Price, *Mesoamerica: The evolution of a civilization,* © 1968, Random House, New York, Figure 10.

RESEARCH STRATEGY—
THE UNILINEAL PARADIGM

Service (1962) has delineated four main levels of social integration: a progression from *bands* through *tribes* (both egalitarian societies) and *chiefdoms* to *states* (both hierarchical societies). His primary emphasis is on changes in social *structure*—particularly kinship. Fried (1967) proposes a basically similar model but has introduced some important modifications of his own, as we shall discuss.

Egalitarian Society (Bands–Tribes)

Our concept of egalitarian society derives both from Service (1962) and Fried (1967) and agrees with Service's original argument that taxonomic variety can be distinguished within the general category. His distinction between band and tribe is essentially a demographic (societal size) and social organizational one, but there are also correlations with subsistence types. Band organization is generally characteristic of hunting and gathering economies, whereas tribes are found primarily among agriculturalists. As Fried points out, however, there are numerous exceptions, as well as considerable overlap in population density, although tribes tend to be denser as well as larger societies than do bands. Both bands and tribal societies are characterized by low population size and density, status differentiation based upon personal achievement within the limits of age and sex, equal access to basic economic resources, and political leadership predicated upon persuasion rather than coercion. For the purposes of the evolutionary model proposed here, which is mainly concerned with the emergence of complex society, we emphasize egalitarian society on the level of tribal agriculturalists.

The major distinction in Service's scheme between band and tribes is that bands are small autonomous local societies, whereas tribes are larger multicommunity societies integrated by such sodalities as theoretical descent groups, voluntary associations, and age sets.

Fried, and lately even Service, do not consider the tribal type of society as a unilineal stage; they rather see it as a kind of social organization that evolved in response to pressures generated by nearby state societies on bands. We feel this argument unconvincing for a variety of reasons. First, it is difficult for us to visualize the evolution of the much larger, more complex, hierarchically organized chiefdom out of the small, single-community, egalitarian society Service calls a band, without some intermediate organization. Since sodality type organizations are also characteristic of chiefdoms, it would seem reasonable, as Service originally proposed, that this intermediate level include sodality organization but without significant ranking—in other words, a tribal society. Finally, and even more important, essentially egalitarian societies with sodalities are such a widespread phenomenon, spatially and temporally, that we find it difficult to believe that everywhere they occur one can explain their presence as due to pressures from states.

We feel that Fried frequently equates the *effects* of pressure from states on well-developed tribal societies with the *evolution of tribal societies as a type*. For example, in the case of the Eastern Woodland, tribes of several thousand people were reported at the time of European contact—for example, the five separate tribes of what later became the Iroquois Confederacy. What contact did do was to create the stimulus for a pyramiding effect in which the five tribes united into a confederate organization, but one still based on egalitarian principles and sodality organization. Three of the matrisibs—Turtles, Bears, and Wolves—were found in all five tribes, and they provided the ideological bonds that formed the tribes into a single unit.

Finally, if one considers the situation from a *processual* point of view and agrees to the proposition that tribes form as the *product of competitive pressures*, why shouldn't competition among egalitarian band societies produce tribes? We feel that the key theoretical variable here is the competition process, and to some degree, therefore, the nature of the organization of the competing societies becomes irrelevant. We say to some degree because there probably are differences in detail between situations where competing groups are equivalent in evolutionary status and where they are not. In any case what is important is the nature of adaptive organizational responses to competition, and these are probably constrained more by the simple structure of band society itself than by the nature of the competitive stress.

In summary, we see considerable merit in Service's original formulation and have retained the tribe as a major stage in social evolution.

Chiefdoms

It is with chiefdoms that a new structural principle for integration of multicommunity societies appears: ranking. In chiefdoms, as defined by Service, lineages are graded on a prestige ladder, and it is characteristic for one of the lineages to reserve right of tenure for the political office that Service refers to as chief. Frequently present is the concept that all members share a common descent from a single ancestor, and that ranking of lineages and individuals will be based on a principle of primogeniture. Everyone in this scheme is related to the chief, and everyone also occupies a unique position of rank that is determined by calculation of the exact degree of closeness (or distance) to the chief. A theoretical result is that true stratification into classes is absent, as there are not large groups made up of people of equivalent rank. In fact, precise position of the mass of the population at the base of the pyramid is operationally irrelevant, since they do not qualify for office and they are frequently distinguished by a single status term, hence partaking somewhat of the feature of a system of stratification. The society is still based on kinship, with ranking mechanisms added as new structural principles. In such societies, the person of the chief is almost sacrosanct, and he frequently plays a vital sacerdotal role. He is surrounded by a retinue of wives, retainers, and assistants, and contact with him is restricted and patterned by elaborate rules of protocol. His life crises of birth, marriage, and—most particularly—death are frequently accompanied by elaborate public ritual. Service refers to the prescriptions for these ceremonial practices as sumptuary rules.

According to Service, the chief's primary economic basis of power lies in his role as a redistributor of goods. In chiefdom societies, local specialization in craft products and in production of foodstuffs and raw materials is highly developed. Characteristically, surpluses of these goods are periodically produced by local kin groups and paid as kin obligations to the chief. He in turn uses these surpluses for maintenance of his court and, more importantly, for redistribution to his subjects. Chiefs in these systems can also command periodic contributions of labor for construction and maintenance of their houses or courts, and of other public buildings, such as temples. These contributions are symbolically rationalized as kin obligations and involve reciprocal payment of the chief in the form of goods, particularly food. The chief derives his power from the sumptuary and redistributive practices just noted. Markets are generally absent or weakly developed, and full-time craft specialization is limited to artisans attached to the chiefly household.

A major problem in Service's definition of the chiefdom as a broad typological category and stage in unilineal evolution is that it is too specific, in reality he is describing a particular kind of chiefdom, characteristic of Polynesia, typified by a ramage structure, with a major focus on redistribution. A rapid perusal of a great number of African societies (Taylor 1975) reveals numerous examples in which the chief has a similar degree and kind of political power as does the Polynesian chief, in which sumptuary rules are equally significant as a basis of chiefly prestige, and in which the chief heads social systems of comparable size; but in these examples the chief's redistributive functions are minor and the chiefdom is organized on the basis of a unilineal descent structure rather than bilateral ramages. In such cases the primary function of the chief is as a war leader, adjudicator of disputes, and patron to the poor. His economic wealth is not based on what he can siphon off from a redistributive network but rather in the productivity of his large herds of livestock and the women of his large polygynous household. The women are derived from the subject communities, and his kin connection with them is primarily affinal rather than consanguineal, in contrast to the Polynesian case. Another source of wealth is fees from adjudication. Some of this wealth is dispensed to visiting subjects in the form of cooked food and drink, and the chief is a symbol and source for hospitality. The position is limited to a particular lineage of a particular sib, and local chiefs under his control tend to come from, but are not always from, the same sib. Other sibs may have the right to titled positions at the chief's court. Although the lineage of the chiefs obviously outrank all others, there is no overall ranking system for individuals and lineages as in the Polynesian system.

What is needed, then, is a definition sufficiently general to include both Polynesian and African types of chiefdoms. Fried's (1967) definition of ranked society is perhaps the best one available, and we will follow it here:

> A ranked society is one in which positions of valued status are somehow limited so that not all of those of sufficient talent to occupy such position actually achieve them. Such a society may or may not be stratified, that is a society may sharply limit the positions of prestige without affecting the access of the entire membership to the basic resources upon which life depends [p. 109].

We would make one modification and say that such a society may *not* be stratified, since we are separating stratified society as a type from ranked society rather than considering it as a subtype of ranked society, as Fried did.

An additional element of the definition is that the society is structured strongly along kinship lines. Division of labor seems to be primarily based on age and sex, with only a limited amount of economic specialization, primarily part-time. Ranked societies also involve a heavy emphasis on sumptuary rules and ritual leadership, as well as a strong element of ranking throughout the society with accompanying negative reciprocity in economic relationships, although such economic relationships do not involve basic goods sufficiently to create stratification.

The problem of redistribution is complex. Peebles and Kus (1977) argue that even Polynesian chiefdoms were not characteristically redistributive economies, at least not to the degree that Sahlins (1958), Fried

(1967), and Service (1962) assert. What were redistributed were primarily status objects that did not filter down to the basal level of the pyramid. Many of the basic goods were produced locally, and most local communities were self-sufficient. When exchanges did occur in basic goods, the system was one of direct or balanced reciprocity between equivalently ranked settlements. The chiefs did exact surpluses in basic food stuffs and did redistribute cooked food in ritual feasts, but the idea of the chief's house as a kind of marketplace for local communities to exchange basic foodstuffs through the ideology of status gifts is probably a misunderstanding of Polynesian economy. Nevertheless, it is probable that the chiefs' position did act as a protective umbrella permitting various kinds of exchanges to occur.

Stratified Societies

Perhaps the most provocative concept, introduced by Fried, is that of the *stratified society*. Briefly, stratified societies are those in which there is differential economic access to basic subsistence resources—that is, capital, productive resources such as land, and water. Such differential access implies accretion of wealth, and all of the internal social stresses related to it. Differential control of wealth confers not only status but the possibility of forming dominant (patron)–subordinate (client) relationships. Wealth becomes a potential political tool in a more fundamental sense than the manipulation of noncapital resources previously allowed. States, of course, have always been recognized as stratified in this manner. For Fried, however, the stratified society, as an evolutionary stage, lacks the complex social, economic, and political institutions that in developed states *maintain* an order of economic stratification. Consequently, Fried emphasizes that this is an all-important but ephemeral, short-term, evolutionary stage. Either it rapidly gives rise to primary state developments, or, in most cases, it breaks down into simpler socioeconomic forms.

Although it is by no means perfectly clear from Fried's presentation, he seemingly postulates the development of stratified societies out of ranked societies as a result of population pressure and the structure of ranked society itself. We retain a distinction between ranked and stratified societies, but only in the context of Fried's restricted use of these terms. Adams (1975) has noted that although Fried's restricted concept of ranking has its uses, social ranking as such occurs in all human societies (p. 167). We recognize that "the ranking of objects inherently involves making a judgement and inherently bestowing value [p. 197]" and that in a society in which some groups have differential control over basic resources they are very likely to be judged, valued, and ultimately ranked differently, and probably more highly, than others. It is almost inevitable that an economically stratified nonstate society will exhibit some forms of ranking, but forms structured differently than in Fried's hypothetical ranked stage.

Two basic problems with the concept are apparent. First, it does not seem necessary, for either logical or ethnographic reasons, to consider stratified societies as developing out of ranked societies. Indeed, it is our position that the characteristic organizational and economic features of ranked society usually reflect a basically egalitarian orientation toward production and redistribution of basic resources and in a very real sense frustrate such a development. Another problem is Fried's assertion that economic stratification, ultimately related to ecological–demographic variables, usually breaks down into simpler social forms. It is unclear from his discussion how this can occur if these variables remain constant. If, for example, a stratified society emerges as an adaptation to population pressure, or differential risk and productivity in a diverse environment, how can it "break down" unless population declines or the environmental context changes? Unfortunately Fried does not explain in any detail what ecological–demographic conditions produce stratified societies.

Fried's conception of economic stratification seems narrower than his own definition of it. Many societies on the egalitarian level exhibit various forms of differential access to scarce productive resources (including women), and such access may serve to structure embryonic power relationships. What is significant is that there are various factors that, in most societies, serve to constrain the consolidation and growth of such power relations. The important questions are what constitutes these constraints and under what unusual circumstances are they removed? In Fried's paradigm an economically stratified society only exists (as an evolutionary stage) when such constraints are absent or ineffective and the potential for rapid evolutionary change is realized. We emphasize the widespread occurrence of low-level economic stratification in order to stress the fundamental evolutionary continuities between Fried's stratified stage and preexisting socioeconomic patterns. Seen in the wider perspective, the mere existence of economic stratification does not, as Fried asserts, indicate that the process of state formation is underway. Nor, we would maintain, do the emergent institutions of early states function *primarily* to maintain an order of stratification, as Fried believes.

We retain the concept of stratified society because of its logical

elegance and because we feel that the problems just noted can be eliminated. We dispose of the first problem simply by denying that stratified
societies must emerge from ranked societies. As for the second, we
maintain that stratified societies *cannot* break down in the absence of a
demographic or ecological catastrophe and must invariably lead to higher
levels of organization. Moreover, we feel that stratified societies may not
be directly related to such demographic variables as absolute size and
density of population. We attempt to define ecological variables, such as
differential risk and productivity, that may lead to economic stratification
in the absence of population pressure. The concept of the stratified
society remains a key element in our own multilineal, evolutionary
model, but not as a necessary link between ranked societies and states.

States

A wide consensus exists concerning the characteristics of the state.
These include (*a*) large, dense populations supported by effective agricultural systems within well-defined territories; (*b*) the presence of highly
centralized organizational foci; (*c*) specialized and centralized political
institutions with several hierarchical levels; (*d*) economic stratification
(unequal access to basic resources); (*e*) complex economic specialization
involving the production of both subsistence and nonsubsistence goods,
with correspondingly complex mechanisms of economic exchange; (*f*)
centralized monopoly of coercive force to regulate the internal status quo
and territorial integrity; (*g*) ranking of whole groups into a class structure,
with class status at least partially ascribed. While these are characteristics
of the state as a *type*, it is the underlying *processes* of segmentation and
centralization which are of greatest concern, and it may be easier to
perceive, from an archeological perspective, these processes rather than
typological markers such as palaces, professional armies, etc.

All ethnographically and historically known states exhibit the preceding features to some degree, but again variety is the rule. A diachronic, evolutionary perspective suggests some qualifications of these
characteristics for early, pristine states and probably for secondary states
as well. In particular we would suggest that monopoly of coercive force
was weakly developed in early states and that kin organization played a
more vital integrative role than it did in developed states.

Finally, Fried has introduced a very important distinction between
pristine and secondary developments. Pristine evolutionary developments
refer to new levels of sociopolitical integration that have emerged
autochthonously—that is, in the absence of influences from more highly

evolved societies. Secondary developments involve evolutionary changes that emerge in the context of, and [possibly] because of, contacts with more advanced societies. According to Fried's model, secondary developments may occur on any sociopolitical level, but he, and most other anthropologists who have used the concept, are mainly interested in the emergence of secondary *states*. It should be noted that Steward (1938:246), with his strong ecological orientation, had previously expressed doubts about the utility of the "pristine" versus "secondary" distinction. Fried uses this concept to discard Service's tribal type of society and regards tribal society as band societies reorganizing themselves in response to pressure from states.

The distinction is valuable primarily because it can be used to extend Fried's model to include societies that, in terms of their size, organizational details, and rates of evolutionary change, depart from the postulated unilineal progression. Despite the fact that the concept has been widely applied, it has proved difficult to operationalize the processual nature of secondary developments and distinguish between the effects of culture contact and indigenous evolutionary potential. This chapter attempts to show that the pristine–secondary distinction can be operationalized and useful given the larger perspective of cultural-ecological theory.

Process and Unilineal Evolution

Although there are important differences between the respective evolutionary schemes of Service and Fried, both, as previously noted, are essentially unilineal in that cultural evolution is seen as progressing through several broad organizational stages. Although they express overtly evolutionary concerns, both have a basically descriptive and typological approach to hypothetical stages of sociocultural evolution, and neither addresses *processes* of evolutionary transformation in any detailed way. Both have primarily developed their models by using comparative ethnographic material rather than by using a diachronic approach that attempts to integrate ethnographic and archeological data (although Service has attempted to integrate synchronic and diachronic methodologies in his book *Origins of the State and Civilization* [1975]).

Service's (1962) primary emphasis is on changes in *social structure*—particularly kinship. Influenced by Steward (1938, 1949, 1955), he introduces ecological variables to explain evolutionary transformations, especially for egalitarian societies. But he does not see them as deterministic in any but a demographic sense. In other words, the productive potential of the environment, coupled with organizational and extractive techniques, influences the demographic patterns (i.e., variability in size and density of population), which in turn bring about adaptive structural changes as society passes from one stage to another.

Service's main deficiency is his lack of a strong systemic viewpoint, which creates an artificial and unnecessary dichotomy between ecological variables on the one hand and societal variables on the other, thus considerably reducing the explanatory and processual utility of his model. For example, he emphasizes conflict (i.e., warfare) as an important factor in the evolution of social organization, but he tends to regard warfare as a process as "superorganic" in nature, rather than an adaptive response to ecological problems that may have evolutionary significance. Little attention is given to details of ecological variation that may affect processes or rates of change, or limit evolutionary potential.

Although Fried has modified Service's model in several important ways, he has retained the same descriptive and typological orientation. Because he is primarily concerned with the evolution of political organization, Fried pays less attention than does Service to details of social structure. The interplay among basic (i.e., capital) resources, wealth, power, and political authority is the central theme of his model. Ecological considerations are appropriate to, even implicit in, this line of thought but are still mainly expressed in terms of their regulations of demographic variables, although environmental variability is singled out as a fundamental precondition for the emergence of ranked political organization. Again there is little appreciation of systemic interrelationships, except on a very high level, and hence few insights into processual changes from one organizational level to the next.

To the extent that either of these authors identifies any kind of "prime mover" in general cultural evolution (and Service, for one, has argued vehemently against it [1971]), it is population growth. Increased population size and density stimulates new, essential, unilineal evolutionary transformations. Earlier unilinealists like Leslie White (1949) emphasized major transformations of the utilization of energy as a prime mover. Although many archeologists have singled out population growth as a prime mover, it has become increasingly clear that variability in observed processes of cultural evolution cannot be consistently related to demographic variables, even though Service's and Fried's main point is seen as valid in the general sense that *when* increases in population growth and density *do* occur (for whatever reasons), old organizational structures eventually prove inadequate and new ones must emerge.

RESEARCH STRATEGY—
THE MULTILINEAL PARADIGM

The major criticism of unilineal typologies has been that although they were useful in elucidating the general process of cultural evolution (the use for which they were designed), they could hardly be expected to explain the great variety of human social behavior with each of the stages. Steward, in his *Theory of Culture Change* (1955), a compendium of earlier papers combined with new ones, tried to resolve the dilemma by proposing a series of sociocultural types intermediate between the general stages proposed by the unilinealists and the highly specific societies described by ethnographers. He further used these intermediate categories to define divergent lines of sociocultural evolution—hence his use of the term *multilineal evolution*.

For example, he defined a number of subtypes of societies that Service would group into a single category of bands; he named them family band, patrilineal band (Service's patrilocal band), and composite band. On the basis of data presented in *Man the Hunter* (Lee and Devore 1968), one could add others: the flexible membership band and the composite sedentary band. We will discuss the adaptive process that produced some of this variety at a later point; here we are concerned only with the scheme as typology. The essential point is that Steward is not talking about specific societies but *types* of societies, and all of them could be included in Service's more broadly defined band society. In actual fact Service denied the aboriginal variety of band societies, considered all bands as patrilocal, and explained all variation as the product of contact with state-level societies. His argument is essentially irrelevant to our discussion here, since we are not concerned with the validity of types but rather the taxonomic relationship between them. If we accept as valid the variety suggested by Steward and the *Man the Hunter* symposium, we could redefine the unilineal type as having the following traits: society consisting of autonomous local groups, with the maximum aggregation having a population less than a few hundred and generally below 100, integrated by coresidential ties, lacking in sodality organization, and having egalitarian patterns of leadership.

Service's tribal type, using a multilineal approach, could be divided into a number of subtypes such as segmentary lineage tribes, dispersed unilineal descent tribes, territorial clan tribes, and age–grade tribes depending on the specific kind of sodality or kin structure that is basic to the functioning of the tribe as a social entity.

With respect to chiefdoms, we have Service's ramage or conical clan type, which in fact was the model he originally assumed for all chiefdoms. Others would be patrilineal and matrilineal chiefdoms. One might also further subdivide these in terms of number of levels of ranking and scale of the redistribution network, as Sahlins (1958) has done.

States could be probably partitioned into a great number of subtypes; examples would be Murdock's African despotism, Wittfogel's (1957) oriental despotism, feudal states, imperial states, republican states etc.

A useful theoretical question is the possible diachronic relationship between particular subtypes of one unilineal stage and those of another. For example, do unilineal tribes always evolve into unilineal chiefdoms, segmentary lineage tribes into conical clan chiefdoms? One could, as Steward did in his study of early civilization (1949), formulate a series of multilineal lines based on this more specific typology.

The most significant value of Steward's work is, of course, his accommodation of ecological and evolutionary theory. The inclusion of the natural environment as a variable provides his approach with the expanded potential to explain cultural *variety*—in other words, specific rather than general cultural evolution—and a strong systemic dimension. His multilinear approach is a direct outgrowth of this cultural ecology paradigm.

Steward's approach to cultural ecology is, as he points out, both a methodology and a theory. In the analysis of a specific ecosystem the methodology involves a series of successive steps: (a) the specification of what resources are used by the group; (b) the strategy of resource exploitation; (c) how the patterns of exploitation affect social interactions; (d) analysis of the relationship between social interaction and social organization; and (e) definition of the ideological correlates of social organization. Implicit in this methodology is the inescapable theoretical conclusion that when a group adapts to a new environment, the process of adaptation historically goes through these same steps. In other words, this is basically the same strategy as that of the unilinealist, but with a stronger and more rigorous materialistic dimension.

Steward uses the same basic method of the unilineal evolutionists— comparative ethnology—in this case comparative ecology. Basically what he attempts to show is that groups with similar generalized patterns of resource exploitation have similar kinds of institutions and ideologies and, if one examines this phenomenon diachronically, similar histories of adaptation.

In order to demonstrate this evolutionary process, one needs typologies of environments, exploitative strategies, social structures, and ideologies that lie between the broad taxonomic categories of the unilineal evolutionists and the very specific descriptions of these phenomena used in the analysis of specific ecosystems.

For example, in general unilineal terms the state, as we noted previously, is a type of society with such broad characteristics as legitimized use of force (usually expressed in codified legal systems, professional judiciary, police, and armed forces), social stratification, and extremely complex internal specialization and differentiation of subgroups.

Wittfogel (1957) has defined a more specific subtype, the despotic oriental state, which has a number of more specific characteristics, such as a weak or absent middle class; poorly developed institutions (other than the central administration itself) with access to economic or political power; state control, construction, and maintenance of such major economic resources as transportation networks, irrigation systems, and military architecture. In terms of process Wittfogel felt that this kind of state evolved in arid regions, where large-scale irrigation was necessary in order to reduce risk and sustain a growing population, and that its functioning required a professional managerial class.

Following the leads provided by the unilineal and multilineal evolutionists, we see three available alternate strategies to explain general social evolution and variation in social evolution.

First, one could use a basically unilineal approach in which all societies, environmental conditions permitting (and here we would exclude only very extreme conditions that limit population size and density), go through the same stages (e.g., Service's or Fried's). The prime mover in this scheme would be population growth and technological (actually energetic) revolutions, producing larger and denser populations, which expand their use of, and eventually put pressure upon, existing resources. This process produces competitive responses eventually leading to differential access to resources, occupational specialization, and centralized political power. In this model *variability* in evolution is seen primarily as one of *tempo*, rather than *kind*, with other environmental factors conditioning tempo (Figure 11.10).

A multilinear model would be one in which variables in the physical environment would direct cultural evolution into different trajectories and population growth would function primarily to condition the tempo of evolution (Figure 11.11).

The third strategy involves a combination of both unilineal and multilineal concepts and is the main theme of this chapter.

Our model, outlined in the following discussion, is essentially a multilineal one, although it utilizes the broad unilineal taxonomic categories. It could probably be used much more effectively if we had

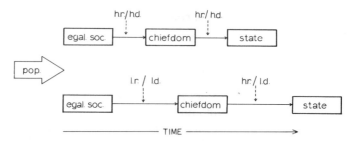

Figure 11.10. General unilineal model as proposed by Service (1962) Fried's (1967) model is essentially similar, except that he would include a stratified stage between chiefdoms and states. Population growth acts as a prime mover and is a constant. l = low; h = high; r = risk; d = diversity.

used multilineal categories of the kind suggested in our discussion of classic multilineal evolution; and we suggest this as a profitable line of research. In terms of causation our model includes a number of variables as factors in cultural evolution—and particularly their interrelationships. To some degree, therefore, our model is systemic rather than lineal. The fact that we ranked the factors gives the model a lineal quality, so that a purist might deny its systemic pretensions. In rejoinder, we would argue that any systemic model—if it is ever to have rigorous value—will have to include quantification of the variables; and if necessary, the result will be inequalities in the strength of the various factors. We have therefore labeled our model a systemic multilineal model.

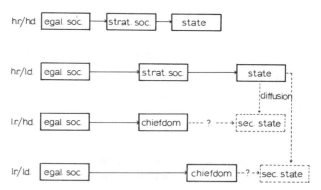

Figure 11.11. General multilineal model incorporating Steward's (1949, 1955) ecological paradigm with unilineal stages. Population growth is a constant. l = low; h = high; r = risk; d = diversity.

A SYSTEMIC MULTILINEAL MODEL

The model proposed here incorporates elements of both the unilinear and multilinear approaches. For the purposes of this presentation we utilize the gross "stages" of the unilineal evolutionists, although we recognize that a more sophisticated typology, as just discussed, has considerably greater potential in the search for an explanation of evolutionary variation. We discard, however, the notion of a single unilinear trajectory in which there is an invariable progression (insofar as evolution occurs) through the sequence of "stages"—which we emphasize rather as organizational types. Our model deals, essentially, with three kinds of variation: (*a*) variation in the *tempo of change* of evolutionary sequences; (*b*) variation in the *organizational level* reached by evolutionary sequences; and, most important, (*c*) variation in the *organizational forms* through which evolutionary sequences pass. Variation is seen as conditioned by distinctive sets of important environmental variables.

Environmental variables can be physical, biological, or cultural, and at this point we would like to reiterate those we see as most significant in cultural evolution or, to be more specific, in the acceleration or retardation of the processes of segregation and centralization. Among the primary physical variables are agricultural risk, diversity, size, and location. The most significant biological factors would be the nature and productivity of the food resource, population size, and population density. Although we are generally resistant toward explaining culture by cultural factors, the technology of a group must also be included as a major cultural factor. Productivity is a complex category that is really a composite of natural, biological, and cultural factors—that is, the size of the environment, soil and moisture conditions, and technology and organization of production.

Our model stresses several possible evolutionary trajectories, each conditioned by a distinctive permutation of environmental variables. Figure 11.12 illustrates these trajectories, and Figure 11.13 diagrams their articulation with the basic environmental variables, as well as with population growth and tempo of change. Since we are primarily concerned with the evolution of complex societies, the lowest evolutionary level considered is that of egalitarian tribal agriculturalists.

The diagramed model departs in several important respects, apart from its multilineal dimension, from the traditional unilineal trajectory proposed by Service and Fried. For one thing, our most important trajectory, (2), which leads to pristine states through a *stratified* level of organization, does not pass through a chiefdom, or ranked, level. We suggest,

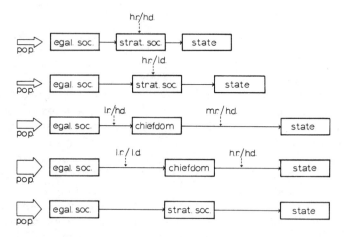

Figure 11.12. Multilineal systemic model with ecological variables controlling various evolutionary trajectories. Population growth is assumed throughout each sequence but is not itself necessarily directly deterministic of tempos or limits of evolution; its importance is greater in some trajectories than in others. *l* = low; *h* = high; *m* = medium; *r* = risk; *d* = diversity.

alternatively, that *most* chiefdoms develop out of egalitarian societies as *alternative* forms of hierarchical organization to the state, under different ecological circumstances (trajectory 1), although some chiefdoms may be transformed into states through processes of secondary development under influences from preexisting states. Moreover, stratified societies do not emerge from ranked societies.

We do feel that under extremely favorable (and unusual) circumstances, chiefdoms may develop into states as a result of indigenous evolutionary processes (trajectory 3). A final provisional trajectory is suggested (4), in which chiefdoms develop out of stratified societies (thus reversing Fried's sequence) as alternatives to the state. We have difficulty in operationalizing this trajectory from the Mesoamerican data described in the following section to explicate the model, although some possible applications are suggested.

It should be noted further that each of these trajectories is characterized by different tempos of transformation, and different population sizes and densities, in addition to different sequences of organizational forms. Indeed, there are important potential variations *within* trajectories if a wide comparative perspective is taken. For example, there would be great variation between the evolutionary histories of, say, central Mexico and lowland Mesopotamia, both of which we would include in trajectory 2.

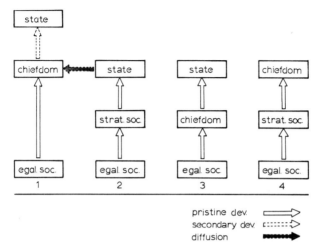

Fig 11.13. Evolutionary trajectories.

CASE EXAMPLES FROM MESOAMERICA

Trajectory 1 or 3—Highland Guatemala

Highland Guatemala is characterized as a low-risk, high-diversity type of environment.

1. *Degree of agricultural risk.* Rainfall over most of the highlands of Guatemala is abundant, although sharply seasonal, and crop losses from drought are a rare phenomenon.

At the time of the Spanish Conquest we estimate the population as between 500,000–800,000 people with a density of only 25–35 per km², a density within the capability of extensive agriculture. This is not to argue that there were no areas of high risk (the Motagua Valley, for example) or that denser population and more intensive agriculture did not occur in some valleys, during some time periods, but there is no evidence that such conditions were widespread at any time period for the highlands as a whole.

2. *Diversity.* The diversity is primarily in the form of nonagricultural resources. Most of the population clusters occur between 1200 and 1600 m, and the same balance of crops is maintained throughout the area. Some variation in productivity does occur if an area larger than a single valley is selected for analysis diversity—particularly in the timing of planting and harvest—is apparent.

The high nonsubsistence diversity would predictably act as a stimulus to local economic specialization, and this should occur early in the sequence of occupation in the region. In the case of the Valley of Guatemala we have evidence of local specialization in ceramics and obsidian processing by Middle Formative times.

3. *Productivity, size, and character of the environment.* Evidence from a number of agricultural studies reveals that the deep soils of the volcanic ash basin of the highlands have very high natural fertility even under intensive cropping. This would suggest considerably greater demographic capacity than the archeological data indicate and that the contemporary population is considerably larger and agriculture much more intensive than in the past. Although the region is topographically diverse, mountain barriers between valleys are minor, in many cases permitting cultivation up to the crests of the intervening ranges. The effect is therefore one of a large continuous, open environment, a condition that would act as a retardation factor in the evolution of complex societies.

The overall conditions would seem to be prime for the relatively rapid evolution of a chiefdom type of society—more specifically the Polynesian kind—followed by little subsequent societal evolution. Joseph Michels (personal communication) and William T. Sanders (1974) argue that this was the case. Very elaborate tombs, including extensive offerings of exotic and local goods, accompanied by sacrificial victims and placed within monumental platforms of earth, appear by 200 B.C., after a preceding occupation of the valley by sedentary farmers around 800 B.C. Also evident is a widespread redistributive network in manufactured goods and raw materials focused on the center of Kaminaljuyu. Succeeding Classic and Post-Classic centers in the Valley of Guatemala and in highland Guatemala generally (one exception seems to be the Conquest period capital of the Quichean polity: Utatlán) seem to reflect little changes in institutions. There is some evidence of possible statelike political organization in the Valley of Guatemala during Middle and Late Classic time, accompanied by a substantial increase in population density (to perhaps 50–75 per km²) and shift to more intensive practices of agriculture. These events might also reflect Fried's secondary state formation, since the Middle Classic is also a period of intensive contact with Teotihuacán.

Trajectory 2—Highlands of Oaxaca

The highlands of Oaxaca contrast very sharply with the highlands of Guatemala. Both land masses are topographically complex, with numerous small valleys at comparable elevations. The Oaxaca valleys, however, are much more arid and occur as tiny oases in a mass of arid uncultivable mountains. The area is characterized by great heterogeneity both in agricultural productivity and other resources, and it is a high-risk environment, with topographical units of much smaller size than those of the Basin of Mexico. The Valley of Oaxaca, the largest topographical unit, is only about one-quarter the size of the Basin of Mexico.

1. *Degree of agricultural risk.* Annual rainfall in the Valley of Oaxaca is comparable to the central and northern portions of the Basin of Mexico. Rainfall effectivity in terms of absolute values of annual precipitation is even less because of the lower elevation (1500–1600 m) and thus the higher evaporation rate. The absence of frost, however, provides some flexibility in planting regions—at least in those areas where natural soil humidity is high, such as riverine terraces or where springs provide water for irrigation. Double cropping is also possible on such lands.

2. *Heterogeneity.* The heterogeneity of the Valley of Oaxaca in terms of agricultural potential is generally comparable to, although perhaps somewhat less than, that of the Basin of Mexico. It should be pointed out, however, that it is a much smaller area. If we included adjacent areas to embrace a total region of comparable size, then the heterogeneity in rainfall, frost pattern, and soil fertility would probably exceed that of the basin. Added to this is the same kind of geologic and topographical complexity that would produce the same kind of localization of key nonagricultural resources.

3. *Productivity, size, and character.* As noted, the topographical and meteorological conditions in Oaxaca create a pattern of scores of small pockets of population, each of high density, but with the isolation of each creating a relatively low overall density. The total area of the watershed of the largest, the Valley of Oaxaca, is approximately 2500 km². Theoretically the small size and high circumscription should result in a much faster rate of evolution during the early phases, as compared with the Central Plateau, but cities and political systems should ultimately stabilize a less impressive level in terms of size and complexity of organization.

With respect to productivity, one could make generalizations approximately comparable with those concerning the Basin of Mexico. The soils are generally poorer in Oaxaca because they derive from much older geologic formations than in the volcanic basins of highland Guatemala and central Mexico, but recent studies demonstrate that they are capable of intensive cultivation with a minimal use of fertilizers. The various types of irrigation seem to have even more striking effects on differential productivity than in the Basin of Mexico. Although the topographical unit is smaller than the basin, the percentage of cultivable land is higher. On the other hand, the productivity of much of the more marginal land seems lower. This would suggest that the localized areas of prime quality land were extremely critical in the evolution of the more complex kinds of sociopolitical systems.

In the case of the Valley of Oaxaca, the environmental conditions would suggest a history of rapid evolution of the Basin of Mexico type, and this is precisely what archeologists record.

Sedentary farmers were living there about the time they occupied the Basin of Mexico. By 1000–800 B.C. evidence of site differentiation between center and dependent village is present. By 600 B.C. a large town emerges at Monte Albán. This political process is accompanied by population growth and rapid expansion of intensive techniques of agriculture, including hydraulic agriculture. Monte Albán became a major urban and political center by the time of Christ. One major difference, aside from the tempo of evolution, emerges when this area is contrasted with the Basin of Mexico. Teotihuacán, in terms of population, level of urban development, and extensiveness of its political and commercial ties far outranked Monte Albán, a contrast that continues into the Post-Classic period in the respective areas. These differences surely relate to the relative sizes and population capacity of the two respective areas.

Trajectory 2—The Basin of Mexico

The Basin of Mexico is characterized as a high-risk, high-diversity environment.

1. *Degree of agricultural risk.* The basin is a large (8000 km^2) topographical unit defined by masses of agriculturally unproductive mountainous terrain and located 2240 m above sea level. It is characterized as a high-risk area due to its highly variable and relatively low rainfall (varying from 450 to 1200 m according to local stations) and the presence of winter frosts. The southwestern third of the basin has higher rainfall values and may be characterized as a low- to medium-risk area. The central and northeastern two-thirds are generally high-risk areas, although the risk can be ameliorated by the use of localized springs for irrigation. The effect of this use would be the creation of a series of physically isolated clusters of low-risk niches within a generally high-risk environment.

2. *Diversity.* The considerable variability in rainfall and a pattern of fall frosts, affected even by minor topographical features, produce major effects on crop productivity. Intermediate elevations have the least frost problem, a situation that is even more favorable in the better watered portions of the basin; at higher elevations and on the flat plains the frost

problem is much more severe. Rainfall and frosts also tend to be highly variable even over short distances within the same sector and elevation band. All of this results in considerable diversity in crop success, yield, and scheduling. Besides those factors that affect agriculture, the presence of both saltwater and freshwater lakes adds another dimension to the diversity of the area, providing such resources as aquatic plants, fauna, and salt. Because of a very complex geologic history, a number of other basic resources, such as basalt, quartz, building stone, lime, and obsidian, tend to be highly localized. Topographical factors produce diversity in wild plant resources and soils for adobe and ceramic manufacture. If we expand our geographic region somewhat to include the adjacent area of the state of Morelos (where population is concentrated in the 1200–1600-m band), then an entirely new dimension to the heterogeneity is added. Resources found there but not obtainable in the basin itself include paper, cotton, tropical fruits, copal incense, a little cacao, tropical root crops, and honey. Added to this is the fact that since Morelos is a frost-free area with abundant irrigation resources, basic crops like maize can be produced in the winter season.

3. *Size and productivity of the environment.* Because of the basin's larger size one would expect a slower rate of sociopolitical evolution than was the case in the small mountain valleys of Oaxaca. But its large size, given the time for infilling, should ultimately permit larger populations and the evolution of larger, more complex political systems and urban centers than developed in the Valley of Oaxaca.

With respect to productivity the situation is extremely complex. Because of the risk problem only a small percentage of the basin is favorable for extensive agriculture—possibly no more than 20–30%. This figure could be doubled with the introduction of such intensive techniques as terracing, spring irrigation, floodwater irrigation, and drainage agriculture. Not only is the cultivable area considerably increased by these methods, but crop yields per planted area are strikingly improved—in part by the reduction of crop losses in bad years, in part because with hydraulic techniques even the input–output ratio is improved. Without such techniques it is doubtful if sufficient surplus could be generated to support more than a chiefdom level of organization, and the evolution of large states and cities is clearly and functionally correlated with the use of such methods of intensive cultivation. An added dimension to the productivity of the basin is the juxtaposition of two ecological zones with the zone of cultivation: the high ranges unusable for agriculture and the lakes, only partially used for cultivation, both being major sources for animal proteins.

The basin was occupied somewhat earlier than the highlands of Guatemala by a sedentary food-producing population, about 1400–1200 B.C. The southern region was the first settled and was consistently the densest settled region throughout the long period of time from 1400 to 200 B.C.—(the Early, Middle, to Late Formative phases). The earliest examples of hierarchical societies occur there, culminating in the site of Cuicuilco. Lacking at Cuicuilco, however, are the sumptuous tombs so diagnostic of the Valley of Guatemala. What is evident is site stratification, with a dichotomy between center and dependent settlement.

By 200 B.C. the central part of the basin, a high-risk area, had drawn abreast of the south in terms of population density and political evolution. There is evidence that this development was associated with intensification of agriculture, including hydraulic agriculture.

Then between 100 B.C. and A.D. 100 the situation changed dramatically. A city of 60,000 people emerged at Teotihuacán, one of the most difficult environments in the basin, but one with major resources for hydraulic agriculture. By A.D. 200 the evidence for a highly urban center with state institutions and political control of the entire basin is conclusive. During the period from A.D. 300 to 600, this center created a commercial–political empire over much of Mesoamerica. We see the overall process in this area as one of evolution from egalitarian to stratified society to state, in which the development during the first phase was at a relatively moderate pace, whereas the following one was very rapid.

Trajectory 1—The Olmec

As another example of trajectory 1 we propose the Gulf Coast Olmec of Tabasco and Veracruz. Ecological factors allowed rapid development to impressive chiefdoms but frustrated further evolution of state-type organization. These factors are summarized as follows:

1. *Degree of agricultural risk.* Risk is virtually nonexistent, either on a yearly or a long-term basis, with the possible exception of floods. Rainfall is both abundant and predictable, and there is no problem with frosts, as there is in the highlands. Moreover, wild food resources, particularly riverine and lagoon animal products, are comparatively plentiful as supplements to agricultural products. For these reasons we expect that the Olmec heartland was very attractive to early agriculturalists, and probably even to earlier hunting and gathering populations, and that initial population increases were rapid.

2. *Diversity.* The Olmec zone in general is characterized by low heterogeneity in terms of nonsubsistence resources. There would have

been little incentive for economic specialization or complex exchange systems. Such raw materials as were necessary for status differentiation were imported from elsewhere.

A similar homogeneity exists in terms of subsistence products. Those agricultural staples central to the Olmec economy, which we assume to have been based upon maize, could have been produced over the entire region, in which, moreover, cropping would have been seasonally synchronous.

Microenvironmental heterogeneity does exist when local agricultural productivity is considered. There is a rather striking productive differential between the rich, well-drained, alluvial levee lands and hinterland areas away from major streams, both in yield and input–output ratios. Not only are yields much greater in the former zones, but these zones are well situated with regard to nonagricultural subsistence resources.

3. *Productivity.* The Olmec undoubtedly practiced a variant of extensive, swidden agriculture. We believe this system to have been highly efficient, as measured by the ratio of energy expended to energy gained, so long as overall population was sufficiently low so that forest or bush–fallow systems could be maintained. Cropping of levee lands was intensive in terms of multicropping and continual use, but even more efficient. Yields per unit of cultivable land were high and, in the case of levee lands, were striking. Furthermore, such lands did not require the labor of clearing and weeding, and therefore the energetic efficiency was very high.

Given an extensive forest or bush–fallow system, overall yields for any large region would have been respectable, but certainly not up to highland standards of intensive cultivation. We envision broad areas of extensive cultivation, with widely separated and restricted, but extremely productive, riverine niches.

4. *Size and character of environment.* The Olmec heartland is a very extensive agricultural niche far surpassing in size any semiarid highland valley. An undetermined portion of the lowland environment is, however, too poorly drained for cultivation. There are no important topographical bounding features, such as mountain ranges. This does not mean, however, that there were not discontinuities in population size and density. Instead of random population scatter in the absence of topographical controls, there was a patchwork pattern of vacant, poorly drained land, higher ground supporting swidden farmers, and dense population concentrations in a few highly favorable riverine zones.

On the basis of the ecological conditions just described, we would postulate a developmental sequence as follows: Initially, the Olmec heartland was an early focus of relatively dense population, perhaps on the hunter–gatherer level, and certainly on the level of egalitarian agriculturalists who were attracted by a low-risk environment. A problem in discussing the Olmec sequence is that we know virtually nothing about the period prior to ca. 1200 B.C. and hence cannot adequately assess the tempo of development. On the one hand, given early indications of agriculturalists in the Maya lowlands at 2000 B.C. or even before, it seems likely that farming populations could have colonized the region at a very early date. On the other hand, given the favorable ecological circumstances, the tempo of sociocultural evolution was very rapid, and early colonization need not necessarily be postulated.

In any case, available cultivable land was probably occupied by ca. 1500 B.C. at the latest, with initial settlements in the productive riverine niches. Population growth was rapid, especially in the latter areas, with overall densities low but with high concentrations near the levee lands. Most Olmec farmers, within limits of available land and seasonal constraints, could produce small per-capita surpluses, whereas those settled on levee lands could produce large surpluses.

By ca. 1200–800 B.C. large political units had formed, centered on those restricted zones of highest population concentration and productivity. We feel that available archeological data on the Olmec indicate that these were chiefdoms. Centers are small but impressive, dominated by ceremonial architecture, and they seem to have had few residents—all consistent with the functions of ceremonial–organizational center and chiefly household. Each center was supported by surpluses derived from adjacent high productivity zones, and drawn from a much wider scatter of hinterland farming populations. By comparison with the highlands, populations were low in density and small in absolute size, but they produced respectable surpluses to support an impressive hierarchical structure, fund its conspicuous displays of imported sumptuary items, produce monumental public architecture, and provide for elaborate burials.

Although we have characterized Olmec political units as chiefdoms, they depart from the classical Polynesian chiefdom model in that low environmental heterogeneity largely negated the redistributive functions so important in Polynesia. Olmec development would probably have been even more rapid had such redistribution been necessary. We see stresses such as competition as more important than redistribution in selecting for hierarchical organization.

By the Middle Pre-Classic populations had reached their height, and the maximum limits of Olmec development were realized. The small Olmec chiefdoms lacked the organizational capacity or economic motivation for successful expansion of political–military authority. Productive capacity had been reached, and the possibilities of intensification, always limited in tropical environments, were insufficient to provide new impetus for population growth or new managerial functions for the hierarchical superstructures. Developments elsewhere in Mesoamerica eventually eclipsed the precocious Olmec development, which was relegated to marginal importance. It is conceivable that the Olmec system could have remained integrated longer, or even experienced further development of a secondary nature, had neighboring societies already passed the threshold of the state. In a sense the precocity of Olmec development, which allowed a very early cultural climax, worked against this possibility.

Trajectory 1 or 3—The Lowland Maya

Cultural evolution in the Maya lowlands produced a highly sophisticated and extremely widespread society under a set of ecological conditions very different from those found in the highlands of Mesoamerica. Although the lowlands have received a great deal of archeological attention, there is still no consensus among archeologists concerning the nature of the Maya evolutionary sequence. Briefly, there are three main positions. Some feel that the Maya never reached the state level but were arrested at the level of advancec chiefdoms. Those who maintain that the Maya did achieve the state differ in that some see this process as a secondary development, whereas others see it as pristine.

We reject the first interpretation of Maya society because we feel that available archeological evidence suggests patterns of state-type organization at least by Late Classic times (after A.D. 600) in some areas. Our own position is that the Maya did achieve the state as a result of internal cultural evolution. Though undoubted contacts with other Mesoamerican societies did occur, they did not fundamentally determine the transformation to the state. Nevertheless this question remains far from settled, and consequently we apply the Maya developmental sequence to both trajectories 1 and 3.

Although we use the term *Maya society*, we recognize that political or economic integration never was realized to any significant extent. Hence we conceive of a mosaic of lowland zones, each with its own local evolutionary history partly determined by interaction within and without the wider Maya culture sphere. We do not believe that evolution progressed at the same rate everywhere, or that all Maya societies necessarily developed into full-fledged states. Our analysis is mainly directed toward the relatively precocious region of the northeastern Petén, where Maya society achieved its most mature form.

The Maya lowlands are seen as having the following ecological characteristics:

1. *Degree of agricultural risk.* As with the Gulf Coast Olmec, risk is very low, with the exception of northwestern Yucatán. Seasonal rainfall is abundant and predictable, as compared with the highlands, and there are no frosts.

2. *Diversity.* The Maya lowlands exhibit low diversity in nonsubsistence products, although commodities such as salt and igneous stone are localized and were traded rather widely.

Although the lowlands are frequently characterized as ecologically homogeneous, significant variations affecting agricultural productivity exist on both a regional and local basis. Regionally, rainfall is much more abundant, and to some extent more predictable, in the southern zone than in northern Yucatán. Some local regions—particularly the northeastern Petén—possess unusually high concentrations of optimally cultivable land. Even within local zones the productive potential of the landscape varies significantly in terms of soil types; most favorable soils are found on well-drained hillsides. In the northeastern Petén we calculate the percentage of optimal land at 40%.

A few riverine and lacustrine niches exist that not only are highly productive but provide access to important wild resources and routes of communication and transportation. Such niches were among the earliest settled.

3. *Productivity.* Even with the use of primitive technology, favorable soils in the Maya lowlands are capable of high yields when bush or forest fallow swidden systems are used. We assume that maize was the dominant cultigen in prehistoric times. Within the limits of available labor and seasonal constraints, Maya farmers could easily provide for the subsistence of their families and produce modest surpluses (ca. 20%).

The Classic Maya swidden system was highly efficient. We calculate an energy input–output gain ratio on the order of 1 : 14. Within local microenvironmental zones there would have been significant variability in energetic efficiency but not on the same scale as between the riverine–hinterland niches in the Gulf Coast.

4. *Size and character of environment.* The Maya lowlands comprise the largest single agricultural niche in Mesoamerica, covering some 250,000 km². There are no strong topographical controls that delimit or isolate local segments. It is essentially a continuous niche, with no impediments to population movement or transmission of cultural information,

nor is there any natural bounding of sociopolitical or socioeconomic units, as there is in the Basin of Mexico. As was the case for the Gulf Coast, such units emerged as population gravitated to, and increased most rapidly in, those zones of highest agricultural potential, such as the northeastern Petén.

The Maya lowlands were probably occupied by agricultural populations at least as early as 2000 B.C., if not well before this date. Initial settlement was along riverine niches (and perhaps coastal areas), and these funneled people at an early date into the northeastern Petén, where we assume the highest-quality lands were first to be occupied. Population growth was rapid, given the productive resource base, but increments of local population could be absorbed for a long time by the continuous agricultural frontier available. There was initially no natural risk incentive for intensification, no striking variations in productivity, and consequently no early economic stratification such as postulated for the basin of Mexico or Oaxaca.

A distinctive feature of the Maya developmental sequence is its slow rate of change in comparison with these highland nuclear areas. Assuming that some Maya groups achieved the state by A.D. 600, the process of state development required a *minimum* of 2600 years from the time of the first agricultural colonization, as opposed to ca. 1200 years for the Basin of Mexico. We feel that available evidence suggests emergent chiefdoms in core areas by ca. 400 B.C., with rapid development of numerous chiefdoms during the Late Pre-Classic (ca. 400 B.C.–A.D. 250). This evidence consists of the appearance of organizational centers of various sizes, characterized by monumental ceremonial architecture. None of these centers seems to have been highly nucleated demographically, which suggests that they were oriented around chiefly households supported by surrounding low-density populations of swidden agriculturalists. Centers are associated with sophisticated art forms, often hierarchical in nature, and sumptuary burials with luxury goods indicate well-developed ranking. As with the Olmec, we see the formation of Maya chiefdoms primarily as responses to competition engendered by demographic imbalances and continued population growth; we would regard the latter factor as a prime mover in the lowland sequence. The oft-cited redistributional functions of chiefdoms as a general stage of evolution were relatively unimportant. Had the Maya environment been highly heterogeneous, with corresponding pressures to develop such redistributive functions, the pace of development to the chiefdom stage would undoubtedly have been more rapid. Maya development was also retarded, to a certain extent permanently, by the lack of rigorous topographical bounding.

At this point we would normally expect that the limits of sociopolitical evolution to have been reached, given the large, continuous ecological
niche, low agricultural risk, and low diversity of the environment. But, as
previously noted, some Maya polities seem to have continued on to the
state level. Basically we see this further development as a response to an
extremely unusual productive potential—perhaps unmatched in other
tropical forest zones—which allowed populations to increase still further,
causing continued change in the lowland systems. Trajectory 3 now
comes into play.

Segments of the Maya landscape were naturally fertile enough to
support unusually dense swidden populations and could even support
some intensification of cultivation, without rapid degeneration. Intensification involved reduction in the fallow cycle, perhaps even continuous
cropping on some areas, so that local population densities of 100–200 per
km^2 were possible with little initial decrease in efficiency. Given these
densities, even small per-capita surpluses were sufficient to underwrite an
elaborate hierarchical superstructure. High fertility even under conditions of intensification is directly related, we feel, to the favorable soil
conditions of the Maya lowlands. Bedrock is high in carbonates, which
provided continued nutrients for plant growth and impeded degenerative
processes, such as laterization, that typify other tropical zones. Bedrock
was also porous, which facilitated drainage and preserved favorable soil
texture, and erosion was not an initially severe problem on moderate
slopes that rapidly recovered their vegetation.

We see competition related to population growth as an important
factor in the emergence of the Maya state. Economic stratification eventually appeared, but as a result of the *interrelationship* between high
population levels and microenvironmental variability in productivity.
Those elements of the population most favorably situated with regard to
optimally productive portions of the landscape initially dominated elite
status positions, and these positions became self-serving (e.g., through
conquest of new land in warfare) in that they *increased* economic stratification. Client–patron relationships were formed as population rose on
more marginal lands and productive efficiency declined. At this point the
Maya system(s) was in trouble as internal stress accumulated. But elite
dominance was buttressed, rather than destroyed because the centralized
political hierarchies exerted increasingly important system-serving
functions related to leadership in warfare, internal adjudication of disputes, and, more importantly, even more intensive forms of agriculture.
The latter include continuous cropping, a possible higher dependence on
root crops, arboriculture, terracing, and the construction of raised field
systems in otherwise uncultivable swamps.

Population reached its height in Late Classic times, with maximum densities in favored areas of 400–500 per km², and the final, mature expression of Maya civilization emerged against the backdrop of a deteriorating environment and ever stronger demands of a burgeoning elite class. Even the Maya zone could not maintain this demographic burden. Soil fertility declined and erosion increased as cropping became more intensive and natural vegetation was eliminated. Unforutnately for the Maya, further intensification, such as extensive irrigation, was precluded by topographical and hydrographic conditions and would, in any case, have been unsuited, given tropical soil conditions and the available staple crops. Some forms of very intensive cultivation, such as raised fields, were attempted, but their potential was too limited in scope and distribution to overcome the ecological stresses in the system.

Maya states not only went through a different evolutionary trajectory at a slower rate than highland ones, but their configurations were highly distinctive. Even the largest of Maya states probably never exceeded a total population size of ca. 70,000 people. Partly because of the nature of the subsistence system, no high degree of nucleation was necessary or possible. Unlike Teotihuacán, Maya centers such as Tikal did not dominate restricted zones of extraordinarily high productivity created by intensive cultivation systems. Lacking a concentration of subsistence resources and population, the centers were not capable of supporting dense urban populations of non–food producers. They had little market potential, in demographic terms, and hence did not attract craftsmen, as Teotihuacán, and later Tenochtitlán, obviously did; complex market institutions never seem to have developed. In any case, the low heterogeneity in nonsubsistence resources would have negated the value of such institutions. Because of the small sustaining populations (by highland standards) and small per-capita surpluses, the Maya elite and specialist classes formed only a small percentage of the total population.

The same factors that lead to slow rates of growth also precluded the kind of political, economic, and military expansion so obvious for highland states. There was no strong economic impetus for establishing far-flung, integrated economic networks and no real adaptive necessity for symbiotic relationships. No one lowland region, moreover, possessed such a striking demographic advantage that differential expansion was possible. Given the small size and fragile organization of the dominant elite, integration of new territory and new populations on a large scale would have been structurally impossible. Existing archeological evidence suggests that such attempts were ephemeral and rather late. The Maya sociopolitical and socioeconomic systems, even in their mature forms, remained highly balkanized.

We have presented the Maya sequence as an example of trajectory 3, which corresponds to Service's original unilineal progression, and this is the interpretation that seems most workable to us. There remains the interpretation that some Maya centers achieved the state level only because of contacts with pristine states already present elsewhere in Mesoamerica. That the Maya participated in the wider Mesoamerican interaction sphere is undeniable. Teotihuacán contacts are apparent in terminal Pre-Classic times and are intense at sites like Tikal during the fifth century A.D. These contacts, undoubtedly of both a political and economic nature, impinge on the Maya systems during their most dynamic stage—the Early Classic—and could be seen as deterministic of subsequent state development. In other words, those Maya societies that evolved into states could be forced into trajectory 1.

In our opinion this interpretation is unnecessary. Given the ecological potential just described, the Maya were perfectly capable of pristine development. If highland influences were so essential, the florescence of Maya society in the Late Classic, after the breakdown of the Teotihuacán horizon, is difficult to explain. That highland contacts may have *accelerated* the pace of development is undeniable, but they did not determine ultimate levels of sociopolitical evolution.

We are unable to operationalize trajectory 4 for Mesoamerica. The problem partly lies in the classical conception of Polynesian chiefdoms, in which chiefdoms are seen as egalitarian in terms of access to productive capital resources. It is difficult to conceive how the chiefdom model could be accommodated to economic stratification. In a sense this is a deficiency of the chiefdom model itself in its classical form. We believe that, in the Old World, pastoral chiefdoms probably emerged through a trajectory 4 evolutionary sequence, since wealth in terms of capital resources characterizes highly ranked leaders in many of these societies, as opposed to Polynesian chiefdoms. We suggest that the same may be true of societies that practice a dual economy in which agricultural and cattle pastoralism are of equal importance—for example, many African and Iron Age European societies.

Two implications of our own evolutionary model, both inherent in the analysis of Mesoamerican cultural evolution just provided, deserve some general comments at this point.

First of all, the pristine-versus-secondary distinction made by Fried comes into play, but it now should be more clear why and how it does so. Very different tempos of cultural evolution within a culture area will inevitably result in contacts between two local developing sequences *whether or not* both are capable of complex cultural development in their own right. Teotihuacán reached the state level quickly and early and exerted widespread influence on other Mesoamerican societies, such as the lowland Maya. It is correct to expect Teotihuacán influence in the Maya sequence, but it is incorrect to assume that this influence is necessarily deterministic in any sense. Such an assumption must be borne out by detailed analysis of the ecological–demographic variables indigenous to a developing cultural system that condition evolutionary processes and mechanisms. In the Maya case the assumption is *not* borne out, since a consideration of those variables indicates that Maya societies were capable of autonomous evolution to the state level. For Kaminaljuyu, on the other hand, the analysis suggests that contacts with already advanced societies elsewhere in Mesoamerica were deterministic of further evolutionary advances.

Another important point is that systemic change itself may condition ecological variables. For example, high agricultural risk may be inherent in the environment as a result of natural constraints. On the other hand, population growth in an environment generally free from risk may ultimately produce risk by causing increased dependence upon more limited, more marginal, more degraded resources. This would be the case for the mature stage of Maya evolution. Similarly, population growth may stimulate colonization of new productive areas where different subsistence resources are produced, consequently creating an agricultural heterogeneity not previously present. The same process may promote specialization in nonsubsistence resources, providing that raw materials are highly localized. Again heterogeneity is promoted. Both of these processes are evident in the Basin of Mexico.

SUMMARY AND CONCLUSIONS

In conclusion, our model of societal evolution has the advantage of explaining much more of the variety in cultural evolution than the older unilineal models. In essence it is a multilineal paradigm comparable to Steward's but goes further in generalization and ranking of the variables that produce culture change. Finally, the model has a systemic character in that the variables are mutual–causal in nature; the fact that we rank the variables does not negate the systemic implications.

Our model assumes that population growth occurs, that rates of growth are constant, and that it is a necessary precondition of all evolutionary trajectories. What we are implying here is that all processes of complex cultural evolution are processes of *growth* as well. Population growth, however, produces variety only in the *tempo* of evolution—in other words, small geographic spaces ought to evolve faster than larger ones, other factors being equal. The carrying capacity of a region may act as a limiting factor in terms of how far evolutionary trajectories go, since there is a correlation between social complexity and population size.

The main factors that condition the variability of cultural evolution, we have observed, are risk, diversity, and productivity. Outlined in the following discussion are the various permutations of these factors along with their proposed evolutionary correlates.

I. *High-risk environments*. This type of region should be colonized by agricultural societies later than regions where risk is low, assuming choices are available. Although extensive techniques of land use may generally characterize initial phases of colonization, the stimulus to more intensive methods of low-risk cultivation is high and such techniques should appear early. Assuming that the relationship between population growth and agricultural systems is a mutual–causal rather than a linear one, population growth should be rapid once the area is colonized. Population distribution should also be uneven, reflecting adaptation to comparatively low-risk zones and zones available for intensification (e.g., frost-free areas, favorable hydrographic and soil conditions, etc.). Without the possibility of intensification population growth would be slow.

A. *Low diversity*. Examples of high-risk, low-diversity environments are probably confined to extensive deserts. Because of the critical variable of water, one would expect a strong stimulus toward economic stratification, but the low diversity would retard economic specialization. The overall evolutionary tempo would be rapid.

1. *Productivity type A*. Under these conditions this trajectory should be a rapid sustained growth from tribe to stratified society to small urban state, large urban state, and empire, assuming that the region is sufficiently large. During the early phase of colonization, the stimulus toward competition, segmentation, and centralization would be low, toward cooperation moderate; during the middle phase, stimulus to cooperation would be high, the other processes moderate, and during the final stage, the stimulus would be high for all four processes.

2. *Productivity type D*. This, in arid regions, is primarily a type characterized by initial high volumes in input–output, followed by a rapid, catastrophic decline due to salinization. Even in low-diversity environments there may be sufficient variety in terms of susceptibility of soils to salinization or in

human manipulation leading to different rates of salinization to raise the stimulus level of cooperation, competition, and centralization above the level of areas with productivity level A. All processes should be under very high stimulus by the later phases. The overall trajectory would be tribe to stratified society to small urban state and then to collapse or a shift out of the region.

B. *High diversity.* Geographic regions of this type are limited to tropical highland settings. The stimulus to both social stratification and economic specialization is very high under such conditions. Sociopolitical evolution generally would be expectably very rapid and probably faster than in the low-diversity high-risk environments.

1. *Productivity type A.* All examples of high-risk, high-diversity environments are generally of this productivity type. The trajectory should be one of sustained rapid growth from tribes to stratified societies to small urban states; evolution to large states would be retarded by the topographical fragmentation. Stimuli toward cooperation, competition, and centralization even during early phases of colonization would be at least moderate in intensity, for segregation it would be high. For the later phases, all processes would be under very high stimulus.

II. *Low-risk environments.* These environments would probably be colonized early by agricultural societies in cases where choices were available; intensive practices should appear later in the sequence. Population growth rates would probably be moderate to high.

A. *Low diversity.* The stimulus toward economic specialization and stratification is low except during the final phase of colonization. Overall cultural evolution would be slow, and population would tend to be evenly distributed during the middle and later phases of colonization. The classic examples of such environments are humid, continental regions with low relief and forest vegetation.

1. *Productivity type 1.* This would be a rare phomemon and when occuring, would be restricted to small sections of the general environment (i.e., levees, riverine floodplains). Such features would occur more commonly in a high-diversity subtype, however, but no environment is entirely homogeneous. The stimulus on the processes of centralization, competition, cooperation, and segregation would be

very low until the final phase of occupation, when population density would be high enough to produce considerable
stress.

2. *Productivity type 3.* This is probably a common mode in
low-risk, low-diversity environments, and agricultural intensification follows the classic Boserup (1965) model as the
direct product of sustained agricultural growth. Under the
conditions of productivity type 3, one would expect low stimulus of all four processes during the early phase, shifting to
moderate levels during the middle of the colonization process, ultimately reaching high values at the end. In situations
where mutual–causal deviation counteracting processes operate to regulate population growth, the trajectory would be
from tribes to chiefdoms and would stabilize at that level. If
populations continue to increase, there may be long-range
deleterious effects in the environment. The resulting trajectory would be tribe to chiefdom to state to collapse. One
argument is that this latter case only occurs under situations
where states have emerged in neighboring high-risk environments. Competition with or stimulus from these states results
in population policies that stimulate continuing population
growth, which ultimately cause the collapse of the state.

B. *High diversity.* This subtype may occur in forest riverine plains
where the presence of water is a central variable affecting productivity (e.g., water for wet rice agriculture in Southeast Asia). The
most common examples, however, are forested mountainous
tropical areas. The stimulus toward economic specialization
would be moderately high even during early phases of colonization, high in the later ones; the stimulas toward stratification
would be low during early phases, moderate during later ones.

1. *Productivity type A.* In contrast to low-diversity, low-risk
environments, productivity type A is commonplace because
of the younger geologic age of the topography and hence
higher natural soil fertility in tropical mountain regions. The
stimulus toward the processes of competition, cooperation,
and centralization would be low to moderate during the early
phases of settlement but would reach higher levels in later
phases. The process of segregation noted previously would
generally be higher because of the need of redistribution but
should stabilize at the chiefdom level. The overall trajectory
would be tribe to chiefdom, or tribe to chiefdom to secondary
state.

2. *Productivity type 2, 3, and 4*. Probably rare in this situation. A possible example of type 4 would be massive erosion. Some upland areas might have only low soil fertility and fall into productivity type 2 or even 3. The evolutionary trajectory could then go from tribe to chiefdom to secondary state to collapse.

We feel that the Mesoamerican evolutionary sequences discussed in this chapter conform more fully to, and are explained more satisfactorily by, our proposed model, which combines controlling ecological variables and multilineal trajectories of change with an overtly systemic evolutionary approach. If refined sufficiently, the model could be applied in a much more rigorous manner than has been done here to any specific sequence, or sequences, of evolution of complex societies. If we have violated the scientific criterion of simplicity as a measure of the sophistication of a model, it is because we feel that the evolution of complex cultural systems cannot be forced into any general, simplistic, unilineal framework.

REFERENCES

Adams, R. N.
　1975　*Energy and structure*. Austin, Tex.: Univ. of Texas Press.
Allan, William
　1965　*The African husbandman*. New York: Barnes and Noble.
Boserup, E.
　1965　*The condition of agricultural growth*. Chicago: Aldine.
Carneiro, Robert
　1970　A theory of the origin of the state. *Science 169*.
Flannery, Kent
　1972　The Cultural Evolution of Civilizations. *Annual Review of Ecology and Systematics 3*.
Fried, M.
　1967　*The evolution of political society:* An essay in political anthropology. New York: Random House.
Lee, R., and I. DeVore
　1968　*Man the hunter*. Chicago: Aldine.
Murdock, G. P.
　1959　*Africa: Its peoples and their culture history*. New York: McGraw-Hill.
Netting, Robert M.
　1972　Sacred power and centralization: Aspects of political adaptation in Africa. In *Population growth: Anthropological implication*, edited by Brian Spooner. Cambridge, Mass.: MIT Press.
Peebles, Christopher, and S. Kus
　1977　Some archaeological correlates of ranked societies. *American Antiquity 42* (3):421–448.

Sahlins, M. D.
  1958   *Social stratification in Polynesia*. Seattle, Wash.: Univ. of Washington Press.
Sanders, W. T.
  1974   Chiefdom to State: Political evolution at Kammoljinju, Guatemala. In *Recon-
          structing complex situations*, edited by C. Moore. Supplement to *The Bulletin of
          the American Schools of Oriental Research* No. 20 (Cambridge, Mass.)
Service, Elman
  1962   *Primitive social organization*. New York: Random House.
  1971   *Cultural evolutionism: Theory in practice*. New York: Holt, Rinehart and
          Winston.
  1975   *Origins of the state and civilization*. New York: Norton.
Steward, J.
  1938   *Basin-plateau Aboriginal sociopolitical groups*. Bulletin 120. Bureau of American
          Ethnology. Washington, D.C." U.S. Government Printing Office.
  1949   Cultural causality and law: A trial formulation of the development of early civiliza-
          tion. *American Anthropologist 51*.
  1955   *Theory of culture change*. Urbana, Ill.: Univ. of Illinois Press.
Taylor, Donna
  1975   Some locational aspects of middle range hierarchical societies. Ph.D. disserta-
          tion, City University of New York.
White, L.
  1949   *The science of culture*. New York: Grove Press.
Wittfogel, K.
  1957   *Oriental despotism*. New Haven, Conn.: Yale Univ. Press.

chapter 12

Environmental Perturbations and the Origin of the Andean State

WILLIAM H. ISBELL

Theories that account for the origins of pristine state government (Fried 1960, 1967; Service 1975) generally invoke transformations in systemic structure that established new, change-oriented, positive feedback loops within an existing sociocultural system. Demographic pressure within a circumscribed region (Carneiro 1970), class conflict (Diakanov 1968), irrigation (Sanders 1968; Wittfogel 1957), rising demand for critical resources available only at a great distance (Rathje 1971), social organizational changes, or a complex combination of these (Adams 1966) have all been considered primary sources of change that promoted still further changes.

The chapter examines a systemic model that has a built-in positive feedback loop selecting for more centralized and efficient decisions at the regional level. The intensity of selective pressures favoring complex decision-making mechanisms increases with the efficiency of past regional organizational decisions, and antecedent innovations such as class formation, irrigation agriculture, or social reorganization—all of which have been considered prime movers—need not be invoked. This model

303

Social Archeology:
Beyond Subsistence and Dating

will also be examined for its fit with data presently available concerning the rise of pristine state government in the prehistoric Central Andes, especially as revealed by the archeological record of the Ayacucho Valley.

Essential for constructing the model is a review of the concept of dynamic equilibrium, or balance between human population and environmental carrying capacity, which underlies many current ideas about culture stability and change. Anthropologists have conducted detailed studies of regional carrying capacity under systems of shifting cultivation. According to Brush (1975), the carrying capacity may be calculated by several formulae that require figures for average period of cultivation, average fallow period, average acreage needed per capita to provide average subsistence, and total land available. Naturally the resulting carrying capacity must be an average carrying capacity—a value that remains constant through time and has neither increases nor decreases unless one of the component values changes. This concept of average carrying capacity, in which population fluctuates around the steady carrying capacity, has been adopted by several archeologists (cf. Jochim 1976; Zubrow 1975).

I submit that if culture process is to be studied in terms of selective pressures operating upon a range of behavioral strategies (Binford 1972), carrying capacity cannot be treated as a constant or average value. Human populations do not adapt to the average carrying capacity of their environment but rather to a range of variation in production, and any model of cultural dynamics that ignores perturbations in production omits a major source of variation influencing cultural behavior. Succession, or evolution, in biotic communities not only involves increases in production and efficiency of energy flow, it also involves the development of complex biological responses and behavioral strategies, such as rhythmic dormancy, energy storage, symbiosis, or migration, that overcome differences in energy from one time to another. Furthermore, if unpredictable energy perturbations are reasonably frequent, complex organisms must maintain internal or external regulatory mechanisms that hold population well below the average carrying capacity. Slow-breeding species such as humans are poorly adapted to dramatic fluctuations in population and would soon become extinct if a population in equilibrium with a local average carrying capacity experienced demographic collapse with each severe local perturbation affecting energy production and demand (consider the 1977 drought in the West and intense cold in the Northeast of the United States, for example).

Human populations subsisting by hunting and gathering generally control expected energy variability by migration and keep population below the average carrying capacity by numerous strategies, including the definition of many edible resources as less desirable. Agricultural societies have a higher investment in production facilities and usually sacrifice mobility. Although population can be stabilized well below a mean carrying capacity by cosmologically defined ideals of community size and distribution, structural points of intracommunity and intercommunity conflict, food taboos, etc. (cf. Chagnon 1968; Goldman 1963; Reichel-Dolmatoff 1971; Siskind 1937a,b), it is clear that averaging strategies are required in order to overcome predictable energy variations as well as less expected perturbations.

Any ecosystem, including a human one, is self-regulating by virtue of its ability to adopt, and remain in, different states. In time, it will come to adopt the most stable state—that in which the number of specialized participating elements and individuals is most constant. The most stable state is one with the greatest diversity, or number of specialized elements that facilitate the most efficient use of available energy. However, systems exposed to energy fluctuations must be rugged and more expensive in terms of the ratio of energy to biomass. The number of specialized elements must be lower, and the intensity of interaction among specialized elements also lower (Ashby 1954, 1956; Leigh 1965; Margalef 1968; McArthur 1955). This means that for a human system to endure significant energy fluctuations, it must not develop efficient energy flow based on highly specialized roles. Rather, it must be composed of essentially redundant individuals whose numbers can be increased or decreased with minimal information loss to the system. Or, the human system must stabilize its population below the level of even severe perturbations.

Growth in the complexity and population of a human system must depend upon buffering the system from energy perturbations. Two kinds of organizational strategies are possible without affecting the actual production potential. Spatial averaging buffers the human system by expanding its resource base, or by combining several adjacent systems, so that energy from contrastive resources subject to different perturbations can be redistributed throughout the larger system. Temporal averaging involves redistribution of energy through time, storing and transferring surplus production of the past to future times of shortage.

It is important to observe that as the efficiency of energy usage increases through a larger number of more intensively interacting elements, the old mechanisms of population stabilization within the human system are interfered with. Population can be expected to increase to a new level, reflecting the increased organizational efficiency. Simultaneously the system becomes subject to the selective pressures of energy perturbations again. Small perturbations are easily handled, but unless major fluctuations can also be managed, selective forces become devastating. Simple systems tolerate variation in biomass, but population loss in a complex system also means organizational collapse. As efficient spatial and temporal averaging establishes a mean carrying capacity for a human system, population rises to approach the mean. Energy perturbations that stretch the capacity of the averaging organization will either depress the organizational and population level or select for progressively larger redistributional spheres and more extensive temporal averaging facilities, and only well-informed, centralized decision-making bodies would be able to guarantee the administrative efficiency required to support a dense population that approximates the mean carrying capacity of a large and variable region.

In this model, the demand for progressively more efficient energy administration selects for a progressively more centralized administrative body directing well-planned spatial and temporal energy-averaging activities. As organization increases within the human component of the system, population variation approaches a smooth line or curve around which energy levels fluctuate. This relationship between energy and population stands in sharp contrast to the models in which energy is assumed to be constant and population is modeled as fluctuating around the average carrying capacity. In the model proposed here, the population may remain relatively stable or follow a curved trajectory through time, depending on investment strategies, technological changes, or other factors. But in either case, strong selective pressures operate in favor of an administrative organization that guarantees minimal energy fluctuation and a smooth population curve. The synergistic process of population increase with improving energy stabilization through progressively more complex organizational structures selects for complex administration that can eventually achieve statehood.

ENERGY PERTURBATIONS AND THE ANDEAN ENVIRONMENT

Sixteenth-century chroniclers claimed that under the Inca regime, no one starved, but later historical records show that food shortages and hunger were commonplace (Murra 1956). Today subsistence farmers also complain of differential yields from year to year. Unfortunately this differential is difficult to measure, since published production statistics for Peru and Bolivia not only are scarce but also represent regional sums from numerous microenvironments. Regional sums reduce the magnitude of perturbations suffered by local economies by providing spatially averaged values.

Highland Andean agriculture depends on many factors that cannot be predicted with precision. Water is generally scarce, especially at lower elevations, where temperatures are warm, but higher fields mature more slowly because of the cool days and may be destroyed by early frosts. Dry years may leave even many irrigated fields parched, whereas wet years retard plant maturation because of the cool cloudy days and crops may rot or suffer frost damage. Hail can destroy plants, and snows at high altitude cover pastures, leaving llamas and alpacas to starve. Pests and diseases vary from year to year, and of course, social disruptions can interrupt the timing of subsistence activities.

The harshness of the Andean environment is ameliorated by its vast myriad of microzones (Tosi 1966). Responding to variation in altitude, exposure to sun, exposure to prevailing wind, slope angle, water resources, soil, and other factors, the mountainous highlands provide many niches with different energy resources. Conditions that damage one set of resources can be benign for others, and it is extremely unlikely that all or most of the products of a region would experience a similar year. With production activities carried out from a few hundred m above sea level to well over 4000 m, completely distinct regimes exist. Manioc, peanuts, achira, and other tropical crops constitute major subsistence items in low elevations. Maize, racacha, beans, tarwi, cactus, avocados, cherimoyas, and others are adapted to intermediate altitudes. High elevations support potatoes, ocas, ullucus, mashua, guinoa, llamas, alpacas, and other cold resistent species.

Variability in production, contrasting energy sources responsive to different environmental factors, and many easily stored products all favored development of complex administrative systems to stabilize prehistoric Central Andean populations.

ENERGY AVERAGING IN
THE INCA STATE

Much of the administrative structure for which the Inca Empire was so famed functioned to average energy production.

Spatial averaging is well documented in several highland ethnic administrative units controlled by the Inca. These pre-Inca polities were integrated into the state with relatively little internal reorganization. Murra (1972) shows that their economies were based upon the exploitation of diverse energy resources in contrasting microenvironments. The Lupaca kingdom included about 20,000 family units directed from Chuquitos, an administrative capital located about 3800 m above sea level on the shores of Lake Titicaca. However, Lupaca colonies exploited lands from sea level on the Pacific coast to the Amazonian Montaña of eastern Bolivia and included specialists in various kinds of agriculture, herding, and fishing (Murra 1968).

The Chupaychu were a much smaller polity of some 3000 family units, but the same economic structure is documented. Administered from Ichu, the seat of the Chupaychu chief, members of the polity exploited resources ranging from pastures at 4000 m altitude to tropical Amazonian crops along the eastern foot of the Andes (Murra 1972).

Centralized temporal averaging is less well documented at these subregional administrative levels. Historical documents suggest that Lupaca chiefs directed, or at least had access to, some specialized storage facilities, and Morris (1967) reports four storage units with a capacity of 30 m³ in the secondary Chupaychu settlement of Auquimarca.

Centralized control of temporal averaging facilities seems to have been developed at the state administrative level. Provincial Inca capitals were distributed along major highways through the four quarters of the state. Cieza de León (1945) commented on the extensive storage facilities attached to these centers, and archeological research at Huánuco Pampa has revealed 497 storehouses with a capacity of about 37,900 m³ (Morris 1967, 1972, 1974; Morris and Thompson 1970). These facilities were dedicated to storage of food, primarily to support the bureaucrats resident in the administrative capital as well as rotating populations of corvée laborers paying their state labor tax. However, in the event of famine, the stored produce could be redistributed to the populace (Rowe 1946). Maize from intermediate altitudes, and dehydrated tubers, or chuñu, from high elevations could be stored indefinitely in cool climates 4000 m above sea level and could be transported to areas where food shortages threatened population and organization.

Both spatial and temporal averaging facilities are apparent at the Inca administrative zenith of Cuzco. Garcilaso de la Vega (1945) claimed that the hinterland of the city consisted of church and state lands within 50 leagues of the capital. Even though the estimate may be inflated, a great range of microenvironments and resources were included. Paved roads with provisioned way stations linked Cuzco to its hinterland, and a large proportion of the estimated 100,000 buildings in the valley were for storage (Rowe 1967). State directed food redistribution to the residents of the capital took place every four days, and Pizarro (1944) stated that there was such an accumulation of goods in Cuzco that it seemed impossible for it ever to be used up. Sancho (1938) was equally startled by the diversity of stored items, which included not only food but every sort of manufactured good. By this policy the Inca buffered their population and administration, giving special attention to the top of the administrative structure, where disruption would be most drastic for a population approaching a mean carrying capacity established by carefully administered spatial and temporal averaging activities.

ENERGY AVERAGING AND
THE PRISTINE ANDEAN STATE

Examination of Inca period energy averaging suggests that the highly diversified Andean environment selected for spatial averaging institutions that initially could be managed by relatively simple decision-making structures. Larger regional averaging spheres would require more elaborate administration and would allow population to rise to a level where equilibrium could only be maintained by highly efficient spatial averaging. However, the close association between large-volume storage facilities with centralized control and state governmental institutions during Inca times suggests that in the Andes, efficient temporal averaging of energy developed along with state administrative institutions.

The interdependence of intermediate-elevation and high-altitude farmers was communicated in Inca ritual by the absolute necessity for both corn and llamas in order to carry out essential ceremonies. Furthermore, Duviols (1974) has demonstrated the existence of a fundamental structural dichotomy in Andean culture that opposes valley people, their religion and identity as original occupants, to the more pastoral people of high elevations, with their religion and identity as conquerors or intruders.

Transhumant migrations between higher and lower altitudes characterized the early hunting and gathering economies of central highlands Ayacucho until about 3000 B.C. From that time on, at least two specialized food procurement systems became apparent in the archeological record. One focused on valley agriculture at intermediate elevations, developing high-investment facilities such as irrigation and terracing while the population became sedentary. The other system involved pastoralism with seasonal migrations between the high pastures, where herding took place exclusively, and slightly lower elevations, where frost resistant crops were also cultivated (MacNiesh, Patterson, and Browman 1975). It is clear that some spatial averaging of energy was already going on between these systems and that this was at least partially responsible for population increases documented by an increasing number of settlements. However, following 1700 B.C. selective forces appear to have given significant advantages to more centralized administration of this interdependence. Intermediate elevation settlements in the Ayacucho Valley began to cluster around central settlements with ceremonial architecture. The greater frequency of high elevation herd animal bones at these centers shows that they were assuming authority over redistributional activities (MacNiesh, Patterson, and Browman 1975).

In the final centuries B.C., a new form of architectural enclosure appeared in the Ayacucho Valley in conjunction with an older ceremonial center (MacNiesh et al. 1975). This may be the earliest evidence for centrally administered temporal averaging facilities, and the architectural enclosures increase in frequency along with population gains through the first half of the first millennium A.D.

By A.D. 600 to 700 Ayacucho Valley settlements show distinct grouping around one large center. Several nonoverlapping community sizes, taken with locations and evidence for administration, demonstrates a level of functional specialization and administrative centralization properly associated with state government (Isbell and Schreiber, in press). The administrative capital has been identified as the huge site of Huari, on the eastern side of the valley.

Contemporary with state administration in Ayacucho, a number of planned rectangular enclosures were constructed throughout the valley as well as at strategic points far beyond Ayacucho. These centers appear to represent a qualitative transformation in the complexity and efficiency of both spatial and temporal averaging institutions (Isbell 1977; Isbell and Schreiber, in press). For example, Pikillaqta near Cuzco (Sanders 1973) appears to be a provincial administrative center for Huari, with functions similar to later Inca counterparts (Morris 1972, 1974; Morris and Thompson 1970). Pikillaqta contains barracks-like quarters appropriate for rotated corvée laborers, and 504 small, oval rooms that would have had a storage capacity of at least 40,000 m^3 (Sanders 1973).

Architectural enclosures similar to Pikillaqta were located near the northern extreme of Huari influence, and a number of such units have been reported near the old Huari administrative center (Isbell and Schreiber, in press). They demonstrate the simultaneous rise of Huari as a state capital and its centrally administered system for both spatial energy averaging among environments and temporal energy averaging in government-maintained central storage facilities.

SUMMARY AND CONCLUSION

Population growth in the prehistoric Central Andes—including the Ayacucho Valley—is still inadequately researched. However, preliminary data tend to confirm that stable population growth in the Ayacucho Valley was associated with progressively more elaborate solutions for energy averaging. Spatial averaging of energy among populations specialized in complementary microenvironments appears to be about as old as agricultural specialization itself. More efficient spatial averaging through centralization of decision making was associated with the rise of ceremonial centers in the second millennium B.C.

Public temporal energy-averaging facilities only appeared after the move toward centralized decision making in regional ceremonial centers. However, the selective advantage that such a strategy confirmed upon its practitioners resulted in rapid population gains and progressively more complex administrative structures until the emergence of state government by about A.D. 600.

The processes involved in this evolutionary sequence are all explainable in terms of the rules or laws that govern the internal regulation of ecosystems (Margalef 1968). Ecosystems will adopt the most stable state—the state in which diversity and integration within the system provide an efficient and constant flow of energy. More highly diversified economic strategies that require efficient administrative integration are selected for inasmuch as they afford greater stability. However, elimination of frequent energy fluctuations permits population to stabilize at a higher level and makes this denser population more dependent upon a constant energy supply. Selective pressures intensify as a consequence and can be expected either to depress a system to a significantly simpler organizational and population level or to impel it progressively toward a structure that efficiently administers energy over a large region and long time period, permitting population to approximate the mean environmental carrying capacity.

REFERENCES

Adams, Robert M.
    1966   *The evolution of urban society: Early Mesopotamia and prehispanic Mexico.* Chicago: Aldine.
Ashby, W. R.
    1954   *Design for a brain.* London: Chapman and Hall.
    1956   *An introduction to cybernetics.* London: Chapman and Hall.
Binford, Lewis R.
    1972   *An archaeological perspective.* New York: Seminar Press.
Brush, Stephen B.
    1975   The concept of carrying capacity for systems of shifting cultivation. *American Anthropologist* 77(4):799–811.
Carneiro, Robert L.
    1970   A theory of the origin of the state. *Science* 169(3947):733–738.

Chagnon, Napoleon A.
1968   *Yanomamo: The fierce people*. New York: Holt, Rinehart and Winston.
Cieza de León, Pedro de
1945   *La cronica del Peru* (1551). Buenos Aires: Colección Austral.
Diakonov, I. M. (editor)
1968   *Ancient Mesopotamia*. Moscow: Nauka Press.
Duviols, Pierre
1974   Huari y Llacuaz, agricultores y pastores: Un dualismo prehispánico de oposición y complementaridad. *Revista Del Museo Nacional* 39:133–191.
Fried, Morton H.
1960   On the evolution of social stratification and the state. In *Culture in history*, edited by S. Diamond. New York: Columbia Univ. Press.
1967   *The evolution of political society*. New York: Random House.
Garcilaso de la Vega (El Inca)
1945   *Commentarios reales de los Incas* (1609), edited by Angel Rosenblatt. Buenos Aires: Emecé Editores, S.A.
Goldman, Irving
1963   *The Cubeo*. Urbana, Ill.: Univ. of Illinois Press.
Isbell, William H.
1977   *The rural foundation for urbanism: Economic and stylistic interaction between rural and urban communities in eighth-century Peru*. Urbana, Ill.: Univ. of Illinois Press.
Isbell, William H., and K. J. Schreiber
in press Was Huari a state? *American Antiquity*.
Jochim, Michael A.
1976   *Hunter–gatherer subsistence and settlement: A predictive model*. New York: Academic Press.
Leigh, E. G.
1965   On the relation between the productivity, biomass, diversity, and stability of a community. *Proceedings of the National Academy of Science* 53:777–783.
MacNeish, R. S., T. Patterson, and D. Browman
1975   The central Peruvian prehistoric interaction sphere. Andover, Mass.: Robert S. Peabody Foundation for Archaeology, Phillips Academy.
Margalef, Ramon
1968   *Perspectives in ecological theory*. Chicago: Univ. of Chicago Press.
McArthur, R. H.
1955   Fluctuations of animal populations, and a measure of community stability. *Ecology* 36:533–536.
Morris, Craig
1967   Storage in Tawantinsuyu. Ph.D. dissertation, Univ. of Chicago.
1972   State settlements in Tawantinsuyu: A strategy of compulsory urbanism. In *Contemporary archaeology*, edited by M. P. Leone. Carbondale, Ill.: Southern Illinois Univ. Press. Pp. 393–401.
1974   Reconstructing patterns of non-agricultural production in the Inca economy: Archaeology and documents in institutional analysis. In *Reconstructing complex societies*, edited by C. B. Moore. *Supplement to the Bulletin of the American Schools of Oriental Research* No. 20:49–60.
Morris, Craig, and Donald Thompson
1970   Huanuco Viejo: An Inca administrative center. *American Antiquity* 35(3):344–362.

Murra, John V.
1956   The economic organization of the Inca state. Ph.D. dissertation, Univ. of Chicago.
1968   An Aymará kingdom in 1567. *Ethnohistory* 15:115-151.
1972   El control vertical de un Máximo de pisos ecológicos en la economía de las sociedades andinas. In *Visita de la provincia de Leon de Huánuco en 1562* (Vol. 2) by Iñigo Ortiz de Zuñiga. Huanuco, Peru: Universidad Nacional Hermilio Valdizan. Pp. 427-476.

Pizarro, Pedro
1944   *Relación del descubrimiento y conquista de los renos del Perú y del gobierno y orden que los naturales tenían* . . . (1571). Buenos Aires: Editorial Futuro.

Rathje, William L.
1971   The origin and development of lowland classic Maya civilization. *American Antiquity* 36(3):275-285.

Reichel-Dolmatoff, Gerardo
1971   *Amazonian cosmos: The sexual and religious symbolism of the Tukano Indians*. Chicago: Univ. of Chicago Press.

Rowe, John
1946   Inca culture at the time of the Spanish conquest. In *Handbook of South American Indians* (Vol. 2), *The Andean civilizations*, edited by J. H. Steward. Washington, D. C.: Smithsonian Institution.
1967   What kind of a settlement was Inca Cuzco? *Nawpa Pacha* No. 5: 59-76.

Sancho de la Hoz, Pedro
1938   Relación para S.M. de lo sucedido en la conquista y pacificación de estas provincias de la Nueva Castilla y de la calidad de la tierra . . . (1534). *Biblioteca de Cultura Peruana*, primera serie No. 2: 117-185. Paris: Desclée, De Brouwer.

Sanders, William T.
1968   Hydraulic agriculture, economic symbiosis, and the evolution of states in central Mexico. In *Anthropological archeology in the Americas*, edited by B. Meggers. Washington, D. C.: Anthropological Society of Washington.
1973   The significance of Pikillakta in Andean culture history. *Occasional Papers in Anthropology* No. 8. Department of Anthropology, Pennsylvania State University.

Service, Elman R.
1975   *Origins of the state and civilization*. New York: W. W. Norton.

Siskind, Janet
1973a   Tropical forest hunters and the economy of sex. In *Peoples and cultures of native South America*, edited by D. R. Gross. Garden City, N. Y.: Doubleday.
1973b   *To hunt in the morning*. New York: Oxford Univ. Press.

Tosi, Juan A.
1966   *Zonas de vida natural en el Peru*. Instituto Interamericano de Ciencias Agricolas de la Organizacion de Estados Americanos, Zona Andina. *Boletin Tecnico* No. 5. Lima.

Wittfogel, Karl A.
1957   *Oriental despotism: A comparative study of total power*. New Haven, Conn.: Yale Univ. Press.

Zubrow, Ezra B. W.
1975   *Prehistoric carrying capacity: A model*. Menlo Park, Calif.: Cummings.

chapter **13**

The Archeological Study of Andean Exchange Systems

CRAIG MORRIS

When archeologists are called upon to rank the success with which they can study the various aspects of extinct societies, the reconstruction of exchange systems usually goes near the top of the list after diet and general ecological adjustments. Of course, not all goods that are exchanged survive in the archeological record, but many important ones do. Furthermore advances in the technical study of many classes of artifacts in recent years allow us to identify the sources of their raw materials, their places of manufacture, and ultimately their routes of movement.

At least since Malinowski (1922) and Mauss (1924) we have known that the exchange of goods often involves factors not adequately covered by the word *trade*. But archeological studies that attempt to deal in a specific way with something more than a mere movement of goods assumed to be "trade" are relatively recent and their number small.[1]

[1] *Ancient Civilization and Trade*, edited by Sabloff and Lamberg-Karlovsky (1975), brings together several important studies of exchange. The research of Renfrew (1969, 1973) and of Pires-Ferreira and her colleagues, which appeared after the paper was prepared from

315

Social Archeology:
Beyond Subsistence and Dating

There are several understandable reasons for this. The anthropological models for understanding nonmarket exchange systems do not seem to have advanced as far since the 1950s as one might have expected. Partly this is because of shifts of emphasis within the discipline. Partly it is because societies of the appropriate range have become increasingly rare, and, of course, certain ranges of social scale of critical importance to the archeologist have never really been observed ethnographically.

More serious, however, than the lack of appropriate models is the lack of appropriate research. This in turn is probably due more to the difficulty and cost of carrying out archeological research on exchange systems than to shortcomings in archeological creativity for producing good research designs. Certainly it is difficult to operationalize certain dimensions of exchange systems for archeological investigation, but the sheer extent of the geographic area that must be explored and the sampling difficulties in tracing the distributions of relatively rare exchange items raise the cost of systematic studies of exchange, particularly interregional exchange. When we add the necessity of contextual information for answering many of the more interesting exchange-related questions, the difficulties are further multiplied.

Ethnographic models of Andean exchange systems are not yet complete or clearly defined, and there remains substantial disagreement on how well various competing interpretations fit the ethnographic and ethnohistorical records. In fact, it is the incompleteness of those records, particularly for the state level, that makes archeological research on Andean economics so imperative. Nevertheless, the ethnohistorical research has been thorough (Alberti and Mayer 1974; Murra 1956, 1972, 1975; Wachtel 1973), and despite problems and minor disagreements, its results suggest an emphasis on nonmarket types of exchange at virtually all levels of the society. The simple rarity of references in the early European sources to large markets and long-distance trading networks contrasts strikingly with the picture for Mexico.

This is not the place to try to recapitulate or evaluate the emerging picture of Andean exchange. I would merely like to pinpoint some aspects of the models that I feel merit additional testing and that lend themselves to archeological study.

which this chapter derives (Pires-Ferreira 1976a,b; Pires-Ferreira and Flannery 1976; Pires-Ferreira and Winter 1976), provide particularly significant examples of how archeological data can be utilized in the study of complex exchange systems.

Funding for the Huánuco Pampa Archaeologica Project, source of much of the archeological data used here, was provided by the National Science Foundation (Grant GS 28815). The project was authorized by the governement of Peru in Supreme Resolutions Nos. 015 and 1030 of 1972 and 371-74-ED.

It is in the essence of reciprocal exchanges that the personal and sociopolitical relationships between the exchanging parties play an important role both in instigating the exchange and in determining its nature. Clearly there are certain aspects of reciprocity, like the reconstruction of a given relationship between individuals—with all its complex components of social positions and feeling tones—which are beyond the access of archeological techniques. If these can be reconstructed at all, it will have to be through other sources, like the study of the contexts and definitions of key Quechua terms in written sources, perhaps supplemented by contemporary ethnographic research.

However, major sociopolitical units can be identified archeologically, and for the contact period the boundaries of these units may be confirmed by written records. What we need to do, then, is to establish the boundaries between relevant units, examine the movement of goods within and between the units, and investigate the nature of the units in ecological and economic as well as sociopolitical terms so as to better understand the kinds of exchanges taking place. As interesting as the reconstruction of exchange networks dealing with sources, routes, comparative quantities of goods, and "central places" is, it is far preferable to be able to spell out the nature of the units engaged in the exchanges.

I would like to look at two major levels of exchange during the Inca period, the community and the state. It must be understood that this is a simplification, since there are frequently intervening sociopolitical and economic levels that may be relevant to exchange. Discussion of the "community" brings us at once to what may well be the single most interesting and difficult problem in Andean studies: What constitutes the community? Indeed, the answer to that question and to those regarding the nature of exchange systems are closely linked.

The Andean region is large and diverse, and much regional variation is apparent. This applies to community form as to other matters, but most analysts agree that the image of a relatively nucleated and neatly bounded geographic unit, or "village," was not a typical Andean pattern. Perhaps the most widely held view is that described by Murra (1972) in his essay on the "vertical control" of multiple ecological zones, although Rostworowski (personal communication, 1975) has suggested that this model may not apply to coastal zones during most time periods, and Duviols (1973) has also suggested some interesting alternatives. Without our going into details of the so-called verticality model in its various forms, the salient point is that a "community," while always having a principal area, or "nucleus," maintains its control over critical subsistence resources in several dispersed zones by keeping "colonies" of its own members in those zones. The written sources imply reciprocity rather than trade as the exchange mechanism that links the various colonies economically, and indeed if markets were to develop, one would tend to postulate the dissolution of the social ties that linked the islands of the "vertical archipelago." If this model is correct, we would have a situation whereby interregional exchange of subsistence goods is handled by intra-community mechanisms.

Unfortunately, the written sources tell us little about the actual movement of goods within the dispersed vertical community. Nor will it be easy for archeology to test and expand the models of Andean exchange. Many of their features would have had only very subtle effects on material remains. For example, labor was a critical part of many exchanges, and the gauging of labor exchange is a difficult task indeed for archeology. But at least the ethnohistorians have provided us with a good beginning, and there are several archeological approaches that should add to our understanding of Andean community exchange systems. I mention only a few.

1.   Studies of the distribution of goods and raw materials outside their primary sources and places of manufacture is one of the ways archeologists have traditionally looked at exchange (e.g., Renfrew, Cann, and Dixon, 1965; Renfrew, Cann, and Dixon 1968) and they do not need a lengthy discussion here. Shell and metals should be very promising materials for study. Obsidian is not as common in the Andes and would not likely provide as much information on movement of goods and raw materials as it has in many other parts of the world. Pottery may offer the best access to both the structure of community units and to certain kinds of movement within and between them. Administrative records from the Huánuco region show that not all settlements produced their own pottery, and the limited archeological studies confirm this. Ceramics are a definite, though not infallible, key to the identification of significant sociopolitical units, and they undoubtedly show economic connections as well. The pots do not by themselves show the nature of the relationship unless one is able to offer convincing interpretations of iconographic elements in their design, but the plotting of categories of ceramics based mainly on stylistic attributes may offer information pertinent to interpreting the kind of exchange involved. If the vertical archipelago model is correct, it should be apparent in the distribution of ceramic styles, revealing a pattern of interdigitation that would be different from the patterns one would predict from trade in the usual sense. In other words, plots of ceramic categories might show the islands of an "archipelago."

2.   In the highly diversified Andean environment even small distances and variations in altitude result in substantial difference in plant and animal populations. This microecological variation makes flora and

fauna a sensitive marker of quite limited spatial units—and of movement between the various zones when plant and animal remains are found outside their regions of natural occurrence. As is the case with other goods, of course, the mere movements of a product do not confirm a particular kind of exchange system, but they can help establish the nature and extent of ecological interconnections.

Most research on plant and animal remains has focused on the more traditional problems of domestication and diet, and such evidence has been seriously underutilized in the investigation of complex societies, where questions of organization and integration usually take priority over the food base. In the Andean case the paleobotanical and archeozoological evidence is of direct relevance in testing the "vertical" model of community organization and resource control. If the model of a community dispersed through multiple zones is correct, we would expect the distribution of the faunal and floral remains, and of products derived from them, to reflect the various zones to which the occupants of any given site had access.

3. Much of the evidence that can ultimately enable us to interpret the character of exchange will come from the contexts in which exchange occurs. The recognition of formal marketplaces is not easy for urban sites; it is likely to be even more difficult for villages, where such areas may not be distinguished by specific architecture. It may be impossible even to note the occurrence of casual exchanges within a community, since they may not take place in a circumscribed activity area. It is obviously even more difficult to establish whether there was concern for establishing equivalences of value in the exchanges or of determining their social nuances. Reciprocal and redistributive exchange are frequently accompanied by ceremony and ritual, during which goods are distributed. We cannot jump to the conclusion that just because there is evidence of feasting and ceremony, we are dealing with some form of nonmarket distribution of goods, but we would have another important piece of the total picture.

Context also has to be looked at even more broadly than the immediate circumstances in which the exchange occurs. We need to comb the ethnographic and ethnohistorical literature thoroughly in order to identify other characteristics that tend to be associated with various kinds of exchange systems and that might be detected in material remains. Perhaps the main point that has to be made in the study of community exchange systems is that no single indicator or test can be taken as sufficient by itself, but rather the existence or absence of several features has to be looked at together. A major weakness in many archeological research designs is that in their zeal to test a few relatively narrow

hypotheses, they fail to properly examine a broad range of other potentially pertinent evidence. The results are often simplistic. Questions must
be rigorously posed, but many different approaches must be employed.
This is especially important in the study of exchange systems we believe to
have been embedded in social, political, and religious affairs.

I now bypass the intervening levels and turn to the state and its
exchange relationships with the people and communities that composed
it. Here we are on firmer ground. The sixteenth-century written data have
provided us with a clearer model with which to work, and we have been
able to undertake more archeological work related to exchange, beginning as early as 1965 and adding to it substantially as part of our ongoing
general study of the Inca provincial capital at Huánuco Pampa. In this
case, then, we are able to present tentative results of archeological work
instead of just programmatic suggestions. Some of this material has been
presented in other papers (especially Morris 1967, 1974), but I think it
useful to draw it together here in its specific relationship to Andean
exchange.

The archeological evidence to date demonstrates fairly convincingly,
I feel, that the relationships between the Inca, or the state, and the people
they ruled, were conditioned by a complex web of reciprocities. Most of
this reciprocity involved "gifts" of cloth, and of food and other forms of
maintenance or "hospitality" on the state's side. The subjects were
obliged to give of their own energies in the state's fields, armies, and on
its public works projects. This verifies part of a model of Inca political
and economic organization advanced by Murra (1956) on the basis
of documentary sources. The archeological evidence, in addition to
confirming the importance of reciprocity and redistribution in the Inca
state, gives us some substantial new information on the scale of such
mechanisms, and on their limitations as well, which are not available in
documents.

Most of the data we have uncovered are related to the state's fulfill-
ment of its obligations to its subjects. The evidence for the other side of
the equation, the so-called labor tax system, is relatively good from the
written record, though that too might be fleshed out with other data. We
have, in essence, two kinds of archeological information: On the one
hand, we have the remains of the massive facilities the state had built in
order to ensure its ability to live up to what appear to have been ever
expanding obligations as its size and power increased. On the other hand,
we have the direct evidence of the consumption or use of goods provided
by the state.

1. First is the evidence for large-scale storage by the state. The
detailed study of storage at Huánuco Pampa revealed a main depository

consisting of 497 storehouses, with a total volume of slightly over 10,000 m³. Evidence suggests that the storehouses were devoted largely to the storage of foodstuffs. Given the fact that the city was built in an isolated area with no evidence of contiguous food production, and that its construction and administration appears to have been largely state controlled, it seems likely that the warehousing facilities were used mainly to provide food for the city's inhabitants. Both documents and archeology suggest that the population of the city was composed largely of the several categories of people who served the state (see Murra and Morris 1975). In addition to their role in maintaining a city under these isolated and rather unusual conditions, the storehouses would seem to be a testament to the state's obligation to support those who served it. There was no evidence of cloth or luxury goods in the Huánuco Pampa storehouses. Although this can be explained in part by poor preservation, I feel that certain classes of luxury goods may have moved in a different "circuit" of exchange from food products. That different circuit took them mainly to Cuzco and may have resulted in their being stored separately from subsistence goods in the provinces (see Morris 1967: chapters IV and V).

From comparative surveys in several other sites, combined with lists of state-built centers in written sources, we can come to a rough estimate of the magnitude of the Inca state's storage operation: The total capacity of the state warehousing system must have surpassed a million cubit meters. This would have put space for more than 30 million bushels of goods at the disposal of the state.

2. The second evidence of the state's provision of certain classes of goods comes from the elaborate craft production complex uncovered at Huánuco Pampa. The 40 workshops and 10 related buildings enclosed in a walled and evidently tightly controlled compound were devoted to textile production on a large scale and probably also to chicha (maize beer) brewing. The production of cloth underscores the importance of that commodity to the ruling elite, which appears to have been centralizing certain aspects of textile production. As Murra's (1962) article entitled "Cloth and Its Function in the Inca State" points out, it was a pervasive item in many different kinds of relationships. And as my own article on nonagricultural production (Morris 1974) suggests, it was crucial not only to maintaining the state's labor supply, but the very processes of expansion and maintenance of political control were also in part dependent on it. It is thus easy to see why the state would have established some form of direct control over cloth production as a key part of its reciprocal arrangements.

3. The ceramics of Huánuco Pampa are highly standardized and appear to have been produced for or by the state, though the exact place

of their production has not been located. The production of pottery can probably be seen as part of the state's obligation to supply the people who worked for it. The high degree of architectural uniformity at Huánuco Pampa suggests that housing was also in a sense provided by the state. Even though construction was almost certainly done by local labor, the building crews would have been fed from state storehouses. Pottery and housing were thus to a large extent on a par with food; they were part of what was expected from the state by those expending their energies, frequently far from home, in its behalf. As we will see, however, not all of the pottery produced at or for Huánuco Pampa was used there; a portion was apparently distributed out to key villages in the surrounding hinterland.

4. The fourth example of archeological evidence pertinent to reciprocity and redistribution was excavated in 1972 and 1974 at Huánuco Pampa by Pat H. Stein. It consisted of two large plazas adjoining what has been interpreted as the palace and/or temple sector of the city. Excavation in the long buildings surrounding these two plazas suggests that one was used for the preparation of food and chicha in large quantities, if the tons of pottery jars involved is any indicator. The other appears to have emphasized the serving of food, but extra caution must be used here, since the analysis of vessel forms, on which determination of function is largely based, is still incomplete (Stein 1975).

The best interpretation of this food preparation and serving area, which covers about 2.5 ha (or over 6 acres) in the most impressive part of the city, would seem to be that it was in essence a center for state or royal "hospitality." The state was providing food and beer for at least a portion of its workers and subjects in a setting of monumental architecture.

5. A further example comes not from the Inca provincial capital, but from the local villages that provided most of the people who populated the city, and the goods that supported it. In our 1965 surveys we had an opportunity to look for evidence of state-supplied goods in the hinterlands of Huánuco. Clearly many of the items that might have come from the state would not have been preserved. The fact that cloth is not preserved is especially lamentable. We do have a limited reading, however, on the distribution of the ceramics associated with Huánuco Pampa. They were found only rarely in the local Yacha and Chupaychu villages, which we know the Inca ruled. In most of the collections from these sites no more than a dozen sherds of "Imperial Inca" pottery were found, and frequently there were none at all. There was one significant exception to this. The village of Ichu, residence of Paucar Guaman, the principal Chupaychu leader, produced sherds from hundreds of vessels. This suggests that pottery at least was not distributed by the state in meaningful

quantities except in the case where a politically important relationship with local leadership was involved. The movement of the special "state" pottery, and any goods the vessels may have contained, almost entirely along politically important lines, suggests the linkage between exchange and political authority.

6. A final bit of archeological information may be added, though it takes the form of negative evidence and as yet is incomplete. Societies that possessed the kinds of specialists and produced the kinds and quantities of luxury goods we can observe for the Inca must have had a far-reaching exchange system. We have looked at Huánuco Pampa for evidence for an alternative to large-scale reciprocity and redistribution—that is, a substantial marketplace. The best likelihood on architectural grounds had seemed to be the plaza areas near the palace–temple sector just mentioned, and these have been demonstrated to have served other purposes.

The importance of the presence or absence of a marketplace to our overall research objectives is such that our search has been unusually thorough. Unless it took a form that was totally unrecognizable to us, no substantial space was reserved for market-like activities. It is of course likely that a certain amount of "casual" exchange took place within the city and perhaps even between its residents and outsiders, but it would seem that consideration of Huánuco Pampa as a large-scale market center can be ruled out.

CONCLUDING REMARKS

From these examples I hope we can begin to see how studies of the distribution of certain artifacts and activities in various contexts might contribute to the solution of even some of the most difficult and complex problems of Andean exchange. Although much remains to be done, I believe we can now confirm some notions of how Andean societies functioned that documents alone could not accomplish. The extent to which the state controlled and supplied some of its big population centers, its direct involvement in the large-scale production of some craft products, the elaborateness of its hospitality measures, and the limited extent that some of its redistributive measures appear to have affected many villages are things we can see better in the archeological record than in the documentary. Hopefully the future will see work that attacks these problems in greater detail at the village level, where our present data are nearly nonexistent, and on the coast, where the preservation of cloth and plant remains should give us a much more complete record of the movement of goods from place to place and context to context.

In closing I would like to stress the special importance the Andean data have for the comparative study of problems of exchange and interaction. The evidence I have outlined points to the case of an economy based primarily on principles of reciprocal and redistributive exchange that had grown to unusually massive proportions. Such principles of exchange are frequently regarded as somehow more primitive or not as efficient as modes of exchange that are less embedded in the sociopolitical system. From that perspective the enormous achievements of the Inca in the political and military spheres are seen as almost paradoxical. But is the situation really paradoxical? It is my view that part of the basis of the incredible growth of Tawantinsuyu rests in the fact that many aspects of the economy remained embedded in sociopolitical organization even as the authority structure became increasingly secular, militaristic, and centralized. The Inca were able to maintain at least fictive versions of the personal and ritual bonds on which reciprocity-like relationships depend. Such bonds would seemingly tend to wither as rulers and subjects are increasingly removed from each other, as both social and geographic distance increase in a highly stratified large-scale society.

The continuing direct linkage between economy and polity enabled the ruling elite to control large amounts of labor and critical natural resources as well as the exchange of certain commodities. It thereby allowed them to wield enormous power. Many of the reciprocal and redistributive aspects of traditional Andean economies had been converted at the state level into what is frequently called mobilization exchange (Smelser 1959), where goods (or labor) flow into central coffers in order to implement the decisions of the ruling authorities. Rather than simply being redistributed to the populace in a purely economic move to even out ecological differences between the regions controlled, the goods are used for purposes that are in large part political. In the case of the Inca, the result was thousands of miles of roads replete with way stations and a network of dozens of administrative cities—all built in less than a century if our chronology is correct (Rowe 1945). It was armies in the hundreds of thousands and state-controlled stores of many millions of bushels. It was one of the three or four largest territorial entities of the preindustrial world. And it was achieved without true writing and with a technology of transportation and communication remarkable for its simplicity.

The most intriguing question in all of this, of course, is how the scale and scope of the economy had been so enlarged while the basic principles of the traditional economy were preserved but bent in new ways to serve new ends. The ability of the Inca to manipulate old institutions into powerful strategies on a larger scale has been noted previously in a variety of contexts (Murra 1968, 1972) and appears to have been a pervasive characteristic of the Cuzco rulers. One of the immediate explanations of the Inca's success in amplifying traditional politico-economic principles is emerging from our research at Huánuco Pampa. The administrative cities built in the provinces were part and parcel of a large nonmarket state economy. The labor and resources mobilized by the Inca were used to produce the goods and build the physical facilities for ceremony and ritual that enabled them to expand the reciprocities and fictive reciprocities to ever larger areas and numbers of people. The Inca ruler needed a residence in every provincial center, not just for his own convenience (obviously he could not have used them personally very often) but as a place where "hospitality" offered in his name could prime the pump of the state economy.

Deeper explanations need to be sought by continuing study of the nature and developmental history of the Andean ecology and economy. At all levels of scale, in the highlands at least, there appears to have been a tendency toward direct administrative solutions to problems of resource management that in other parts of the world would have been handled by simpler forms of trade. Such practices were almost certainly very old, and thus by Inca times there was a great receptivity to and understanding of these kinds of solutions. This approach to resource management may have been the result of a kind of underlying ecological marginality in parts of the highlands, which made the area highly susceptible to drought and other causes of famine as Lanning (personal communication, 1971) has suggested. In this view the most effective way for certain highland populations to obtain adequate food during times of crisis would be by direct control of other more stable zones. Isbell's concept of "energy averaging" (Chapter 12, this volume) takes a rather similar position, and we may find that economies that rely heavily on stored goods function better when production and exchange can be tightly controlled from above, assuring that goods will be channeled to the warehouses and enabling long-term economic planning.

Much work lies ahead in the archeological study of Andean exchange. Variables such as the spacing of various resources in the environment need to be looked at closely in terms of the efficiency of their exchange. We also need to examine the scheduling of planting, cultivation, harvest, and other activities. Lynch (1971) and others have emphasized the importance of transhumance between highland ecological zones in the preceramic, and even during Inca times much of the movement that took place was of people rather than goods. Although settlements were permanent, there was substantial movement back and forth between them, and much of the movement was to transport human energy itself, not material products. Even the "urban" centers are felt to have been based in part on highly organized population transfers. It may have been that the most efficient way to exploit certain seasonal resources, even in a settled agricultural economy, was to move labor to zones where it was needed when it was needed. This would have had to be tuned to fit an elaborate seasonal schedule, which, when practiced on a large scale, could be most effectively coordinated by strong central authority.

For most of these questions we have to reach back into the early and still poorly understood formative periods. I suspect that in some respects the differences in exchange systems between the Andes and areas such as central Mexico are so profound that they followed different developmental courses from quite early times.

REFERENCES

Alberti, Giorgio, and Enrique Mayer (Editors)
  1974   Reciprocidad e intercambio en los Andes peruanos. Lima: Instituto de Estudios
          Peruanos.
Duviols, Pierre
  1973   Huari y Llancuaz, agriculturoes y pastores: Un dualismo prehispánico de oposi-
          ción y complementaridad. Revista de Museo Nacional 39:153–191.
Lynch, Thomas F.
  1971   Perceramic transhumance in the Callejón de Huaylas, Peru. American Antiquity
          36(2):139–148.
Malinowski, Bronislow
  1922   Argonauts of the western Pacific. London: Routledge & Kegan Paul.
Mauss, Marcel
  1923–1924 Essai sur le don: Forme et Raison de L'Échange dans les Sociétés Archaiques.
          Paris: L'Annee Sociologique.
Morris, Craig
  1967   Storage in Tawantinsuyu. Doctoral dissertation, Univ. of Chicago.
  1974   Reconstructing patterns of non-agricultural production in the Inca economy:
          Archaeology and documents in institutional analysis. In Reconstructing complex
          societies: An archaeological colloquium, edited by C. M. Moore. Supplement to
          the Bulletin of American Schools of Oriental Research No. 20:49–68.
Murra, John U.
  1956   The economic organization of the Inca state. Doctoral dissertation, Univ. of
          Chicago.
  1962   Cloth and its function in the Inca state. American Anthropologist 64: 710–728.
  1968   An Aymará kingdom in 1567. Ethnohistory 15(2):115–151.
  1972   El control vertical de un máximo de pisas ecológicos en la economía de las
          sociedades andinas. In Visita de la provincia de Leon de Huánuco en 1562 (Vol.
          2),(Iñigo Ortiz de Zúñiga. Huánuco, Peru: Universidad Nacional Hermilio Valdi-
          zan. Pp. 427–476.

1975   *Formaciones económicas y políticas del mundo andino*. Lima: Instituto de Estudios Peruanos.
Murra, John V., and Craig Morris
1975   Dynastic oral tradition, administrative records and archaeology in the Andes. *World Archaeology* 7(3):167–170.
Pires-Ferreira, Jane W.
1976a   Obsidian exchange in formative Mesoamerica. In *The early Mesoamerican village*, edited by Kent Flannery. New York: Academic. Pp. 292–306.
1976b   Shell and iron-ore mirror exchange in formative Mesoamerica, with comment on other commodities. In *The early Mesoamerican village*, edited by Kent Flannery. New York: Academic. Pp. 311–326.
Pires-Ferreira, Jane W., and Kent V. Flannery
1976   Ethnographic models for formative exchange. In *The early Mesoamerican village*, edited by Kent Flannery. New York: Academic. Pp. 286–292.
Pires-Ferreira, Jane W., and Marcus C. Winter
1976   Distribution of obsidian among households in two Oaxacan villages. In *The early Mesoamerican village*, edited by Kent Flannery. New York: Academic. Pp. 306–311.
Renfrew, Colin
1969   Trade and culture process in European prehistory. *Current Anthropology* 10:151–169.
1973   Monuments, mobilisation, and social organisation in Neolithic Wessex. In *The explanation of culture change: Models in prehistory*, edited by C. Renfrew. London: Duckworth. Pp. 539–558.
Renfrew, Colin, J. R. Cann, and J. E. Dixon
1965   Obsidian in the Aegean. *Annual of the British School of Archaeology at Athens* 63:45–66.
Renfrew, Colin, J. E. Dixon, and J. R. Cann
1968   Further analysis of Near-Eastern obsidians. *Proceedings of the Prehistoric Society* 34:319–331.
Rowe, John Howland
1945   Absolute chronology in the Andean area. *American Antiquity* 10:265–284.
Sabloff, Jeremy A., and C. C. Lamberg-Karlovsky
1975   *Ancient civilization and trade*. Albuquerque, N. M.: Univ. of New Mexico Press.
Smelser, Neil J.
1959   A comparative view of exchange systems. *Economic Development and Cultural Change* 7:173–182.
Stein, Pat H.
1975   The Inca's hospitality: Food processing and distribution at Huánuco Viejo. Paper read at the 40th annual meeting of the Society for American Archaeology, Dallas, Tex.
Wachtel, Nathan
1973   *Sociedad e ideología*. Lima: Instituto de Estudios Peruanos.

chapter 14

Mesopotamian Urban Ecology: The Systemic Context of the Emergence of Urbanism

CHARLES L. REDMAN

In recent years there have been frequent attempts to explain the emergence of urban society in terms of the effects of one or more major forces (Adams 1966, 1972; Carneiro 1970; Diakonoff 1969; Flannery 1968, 1972; Gibson 1973; Johnson 1973; Rathje 1971; Sanders and Price 1968; Wright 1972; Wright and Johnson 1975). Whereas each of these attempts has provided useful insights and stimulating explanations, it is useful now to attempt an integration of some of these diverse factors and discuss their interrelationships during the emergence of Mesopotamian urbanism. The purpose of this chapter is to focus on the interaction of multiple factors that were prompted by the conditions of the natural situation and previous cultural developments. This general interpretive context can be operationalized by defining the actual factors that could be tested in archeological instances. Further details on the cultural historical background for Mesopotamian urbanism can be found in a variety of epigraphic and archeological sources (see Redman 1978).

Social Archeology:
Beyond Subsistence and Dating

NATURE OF SYSTEMS EXPLANATION

Although systems theory has offered no easy answers to archeologists, it does provide a useful framework that enables the researcher to specify the interrelationship of relevant variables, deduce
critical implications for testing the model, and formulate the methodology for conducting investigations. To explain the appearance of new
phenomena or changes in existing systems, it is necessary to outline
explicitly the existence and interrelationships of relevant variables and
stimuli (Hill 1971). The proposed relationships of variables and their
products should be subsumed under already confirmed general relationships within the social sciences. Because a codified body of such relationships or laws does not exist in a usable form, assertions on the nature and
outcome of specific relationships are described in terms of logic and
inferences drawn from archeological, historical, and ethnographic investigations.

Three sets of factors are interrelated in the systems model presented:
(a) environmental and/or cultural stimuli that set up and initiate the
positive feedback relationships; (b) positive feedback cycles between variables that promote change; and (c) stabilizing, regulation mechanisms
that emerge to control and integrate changes that have occurred.

On the basis of an effective systems model, the researcher should be
able to predict the course of developments given the previous situation,
the initial stimuli, and the potential feedback relationships. An adequate
explanation implies a thorough understanding of the phenomenon, including answers to the questions of how and why a particular process
occurred and the insight needed to predict it. This seemingly deterministic approach might appear unrealistic to some social scientists, but it
should not. I acknowledge that prehistoric communities were composed
of individuals who made decisions based on a series of rational and
apparently irrational bases. With the emergence of an administrative elite
composed of a small proportion of the population, the decisions and goals
of a few may have influenced particular events of widespread significance.
However, I do not interpret these as reasons for eschewing what has
recently been termed a "gradualist–systemic approach [Adams 1974]." To
the contrary, the positive feedback relationships outlined in Figure 14.2
rely on the motivation of individuals involved in accumulating increasing
amounts of wealth and power. This is particularly crucial when evaluating
methods by which the emerging elite fostered situations and institutions
that increased their growing control. I assert that when dealing with large
population aggregates and long periods of time, one can adequately
account for the goals and aspirations of individuals in statistical, cumula-

tive, behaviorist terms. Apparently unpredictable actions of single individuals may cause minor perturbations in the course of development, but unless these changes are more widely adopted and incorporated into ongoing feedback relationships, they will not be of long-term, major significance. I suggest that when the decisions made by individuals or groups were in accordance with the interrelationships outlined in Figure 14.2, these people were more successful than were those who acted otherwise. Hence, not all communities nor all individuals behaved according to the proposed model, but those who did were at an advantage, and hence, there was a selective pressure for the set of decisions and goals I have suggested. Accepting such a position does not deny the importance of great individuals in history, nor does it deny that entrepreneurship played a crucial role in early civilizations.

I. THE PROCESS: BACKGROUND AND STIMULI

The process of urbanization was not a linear arrangement of one factor causing a change in a second factor, which caused a change in a third, and so on. Rather, the rise of civilization should be conceptualized as a series of interacting incremental processes that were set up and triggered by a favorable ecological and cultural situation. The changes caused by these processes increased through a series of mutually reinforcing interactions. Five positive feedback interrelationships crucial to the developmental process are described in the following discussion. Three of these relationships (A, B, and C in Figure 14.2) were prompted by the ecological situation and gave rise to institutions that characterized early Mesopotamian cities. The fourth and fifth positive feedback relationships (D and E in Figure 14.2) were stimulated by early urban developments and helped transform the independent cities into members of a series of centralized nation states. These feedback relationships did not function for a long period of time in an administrative vacuum until the sudden appearance of an administrative elite "full blown" to control the already developed institutions. Rather, each of the institutions started at a simple, low level and increased by small increments. These processes deepened the growing divisions within society that came to be institutionalized as economic strata within a hierarchical society. These feedback relationships also stimulated the growth of a class of administrators who increasingly controlled the productive resources of society and who reinforced the emerging divisions in the class structure. At the same time, these factors also gave rise to a series of negative feedback situations that regulated urban growth to certain limits.

Effective utilization of a systems approach involves the analysis of two different aspects of a developmental process, each represented by a diagram. One diagram portrays the alternate possible states for the system and the linkages among them (Figure 14.1). The second diagram represents the interrelationships of cultural variables within this system at any point in time (Figure 14.2). Figure 14.1 is a diagram of the successive phases of urban development in Mesopotamia. As development proceeded, not all communities grew nor followed this simplified scheme. Many towns and villages continued to exist and function within the emerging civilizational network. However, the structure of Mesopotamian society was profoundly influenced by the larger communities, which were the focus of institutional developments. Hence, although it is necessary to study both large and small settlements to understand an urban society, this model focuses on changes that led to the differentiation of community types.

A meaningful variable by which to measure the development of urbanism is the relative increase in formalized internal complexity, as represented by the emergence of stratified society. This assumes its relevant form in the increasing importance and control of an administrative elite. Figure 14.2 is a portrayal of the feedback between elements of early Mesopotamian society that affected the growth of an administrative elite. This figure is not arranged chronologically from left to right but is a description of the interrelationships of the factors at work at all times throughout the process.

A favorable ecological situation was instrumental in the formation of Mesopotamian civilization. At about 5500 B.C. there was an enormous and potentially productive ecological niche that was unoccupied. The southern Mesopotamian plain was at most sparsely inhabited by seminomadic collecting communities, and apparently void of farming

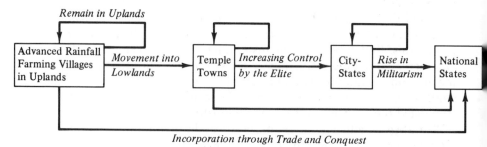

Figure 14.1. Trajectory of the development of dominant community forms during the emergence of urbanism in lowland Mesopotamia.

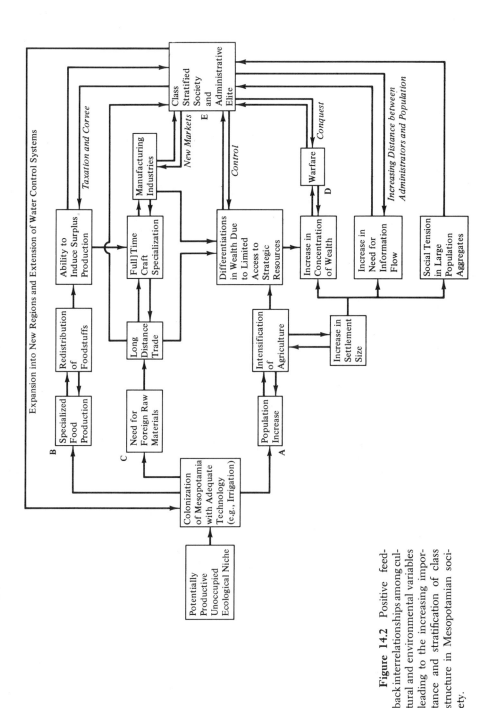

Figure 14.2 Positive feedback interrelationships among cultural and environmental variables leading to the increasing importance and stratification of class structure in Mesopotamian society.

333

communities. The limitations were insufficient rainfall for dry farming, and inability of the upland plants and animals to tolerate the summer heat or the salinity of the lowland river valley soils.

With the appropriate technology, the agricultural potential of land adjacent to the natural water courses was immense. However, by 5000 B.C. important strides toward forming the basis for Mesopotamian urbanism had already taken place. The distribution of village farming communities had spread from areas where plants and animals had first been domesticated. Some of the new areas imposed environmental stresses on the plants and livestock, stresses that selected for more tolerant strains. At the same time, it appears that some of the communities that had moved to the margins of the southern Mesopotamian lowlands, such as the people of Tell es-Sawwan or Choga Mami, were beginning to rely upon simple forms of irrigation to supplement the meager rainfall. In addition, there is evidence that these communities had developed more complex forms of organization than had their early village predecessors. Ranked society in Morton Fried's terms (1967) and a chiefdom level of organization in Elman Service's model (1962) had emerged. Hence, these four advances—heat tolerant animals; saline resistant plants; simple irrigation systems; and ranked, chiefdom organization—laid the groundwork for the rapid emergence of urbanism in lowland Mesopotamia. With these advances in subsistence and organization, the potentially productive, but until then largely uninhabitable, agricultural niche on the Mesopotamian plain could be successfully colonized.

The movement of advanced farming communities into the Mesopotamian lowlands and their occupation of this as yet vacant niche led to several major changes, creating three deviation-amplifying relationships that eventually led to class stratified society (A, B, and C in Figure 14.2). Although the expansion into lower elevations by the villagers of the sixth millennium, and later movements of advanced villagers onto the Mesopotamian plain, set in motion the feedback processes encouraging urbanism, I do not suggest that the participants necessarily recognized the entire importance of the actions they had taken. Rather, this whole process of movements of peoples, colonization of new regions, and stimulation of important feedback mechanisms can be understood in terms of natural, incremental processes that required people only to react to what they perceived at their most advantageous short-range choices. Hence, it was the environmental, technological, and social systems that primarily directed the evolution of these societies. Although individuals and unique circumstances may cause minor deviations in the process of civilization, its general course was charted in a seemingly irreversible manner given the initial steps just mentioned.

The slow growth in population during the village farming era led to a multiplication of the number of farming villages. This increase prompted the movement of villages into new regions, including lower elevations and eventually the Mesopotamian alluvial plain itself. Emigration to adjacent valleys was probably a common solution to the problem of a growing population. During the course of seasonal migrations of the herding segment of semisedentary villages, the early farmers came to know both upland and lowland areas. Given the slow movement of groups due to either population growth, soil depletion, or a combination of these, it is logical to suppose that over a 2000-year period (possibly 80 generations) people would attempt to live at lower elevations among other alternatives. Not every village established in the lower, piedmont areas succeeded, but those that used irrigation water and relied on hardy strains of plants and animals were more often successful. This process does not necessitate foresight, nor the desire of people to move into Mesopotamia, nor any conception of the complex society that would develop there. Instead, it relies on the natural small-scale movements of human groups, and the combination of factors necessary for survival of a community in the Mesopotamian lowlands. If successful, these same factors would enable further downslope movement while maintaining the agricultural success of the community.

II. PRIMARY POSITIVE FEEDBACK RELATIONSHIPS

The establishment of agricultural communities along the natural river courses of lower Mesopotamia stimulated three processes that set up crucial positive feedback relationships (Figure 14.2): (a) a slow but general trend toward population growth within a circumscribed (practically/culturally) productive region; (b) specialized food production by different units within the society; and (c) foreign raw materials needed for utilitarian purposes.

The increasing population of the Mesopotamian plain, resulting from a probable combination of internal growth and immigration, initiated several crucial transitions. Unlike rainfall-agriculture areas, where the prime determinant of productive locations is the fertility of the soil, the alluvial plain presented a different situation (Adams 1966). The land itself was relatively extensive, but it was agriculturally productive only if water was available. With small-scale irrigation works, this meant that the best land was close to the natural courses of the major rivers. As the number of inhabitants increased, the amount of farmland utilized was increased, and the point was soon reached where some farmers had to cultivate land without direct access to the river, obtaining water only from canals that ran through the land of other farmers. This situation might be workable so long as the farmers remained amicable and there was sufficient water for everyone. However, in dry years the farmer with primary access to the river might use all of the available water on his fields. The frequency of such a situation would increase as the population grew because all of the favorable land was occupied so that less desirable land would have to be cultivated. There were two cumulative results to the filling up of farmland in a situation where productivity is related to a spatially limited variable, irrigation. First, some land produced more crops per work-hour than did other land. Second, some farmers found that they had power over their neighbors. The stimulus was for more irrigation works to be built that would water greater areas. Even with an extensive canal system, farmers close to the source of the irrigation water would still be in an advantageous position.

The more people and the more land under cultivation, the more advantageous it became to control the land with direct access to irrigation water. The differential wealth produced by having better land would allow these farmers to acquire status and/or additional favorable land. The control of sources of irrigation water also meant that the already wealthy farmer would be the first to benefit by any further construction of canals that passed through his land. All of these tendencies toward differential land values would encourage among the fortunate the concept of individual or group ownership rather than communal property. Inheritance of property and wealth would be a logical next step, prompting the recognition of ascribed status, one of the basic regulating mechanisms within early civilizations. Hence, a vicious cycle of the rich getting richer and more powerful was initiated 6000 years ago. As Adams (1966) has pointed out, this successive intensification of agriculture and the ensuing differential access to strategic resources were a major cause for the emergence of class-stratified society.

It has been suggested on the basis of contemporary villages in Iraq and the absence of early historical references that major irrigation works and planning were not necessary nor present in the earliest urban societies of Mesopotamia. Nevertheless, even though small-scale irrigation works were sufficient for an adequate agricultural livelihood on the Mesopotamian plain, managed irrigation and overall agricultural planning were more effective, leading to greater success. The trend toward centralization, administration, and large-scale irrigation works was incremental, only becoming obvious in the archeological and textual records once they had reached major proportions.

There are several elements in this situation that reinforce each other and lead to a complex positive feedback relationship:

1. The more people there are, the more land that must be cultivated and/or the more intensive must be the cultivation of each field. The more intensive the agriculture, the more food that is available for a growing population.
2. Another method for increasing agricultural production for a growing population is through the centralized planning and administration of agricultural activities. Among other things this includes the construction, maintenance, and management of irrigation works.
3. A growing population in a relatively circumscribed productive area is forced to live closer together. Settlements increase in size. This, in turn, necessitates increasingly intensive agriculture, especially in the vicinity of large settlements.
4. The outcome of this intensification of agriculture in the Mesopotamian situation was differential access to strategic resources (i.e., irrigable farmland) and the basis for a growing administrative elite.

A secondary effect of the general population increase was the impact of larger communities. The concentration of large numbers of people in nucleated settlements, together with their stored food supplies and tools, created concentrations of wealth of dimensions previously unknown. The presence of members of wealthier families in these large settlements would further accentuate this concentration stimulating a concern for defense. This led to standing armies, which evolved into an institution that regulated and maintained the growing divisions within society. Another need created by the growth of large settlements was for better mechanisms of information flow in order to maintain social and economic order. Kinship ties and face-to-face relationships were no longer adequate to regulate large agglomerations of people. Formalized roles and rules were means of conveying technical information concering the productive economy. Tasks such as these seem to have been taken over by the temple community in early Mesopotamian cities, with writing and standardized representational artwork being the two major mechanisms used. A third impact of large settlements was the social tension created by these dense masses of people. New integrating mechanisms, closer regulation, and adjudication of conflicts would be necessary. This need was fulfilled in early cities by the administrative elite associated with the temple and promoted through rituals, social sanctions, and the newly emerging military establishment.

The colonization and subsequent population growth within lower Mesopotamia created an agricultural system that soon led to differential wealth and power, and by creating large settlements these factors also prompted the need for an administrative organization. The administrative elite that organized activities within the entire community was drawn from members of the wealthy and powerful landed families, officers in the growing military, and officials of the temple community. By being the administrators, the elite encouraged the growth of institutions that continued their differential access to strategic goods and created new sources of wealth and power for themselves.

The agricultural potential of the Mesopotamian plain and the intensification of food production through the widespread use of irrigation created a situation in which it was advantageous for production to become specialized. It is possible to achieve greater production in a number of ways: (a) by utilizing more land; (b) by producing more food per unit of land; or (c) by increasing specialization and exchange. All three of these potential avenues were pursued in Mesopotamia. The specialization of productive tasks led to the creation of groups of workers who were strictly fishermen, herders, or farmers. Each could do his job more effectively on a full-time basis than if each family had to accomplish all three tasks (cf. Lees and Bates 1974). This specialized food production created the need for a means of exchanging goods. In Mesopotamia a system of collection and redistribution was organized by the temple. The temple directly employed a large portion of the city's population in productive tasks.

The redistributive economy increased the efficiency of food production, but more important than this for the emergence of urbanism, it placed additional power in the hands of the administrative elite, especially those in the temple community (Polanyi, Arensberg, and Pearson 1957). One of the major requirements of a complex society is that a surplus of food must be accumulated from the productive segment of society to support craftsmen, traders, and the elite. A redistributive system allows the administrator to set the required amount of input of food a farmer must contribute to get a certain quantity of fish or meat in return. In this manner, the temple elite could encourage the production of a surplus by setting high requirements. It also gave the administrators another weapon against deviants. The mechanism of specialized food production, therefore, both created the need for a managerial elite and vested in their hands the means for supporting themselves and other non-food-producing specialists.

The third major process that was stimulated by the movement into Mesopotamia was the need for raw materials from other regions (C in Figure 14.2). Southern Mesopotamia did not have adequate building stone, timber, bitumen, metal, or stone for tools, grinding slabs, or vessels. Substitute materials were used in some circumstances, such as baked clay tools instead of stone and mud brick architecture instead of stone masonry, but nevertheless, significant amounts of material had to be imported.

Trade can assume a number of forms, depending on social organization and need for goods. Frequently, raw materials are procured directly from the people who manufacture or mine them, whereas in other situations intermediaries may be involved in the exchange. The exchanges are a form of reciprocal interaction. Often the exchanges involve goods of equal value, but frequently one side may give more than it receives in an effort to maintain the trading relation or establish an alliance. Ceremonies may accompany the exchanges in which "gifts" are given and solidarity reaffirmed.

In order to understand how the trading network affected social organization, it is necessary to identify the individuals or groups conducting the trade and discover how the goods were distributed and local goods procured for payment. Although archeological evidence is inconclusive for the fifth and fourth millennia, it is likely that long-distance trade was conducted through the temple community. Trading parties may have been sent to procure needed goods to regions where they were available. It appears that by the fourth millennium villages concentrating on extraction and production of raw materials, such as copper and obsidian, existed in Iran and Turkey, The Mesopotamian traders may have exchanged textiles, pottery, foodstuffs, or craft goods for the raw material. As early as the Jemdet Nasr period it appears that there were communities of Mesopotamian traders living in distant centers to carry on trade, Godin Tepe in Iran and Tell Brak in northern Syria. Once the goods were brought back to the Mesopotamian center, they would become part of the temple community inventory to be processed into manufactured goods and subsequently distributed to the population or retained in the temple. At first, this trade may have been in utilitarian commodities, but within a short time it also involved the importation of rare metals, semiprecious stones, and other exotica. The emergence of wealthy classes and people in positions of authority stimulated the need for status goods that were dependent on trade. The increasing scale of trade had several important effects on Mesopotamian society. Long-distance trade can be carried out more efficiently by a central administration that can evaluate or create the demand for the goods. Agricultural surplus was used to support the full-time traders.

It is hypothesized that the earliest traders were functionaries of the temple. However, during the second half of the Early Dynastic period, when historic texts are more explicit, the assumption that traders were government employees is less certain. Traders acted for the temple but also on behalf of the newly emerging king and wealthy citizens. In addition, traders may have carried on some business for their direct benefit, leading to a semiindependent class of traders that conducted both official and private transactions (Adams 1974).

The importation of these goods often meant that goods had to be produced in order to pay for raw materials. Mesopotamian cities excelled at two categories of production: manufactured craft goods and agricultural foodstuffs. The ability to collect a surplus of food supplies from the agrarian population enabled the administrators to support a class of full-time craftsmen. These workers fabricated pottery, textiles, sculpture, metallurgy, and perhaps architecture. The craftsmen became well organized, and there is good evidence for mass-production industries for certain goods at a very early date (e.g., pottery by 3000 B.C. and textiles by 2700 B.C.). These manufacturing industries required administration, and their control had to be coordinated with the control of the trading networks. Hence, the movement into Mesopotamia necessitated trade in utilitarian objects and created an institution that soon stimulated craft specialization and industrialization within the city, which in turn created far greater demands for the trading network. In this way, trade and industry was a part of, and further stimulated, the increasing complexity that characterized urban society.

A fourth feedback relationship partially owes its existence to the transformations caused by the original three feedback mechanisms (D in Figure 14.2). The increasing size of individual settlements plus differential wealth created major concentrations of wealth—for example, stored agricultural produce, portable equipment, and status goods. This was a temptation to raiders from outside the community, or from inside (i.e., the poorer classes). In either case, the wealthier classes and, to a certain extent, all members of the society would require some sort of military force to protect themselves. At the same time, the increasing concentration of wealth would be a stimulus for assembling military forces for offensive campaigns. These armies might be used to settle disputes about land, protect trading routes, or loot goods from other communities. The greater the threat by the armies of others, the greater the necessity for supporting the full-time core of an army of one's own. However, once an army is formed, even for defensive purposes, it does not usually remain idle. Consequently, the concentration of wealth in cities prompted defensive armies, which in turn stimulated offensive armies, which encouraged further concentration of wealth within defensible city limits. This vicious cycle of plunderable wealth leading to militarism leading to greater concentration of wealth is a cycle that has continued to the present day.

The growth of militarism had important effects of the growth of urbanism. First, the core of the army had to be supported by surpluses accumulated by the administrative elite. In return, the army helped to enforce the directives of the elite. Second, in times of instability, militarism may have encouraged the occupants of the countryside to move into the defensible cities, which brought these peasants under more direct control of the urban elite than before. Third, militarism soon became an independent force of its own within the emerging civilizational hierarchy of administrative groups. Whereas the elite of the temple community might be able to exert power by informational, ritual, and economic means, the army could assert its authority directly through the use of force. This factor became extremely important once cities had been established and is instrumental in the formation of secular state governments.

The processes just described were reasonably independent, yet interrelated, situations that came into being due to the circumstances created by the colonization of the Mesopotamian plain by agriculturalists. The institutions that emerged to administer these situations grew to importance on the basis of mutually reinforcing relationships among various economic, social, and environmental factors. Each of these institutions was instrumental in providing the economic base upon which the complex hierarchical society was structured, as well as providing a strong stimulus to the formation of a managerial elite. This elite either may have been a single group or may have been composed of multiple groups each attempting to extend the scope of its authority. It was logical for the administrative elite to encourage the further growth of managerial institutions to regulate the positive and negative feedback relationships. By doing so they increased the scope of their control, making society more dependent on the activities of the elite. Each of the regulating institutions was a source of economic and administrative power for their respective managers. Various social codes and ethics were established to maintain and extend the power of these emerging elites. Ownership of property by individuals or institutions; ascribed status; differential access to productive resources; military force; and elements of religion, myth, and artwork all contributed to the newly created social divisions. The growth in complexity, social stratification, and the emergence of managerial institutions were initially caused by a series of interrelated systemic ecological factors. However, the elite they created were participants in the fifth positive feedback relationship—that is, purposeful strategies of the elite to stimulate further growth of the institutions that gave them their power and wealth (E in Figure 14.2).

Although the course of cultural change is determined by a diversity of factors, an important element is the cumulative decisions made by the participating population. These decisions are made with the information at hand and are not always recognized as significant by the participants. Before the emergence of urbanism, the decisions made by every individual had relatively equal significance. This situation changed with complex society. In an urban society decisions made by a small elite group influence the course of events for a large population. Even decisions made by the entire population are affected by the elite, who formulate courses of action for the populace to choose from and who influence opinions. This power of the elite might be especially evident in times of crisis or in response to an event of particular importance. Strong individuals or groups may gain power or change institutions rapidly under these conditions and may be unwilling to relinquish the power after the crisis has apparently passed. The growing influence of the elite does not mean that complex societies no longer react to their environmental settings or economic exigencies; nevertheless, the elite serves as an intermediary that both interprets the situation and provides the acceptable alternatives. The elite often has enough control so that its members can direct societies in courses initially at odds with the necessities of the environment and their own social system. Eventually, however, these nonadaptive decisions must fail. By examining length of occupation and patterns of population growth, it is possible to determine from archeological evidence which societies were successful in coping with complexity and which remained at a lower level or disappeared altogether.

III. PRIMARY NEGATIVE FEEDBACK RELATIONSHIPS

The positive feedback relationships outlined in the preceding section were responsible for changes that prompted the rapid growth of complexity in Mesopotamian society. In addition there were numerous negative feedback relationships set up by the conditions in Mesopotamia that had a regulating or inhibiting effect on the growth of urbanism. It is the articulation of the positive and negative relationships and their relative importance that determine which systems grow, remain static, or diminish. No society steadily continues in increase in size and complexity without interruption. Mesopotamian civilization developed in a series of phases, each one attaining a level of stability and then retrogressing in terms of size and complexity. The negative feedback situations are crucial in determining the level and nature of these states of stability and the institutions that emerged to regulate the changing society.

Many of the factors outlined in Figure 14.2 have potential negative interrelations; however, two stand out as critical: production of agricultural surplus and increasing militarism.

The production of agricultural surplus is central to the development of Mesopotamian civilization. It enabled a redistributive economy, crafts, trade, and industries. Agricultural surplus was also used to support the growing administrative elite and other specialists that were at the core of early urbanism. However, various processes involved in the growth of urbanism had a negative effect on the production and utilization of agricultural surpluses:

1. Short-term efforts at increasing production led to overintensification, which frequently resulted in long-term economic disasters. Decisions to not allow sufficient fallow periods between crops or to continuously irrigate without proper precautions increased the probability of the water table rising and the farmland becoming salinized and unusable (Gibson 1974). Hence, administered efforts to increase production might, over a period of time, diminish production or even lead to complete abandonment of a region.

2. In Mesopotamia I visualize surplus production and a redistributive economy leading toward a differentiation of wealth and a system of institutionalized control. However, there are ethnographic examples of situations where redistribution is used as a mechanism to equalize wealth. I believe that redistribution did not frequently act as a leveling mechanism in Mesopotamia because of ethical considerations created by the productive situation. Much of this is embodied in the shift from ranked to stratified society, using Fried's (1967) terminology. In ranked society status is maintained through accomplishments and redistribution of wealth, whereas in a stratified society status is formalized, not requiring the continual affirmation of one's position through distribution of wealth. What caused this change in ethics in early Mesopotamia is more difficult to pinpoint, but the unequal land values and need for imported utilitarian goods were probably important.

3. The concentration of population in cities reduces the amount of land that could potentially be cultivated. The ideal agricultural situation would be an even distribution of people over the entire agriculturally productive landscape. Concentrations of people can be supported by intensifying agriculture in the vicinity of the city, but there are limits. Better transportation due to canal construction allows for larger urban centers, as does the importation of foodstuffs. However, the trends toward urban growth and potential agricultural production are inversely related.

4. The increasing size and wealth of the administrative elite drained capital from the productive segments of society. Excessively large classes of administrators and bureaucrats consumed an increasing proportion of

the available agricultural surplus. This trend was intensified by the desired of the elite for status goods and the periodic immobilization of these goods in burials. Because of this trend less surplus would be available for investment in improving agriculture, supporting craft production, or industry. The overall trend would be for an increasing gap between the wealth of the elite and that of the productive elements in the population. This would stimulate internal strife from the poorer classes and prompt external invasion due to the concentration of portable wealth.

The increasing frequency and intensity of military activity is implied by several kinds of evidence for the Early Dynastic period in Mesopotamia. The establishment of a standing army would vest power in the hands of its leader and create a source of wealth for the city through conquest and tribute. The instability of the countryside during periods of military activity would also encourage rural folk to migrate into the city. However, militarism also had several negative impacts on the processes leading toward greater urbanism:

1. The insecurity of the countryside encouraged farmers to move into the city and, hence, reduced the amount of land that could be cultivated and the quantity of agricultural production.

2. Militarism and instability in the region inhibited long-distance trade by making it hazardous and more costly to protect.

3. The support of a standing army and an active state of militarism funneled off large amounts of potentially productive resources. The manpower and subsistence needs of the army itself reduced productive capabilities that could be channeled elsewhere. The defensive constructions around the city and equipment of the army required large quantities of labor and raw materials. The act of warfare itself with its killing and destruction destroyed potentially productive capital resources and already accumulated wealth.

The growth of urbanism was stimulated by militarism yet was periodically inhibited by negative feedback relationships that acted to keep societies from developing into totally militaristic enterprises.

FUTURE RESEARCH AND EVALUATION

The systems model diagrammed in Figures 14.1 and 14.2 is an attempt at further specifying the interrelationships among variables that prompted the emergence of Mesopotamian civilization. However, general models of formation processes are difficult to test with data from the archeological record. Simple answers are not offered, nor should this approach be considered a total departure from previous attempts. Rather, it provides an intellectual framework within which research can proceed and current results can be evaluated.

Three directions for further investigations are suggested:

1. Terms and categories must be precisely defined as they relate to the development of urbanism in Mesopotamia. These include the nature of class divisions, composition of administrative elites, activities of ethnic groups, mechanisms of trade and industry, and power bases of early city rulers. It is necessary to develop the relevant archeological yardsticks to measure civilizational variables in the archeological record. Methods of recognizing economic classes, conical clans, ethnic groups, mechanisms of trade, and patterns of control are poorly developed in our discipline. A rigorous methodology based on a quantitative approach and historical inferences is essential to future investigations.

2. Comparisons should be made with the variables present in regions where urbanism did not develop. Although this model is constructed for Mesopotamia, it does have elements of general significance. A comparative study could suggest the crucial variables that were necessary for urbanism. An examination of why Çatal Hüyük apparently did not evolve a centralized administrative elite is an example of this type of study. Çatal Hüyük's early growth was the result of villagers moving into an unoccupied ecological niche and becoming irrigation agriculturalists on the Konya Plain. Although Çatal Hüyük became the largest known demographic center in its time period, it lacked several key variables that were present in Mesopotamian civilization: Çatal Hüyük's economy was based not so much on the importation of major raw materials as on exporting them to less developed trading partners; the size of the Konya Plain was small in comparison to southern Mesopotamia; specialization of subsistence pursuits was not encouraged; and there were no competing centers of population to threaten hostilities. Although major developments occurred, the centralized administrative structure necessary for urbanism did not emerge. Consequently, Çatal Hüyük was unable to increase or even maintain its size and complexity.

3. One of the most direct tests of a theory such as the systems ecological model proposed here would be to investigate the societies directly preceding the formation of states and cities to see whether the institutions discussed were already at work before the total crystallization of the administrative elite (Wright and Johnson 1975). Support for the interpretation summarized in Figure 14.2 would include good evidence for increasingly intensive agriculture, redistributive economy, differential wealth, small-scale warfare, and increasing trade and manufacturing

during the fifth and fourth millennia in Mesopotamia. If these institutions took on importance *after* the formation of the state, then they were not essential elements in the formation of a stratified society with an administrative elite.

Interpretive theories for the rise of civilization remain in the form of plausible stories—logical, but not objectively confirmed. This situation is now in rapid flux. By organizing research around a systems model framework, it is possible for us as archeologists to better specify hypotheses, develop new methodologies, and rigorously test trial formulations. The ultimate result is that we would be able to propose and differentiate objectively among competing intellectual positions and to present a verifiable theory for the origins of urbanism in Mesopotamia and elsewhere.

ACKNOWLEDGMENTS

My research experiences in the Near East and many of my ideas on Mesopotamian urbanism have come from Robert McC. Adams, Robert J. Braidwood, and Patty Jo Watson. They have also read and commented on an earlier draft of this chapter. Although my debt to them is profound, the actual content and implications of this chapter are my responsibility.

REFERENCES

Adams, Robert McC.
  1966   *The evolution of urban society.* Chicago: Aldine.
  1972   Patterns of urbanization in early southern Mesopotamia. In *Man, settlement and urbanism*, edited by P. J. Ucko, R. Tringham, and C. W. Dimbleby. London: Duckworth. Pp. 735–749.
  1974   Anthropological perspectives on ancient trade. *Current Anthropology* 15:239–256.
Carneiro, Robert L.
  1970   A theory of the origin of the state. *Science* 159:733–738.
Diakonoff, Igor M.
  1969   The rise of the despotic state in ancient Mesopotamia. In *Ancient Mesopotamia, a socio-economic history*, edited by I. M. Diakonoff. Moscow: Mauka Publishing House. Pp. 173–203.
Flannery, Kent V.
  1968   The Olmec and the Valley of Oaxaca: A model for interregional interaction in formative times. In *Dumbarton Oaks Conference on the Olmec*, edited by E. R. Benson. Washington, D.C.: Dumbarton Oaks Research Library and Collection. Pp. 79–110.
  1972   The cultural evolution of civilizations. *Annual Review of Ecology and Systematics* 3:399–426.
Fried, Morton H.
  1967   *The evolution of political society: An essay in political anthropology.* New York: Random House.

Gibson, McGuire
1973   Population shift and the rise of Mesopotamian civilization. In *The explanation of culture change: Models in prehistory*, edited by C. Renfrew. Pp. 447–463.
1974   Violation of fallow and engineered disaster in Mesopotamian civilization. In *Irrigation's impact on society*, edited by T. E. Downing and M. Gibson. *Anthropology Papers of the University of Arizona* No. 26.
Hill, James N.
1971   Seminar on the explanation of prehistoric organizational change. *Current Anthropology* 12(3):406–408.
Johnson, Gregory A.
1973   *Local exchange and early state development in southwestern Iran.* Ann Arbor, Mich.: Museum of Anthropology, Univ. of Michigan.
Lees, Susan H., and Daniel G. Bates
1974   The origins of specialized nomadic pastoralism: A systemic model. *American Antiquity* 39:187–193.
Polanyi, Karl, C. Arensberg, and H. W. Pearson (Editors)
1957   *Trade and market in the early empires.* New York: Free Press.
Rathje, William L.
1971   The origin and development of lowland classic Maya civilization. *American Antiquity* 36(3):275–285.
Redman, Charles L.
1978   *The rise of civilization: Early farmers to urban society in the ancient Near East.* San Francisco: W. H. Freeman.
Sanders, W. T., and B. Price
1968   *Mesoamerica: Evolution of a civilization.* New York: Random House.
Service, Elman
1962   *Primitive social organization: An evolutionary perspective.* New York: Random House.
Wright, Henry T.
1972   A consideration of interregional exchange in greater Mesopotamia: 4000–3000 B.C. In *Social exchange and interaction*, edited by E. N. Wilmsen. University of Michigan, Museum of Anthropology, Anthropological Papers No. 46: 95–105.
Wright, Henry T., and Gregory A. Johnson
1975   Population, exchange and early state formation in southwestern Iran. *American Anthropologist* 77:267–289.

chapter 15

The Keresan Bridge:
An Ecological And
Archeological Account

FRED PLOG

INTRODUCTION

The Pueblo settlements of the American Southwest have attracted considerable anthropological interest for close to a century. The reason for this attention is, I suspect, simple. Viewed from a cultural perspective, the Pueblo are remarkably similar, but from a strictly social structural perspective, the variation among them is immense; the manner in which they are organized is remarkably diverse.

The purpose of this chapter is to add to our understanding of the nature of this variation within similarity. It is not an effort to account for all of the variation, but it hopefully will help clarify some aspects of the variation, especially those related to Pueblo environment and subsistence practices. I intend to:

1. describe the nature of variation in the social structure of Pueblo settlements.
2. describe the hypotheses that have been introduced to account for this variation.

349

Social Archeology:
Beyond Subsistence and Dating

3. discuss the nature of variation in subsistence practices.
4. attempt to show the relationship between the patterns of variability in each of these three (social structure, environment, subsistence) areas.
5. attempt to show the relationship between the patterns of variation in existing Pueblo populations and those that existed in the prehistoric past.

CULTURE AND SOCIAL STRUCTURE

The contrast between purely cultural and purely social structural approaches to the study of society is perhaps nowhere clearer than in the Pueblo Southwest. From a strictly cultural perspective, as Driver and Coffin's (1975) analysis of North American groups indicates, the area of Arizona and New Mexico inhabited by the Pueblo is extremely homogenous. Throughout the area, people occupy nucleated settlements consisting of stone and adobe houses, arranged in apartment-like structures. Their subsistence practices are largely agricultural, although herding, fishing, hunting, and gathering contribute to the subsistence base in varying degrees. Pottery is made in the vast majority of the settlements, and material culture is quite similar from one to another. Although there is some dispute, religious beliefs, "world view," and ritual organization also share important features. Yet, each of the settlements is autonomous. And, given this autonomy, there is substantial diversity in the social structure and social organization of the communities.

Table 15.1 summarizes the major aspects of organizational variation among the Pueblo.[1] Let me comment on each of the dimensions.

Ethnographic discussions of the Pueblo do not clearly distinguish between families and domestic groups. On the one hand, great emphasis is placed on units for which the Pueblo occupying particular settlements have terms. On the other, while there are few good summaries of the actual composition of households within communities, it is clear that behavioral observations have informed the conclusions of most Pueblo ethnographers, that the descriptions of family form are not entirely conceptual. In that sense, it is probably safest to think of the descriptions as averages, with little sensitivity to intracommunity variation. Given these

[1] Materials summarized in the table and throughout the chapter are drawn from 50 years of Pueblo research. Thus, the description is not of the Pueblo today but of some "average" point in the earlier part of the century.

Table 15.1

VARIATION IN SOCIAL STRUCTURE AMONG PUEBLO SETTLEMENTS

	Family	Residence	Descent–inheritance	Kinship	Clans	Moieties	Kivas
Western Pueblo Hopi, Zuni	Large extended	Matrilocal	Matrilineal	Crow	P	A	6–7
Western Keresans Acoma, Laguna	Large extended	Matrilocal–ambilocal	Matrilineal	Crow	P	A	multiple
Central Keresans Santa Ana, Zia	Samll extended	Ambilocal–neolocal	Children, either sex	Hawaiian? Crow	P	P	2
Eastern Keresans Cochiti, Santo Domingo, Felipe	Small extended	Ambilocal–neolocal	Children, either sex	Iroquois–Crow	P	P	2
Eastern Pueblo Tewa, Tiwa, Towa	Nuclear	Neolocal	Children, either sex	Eskimo	A	P	2²

² While two kivas is the most common pattern, one village has six. Still greater variation in the past is clearly possible.

qualifications, there is a continuum from large extended to small extended to nuclear families moving from western to eastern communities within the Pueblo area.

Many of these same qualifications hold in discussing residence rules: The net result is a description that is somewhere between an idealized model and a characterization of actual behavior. Given these qualifications, there is a continuum from matrilocal to ambilocal to neolocal residence among the different Pueblo communities.

The description of the systems of descent in the different Pueblo groups is somewhat more straightforward. In no case that I know of is there a substantial discussion of "descent behavior." The variation between matrilineal and "bilateral" descent is an exclusively normative characterization of the society, at least at present.

Kinship is perhaps the most problematical consideration of all. At the ends of the continuum moving from west to east are Crow and Eskimo systems, with Hawaiian (?) and Iroquois systems intervening. Simply, perhaps oversimply, it may be regarded as a continuum from lineal to bilateral terminological systems. But, there are problems, only some of which are unique to Pueblo ethnography. First, there is widespread disagreement among students of the Pueblo settlements as to the most accurate description of each settlement's system. Moreover, the evidence that the boundaries between such systems are less than watertight is growing. First, analyses such as Buchler and Selby's (1968) study of the Iroquois systems and Lounsbury's (1964) study of the Omaha and Crow systems clearly indicate that there is far more than random variation around and between each. Given this variation, it is necessary to wonder about the time depth and duration of most systems. Second, there is increasing evidence of situational variation in not only the use of kin terms but the nature of the kinship system employed.

Robin Fox (1967) points out that the Cochiti Pueblo use Kariera (Iroquois) in day-to-day affairs but Crow in ritual contexts. Nevertheless, to employ the conventional model, a highly lineal system (Crow) is used in the western area, a bilateral system (Eskimo) in the eastern area, with variations in between.

Clans are present in the western and Keresan groups, but not in the eastern. Moieties are present among the Eastern Pueblo, and Eastern and Central Keresans, but not among the Western Keresans or Western Pueblo. The number of kivas, round or square ceremonial structures present in the settlements, is substantially varied: multiple kivas among the Western Pueblo and Western Keresans, two kivas among the Central and Eastern Keresans, and two among the Eastern Pueblo.

ASKING THE PROPER QUESTION

As indicated earlier, the history of describing and attempting to explain the diversity of Pueblo organization is a long one (Aberle 1948; Dozier 1970; Eggan 1950; Ellis 1964; Fox 1967; Hawley 1950; Ortiz 1969; Parsons 1929; Schneider and Roberts 1956; Steward 1937; Strong 1927; Titiev 1944; White 1939; Wittfogel and Goldfrank 1943). The first lasting contribution is the "irrigation" hypothesis of Wittfogel and Goldfrank (1943). According to them the case is a relatively simple one. On the one hand, there is the organizational contrast between the Eastern and Western Pueblo: the Eastern Pueblo have moiety organization, and the Western Pueblo do not. On the other hand, the subsistence strategy of the Eastern Pueblo involves a heavy investment in irrigation agriculture, whereas that of the Western Pueblo does not. The explanation of the organizational diversity is therefore the difference in subsistence strategy; irrigation agriculture required the more complex and centralized moiety system. Despite some of the shortcomings of this approach, it has been important to the arguments of other anthropologists—especially Eggan (1950) and Fox (1967). Although not disagreeing with the Wittfogel–Goldfrank position, Eggan (1950) has added to it a new set of concerns. He focuses considerable attention on the important differences in kin terms and lineal organization among the Pueblos. The Western Pueblo are Crow in their system of kin terms; "lineal organization" is important in these settlements. Both in their kin terms and in their organization, "bilaterality" is far more characteristic of the Eastern settlements. Eggan also notes that there is substantial variation among some Eastern Pueblos, especially the Keresan groups. These differences he explains by what Fox (1967) has called a time of arrival–length of survival explanation:

> All of the Pueblos were once of the Western type, however developed and derived. The divergencies in type that we now notice amongst the Pueblos represent a gradual running-down of this Western type amongst the Rio Grande groups in response to irrigation conditions, a development which was accelerated by the Spanish and Americans. The Keres, coming last to the Rio Grande, preserved their Western structure the longest and this is evidenced by the existence of clans though these are practically functionless now [p. 31].

Although Eggan's efforts were based on new and insightful analyses of Western Pueblo organization, the organization of the Eastern Pueblo was as yet poorly defined, by modern standards. Disagreements existed over the most fundamental issues. In retrospect, this situation may very well have led Eggan to see Eastern Pueblo organization as a degraded Western form.

Precisely because he devotes considerable attention to these conflicts and disagreements for at least the Eastern Keresan Pueblo if not all Kerasans or even all Eastern Pueblo, Fox's (1967) work refines the case further. Table 15.1 would not be possible without Fox's clear definition of many previously confused points. Of particular importance is the evidence he develops suggesting that the organization of the Eastern Keresan Pueblos is not some vague form of bilaterality but rather a precise system of "dual descent–dual affiliation."

Fox finds evidence of the coexistence of two very different kin term systems—a Crow-like system used in largely ritual contexts within an overall system approximating Kariera. Such a situation, he argues, would be less likely to result from the replacement of clans by moieties (Crow to bilateral) than from the invasion of exogamous patrimoieties by matrilineal clans that took over the exogamy function. Thus, Fox argues that the system of the Eastern Keresans is much more than a degraded form of Crow and that to the extent that lineality can be inferred in the situation, the direction is likely to be the opposite of what Eggan suggests.

While Fox's analysis clearly adds greater detail to our understanding of organizational variation, this greater detail is not so germane to his argument as one might suppose. The new evidence is simply used to argue that Eggan had the sequence backward. I would like to suggest that many of the implications of Fox's formulation go well beyond his position. I will set aside the issue of organizational variation for the moment and examine, in far more detail than the "irrigation hypothesis" suggests, the precise patterns of variation in key environmental variables and subsistence strategies in the two areas and to replace speculation about what happened in the past with evidence.

THE PUEBLO ENVIRONMENT

The precise nature of the environment inhabited by the Pueblo is the subject of considerable disagreement. Eggan (1950) has observed that the environment is "remarkably uniform," flora and fauna relatively similar, the climate basically the same. He does note that because the east is higher in altitude, the rainfall is a bit greater and the temperature a bit cooler. Moreover, the Rio Grande furnishes a permanent supply of water to the Eastern Pueblos, which is simply not available in the west.

Ford (1972) has suggested that this characterization is inadequate because it fails to identify important variation in critical climatic factors. Although his analysis is specifically focused on the Tewa, he mentions the following:

1. Soil nutrients vary considerably from one field to another.
2. Some fields receive more rainfall from year to year than do others, and this pattern changes annually.
3. Severe summer storms may destroy crops in one area but not those only a short distance away.
4. The dates of the last spring frost and the earliest fall frost vary considerably.
5. Insect and animal pests have a substantial but capricious effect on different fields.

Although I basically agree with Ford's argument that a position more sensitive to the variation within the region than Eggan's is necessary and I believe that the patterns of variation that Ford has described are generally characteristic of the Pueblo region, I suggest that his analysis obscures some important aspects of the variation. Significantly, Ford has put his finger on the problem in underscoring the tendency of anthropologists to focus on average data rather than data describing variation. If one examines average environmental information for the area occupied by the Pueblo, it does indeed appear to be relatively homogenous. But if one instead considers the pattern of variability within it, extreme differences emerge.

Specifically, there are differences between the areas inhabited by the Eastern and Western Pueblo with respect to precipitation, hydrology, temperature, soils, and wind. Although it is undeniably the case that variation occurs within each of these regions and that the average conditions in the two areas are much the same, the following differences are evident.[3]

Precipitation

Relative to the Western Pueblo area, the Eastern Pueblo area has (a) a higher percentage of rainfall during the crop-growing season; (b) more rain in May and June, the two months during which moisture is most critical for the germination of seeds; (c) fewer 14-day periods during the crop-growing season in which no rain falls; (d) fewer years in which rainfall is less than 75% of normal; (e) an "average dry year" that is wetter; and (f) in dry years, more rainfall in May and June (all of the preceding from Visher [1954]).

[3] Southwestern archeologists using dendroclimatological techniques are currently projecting average data well into the prehistoric past. It is not currently possible, however, to suggest how reflective of past conditions these various measures of variation may have been.

Hydrology

In respect to hydrology, there are also substantial differences. There is no major permanent stream similar to the Rio Grande in the Western Pueblo area. Moreover, for the nonpermanent streams in both areas, the drainage basins in the Eastern Pueblo areas have watersheds extending to higher elevations, which implies a higher probability of both winter snows and summer rains. Moreover, in the Eastern Pueblo area, there is a lower rate of runoff. More water seeps into the ground and is retained as soil moisture, and there is less evaporation of surface waters.

Temperature

Average temperature and variation in temperature appear to be about the same in the Eastern and Western Pueblo areas. Nevertheless, it is important to keep in mind the fact that the greater abundance of water results in more rapidly maturing crops in the Eastern Pueblo area, rendering temperature a somewhat less critical variable.

Soils

Soils in the Eastern Pueblo area have a higher average level of moisture, a higher level of soil nutrients, and a better structure for drainage, resulting in a lower probability of saline conditions developing within the soils (U.S.S.C.S. maps).

Wind

Valleys in the Eastern Pueblo area are smaller, more enclosed, and less exposed to prevailing wind currents, rendering the probability of wind damage less substantial.

(In relation to the Sanders and Webster presentation, Chapter 11, one might characterize the Western Pueblo as a high-risk, low-diversity area with correspondingly low population, whereas the Eastern Pueblo area is lower in risk in higher in diversity and population.)

IRRIGATION AND DRY FARMING

The subsistence practices of the Pueblo are usually described as irrigation agriculture among the Eastern and dry farming and Western

Table 15.2

ELEMENTS OF HOPI AGRICULTURAL STRATEGY

	Water	Temperature	Soil	Wind
Strains of corn	+	+		+
Dispersion	+		+	
Deep planting	+	+		
Northeast slopes	+	+		
Cluster planting	+		+	+
Topography	+		+	
Elevation along	+	+		
Elevation across	+	+		+
Early–late crop		+		
Kiva hothousing		+		
Beans–corn			+	
Technology	+	+	+	+

Pueblo.[4] Most of us are relatively familiar with at least some of the prerequisites of an irrigation system—the engineering skills and labor required to construct the ditches, the maintenance that must be regularly performed, and the allocation decisions that must be made. (But there is considerable disagreement about the time and degree of centralization in social structure required by these activities.)

But dry farming tends to be either an unfamiliar or a deceptively familiar term. Saying, as so many anthropologists have, that the Eastern Pueblo have irrigation and the Western Pueblo don't—even saying that the Eastern Pueblo have irrigation and the Western have dry farming— prepares us only poorly for the substantial differences that exist between the two groups because such statements fail to elucidate the complexity of Western Pueblo agricultural practices. Let us consider the Hopi as an example of Western Pueblo dry farming strategies.

Table 15.2 summarizes some of the planting strategies that the Hopi use (Bradfield 1971; Forde 1963; Hack 1942; Whiting 1937) and one or more environmental contingencies that each strategy helps to meet. Let us examine each of these strategies.

1. The Hopi carefully maintain different strains of water-, frost-, and

---

[4] Here and in other parts of the chapter I am contrasting the Hopi and Tewa as extremes on the continuum. There is some dry farming in the east; some irrigation in the west, for example. I am certainly aware of the diversity between those two extremes that exists in modern pueblos and of the far greater diversity that probably existed in the past. Understanding the nature of these equally real extremes is ultimately a source of insight into the variation between them.

wind-resistant corn. (In an area where environmental variation is so extreme, a hybrid with average tolerance would clearly be maladaptive.)

2. All of the strains of corn the Hopi have are adapted to planting at great depth, 10–14 inches below the ground surface. In the early spring months, soil at this depth is likely to be wetter, increasing the chances of germination, and warmer, decreasing the chances of frost damage to the just-sprouted seed.

3. Only about 5% of the land in each drainage is planted.

4. Fields are located on northeast-facing slopes (which are also sometimes terraced). Winter snows accumulate on these slopes, and the ground moisture is, therefore, likely to be higher at planting time. Moreover, this is the slope that catches the first light of the morning sun, the slope on which a frost will be broken earliest in the day.

5. The Hopi plant their crops in clusters rather than in rows. On the one hand, this packing together of several plants protects the inner ones from wind. On the other, it results in a lower overall density of plants in a field, decreasing the water requirements as well as the drain on soil nutrients for a field as a totality.

6. Topography is important to Western Pueblo practices; especially important is the selection of large and small alluvial fans. Fields in such locations will more probably receive water, and that water will more probably seep into the ground surface (a situation also characteristic of "dune" fields) rather than run off. Moreover, soil including both organic and mineral nutrients is deposited on these fans.

7. Fields are located at different elevations along the course of a wash. It is necessary that some fields be planted from 20 to 40 miles from a village to generate the needed differences in elevation (Hack, 1942; Dittert, personal communication). The summer rainfall regime in the Southwest is either hot and dry or cool and wet. In a hot dry summer, fields in the drier lowlands will receive insufficient water to produce a crop. Whatever rains that fall will do so in the high areas, where the growing season will probably be long enough for a successful harvest. In a cool wet summer, the growing season will probably be too short for crops to mature, but sufficient water will reach the warmer and lower-lying areas to produce crops there.

8. Crops are also planted at different locations across the arroyos—in the bottom, on the lower terraces, and immediately adjacent to the arroyo. In a dry year there will probably be enough water, at least subsurface water, in the arroyo bottom plots for a crop to be produced. In a wet year these crops will be washed away, but those on the terraces or away from the arroyo will be well watered. In regard to temperature, the sandy arroyo walls collect radiant energy during the day and release it

during the night, somewhat diminishing the chances of frost damage. Planting in the arroyo bottoms also provides some protection against the wind.

9. The Western Pueblo plant an early and a late crop each year, one in April and the other in May. The early crop runs the risk of being affected by a late spring frost, the late crop the risk of being destroyed by an early fall frost. In all but the most extreme years, one of the crops should come through.

10. Some of the plants put out in the second planting are beans, corn, and squash that have been "hothoused" in the kivas—that is, they are set out as young plants, not seeds. These young plants can also be saved for a period of days or a week in the hope that a cold spell will snap or that rains will fall.

11. Beans are planted along with the corn in order to replace some of the soil nutrients the corn removes.

12. Some water and soil control technologies are used, including the terracing of some northeast-facing slopes to catch winter snows and summer water and to slow erosion. Small ditches are built to carry water from springs and seeps to fields. "Water spreaders" are built across arroyos to divert water to nearby fields.

In summary these strategies are based on planting crops in a diversity of situations, in the expectation that not all but only some plots will bear fruit, as determined by the weather conditions of a specific summer. The travel and informations costs of such strategies are quite high. But they provide the only basis for dealing with the immense environmental variation of the area and a generally harsh environment.

SOCIAL STRUCTURE REVISITED

In my initial characterization of variation in social structure among the Pueblo settlements, I focused on different structural characteristics. Yet, these characteristics are at one level simply different ways of describing what at another level is the single structure of each Pueblo community. Although I am in substantial sympathy with the emerging tradition of decision theory in anthropology (Quinn 1975), I intend in this analysis to focus on structure in both a conceptual and a group sense, principally because the evidence that one would want to use to investigate social structure from a decision perspective is simply not available.

In Table 15.3, I have attempted to summarize the structure of Western Pueblo, Keresans, and Eastern Pueblo in respect to some of the more important activities that occur in these and any other villages. Taken

Table 15.3

VARIATION IN SELECTED ROLES AND ACTIVITIES AMONG THE PUEBLO

	Western Pueblo	Keresans	Eastern Pueblo
Domestic activities	Matrilocal extended family	Nuclear–matrilocal–patrilocal extended family	Nuclear family
Agricultural activities	Matrilocal extended family	Men	Men
Political offices	Clan–ritual household	Moiety, A	Moiety, A
Political activities	Clan–ritual household	Village	Village
Ceremonial offices	Clan–ritual household	Moiety, B, C, etc.	Moiety, B, C, etc.
Ceremonial activities	Societies	Village	Village
Kivas	Clan	Moiety	Village
Conflict	Clan	Village	Village
Landholding	Clan	Familial	Familial
Inheritance	Matrilineal	Partitive	Partitive

individually, the meaning of each of these activities is clear. Domestic activities are the domain of the matrilocal extended family among the Western Pueblo; the family group, whatever its definition, among the Keresans, and the nuclear family among the Eastern Pueblo. Agricultural activities are a common concern of all members of the matrilocal extended family among the Western Pueblo but are reserved for the men of the family among the Keresans and Eastern Pueblo. Political offices are substantially ascribed and associated with a particular clan or ritual household among the Western Pueblo, whereas they are associated with moieties in the latter groups. Political activity tends to be within or directly between clans in Western Pueblo communities, whereas it occurs far more substantially at the village level among the Eastern Pueblo and Keresans.

Ceremonies, ceremonial offices, and kivas belong to the clans among the Western Pueblo, whereas they are the concern of either moieties or the entire village among the Keresans and Eastern Pueblo, respectively. Land is held by the clan and inherited matrilineally among the Western Pueblo, whereas it is held by the family and inherited by children of either sex from either or both parents among the Eastern Pueblo and Keresans.

Two critical elements are not evident in Table 15.3. First, whatever the common anthropological usage, the minimal definition of a clan among the Western Pueblo is a single matrilocal extended family, a "ritual household" as Fox (1967) has called it. Second, although moiety organization in one form or another is present among the Keresans and Eastern Pueblo, the system is not a singular one. Different moiety divisions are used for different purposes. Any given individual can be a moiety, or society mate, with a particular group of individuals in one context but with a partially, substantially, or completely separate set of mates for other purposes.

A significant pattern is evident once this information is in hand. Among the Western Pueblo, there is basically only a single organizational unit: the matrilocal extended family or groups of such families. These families are the basic domestic group and entail the offices, ceremonies, and activities that are necessary for activities of the community as a whole. The matrilocal extended families are held together by (a) the overlapping membership of the ceremonial societies, and (b) the fact that men are members of two households—a ritual household into which they were born and a domestic household into which they married (Fox 1967). But beyond ritual there is little or no specialization in the role that a clan plays in village affairs. Each such unit, allowing for demographic and concomitant differences, is a structural parallel and to a substantial degree a behavioral parallel of every other such unit.

The situation among the Keresan and, especially, the Eastern Pueblo groups is fundamentally different. On the one hand, there are nuclear or small extended families. On the other are a large number of villagewide activities carried out by village officials themselves or by the societies or moieties. The roles of the village officials are specialized, and so are those of the moieties. Given that the different moieties do not and cannot be precisely aligned, the family unit inevitably contains individual members with a variety of different moiety commitments, creating multiplex ties among individuals and families.[5]

In short, the residential group among the Western Pueblo is the effective group for a wide variety of different activities that occur in the community. The residential group among the Eastern Pueblo is important in areas of subsistence and socialization but only to a limited degree in any other spheres. Panvillage affairs among the Western Pueblo substantially involve interaction among the residence groups in their ritual mold. Among the Eastern Pueblo and the Keresans a variety of different specialized organizations and offices exist to handle these same functions.

---

[5] Wives can change moiety affiliation at marriage. Children are sometimes assigned to moieties in alternating order of birth.

The Western Pueblo clan is a self-contained and self-sufficient unit. There is no parallel unit of equal self-sufficiency below the village level among the Eastern Pueblo and the Keresans.[6]

Having characterized social structure in this fashion, I want to return to the issue of explaining the diversity, focusing on four tentative, but I think not tenuous, connections between social organization, subsistence, and environmental variation.

The first of these connections is irrigation. It is evident that the original Wittfogel–Goldfrank formulation is a crude and mechanical one. It is based upon assumptions about the demands that an irrigation-based subsistence strategy places on its practitioners, and it has been justifiably criticized for this fact. At the same time, I feel little sympathy with the many suggestions that seem to reduce to the notion that irrigation is easy and nonproblematic. Several years of research in modern American farming communities on the Colorado Plateau—examining historical records of decades of intracommunity and intercommunity conflict, and seeing the substantial initial costs of constructing these facilities, the strength of the organizations brought into play yearly simply to maintain the ditches as viable facilities, and the ultimate failure of many communities as farming groups—convinces me that at least in this environment managing an irrigation system is no simple task. (And there is evidence of parallel problems among the Pueblo [Fox 1967: 10; Dittert, personal communication]). At the same time, none of the anthropologists who have commented on this issue, whichever side he or she has taken, has performed studies that allow one to assess the labor costs or the extent of conflict that accompanies such a system, and, until such studies are carried out, the extent to which irrigation may act as a strong selective pressure for relatively specialized organization at the village level will remain unclear.

A second and more direct and obvious relationship between environment, subsistence, and social organization is in the area of land use. The subsistence strategy practiced by the Western Pueblo requires that each domestic unit have access to lands in a variety of different microenvironmental situations, and compared with the Rio Grande Valley, the territory occupied by the Western Pueblo is extremely fine grained. The potential effects of a familial or partitive inheritance pattern in such circumstances are clear. Over time, it would randomize the location of the land holdings of any one group. Such a randomization process is maladaptive in the context of Western Pueblo subsistence strategies.

---

[6] Societies among the Eastern Pueblo are in some ways counterparts of clans in the West. While their importance in village affairs should not be minimized, they are neither as formal nor as enduring a social unit as the clan.

Dispersed clan land holding plus the option of obtaining land from ritual households allows each domestic group at least two sources to draw on. Among the Eastern Pueblo, there is no such necessity. In fact, given that the factors that have a negative impact on the success of crops are random events within a generally coarsely grained environment, a familial–partitive inheritance pattern may very well serve as a leveling mechanism. Not only is inheritance partitive among the Eastern Pueblo, but unused land reverts to the village council for reallocation to individuals (Brandt, personal communication). In any case, in the Western Pueblo area there would be strong selection against a group practicing a form of inheritance that was not lineal, that did not maintain access for individual domestic units to land in a variety of different locations (or that did not provide a substantial redistributive mechanism to overcome the resulting inequities).

As important if not more important than the land itself is the nature of the cropping practices. As we observed earlier, the Western Pueblo consciously maintain different strains of corn resistant to different environmental contingencies. Whiting (1937) notes that these strains are owned by matrifamilies, and that 85% of the seed corn a household uses in a year is obtained through inheritance. Mothers give sons seeds at the time of marriage. Great care is taken in selecting the seed corn in order to remove any hybrid ears. They refuse to plant corn that they believe to be from hybrid ears. Moreover, although some seed corn is exchanged between groups at spring ceremonies, there is a strict prohibition against saving any of the seed for next year's crop; it must be eaten.

Thus quite apart from the obvious steps that the Hopi take to ensure the integrity of the various corn strains, matrilineal inheritance is clearly important. At any one point in time, a domestic household has a variety of strains brought by the husbands who have married into the household. It may obtain temporary but not permanent access to other strains through purchase or ceremonies. But the strains are the possession of the matrifamilies.

In this same regard, the matrilineal inheritance of land and that of seed are clearly not independent. The probability of hybridization is much higher if seeds of different strains are planted in proximity to one another. When planting is done in dispersed locations, this problem is ameliorated.

The Eastern Pueblo do not have to cope with the same environmental contingencies and do not retain so many separate strains of corn.

A final but inconclusive factor is the demographic situation of the different Pueblo settlements. It is evident from the characterization of the social structure of the different groups that there are strong structural units within any Western Pueblo village but not within either Eastern Pueblo or Keresan villages. Moieties crosscut one another too much to be strong. In this sense, any Western Pueblo village is at least potentially a number of different villages, whereas the Eastern Pueblo village is a village, period. (I am not suggesting that clans always become new villages, but they could and did serve as structural foci for them.)

It could make a compelling argument on this issue if I could suggest that there is substantially more evidence for fission among the Western Pueblo—that clans continuously or even occasionally split off to find new villages. Unfortunately, I cannot. The demographic data for the Eastern Pueblo do indicate that there is no recurrent process of fission, but the Western Pueblo are poorly described demographically. There are occasions during the last century when splits were recorded, new villages were founded (Titiev 1944). The individuals who founded the new villages are clearly nonrandomly distributed with respect to the clan structure of the old. But a fission process cannot be established. Indirectly, one must suspect that a group growing two to three times as much food as is needed in a given year and employing strategies that are exceedingly costly in time and labor input must have become adapted to relatively extreme environmental contingencies, especially in contrast with the Eastern Pueblo, who produce only an 18% surplus (Ford 1972) and grow crops in the more immediate vicinity of their villages. But the case is ultimately only suggestive, not conclusive. (It is worth noting in passing that the documented cases of fission among the Hopi are greatest for Third Mesa, which has the least amount of arable land.)

This same argument can be approached from a slightly different perspective. If the likelihood of survival of a social unit is low, the likelihood of specialization is low, even given the increments to output per unit land or labor and/or reduced costs of information transfer and processing that are realized from specialization. Thus, one might argue that the Eastern Pueblo are specialized principally because they can afford it.

In summary, I am suggesting important links between variability in environment, variability in subsistence, and variability in social organization. In a high-risk environment, subsistence strategies based on a diversity of specific cropping practices will be selected for. No single strategy is adequate given the variation in conditions that occurs, and, therefore, hedging bets by using a variety of different strategies, only some of which will result in the production of usable resources during a given growing season, is the only viable alternative. I then argue that the *maintenance of this diversity requires a strongly lineal organization*. In general, I am suggesting that it is more difficult for societies to maintain patterned diversity than norm-focused but "normally distributed" behavior. In addition, specialization is problematic given that even the practice of a diversity of subsistence strategies is insufficient to prevent periodic breakdown and fissioning of population aggregates. A strongly lineal organizational pattern is one means of structuring the requisite diversity and of providing a unit within villages that will serve as the germ of a new settlement (although some members will almost certainly come from other clans) when fission is necessary. Lineality is, thus, of some structural, if not behavioral, consequence, but of great consequence during periods of stress.

There is some substantial similarity between this argument and one recently advanced by evolutionary biologists (S. Gould 1975). In the past, evolutionary biologists assumed that organisms living in unstable environments would possess great genetic variation in comparison with those living in stable environments. In unstable environments, they believed, genetic variation was necessary so that the population would survive extreme changes in environment. In stable environments, it was assumed, one pattern would prove most successful. Field studies showed the situation to be both different and more complex. In unstable environments genetic variability is limited, in stable environments it is great—a thousand flowers can and do bloom. The limited genetic variability in the unstable environments, however, programs organisms with great physiological and behavioral plasticity. That is, they respond to environmental changes through physiological and behavioral plasticity, which is maintained by a rigid genetic structure.

Similarly, I do not argue that the Pueblo behave in either a rigidly bilateral or a rigidly lineal fashion. The subsistence strategies of the Western Pueblo are behaviorally more varied, more plastic. This variability is maintained in a variety of ways, probably more ways than I have enumerated in this chapter, by a relatively more rigid, less varied, structure.

THE ARCHEOLOGICAL EVIDENCE

We need not, however, leave the case at the level of suggesting that these selective pressures may have operated. The archeological record of the southwestern United States is an extremely rich one. Unfortunately, it has not typically been interpreted in a fashion suitable to questions such as those we have been considering. Yet, although it is not possible to speak to the details of these selective pressures, it is possible to speak of them in a broad form.

Subsistence Strategies

Let us turn first to the issue of subsistence strategies. The most common understanding of the prehistoric subsistence pattern in the Southwest is that agriculture had been present for a considerable time prior to Spanish contact. Whether or not this is the case depends in large part on the kinds of evidence that one chooses to emphasize. The oldest remains of corn in the Southwest are indeed 4000 to 5000 years old. But, there are ethnographically known groups in the Southwest that planted crops and did not tend them but returned to see if there was a harvest in the fall. And there is certainly no abundant evidence of agriculture for many thousands of years after the first corncob.

The first sedentary settlements, which some archeologists see as a prime indicator of agriculture, do not appear until the second or third century A.D. (Haury 1967). And these villages are a temporary phenomenon. Between A.D. 500 and 900 there is little evidence of other than scattered settlements of one or two houses over most of the Southwest. The new strains of corn on which southwestern agriculture is ultimately based were not in evidence until about A.D. 850 (Schroeder 1965). Evidence of substantial agricultural practice in the form of abundant subsistence remains is not much earlier.[7] On the Colorado Plateau the first evidence of irrigation systems dates to about A.D. 900–1000 (Vivian 1974). In short, there is not firm evidence of subsistence strategies based on agriculture until well into the Christian era, perhaps no earlier than around A.D. 1000. In this sense, the southwestern populations even at contact time should not be considered as developed agriculturalists but as populations that were still experimenting with agricultural subsistence strategies.

And there is substantial evidence of this experimentation that pertains directly to the issues we have been discussing. Everywhere that archeologists have looked for evidence of irrigation and technologically complex agricultural strategies in the territory that is now inhabited by the Western Pueblo, they have found it. It is reasonable to conclude that at about A.D. 1100 the typical agricultural practice on the Colorado Plateau was the irrigation strategy now practiced by the Eastern Pueblo.

[7] Wilcox (1976) has argued that shifting agriculture was a predominant pattern in the early agricultural history of the Southwest. I suspect he is correct, in which case there was a somewhat heavier reliance on agriculture than is indicated. At the same time, Dittert (1959) and others have argued that ethnohistoric and ethnographic data greatly underestimate the importance of hunting–gathering among all Pueblo groups. Finally, I am convinced that by A.D. 1000 there is now and will continue to be evidence of a shift to a reliance on technologically based strategies.

One hundred to 200 years later, a very large percentage of the Plateau was "abandoned." I would suggest that this abandonment is a misnomer; there was no abandonment. What we are observing is the perfectly expectable outcome of an experiment with a new subsistence strategy; many if not most of the initial efforts failed. Earlier we saw compelling evidence that an irrigation-based strategy is unlikely to succeed in the complex and comprehensive environmental variation in the Western Pueblo area, most of the Colorado Plateau. It did not succeed, nor has any such strategy practiced by more recent groups. The strategy survived along the Rio Grande—an area with climatic and environmental characteristics suitable to its practice. In the Western Pueblo area a new strategy began to emerge, the strategy now practiced by the Hopi. Although proof is obviously not possible in such circumstances, I would venture that were it not for the arrival of the Spanish, much of the Colorado Plateau would have been repopulated by people employing Western Pueblo subsistence strategies. (Thus, if the equation of irrigation agriculture and bilaterality is accepted, Fox's position then receives greater support from the archeological evidence than does Eggan's.)

Social Organization

A similar picture emerges in the case of social organization. I do not use this term in reference to recent attempts to infer postnuptial residence practices but in reference to what I regard to be far more basic indicators of structural variation: the extent to which villages are planned or unplanned; the extent to which villages grow by simple familial expansion as opposed to the addition of larger social aggregates; the manner in which functionally different rooms—rooms used for habitation, storing, and ceremonies—are associated; the ratio of rooms to kivas (e.g. Steward, 1937). These are measures of variable social structures in a far more direct sense than is prehistoric matrilocality.

Unfortunately, southwestern archeological data have been used to make inferences about migrations rather than organization. Thus, Ford, Schroeder, and Peckham (1972) associate the Western Keresans with Mesa Verde Black-on-white, the Tewa with Santa Fe Black-on-white, the Tiwa with Taos Black-on-white, and so on. In fairness, they do note that "the basic assumption that major pottery styles can be correlated with particular linguistic groups has never been rigorously tested [p. 37]." In fairness, Fox, Eggan, and other ethnographers have accepted such conclusions. But does this proposition need to be tested? Or is it sufficiently absurd and insulting to the populations who are accused of such stereotyped behavior that is can be abandoned? In any case, such conclusions are supportable only when one ignores the bulk of the ceramic evidence from most areas.

In the final analysis, the position that one wishes to take on such inferred migrations is of importance to the current discussion insofar as one can show that different organizational patterns existed in restricted regions of the Southwest, regions that might have been the ancestral home of modern groups. What was the situation?

In relation to the earlier discussion of social organization, three questions can be posed that are answerable without an exhaustive review of southwestern architectural patterns, a review that is beyond the scope of this chapter. First, when did the village as an organizational form arise? The existence of a village is basic to both Eastern and Western patterns. Thus, before these settlement patterns are in evidence, a pattern different from either, one must presume, must still have been in existence. Second, what is the relationship between kivas and other architectural units on sites? Substantially different patterns exist among the modern Pueblos. To what extent can these be documented archeologically? Finally, what and where is the evidence of planned villages? Planning implies the existence of a substantial organizational entity at the village level, an Eastern Pueblo–like organization.

Village Size

According to conventional views of the prehistoric Southwest, populations lived in villages of 30–100 rooms before the abandonment epoch, hundreds of rooms afterward. There are still no data available that allow one to describe the size of the typical southwestern site either for all time periods or for any specific time period. However, members of the Southwestern Anthropological Research Group (Euler & Gumerman, 1978) have gathered information on nearly 3000 archeological sites generally distributed over the southwestern area. The average site with structures in these files has 6.5 rooms. At about A.D. 1000 the average site had 3 rooms. At about A.D. 1300 the average site had 10 rooms. Until very late in southwestern prehistory, people lived in sites that probably held a single family. Even if such sites were seasonal, there were vast areas of the Southwest without large centers from which people might have been moving; if their behavior was seasonal, they moved from one family-size domicile to another. And even during periods when some parts of the Southwest were occupied by people living in large settlements, available evidence suggests that they represented a significant minority of the total population (Plog, Effland, & Green 1978). Thus, the village as a settlement type and an organizational form was a late development. Aggregation into villages may very well have been one element of the "abandonment" period. Perhaps people concentrated into such villages in an effort to localize manpower for building more substantial irrigation networks. Perhaps such villages represent the development and success of nontechnologically complex agricultural strategies. But they are part of what began to happen as the Southwest was abandoned, not a part of the "Classic" period. Moreover, there is currently no evidence of regional patterning specific to homelands of the modern groups.

Kivas

Steward's (1937) discussion of the increasing scope of integration in the Southwest, as evidenced by growth in kiva–ratios, suggests that there was a substantial and strongly linear evolutionary pattern toward Eastern Pueblo organization in the Southwest taken as a totality. Was this the case? Although Steward's argument is provocative and his approach was pioneering, the case he makes is ultimately suspect. His tabular summary is based upon sites distributed all over the Southwest. For each site there are contemporaries that deviate significantly from the ratio. This argument stands whether one considers the case of Great Kivas or small room-size kivas. Consider the case of Great Kivas in Chaco Canyon alone. Sites with three kivas are contemporaneous with sites with none. And the same pattern can be found in region after region of the Southwest. No demonstration that there is a typical ratio of rooms to Great Kivas exists, and I doubt that a case can be made for such a ratio.

Moreover, the context in which Great Kivas are found is highly varied. In the Upper Little Colorado area of Arizona, for example, Great Kivas south of Winslow, Arizona, have no evident associations with room blocks. Farther east, near Show Low, they are generally associated with blocks of 10–25 rooms. Further east still, near Springerville, they generally occur in sites with 100 or more rooms. A similar pattern characterizes small, or room-size, kivas. In the Hay Hollow Valley of Arizona sites have such features. Less than 50 miles away, in the Chevelon and surrounding drainages, there is no evidence that they even existed. In the Mesa Verde area, the number of such kivas on sites varies substantially (Plog 1974). Thus, the evidence on kiva–room patterning suggests substantial variation all over the southwestern area; little regional patterning has been demonstrated, certainly none sufficient to define ancestral homelands.

Planning

And the same evidence exists when one considers evidence of planning, whether that evidence is in the form of the regularity of village plans or bonding–abutting patterns. Sites organized around several large plazas, suggestive of moiety-like divisions, do indeed occur near and in the Rio Grande Valley. But, Homolovi IV, near Winslow, Arizona, is identical to many of these sites and is claimed as an ancestral home by one Hopi clan. At Chavez Pass, near Winslow, one block of several hundred rooms is regularly layed out around a plaza, whereas a second cascades down a hillside with little indication of any formality or planning. Dean's (1972) analysis of architectural patterns at the nearby ruins of Betatakein and Kiet Siel suggest very different growth processes for these sites. Again, I would suggest that there is currently no evidence that the formality of village plans or processes of village growth show any distinctive patterning from west to east within the Pueblo area. The Classic was a time of great diversity in settlement and of small settlements. There is not evidence of a singular successful subsistence or organizational strategy over the Southwest. (We probably would not see the abandonment as an abandonment if we ceased to view the Classic as "classic," imputing the notion of a group of folk who "had it made.")

Given this, it makes no sense to argue that particular Pueblo groups already equipped with distinctive organizational patterns moved from different ancestral areas. Western Pueblo, Keresans, and Eastern Pueblo may well have originated in geographically distinct areas of the Southwest. But there are at present no studies defining such organizationally distinctive ancestral areas. Diversity was far greater than what such a construction allows. Moreover, their origins reflect a common evolutionary process—experimentation with subsistence strategies, experimentation with organizational patterns, and the survival of a few relatively more successful combinations.

ACKNOWLEDGMENTS

A preliminary version of this chapter was critically reviewed by Betsy Brandt, Jim Eder, Ed Dittert, Mel Firestone, and David Wilcox. Their criticisms have resulted in many improvements in it. There remain many arguments with which one or more of them would disagree.

REFERENCES

Aberle, D.
  1948   The Pueblo Indians of New Mexico: Their land, economy, and civil organization. *American Anthropological Association Memoir No. 70*
Bradfield, M.
  1971   Changing patterns of Hopi agriculture. *Journal of the Royal Anthropological Institute No. 30.*

Buchler, J. & H. Selby
    1968   *Kinship and social organization*. New York: Macmillan.
Dean, J.
    1970   Aspects of Tsegi Phase social organization: a trial reconstruction. In *Reconstructing prehistoric Pueblo societies*, edited by W. Longacre. Albuquerque: University of New Mexico Press. Pp. 140–174.
Dozier, E.
    1970   *The Pueblo Indians of North America*. New York: Holt, Rinehart, and Winston.
Driver, H. & J. Coffin
    1975   Classification and development of North American Indian Cultures: A statistical analysis of the Driver-Massey sample. *Transactions of the American Philosophical Society 65*: Part 3.
Eggan, F.
    1950   *Social organization of the Western Pueblo*. Chicago: University of Chicago Press.
Ellis, F.
    1964   A reconstruction of the basic Jemez pattern of social organization with comparisons to other Tanoan social structures. *University of New Mexico Publications in Anthropology No. 11.*
Euler, R. and G. Gumerman
    1978   *Investigations of the Soutwestern Anthropological Research Group*. Flagstaff, Arizona: Museum of Northern Arizona.
Dittert, E.
    1959   Culture change in the Cebolleta Mesa Region. Unpublished doctoral dissertation, Department of Anthropology, University of Arizona.
Ford, R.
    1968   An ecological analysis involving the population of San Juan Pueblo, New Mexico. Unpublished doctoral dissertation, University of Michigan.
    1972   An ecological perspective on the Eastern Pueblos. In *New perspectives on the Pueblo*, edited by A. Ortiz. Albuquerque: University of New Mexico Press.
Ford, R., A. Schroeder, and S. Peckham
    1972   Three perspectives on Puebloan prehistory. In *New perspectives on the Pueblo*, edited by A. Ortiz. Albuquerque: University of New Mexico Press.
Forde, D.
    1963   *Habitat, economy, and society*. New York: Dutton.
Fox, R.
    1967   *The Keresan bridge*. London School of Economics Monograph in Social Anthropology No. 35. London: The Athlone Press.
Gould, S.
    1975   A threat to Darwinism. *Natural History 84*:4–9.
Hack, J.
    1942   The changing physical environment of the Hopi Indians of Arizona. *Papers of the Peabody Museum No. 35.*
Haury, E.
    1967   The greater American Southwest. In *Courses toward Urban Life*, edited by R. Braidwood and G. Willey. Chicago: Aldine. Pp. 106–131.
Hawley, F.
    1937   Pueblo social organization as a lead to Pueblo prehistory. *American Anthropologist 39*: 504–522.
    1950   Big kivas, little kivas, and moiety houses in historical reconstruction. *Southwestern Journal of Anthropology 6*:286–302.

Lounsbury, F.
1956   A formal account of the Crow- and Omaha-type kinship terminologies. In
        Explorations in cultural anthropology, edited by W. Goodenough. New York:
        McGraw-Hill.
Ortiz, A.
1969   *The Tewa world*. Chicago: University of Chicago Press.
Parsons, E.
1924   Tewa kin, clan, and moiety. *American Anthropologist* 26:333–339.
Plog, F.
1974   *The study of prehistoric change*. New York: Academic.
Plog, F., R. Effland, & D. Green
1978   Inferences using the SARG data Bank. In *Investigations of the Southwestern
        Anthropological Research Group*, edited by R. Euler and G. Gumerman. Flagstaff,
        Ariz.: Museum of Northern Arizona.
Quinn, N.
1975   Decision models of social structure. *American Ethnologist* 2:19–45.
Schneider, D. & J. Roberts
1956   Zuni kin terms. *University of Nebraska Laboratory of Anthropology Notebook No.
        3.*
Steward, J.
1937   Ecological aspects of Southwestern society. *Anthropols* 32:87–104.
Strong, W.
1927   An analysis of southwestern society. *American Anthropologist* 29:1–61.
Titiev, M.
1944   Old Oraibi. *Papers of the Peabody Museum of American Archaeology and Ethnol-
        ogy* 32: No. 1.
Visher, S.
1954   *A climatic atlas of the United States*. Washington, D.C.: U. S. Government
        Printing Office.
White, L.
1939   A problem in kinship terminology. *American Anthropologist* 41:566–73.
Whiting, A.
1937   Hopi Indian agriculture II. *Museum Notes. Museum of Northern Arizona* 10:11–
        16.
Wittfogel, K & E. Goldfrank
1943   Some aspects of Pueblo mythology and society. *Journal of American Folklore* 56:
        17–30.
Wilcox, D.
1976   How the Pueblos came to be as they are: The problem today. Manuscript,
        University of Arizona, Tucson.

chapter **16**

Le Projet du Garbàge 1975: Historic Trade-offs

WILLIAM L. RATHJE

Each day the city of Tucson, Arizona, expends a tremendous effort to discard the 250 tons of material resources it generates at the household level, which will perhaps become the basis for studies by archeologists of the distant future. But these data need not be wasted by contemporary archeologists. The fact that household discard of commodities is observable as a process in our ongoing society provides archeologists with an interesting analysis potential.

Analyses of contemporary industrial societies using traditional archeological methods and measures can make behaviors today comparable to those of the past. This comparability provides a link to the work of other archeologists in the form of a cap to the long time sequences they have reconstructed and produces a unique perspective that relates past to present.

An archeological focus also provides a unique materialist perspective on our present society that contrasts to most sociology and psychology studies based on interviews. The kinds of observations archeologists record on human behavior–material culture interactions are easily quanti-

373

Social Archeology:
Beyond Subsistence and Dating

fiable on standard scales. In addition, the measurements and measurers themselves need not intrude on the activities they seek to record. (Interview–garbage comparisons, at both the census tract and household level, demonstrate that (a) there are significant differences between "front door" and "back door" data; and (b) these differences are patterned. For beer and cigarettes, garbage data recorded significantly more drinkers and smokers and higher rates of consumption than reported in interviews in the same neighborhoods.) This advantage of material–behavior studies has attracted the attention and even some emulation from sociologists.

Using an archeological perspective, researchers can analyze modern industrial societies in order to contribute to long-term and short-term views of the workings of complex social–material systems. This potential can be illustrated with a few comments about one aspect of the University of Arizona's Garbage Project—specifically, the analysis of resource discard from both a long- and short-term perspective (for more detailed studies see Rathje and Hughes 1975, Rathje and McCarthy 1977, Rathje and Harrison 1977, and Rathje in press).

The rationale for garbage research is clearly drawn from archeology. From this discipline has come an emphasis on the unique kinds of information that material culture contains about human activities and an appreciation for the significant part played in these activities by material commodities. Archeologists have developed methods to analyze old garbage in order to discover the relationships among resource management, urban demography, and social and economic stratification that once existed in ancient urban centers. Contemporary garbage can be used to obtain a new insight on the same relationships.

All archeologists study garbage; the Garbage Project's raw data are just a little fresher than most.

Each bag of household refuse is a neat time capsule of diverse, but directly related, behavior sets. Over 140 variable categories were selected to record garbage data in a way to meet as wide a range of problems as could be foreseen covering health, nutrition, personal and household sanitation, child and adult education and amusement, communication, and pet-related materials. Each item (usually clearly labeled food packaging) in sampled refuse is recorded by general category, specific type, input volume, cost, brand, material composition, and weight of any edible food discard (not including bones, skins, peels, rinds, or tops). The project's sampling design was based on grouping Tucson's 66 urban census tracts into 7 clusters derived from 1970 federal census population and housing characteristics. From 1973 up to 1977, household samples have been consistently drawn from 13 census tracts selected to be representative of Tucson's 7 tract clusters. The total recorded garbage represents around

3000 3.5-day household refuse accumulations—more than 140,000 individual items. The raw data were collected by Tucson Sanitation Division foremen, who randomly selected households within the sample tracts. Data recording was done by more than 100 student volunteers—the real core of the project—who were forced to submit to immunizations and coerced into wearing lab coats, rubber gloves, and face masks.

To protect the anonymity of specific households, garbage samples were recorded only by census tract. No names, addresses, or other specific personal data were either examined, recorded, or saved. To place present types of resource discard into a meaningful frame of reference, long-term data are needed. Without these, modern data are often equivocal or misleading.

Because we have so little comparative data, we often think of ourselves today as ardent recyclers. Coors, Olympia, the beverage industry, the Iron and Steel Foundation, Alcoa, Reynolds, and everyone else seems to be recycling metal cans. Until the slump in the building industry, there were incessant newspaper drives. At Christmas we all receive an onslaught of Christmas cards printed on recycled paper. Our potential conceit is placed in some perspective by the fact that at present, generally, we are recycling less than we did in the recent past. For example, today only 19% of all wood fiber is recycled. This stands in marked contrast to the 35% that was recycled during World War II.

Analyses of even older data indicate exponential changes in rates of reuse, recycling, and resource discard. Bunny Fontana's classic study of bottles excavated from mid-1800s trash deposits in Magdalena, Mexico, is an example (Fontana 1968). Fontana noted that after glass containers were first introduced, only broken bottles were found in trash, and in each case where bases were recorded, they were worn almost paper thin from long-term reuse. Even after bottles became more common and the infrequent discard of whole bottles began to appear, all bases, on both whole and broken bottles, continued to show signs of long-term reuse.

Garbage Project data from modern Tucson are a striking contrast. The average Tucson household discards 500 whole glass bottles each year. Around 50 of these bottles (10%) are made of returnable glass and could be reused, ideally, up to 40 times if returned to distributors. The other 450 bottles could be turned in to local recycling plants and ground into cullet for making additional bottles. Nevertheless, almost all bottles seem to be discarded as soon as the original contents are emptied; none show any trace of reuse.

Another example of time depth in resource discard may be nearer and dearer to the hearts of archeologists. A change in the discard of ceramics is illustrated by data presented by Deetz (1973) and excavated at

Plymouth Plantation in New England. The Joseph Howland site was occupied for 50 years, between 1675 and 1725. Deetz's photograph of the ceramics from its trash pits shows eight puny piles of broken pieces spread out on a spacious lab table. The same table is smothered by a deep layer of ceramics from a century later. The majority of the later pottery seems only slightly damaged by cracking and chipping, and an almost complete eight-place table setting is discernible in the piles of porcelain. This entire load was produced by a single family in only 5 years, between 1830 and 1835.

Tucsonans today do not often discard serving items, they concentrate instead on high-turnover packaging materials. The average household each year discards 1800 plastic items, both wraps and containers; 850 steel cans; 500 recyclable all-aluminum cans; and more than 13,000 individual items of paper and cardboard (largely packaging). The EPA estimates that as a nation in 1966, the United States produced 55 billion pounds of food packaging; most of it was discarded after a single use and disposed of in dumps and landfills at a cost of over $400 million. The majority of this packaging was developed to decrease food discard due to spoilage, and for this purpose it has been effective. Although considerable variability between sociodemographic groups has been identified by the Garbage Project and although the only other large-scale food discard data for households were presented almost 50 years ago without any clear statement of methodology of collection, it seems fair to say that packaging (along with other technological changes) has cut household food discard from 20 to 25% of total input by volume during World War I to between 10 and 15% of input by volume today in Tucson.

However, this technological solution to waste has been bought by a trade-off of nonrenewable resources (iron ore, oil, bauxite for aluminum) or slowly renewable resources (forests) in exchange for such rapidly renewable resources as corn, beef and apples.

It is important to study the development of this trade-off and to quantify various aspects of it now because many ramifications of our material–behavior interactions go unrealized while our response alternatives become increasingly limited by the size and inelasticity of our resource demands.

This resource–discard trade-off is a good long-term problem for archeologists to develop because their data base can place resource trade-off behaviors in an extremely useful perspective for modern consumers as well as provide unique data to test general regularities in long-term man–material interactions. Long-term trade-offs to decrease edible food discard lead into a study of food waste at the household level over the short-term—specifically, over the last 3 years in Tucson, Arizona.

Edible food discard has long been a concern of the government (most notably the USDA), consumer educators and nutritionists, and household managers; but it is not easy to obtain data on its extent, much less useful information on its social and behavioral correlates.

The limitations of traditional interview–survey techniques present problems for gathering accurate data on household-level food discard behavior in the U.S. The concept of "food waste" is fraught with moral implications. Few Americans will admit that they unnecessarily discard edible food even to themselves, and mere participation in a study of waste behavior is sure to bias results (Adelson et al. 1961, 1963).

On the other hand, garbage provides quantifiable data on food discard unbiased by the kinds of problems facing interviewers. There are, of course, other biases—garbage disposals, pets, fireplaces, and compost piles; but all these factors work in one direction: to minimize food discard. Thus, garbage data represent minimum levels of food utilization and waste. As a data base developed in 1973 and 1974, the Garbage Project began to correlate edible food discard patterns with sociodemographic population segments. Although patterns emerged around group means, there was a great deal of variability that cut across these groups and the question was clearly, Are there more general and useful correlates of food discard behavior?

Data from the 1973 beef shortage provided an initial clue. As prices went up and beef became less available, household purchase behaviors changed rapidly and radically: Shoppers bought new cuts, they bought in new quantities (either trying to stock up or trying to cut down), and they bought more or less frequently than usual. As this variety came in the front door, an all-time high waste of beef—9% of the volume purchased (not including the weight of bone and fat)—spilled out the back.

As beef purchase behaviors stabilized in 1974 and 1975, however, the quantity wasted decreased drastically to 3% of input volume. These data led to an hypothesized "food discard equation." This simple formula states that the amount of regularity in purchase–consumption behaviors varies inversely with the percentage of food input that is discarded. This waste equation is only an hypothesis and must be tested rigorously with our current data; however, we have had success in predicting retro-dicting relative waste rates among different population segments over a 3-year time frame for a wide variety of food commodities. Nevertheless, the formula remains applicable only to southwestern U.S. communities that purchase modern processed foods that are prepared and consumed at the household level.

From this formula we were able to anticipate food discard behavior in relation to the sugar shortage. As the variety of purchases increased along with sugar prices and scarcity in the spring of 1975, the quantity of waste of pastries, kiddie cereals, candy bars, and even sugar in granular form was double its previous rate.

The formula is also useful in evaluating the waste associated with commonly utilized commodities that do not rapidly fluctuate in price under normal conditions. "White" bread is an example. Bread discard associated with standard 24-ounce and 16-ounce packages is less than 5% of total input. Bread packaged in less than 16-ounce wrappers is less than 5% of total input. Bread packages less than 16-ounce are usually a special variety of sizes. As expected, the waste associated with these less regularly utilized breads is high, almost 10% of total bread waste.

Food discard may be at a lower rate today than in 1918, but edible food in refuse adds up to as much as 8% of the total weight of household garbage, and a considerable quantity of nutrients end up in dumps and sanitary landfills. Extrapolations from Garbage Project data suggest, for example, that in 1974 the 360,000 plus residents of Tucson discarded more than 9500 tons of edible food, worth between 9 and 11 million dollars. But to make any kind of dent in this behavior, the basic correlates of food discard must be identified, and attempts by consumer educators and nutritionists to modify behavior must be evaluated. It is obvious that if the discard formula is correct, awareness of waste is not enough to decrease discard; purchase behavior must be modified. It is now important for the Garbage Project to refocus on the sociodemographics of households in order to identify their correlation with specific patterns in food purchases and the effect of these patterns on food discard. The general implication of this short-term study and its tentative food discard formula for the study of long-term resource discard is that it too may be understandable in relation to general patterns and regularities of the interaction between human behavior and material culture.

This kind of synergism between long-term and short-term analyses is what the Garbage Project seeks to develop in its continued short-term archeology of household refuse and in its long-term comparisons of these data with the remains from much older household middens.

ACKNOWLEDGMENTS

Major portions of this research were supported by Grant AEN716371 from the Research Applied to National Needs Division of the National Science Foundation. Work is continuing through grants from the Environmental Protection Agency and American Can Company.

Appreciation is due to: Tom Price, Director of Operations, City of Tucson; Carlos Valencia, Director of Sanitation, City of Tucson; the personnel of the Sanitation Division; and the dedicated student volunteers who made the Garbàge Projet possible.

REFERENCES

Adelson, S. F., E. Asp and I. Noble
1961   Household records of foods used and discarded. *Journal of the American Dietetic Association* 39 (No. 6): 578–584.
Adelson, S. F., I. Delaney, C. Miller and I. Noble
1963   Discard of edible food in households. *Journal of Home Economics* 55 (No. 8): 633–638.
Deetz, J. J. F.
1973   Ceramics from Plymouth, 1635–1835: The archaeological evidence. In *Ceramics in America*, edited by I. M. G. Quimby. Virginia: The University Press of Virginia. Pp. 15–40.
Fontana, B. L.
1968   Bottles and history: The case of Magdalena de Kino, Sonora, Mexico. *Historical Archaeology* 1968: 45–55.
Rathje, W. L.
n.d.   Archaeological ethnography. In *Ethnoarchaeology: From Tasmania to Tucson*, edited by R. A. Gould. School of American Research and the University of New Mexico Press. (in press.)
Rathje, W. L. and G. G. Harrison
1977   Monitoring trends in food utilization: Application of an archaeological method. *Proceedings of the Federation of American Societies for Experimental Biology* 37 (No. 1): 49–54.
Rathje, W. L. and W. W. Hughes
1976   The Garbage Project as a nonreactive approach: Garbage in . . . garbage out? In *Perspectives on attitude assessment: Surveys and their alternatives*, edited by H. W. Sinaiko and L. A. Broedling, Champaign–Urbana: Pendleton Publications. Pp. 151–167.
Rathje, W. L. and M. McCarthy
1977   Regularity and variability in contemporary garbage. In *Research strategies in historical archaeology*, edited by S. South. New York: Academic. Pp. 261–286.

chapter 17

Prehistoric Populations of the Dinaric Alps: An Investigation of Interregional Interaction

EUGENE L. STERUD

INTRODUCTION

In the theoretical and analytical literature of European prehistory there is a paucity of work devoted to the processes involved in the origin and subsequent developmental history of early food production. In the context of the culture-historical tradition of European archeology, changes are customarily attributed to the broad and overly general concepts of *diffusion, migration,* and/or *autochthonous development.* Seldom has the espousal of such notions been followed up by detailed demonstrations of the reality of the forces claimed.

European archeologists have drawn heavily upon studies that were accomplished in southwestern Asia on early and primary food production, attributing the spread of food production into Europe and about the Mediterranean basin to demographic pressures farther to the east. The influences issuing from southwestern Asia are repeatedly in evidence in citations made of the work of Braidwood and Howe, Kenyon, Mellaart, and others, by the discussions involving the question of a possible

Social Archeology:
Beyond Subsistence and Dating

"Aceramic Neolithic" in Europe similar to that in the Near East, and the ready acceptance of the notion of Neolithic populations being sedentary villagers with the full range of supportive technological accoutrements that characterized the food producers of the Near East.

Although herding has been recognized as a regular component of early food production, there have been few serious discussions of pastoralism as a major strategy or focus of such Neolithic populations. Exceptional in this regard must be the observations of O. Menghin (1931) who did suggest at a very early point in time that some predominantly pastoral Neolithic groups may have existed. These, he suggested, might be identified by reference to the preponderance of domesticated animal bone over cereal remains in certain sites. Narr (1956) likewise raised the question of the role of pastoralism in the development of the European Neolithic as well as of later periods. Although expressing interest in the possible role of pastoralism, he laments that the identification of such food production strategies is most difficult. He too observes that differential patterns of faunal remains are the most useful kinds of data that can be brought to bear upon the subject. More recently, some writers have begun to take a closer look at the role of transhumance in Mediterranean Europe. Sherratt (1973) notes the likelihood of an extensive transhumant pastoralism as an important and locally developed land-use strategy. Barker (1975), utilizing site catchment analyses, questions the long-standing model of stable Neolithic food production shifting to a fully transhumant economy in latter Bronze Age times; he suggests instead a shift, already in Neolithic times, toward a more intensive pattern of land use that he sees as the possible result of population pressures. These suggestions, yet to be tested in any rigorous fashion, do represent some significant departures from traditional discussions of early food production in Mediterranean Europe.

Another factor that seems to have impeded serious consideration—at least by American anthropologically trained archeologists—of the role of transhumant pastoralism is the fact that the investigation of pastoralism in Europe has largely been ignored by sociocultural anthropologists and, instead, has been considered the domain of the cultural geographer. Thus, American-trained archeologists have not taken advantage to date of a vast corpus of potentially valuable data. By contrast, in southwestern Asia, where a number of sociocultural anthropologists have been involved in the study of pastoral populations, there has been a significantly greater awareness of the potential utility of pastoral studies in the development of models of early food production (e.g., the work of F. Hole, who has been pursuing a series of "ethnoarcheological" investigations of contemporary transhumant herders in the Zagros Mountains).

A MODEL FOR EARLY FOOD
PRODUCTION IN THE DINARIC ALPS

The basic proposition put forth in this chapter is that, during the earliest stages of food production in the Dinaric region, and perhaps in other regions of Mediterranean Europe as well, there was a heavy reliance upon pastoralism. This may well have taken the form of a transhumant strategy whereby herds were seasonally moved to areas where grazing was most readily available. During later Neolithic times, there was a shift away from such an extensive land-use pattern toward a more intensive pattern, involving more permanent settlement and a changed man–animal–habitat relationship.

Basic to this argument is the generalization that, given the repertoire of food management techniques available to early food producers in Mediterranean Europe, the less conducive the landscape for food production, the more extensive will be the pattern of land utilization. It will become clear in the subsequent discussion that in the case of the Dinaric region, one is dealing with a variety of ecological situations, some of which would seem to have been rather high-risk environments that would have placed some restraints upon the early food-producing populations under consideration here.

Transhumance, An Economic Strategy

Strictly speaking, transhumance involves the economic strategy of moving herds of domestic livestock from one place to another on the landscape in order to provide suitable pasturage for the animals. Although in most cases it is just one of several options open to a food-producing population, there are generally some environmentally based factors that figure prominently in the decision. These might include a seasonal shortage of water, absence of suitable pasturage locally, the difficulty of providing sufficient fodder for the animals during winter months, the harshness of the winter, or even the relative safety of the mountainous regions in times of political instability.

Transhumance can be viewed as a risk-reducing economic strategy in an environment that is, in some sense, marginal or instable or where there is some threat to the livelihood of the human populations or their economic resources. Risks are reduced as the people transport the animals to the available foodstuffs, thus utilizing the landscape in an extensive manner. It might serve to eliminate the threat of the "bad year" locally, or the unpredictably long and overly severe winter or summer drought.

There is, however, the ever present danger of degrading the landscape through overgrazing. Especially in marginal lands, overgrazing can permanently destroy the grass cover. This seems especially to be the case on limestone rich surfaces, where plants do not develop effective and durable root systems and, once removed, tend to be replaced only with great difficulty. Deforestation, for the purpose of opening up new pastures, may be a short-term strategy of some utility to the herder that, in the long run, may have disastrous effects upon the countryside. Although wild animals tend to graze much the same areas as domestic herds, the fact that the domestic animal movements are human-directed means that their grazing patterns may be markedly different, especially in the amount of time spent at any one place. What is involved in the grazing of domestic animals on wild lands is an interruption of the natural plant succession so that the plant communities never achieve the energy conservative climax stage of the succession. Grazing, or burning off areas to prepare better grazing conditions, repeatedly sets an area back to a primary stage of the plant succession and, in the process, threatens its existence. Grazing animals consume mineral-containing organic materials and remove those minerals from the region. In higher altitudes, where there are no earthworms, burrowing rodents aerate and mix the soils and are thus extremely valuable in maintaining the quality of the vegetational cover. Where overgrazing occurs, the vegetational cover is reduced and the soils turned up by the rodents tend more easily to be washed away, which accelerates erosional forces (Darling 1956).

Natural Conditions in the Dinaric Region

The natural conditions of the Dinaric region provide an important backdrop to the study of early food production. The geographic region under consideration is restricted to the portion of the Balkan peninsula that today constitutes the modern nation of Yugoslavia. Although this is a somewhat arbitrary unit, the Alpine range to the north does provide a natural boundary. The nearly total lack of archeological evidence issuing out of Albania restricts us to the south. The Danube basin, including the major tributaries above the modern city of Belgrade, comprises the eastern periphery of the study area. The main focus will be the Adriatic coast, the High Karst region just inland, and the rows of gradually descending mountain ranges to the northeast of the Dinaric mountain range.

The Adriatic Littoral

Along the Adriatic coast one finds a generally quite narrow coastal plain, wide from Istria to Šibenik, becoming a series of coastal terraces

	January	Minimal	July	Maximum
Adriatic Littoral	5–9° C	−4 – −8.7°	C20–26° C	40–45° C
High Karst	−3.5 – −3.8°	−24 – −34°	14.8–16.8°	30–36°
Eastern Karst	−3.5 – −6.8°	−24 – −34°	14.8–16.9°	30–36°
below 800 m	−10 – −3.5°		21.3–21.7°	
Sava-Danube Basin	c. −1.5°	−26°	c. 23°	41.8°

Figure 17.1.   Temperature ranges in the Dinaric region. (All temperatures in degrees Celsius.)

ending in cliffs broken only by river valleys, such as the Neretva. Offshore, a series of long, low, narrow islands parallel the coast. These are the remains of partly submerged limestone ridges.

The soils on the coastal terraces tend to be moderately fertile, with outcrops of *flysch* (clay and sandstone deposits left by sedimentation processes during the formation of the emergent Alpine range). The lower valleys of rivers contain alluvial flats. Due to its relatively flat topography, the broad coastal plain north of Šibenik has not suffered as severely from erosion as have the steeper slopes. Figure 17.1 illustrates the wide temperature fluctuation from winter to summer. Precipitation is highly variable, dependent upon microgeographic conditions; year-to-year fluctuations tend to be great along the coast, but generally below 1000 mm. Mostar, in the valley of the Neretva, has an annual accumulation of ca. 1400 mm. The precipitation is primarily in the form of winter rains.

The High Karst

Inland from the coast, the Dinaric range, the so-called High Karst, rises abruptly, forming one of the most rugged and formidable mountain chains in Europe. With peaks as high as 2538 m, it creates a climatic divide between the Mediterranean climate on the Adriatic and a continental climate immediately to the east. It has long been considered to have been a serious barrier to communication and is today traversed at only three or four places. This is a region of "classical" *karst* topography. Although the Adriatic slopes enjoy some of the heaviest rainfall in the Mediterranean (4500–5300 mm), the porous limestone quickly absorbs the water into cracks and fissures, draining the surface and leaving the landscape parched. The waters form underground torrents that ultimately emerge as rivers. In some cases, the underground waters have hollowed out enormous caverns, which subsequently collapse and are filled in forming various-sized sinkholes (dolines) or vast depressions (poljes). These are areas of greater moisture and soil fertility. In the fall the rains induce temporary flooding; in the spring the poljes are filled with melt water from snows melting on the high slopes. One often finds the permanent lowland villages today established on the margins of these basins.

Water is a scarce commodity, and there are many methods practiced to locate and preserve this critical resource. Cisterns are dug, fissures are stopped up, water is strenuously extracted from caves or deep crevices by long queues of villagers handing jars of water out of these fissures. In the mountains snow is collected in the spring and covered with straw or leaves to retard melting.

The soils of the karst slopes are thin, leached, and infertile (terra rosa), the limestone base seriously affecting the durability of the grass cover.

The Eastern Karst

Although lower in altitude, the mountain ranges just east of the High Karst are still formidable and difficult of access and travel. This area consists of a series of ranges running parallel to the High Karst, separated by valleys through which rivers have cut deep gorges as they flow northeastward to enter into the Sava, a major tributary of the Danube. V. Gordon Childe (1929) described these intermontane areas as follows:

> To cross the many parallel ranges into which the Bosnian highlands are broken can never have been easy. The passage from the Upper Drina to the headwaters of the Bosna by the present railway route involves the negotiation of many narrow canyons carved out by mountain torrents that now swirl along at the very foot of the perpendicular walls of rock [p. 2, footnote 1].

The Bosna River, mentioned by Childe, which has its origin as an underground river that emerges near the modern city of Sarajevo and that cuts its way to the lowland Sava plain, marks the focal point of the currently discussed researches, and it is on this river and on some of its primary tributaries that one finds the greatest evidence for early farming populations in this intermontane zone.

Although the Eastern Karst is still predominantly a limestone range, with occasional karst characteristics, there is a considerably greater soil cover here, which has historically supported the growth of trees, resulting from slope wash and other fluvial activities (fluviokarst) and creating water tables between the depositional surface and the underlying limestone.

The precipitation pattern in the Eastern Karst ranges from 1000–1200 mm in the higher altitudes (e.g., around Sarajevo, at the headwaters of the Bosna) to 700–900 mm at the lower altitudes. This occurs as spring and fall rains as well as moderately heavy snowfalls in winter.

The Sava–Danube Drainage Basin

As the lower elevations are reached, the valleys open up into the rolling hills and undulating plains of the Sava–Danube basin. The Sava, as a major tributary of the Danube, drains the whole western region. The soils of the central Danube basin are today quite fertile, due to the continuing alluviation along the Danube and its major tributaries. Especially to the east of the Danube itself, one finds extensive loess layers that are relatively light and fertile. It is this fertile riverine plain that attracted the interest of archeologists from the time of Childe until now. Childe made a great deal out of the corridor of loess deposits that ran parallel with the river drainage system, viewing this as the route along which early farmers moved into north-central Europe (Childe 1929:3,4, Map I). But the advantages of the soils of the Danube basin for early farmers have been challenged (Barker 1975). The basic argument is that (a) in spite of high precipitation, the evaporation is so great as to make the soils of the area moisture deficient; (b) the loess soils, being thick and dry, would have required a level of technology that was unavailable to the early farmers; and (c) the low gradient of the plain would have been regularly subject to serious flooding.

As one approaches the intersection of the Sava and Danube rivers, the relief is quite low, the entire area falling below 200 m. Discussing the flooding dangers, Barker (1975) remarks that

> much of the Vojvodina and the Hungarian plains to the north lies between 5 and 10 m above the mean water level of the two rivers (Danube and Tisza). With river maxima in late spring, large areas are liable to very serious flooding for up to several miles on either side of the river course, destroying the standing crops. The Sava, Drava and Tisza flood waters may even hold back the flow of the Danube causing the Tisza to flow backwards [p. 100].

Because of these factors, which Barker feels would have limited the potential for the development of a fully sedentary agricultural way of life in the Danube basin, he suggests that, in the earliest stages of the Neolithic, the local Štarcevo populations would likely have depended to a considerable degree upon herding practices.

The Sava region receives an annual precipitation of ca. 1000 mm, falling predominantly in the late spring (May and June). The winter months have a minimum of precipitation and the summer months are generally quite dry. There is a high evapotranspiration rate, which, as previously mentioned, does reduce the effect of the relatively high spring rainfall.

From the evidence just presented, it should be clear that the agricultural potential in the different zones of the Dinaric region is quite variable. Each zone has certain natural characteristics that would figure either positively or negatively into any discussion of the kinds of early food production that could have been practiced. It is, for example, interesting that one finds early food-producing Neolithic settlements in the Eastern Karst region at all when one considers the long, severe winters, short growing seasons (reduced numbers of frost-free days in contrast to low-lying zones), restricted amounts of arable soil, poor soils (leached or eroded), and the necessity for collecting and storing substantial amounts of foodstuffs for human consumption as well as fodder for the livestock.

Transhumance in the Dinaric Region—Historical Evidence

In the Dinaric region there is a long history of the practice of a transhumant form of pastoralism. Such was the pattern of many of the Dinaric inhabitants at the time of the Roman conquest. There are Classical references made to the fact that the Dinaric soils were ill suited to farming but that the region was quite adapted to sheepherding. The wools were coarse; the cheeses of the finest. The interior lands supported a pastoral economy with seasonal migrations of the flocks. Hunting and fishing supplemented this economy (Wilkes 1969:178–180). Indigenous Illyrian groups were described as inhabiting the mountainous lands of the region and relying heavily upon pastoral pursuits.

During the early Christian centuries, herding populations called Vlahs—whether correctly or not is disputed—were reported in these regions. From the fourteenth and fifteenth centuries come references to Vlahs in Bosnia. They were regarded as exclusively herding peoples. From the fourteenth century onward, there is increasing documentary evidence of the rich pastoral life existing in the Dinaric region.

Vlajko Palavestra, in 1971, published an interesting and relevant study of "Folk Traditions of the Ancient Populations of the Dinaric Region," which he utilizes a rich ethnographic collection dating back into the late nineteenth century. He was concerned with the folk beliefs regarding the identification of the previous inhabitants of the Dinaric region. Who were they? The most common answer was "Greeks." They were often considered to be wealthy, the wealth being in the form of livestock. A number of accounts refer to wooden troughs (which once carried water to the lowlands) as pipelines for transporting out of the mountains the milk derived from these herds—so rich was the pastoral economy! A common exaggeration described the size of the herds: "thousands of white sheep and thousands of black ones, the first arriving at their pens, the last still in the mountains." Why did they disappear? Their departure was variously attributed to "severe winter," "cold," "snow falling continually for several years," "snow falling during summer," "snow, frost, ice," "drought." Palavestra concludes that the widespread practice of transhumance, whereby herders brought their herds into the mountains each spring and kept them there until the fall when the first snow fell or when the weather turned cold, was the ultimate basis of the folk tradition. The annual visit and departure at the first signs of winter's approach, was altered into a single, final reason for the disappearance of the pastoralists (Palavestra 1971).

The transhumant way of life was severely reduced by the Turks, who did not wish to practice a pastoral life themselves but who, for some time, permitted the "Christian" herders to do so. They did, however, force the Muslim religion upon them. Dedijer (1916) relates a tradition to the effect that these pastoral converts practiced Islam in winter, while they were in their lowland villages, but in summer, when they moved with their flocks to the mountain pastures, they reverted to their ancestral orthodox beliefs. In the Middle Dinaric region, the transhumant way of life continued to be practiced during Turkish occupation, for they often found it possible to find protection, with their possessions, families, and livestock, from Turkish oppression by retreating, when necessary, to remote mountainous areas. It is no accident that Christian villages subsisted during Turkish times from herding whereas the Muslim villages were agricultural—a pattern that is still somewhat in evidence in Bosnia today.

Varieties of Transhumant Practices

In reviewing the literature from the Dinaric region, the reader is struck by the great variety of alternative measures practiced to provide a suitable adaptation to local circumstances.

Two basic types of transhumance are known for Mediterranean Europe. They are *normal transhumance* (Mediterranean transhumance), in which the winter settlement, the permanent village base, is maintained at low altitudes. Here the herds are moved to high mountain pastures in summer. The second is *inverse transhumance* (Alpine transhumance), in which the permanent village is maintained in the mountains; the animals are moved down into low-lying areas at one or more times during the year. I have counted at least twelve different patterns of transhumance, in the literature dealing with the Mediterranean-facing Dinaric slopes, which were operative as recently as the beginning of the present century. Still other patterns are described for the Eastern Karst zone.

The forms of transhumance practiced on the Adriatic slopes of the

Dinaric range all fall under the heading of *normal transhumance*, though varying greatly within this category. The implications that these strategies might possibly have in a consideration of early food production in this region make it useful to consider some of these variations in some detail.

In cases where highlands greater than ca. 1300 m exist close to the permanent lowland village, the flocks are kept close to home. Where this is not the case, some form of transhumant strategy is effected. The permanent village is generally placed strategically to accommodate the seasonal movements, often between the mountains and a large polje. In the spring the herders will take their herds to the high mountain pastures, where they have cabins. In the fall, when they return, they may remain in the vicinity of their village. Later they might take their herds farther down into the polje. Alternatively, upon their return from on high, they might go directly down onto the margins of the polje to take advantage of the grazing possibilities resulting from the increased retention of moisture there. The flexibility involved here is suggested by examples where herders, returning from the mountains to find the summer drought continuing longer than usual, will take their animals to poljes until the fall rains make it possible to return to their winter villages. Such cases that are triggered by drought are untypical moves by the desperate herder and, according to the ethnographic examples, set off arguments over grazing rights and trespass (Dedijer 1916) (Figure 17.2).

Yet other groups move up to the High Karst and back down again in a series of six or more stages, with temporary stops at each stage. In cases where there are multiple grazing areas with the annual trek of the herders, it seems clear that these are planned responses to a recognition of the fragile nature of grazing potential and that shorter stays at a number of different places cause less damage to the critical grass cover than do longer visits (Matley 1968) (Figure 17.3).

There are a few cases of herders who are essentially nomadic, spending 6 months wandering with their families and all of their possessions and spending the other 6 months in a low-lying village where they live in simply constructed houses, sometimes of straw, which offer the barest shelter from the rains. Their dwellings are more like caves than true houses (Dedijer 1916).

For our present purposes, the most interesting pattern that has been recorded is that of the Adriatic herders who take their flocks to the mountains every summer where they have established cabins. In a number of cases they have established in these high areas more permanent settlements called *villages of summer*, where they live with their herds until late December, at which time they return to their lowland winter villages. They have, in truth, double villages, a phenomenon also common in southern Bosnia. Dedijer (1916) describes them:

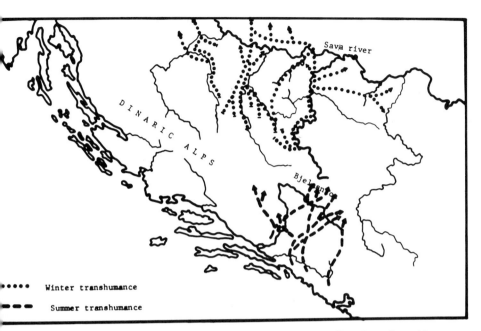

Figure 17.2. Winter and summer transhumance patterns, Dinaric region. After Popović (1971:104, Map I).

> In reality, they represent a form of transition of which one finds numerous traces. The establishment in several elevated regions, begun, in effect, by the cabins which later became villages of summer, were yet later transformed in their turn into permanent villages. . . . The existence of these villages can be explained by the need of a particularly extensive economy [pp. 355,356].

Some of these herders take their flocks quite high into the mountains at the border of the Middle Dinaric zone, summering at heights of greater than 1880 m on the slopes of Bjelašnica, which overlooks the Bosna Valley, just above Sarajevo. Since herders from the Bosna Valley also use these slopes, sometimes camping within a few miles from the Adriatic herders, there are numerous opportunities for information exchange, trading of goods, etc. In one area, there are some 14 villages populated by those who originally were Adriatic herders and who, after having established summer villages there, finally settled permanently in the mountains. They took on the identity of their new environment and, when they were quizzed as to how long they had been here, replied: "as long as the world has existed [Popović 1971:112]." Their transhumant pattern, though altered by their new permanent residence, was not halted. Instead, in March, from Bjelašnica, they moved their flocks down into the Bosna River valley and farther downriver, where some of them halted near Visoko (the

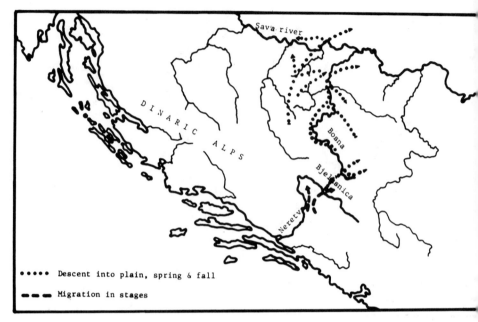

Figure 17.3. Multistage transhumance and spring–fall transhumance patterns, Dinaric region. After Popović (1971:110, Map II).

vicinity of several of the early Neolithic sites in this Middle Dinaric region, including the sites of Obre I and II, which will be discussed shortly); others continued down to the Sava plain, staying there during the spring lambing. In early May they returned to the mountain village, where, if they had sufficient fodder, they would keep their livestock in pens in the permanent mountain village through winter. This is, then, an interesting pattern of change in which their specific strategies changed as they adapted to the intermontane environment while at the same time they maintained their basically pastoral way of life. Such behavior as this must bring into question models of prehistoric settlement that view mountains as fairly efficient boundaries between groups.

Within this Eastern Karst or Middle Dinaric zone, the transhumant practices are of the *inverse* type, with the permanent villages well up in the mountains or in the high valleys. From here, a variety of migrations take place. Some winter on the Sava plain, having moved down there from Bosnia with their herds in the fall, after the harvests and haying have been completed by the farmers there. The herders graze their herds on the stubble, paying for these rights with dairy products or simply being allowed to graze there, since the manuring accomplished by the herds on the fields is of sufficient value to the local inhabitants. After the spring lambing has taken place, they return with their flocks to the mountain villages (Figure 17.2). Other Bosnian herders, who keep their flocks in their upland winter villages during the winter, will descend onto the Sava plain in the spring, returning in summer and then again in autumn. This is apparently a strategy designed to economize on the amount of local forage and fodder required from around the permanent village as well as to permit the lambs to be born in milder conditions (Figure 17.3).

There are indications that pastoralists permanently based on the Sava and Danube plains moved their flocks out of the low-lying areas as well and into the adjacent mountain valleys. Some of the archeological implications of such pastoral patterns in the Danube, Morava, and Vardar basins have been explored by Barker (1975).

A consideration of transhumance as a risk-reducing economic resource management strategy—because of its great time depth in the Dinaric region, on the Balkan Peninsula, and about the Mediterranean basin generally—and because of its considerable complexity and variety, all combine to suggest the potential usefulness of this tactic. The examples briefly described in the foregoing discussion offer some suggestions as to how the initial introduction of food-producing groups into such intermontane uplands as the Middle Dinaric zone might have been accomplished. Moving animals into this area during certain seasons and moving them out again could, as in numerous modern examples, have ultimately led to more permanent settlement without necessarily disrupting seriously the herders' basic pastoral pattern. In such areas that we might today regard as having been marginal, these risk-reducing strategies, which enabled the food producers to use the landscape in an extensive manner, would have made the region more capable of supporting viable human populations. The mobility involved in the seasonal herding practices would have afforded numerous opportunities for the exchange of valuable goods as well as information flow and genetic interaction.

RECENT INVESTIGATIONS OF EARLY FOOD PRODUCTION IN THE MIDDLE DINARIC REGION

Stimulated by the investigations of early food production in southwestern Asia, workers in southeastern Europe have begun to investigate in greater detail the subsequent spread of food production into Europe and around the Mediterranean basin. In Yugoslavia, this interest has further been stimulated by the opportunity for cooperative work under the sponsorship of the Smithsonian Institution. Local scholars graciously extended invitations to American colleagues, and a number of joint expeditions resulted. It is as a result of one of these projects, at the sites of Obre I and II in the Middle Dinaric region of Bosnia, that the issues treated in this chapter came under investigation (Figure 17.4).

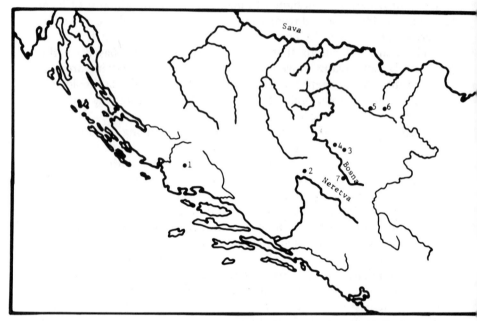

Figure 17.4. Map of Neolithic sites of the Dinaric region mentioned in the text. (1) Danilo; (2) Lisičići; (3) Obre I and II; (4) Kakanj; (5) Donja Tuzla; (6) Gornja Tuzla; (7) Butmir.

Obre I and II

The adjacent sites of Obre I and II are located on low terraces of the Trstionica River, a tributary of the Bosna River, in central Bosnia at about 500 m above sea level. The earlier of the two sites, Obre I, has, in its earliest levels, materials that unquestionably relate the earliest inhabitants here to the Danube-based Starčevo culture, in other words, the earliest known food-producing populations known in the continental parts of Yugoslavia. However, in these same levels are small quantities of ceramics that relate clearly to the Impresso culture of the Adriatic coast, that is, the earliest food producers in the Mediterranean basin. It is interesting to note that the latter ceramics represent a very limited segment of a rich and stylistically varied *fine* ware, whereas the coarser utilitarian wares are totally absent. At the same time, the Starčevo pottery is represented by a full array of *fine* and *coarse* wares. The upper layers of Obre I consist of a continuation of Starčevo elements, but with a number of new, apparently coastal, ceramic characteristics, again representing a limited, but stylistically *fine* ware. Outstanding are certain vessel forms that the local scholars recognize as being stylistically Adriatic (Benac 1973:383) and an uncommon form, a four-footed *rhyton*, a vessel with four fat anthropomorphic legs supporting a bowl, the mouth of which is oval and rises diagonally or nearly vertically. A large basket handle is affixed to the top of the bowl. The interested reader can see the parallel form from the Adriatic coast, as well as some examples from Greek sites, in Weinberg (1965:195–199, Figures 4–6).

Obre II, about 300 m upriver, exhibits, in its earliest levels (according to my determination), a continuation, with some modifications, of this so-called Kakanj culture (or late Starčevo). After the initial Kakanj-like horizon, my examinations gave evidence of a quite sharp break in the material inventory, a change that crosscut all categories of material remains studied and that was evident in the faunal remains as well. The layers above this break (there were no signs of a hiatus) were classically of the local later Neolithic Butmir culture (again, according to my determinations), in no major way distinct from those that had been discovered in the famous Austrian excavations during the 1890s at the Butmir site, located near the source of the Bosna River in the Bosna Valley just at the base of Bjelašnica Mountain. The remainder of the Obre II deposit, except for some obviously much later Copper Age pits at the surface, consisted of a series of Butmir levels in which there was a high degree of internal similarity and evidences of gradual changes taking place (Sterud 1976; Sterud and Sterud 1974).

From the Obre excavations came the largest collection to date of economic data from an early food-producing settlement in Yugoslavia, ca. 60,000 pieces of animal bone, a sizable sample of cereal grains, and a series of 31 radiocarbon determinations.

Some Alternative Investigative Directions

In the course of attempting to reconcile some disagreements regarding the nature of the transition from the early to the later Neolithic periods, it became clear that a reorientation of research into the nature of early food-producing populations in the Dinaric region was needed (Sterud 1976), and in place of the continuing preoccupation with site specific and basically culture-historical concerns, efforts should be made to determine, if possible, why early food production in the Dinaric region took the form that it did. Some beginnings have already been made to investigate the processes involved.

A number of alternatives seemed possible. The intermontane Middle Dinaric region, located as it is between the two areas of early food-producing cultures, the Adriatic and the Danube, might have functioned as an intermediate point in an interregional trading network. The presence in the regions in question of two river systems—the Neretva, which begins in the Dinaric Mountains and flows into the Mediterranean, and the Bosna, which also begins in the Dinaric Mountains, not greatly removed from the headwaters of the Neretva, and flows northeastward into the Sava, a major tributary of the Danube—would seem to be likely places to begin to investigate this possibility. Although at Obre one does find small quantities of exotic materials (obsidian, marine shell, amber, copper) as well as ceramics that appear to be introduced from one or other of the major spheres of early Neolithic development, at the end points of this postulated network there are no clear evidences of such an active flow of goods as one might expect from such a trade route.

A second possibility is that the intermontane region controlled certain valuable natural resources that were considered valuable (either regularly or intermittently) by the lowland populations. There is little of a tangible nature to suggest this. Most of the imaginable resources (dairy products, hides, etc.) are not likely to be found regularly in the archeological record. Stone for either chipped or polished implements must be rejected on the basis of present knowledge. From period to period within the Middle Dinaric region, the same raw materials recur repeatedly from site to site, although differing from period to period. An examination of sites peripheral to this region reveals the use of other raw materials that were apparently available locally. There is thus little to suggest interregional movement of lithics; rather there is some evidence for a regionwide adoption of a particular set of raw materials, a pattern that differs strikingly from period to period. Salt, although not a resource that preserves well in the archeological record, is a valuable commodity for animal-keeping populations and might qualify. At the northeastern fringes of the Middle Dinaric region, at the present city of Tuzla, is located one of the chief modern sources of salt for Yugoslavia today. Here one also finds the prehistoric site of Donja Tuzla, which, although only investigated to date in a limited fashion, appears to be a long-occupied Neolithic site at which the richness of the ceramics (in terms of sheer density of sherds) was noted as quite unusual (Dj. Basler, personal communication, 1971). Nearby is a second site, Gornja Tuzla, with early

Neolithic remains of a comparable age and composition as the early levels at Obre I; this site continued to be occupied into the Copper Age and has a total site accumulation of 5.45 m. Whether the local salt resources played an important role in the economy of these sites remains to be demonstrated. To date, these seem to be the only possible cases for the development of the Neolithic here as a response to the development of local natural resources.

A third alternative that has been under investigation is the possibility that early food-producing populations in the Adriatic and Danubian regions were forced by internal population growth, by the introduction of new people from the outside, or by some changes in the carrying capacity of the lowlands (e.g., soil depletion) to exploit this peripheral intermontane area as needed. It would have functioned for either or both of the lowland areas as a safety valve in times of demographic or environmental pressures. Somewhat supportive of this suggestion is the fact that one does see evidence, in the form of characteristic pottery elements, of both Danubian and Adriatic contact in the intermontane region. At Obre, for example, prior to the previously mentioned discontinuity (Kakanj–Butmir), the Danubian region is more strongly represented; after the break, the Adriatic (i.e., the Danilo culture) is more in evidence.

It is, however, with one last alternative that this chapter is primarily concerned, namely, the view that this intermontane zone was not necessarily a refuge zone but rather an integral part of the economic universe of early food-producing populations well adjusted to a pastoral routine that reduced risks by utilizing the landscape in an extensive manner. It will be argued in the following discussion that this strategy was modified for some reason to a more intensive exploitation of the environment through the conversion of the local site environments to satisfy their needs.

THE EVIDENCE FOR PASTORALISM IN THE DINARIC NEOLITHIC

The balance of this chapter will be devoted to a discussion of the proposition that during the early Neolithic in the Danube–Sava basin and along the Adriatic coast, considerable reliance was made upon pastoral pursuits and this involved a pattern of seasonal transhumance, whereby herds were moved into the intermontane region where grazing was most readily available. Given the marked contrasts in the environments of each of the two low-lying regions as well as the Middle Dinaric uplands, one might expect these strategies to have been complex and varied, reflecting those differences.

Essentially, the pattern of early Neolithic food production would seem to have been one of an extensive use of the landscape, as might be argued from the quality of the landscape viewed in the light of the exploitative (technological) capabilities of the early food-producing populations.

During later Neolithic times, resource management strategies appear to be different. There is a suggestion of greater stability of population in the Middle Dinaric region as well as in the lowland zones, which may indicate the development of a more intensive food-producing strategy involving environmental alteration rather than the transportation of the consumers to the scattered resources. The required alteration of a particular environment in close proximity to a settlement location could be accomplished through such things as the selection of those domestic animals that could best be accommodated to such a strategy, supporting such animals through the increased accumulation of fodder, reliance upon pasturages near to the settlement, and the increased use of penning. The selection of cereals and/or pulses that would thrive in the upland environment would increase the dependability of the field crop and allow for an increase in production of such commodities in the lands close to the settlement.

Examining the faunal evidence from Obre I and II (Figure 17.5), one is struck by the pattern of animal exploitation. The proportion of domestic to wild animals throughout the Neolithic occupation of the Obre sites is extremely high. This argues for a relatively heavy reliance upon domestic animals in the overall economy. Unfortunately, one cannot quantify cereal remains in the same way that one can the faunal remains. There is, however, the suggestion that husbandry is of more importance than field cropping.

In the early period of settlement at Obre by Starčevo populations from the Danube basin (assumedly), cattle and sheep–goat, both readily transhumant animals, are the most common. It is interesting to note that in later prehistoric periods, as well as today, the temperate conditions of the Danube basin were ideal for the exploitation of pigs. The early Starčevo populations in the Danubian region did not, as one might at first glance have expected, utilize pigs to any great degree. This might suggest an exploitation of more mobile stock (Barker 1975:101).

In the later periods of settlement (Butmir) at Obre, there is a marked shift in the composition of the domestic animals; pig, not a transhumant animal (although rare accounts of pig transhumance do appear in the literature for Mediterranean Europe), has replaced sheep–goat in popularity. Cattle remain the primary domesticate. It could be argued from this that there is a shift, however stimulated, toward a more intensive

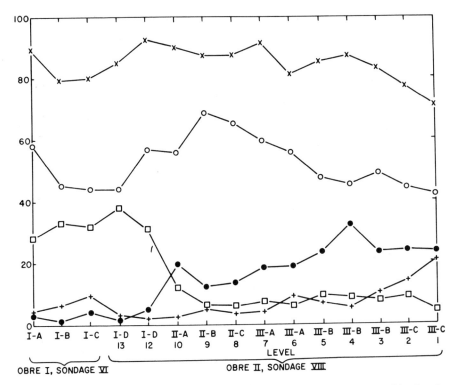

Figure 17.5. Distribution of percentages of wild and domesticated fauna, Obre I and II. × = domesticated; ○ = cattle; □ = sheep–goat; ● = pig; + = red deer. Based on Bökönyi 1974.

economic exploitation strategy involving a more localized site environment utilization. It is interesting to note that, although the ceramic inventory strongly points to an Adriatic-oriented (Danilo) population, the domestic faunal record does not. What faunal evidence we have from the Adriatic coast (and it is very scanty and only expressible in qualitative terms) points to an expected concentration upon sheep–goat. Pig is not of any consequence. At this time, however, in the Danubian region, there was a marked increase in the utilization of domestic pig.

At Obre one finds the first occurrence of postholes in areas outside of houses in the Butmir layers. Whether or not this is to be seen in connection with penning practices can only be speculated upon here (see Benac 1973).

Although the Starčevo settlements in the Middle Dinaric region, as evidenced by Obre I and Gornja Tuzla (basal levels), are thin and do not appear to represent any great intensity of local use of the area, at these sites and at increasing numbers of other sites in the Middle Dinaric region, there are evidences of more stable and continuously occupied settlements from later Starčevo (Kakanj levels at Obre I) and middle Neolithic times outward. At Gornja Tuzla, for example, the Starčevo levels are about 50 cm thick, whereas the succeeding Vinča and later levels reach nearly 5 m of deposition. The same pattern is common in the Danubian zone, where, for example, at the site of Vinča, the basal Starčevo levels are very thin; there exist at least 8 m of Vinča materials above these. We may be witnessing an initial movement of pastorally oriented Starčevo populations into the upland Bosnian region on a seasonal basis, a process that may, as suggested by the behavior of modern transhumant herders, have resulted in the establishment of more permanent settlements there. That this could have been done without any serious disruption of their normal economic patterns is again suggested by the modern examples. Such a settlement would certainly be more realistic than the often postulated waves of migrants sweeping into the area from some unnamed region. The contrasts in thickness of deposition in the earlier and later Neolithic settlements in the Adriatic region are quite in keeping with the changes just described.

Although there is rather little in the way of exotic goods discovered at Obre, it does appear that there is a greater evidence for trade of obsidian in the earlier phases. If the trace element studies accomplished to date are correct, these materials are ultimately derived from Sardinian (hence, Mediterranean) sources. Mediterranean spondylus shell, a few sherds of exotic pottery that appear to be traceable to Italy (Serra d'Alto), and the *fine* wares from the coast suggest a flow of information during earlier Neolithic times. The discussions of possible routes of communication, centering as they have until now upon the riverine connections, with little success in locating evidences of routes through the mountains, may, if the pastoral model is correct, be directed to the wrong places. The existence in recent years of summer pastoral groups from the Adriatic coast and from the Bosna Valley on the high slopes of Bjelašnica (above 1500 m), within 5 miles of one another, might suggest as likely a context in which early Neolithic exchange might have occurred (Benac 1973:Plate XLII, No.8, 190).

If, during the later Neolithic, there was a greater intensity of economic exploitation, there should be some indication of this with respect to the plant remains. Only two possible indications of this are apparent at Obre. One finds with the later, Butmir, culture that "six-row barley was beginning to be grown more widely as a crop [Renfrew 1974:52]." Locally, this same trend is also apparent at Lisičići and Butmir, both representing the later Neolithic of the region. Barley, although not tolerant of extreme cold, is less exacting as to temperature and soils than the early wheats. Its tolerance of alkaline soils makes it a valuable crop in areas such as the Dinaric region, much of which is derived from limestones (Renfrew 1973:81).

Yet another circumstantial argument for a greater reliance upon local field agriculture in the Obre economy is the observation made by Benac (1973:345) that with the Butmir culture there was a marked increase in grinding stones used in the processing of cereal foods.

One final observation in connection with Figure 17.5. The rise in the proportions of red deer in the late stage of occupation has been attributed by Bökönyi (1974) to the increase of rainfall and a consequent increase in forest habitats. To date the absence of suitable pollen data or other forms of confirmation of this opinion leaves the matter open to speculation. Another alternative might be the increased stability that an intensive economy might produce, leading to the opportunity to diversify by expanding the utilization of wild animals. Further research will be required to determine which of the two ideas has greatest merit.

The evidence bearing upon the proposition that the beginnings of food production in the Middle Dinaric region were closely tied into widespread pastoral practices and that, through time, there was a shift from an extensive to a more intensive pattern of land management and resource utilization is far from conclusive. It is felt, however, that the generation of propositions such as this, inasmuch as they do provide the possibility of being tested through properly designed field researches, are of importance at the present stage of Neolithic research in southeastern Europe. The ultimate confirmation of such patterning in this area would seem to have important implications for the origins and development of food production in Mediterranean Europe generally.

Stock-Raising Patterns in Early
Mediterranean and Temperate Europe

When one begins to examine the pattern of early food-producing populations in Mediterranean Europe and in the more temperate areas of southeastern Europe, it becomes evident that there are some fairly consistent stock-raising practices. To illustrate this, I've used three-pole graphs to illustrate the proportions of the three early domestic animals that figured in the Neolithic economy. Figure 17.6 treats primarily those sites in the central Mediterranean basin for which proportions of these domesticates are available. Included are data from Franchthi, Nea Nikomedeia, Otzaki, Argissa Magula, Anzabegovo, and Ruk Bair—all of which are

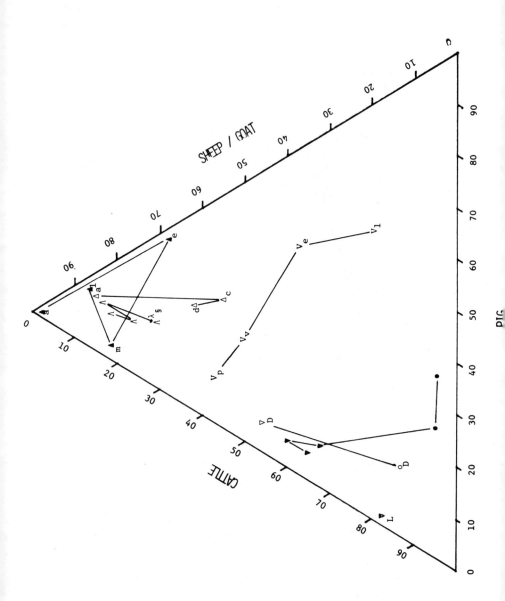

SHEEP / GOAT

CATTLE

PIG

located in Greece or in Macedonian Yugoslavia. They demonstrate that in the early Neolithic there was a heavy reliance upon sheep–goat and that in the semiarid environment of the Mediterranean there were only moderate changes through time. Certainly the nature of the environment—the soil characteristics, the grass cover, and the scarcity of water—contributed to make this pastoral pattern the most suitable one given the restraints of early Neolithic technology. The only striking departure from this pattern is that of Otzaki, a multicomponent Neolithic site located near Larissa in Thessaly. There the most obvious change in the economic pattern is a dramatic and unidirectional shift toward the increased utilization of pig.

On the same graph is shown, for comparative purposes, the pattern of animal-keeping changes that marked the sites of Obre and Divostin from early (Starčevo) to later prehistoric periods. The Starčevo levels at Lepenski Vir are also included. Here the reliance upon a combination of cattle and sheep–goat is indicated; in later periods, there is a shift to a greater utilization of pig. There is thus a clear contrast between the pattern illustrated for Mediterranean Europe and that of more temperate surroundings in the central Balkans.

Figure 17.7, another three-pole graph that concentrates upon a longer sequence of food-producing populations in southeastern and central Europe, offers several additional insights into this matter of stock raising in more temperate lands. Note first the distribution of the Körös sites of Hungary. These represent the earliest Neolithic populations there. It is of great interest to note that the pattern here is much more closely similar to that of the Mediterranean early Neolithic population than to the neighboring and contemporary Starčevo populations (Lepenski Vir, Divostin, and Obre are repeated on this graph). Since it is generally agreed that the beginnings of animal keeping in the Mediterranean and southeastern Europe were the result of the introduction of sheep–goat from southwestern Asia, where they were indigenous, a notion seemingly corroborated by recent investigations at Franchthi (Payne 1975), one might well expect that the earliest developments of food production in neighboring temperate areas might to some degree reflect these early patterns. The developments that took place in later Neolithic times, as

---

Figure 17.6. Three-pole graph plotting of proportions of domestic fauna emphasizing sites in Mediterranean environments. ∇ = Starčevo: L = Lepenski Vir, D = Divostin; $\blacktriangledown$ = Starčevo–Obre; $\bigcirc$ = Vinča; $\bullet$ = Butmir–Obre; Λ = Anza (I–IV); λ = Ruk Bair; $\S$ = Nea Nikomedeia; Δ = Argissa Magula (aceramic, ceramic, Dimini); $\blacktriangle$ = Franchthi: a = aceramic, e = early Neolithic, m = middle Neolithic, l = late Neolithic; V_p = Proto-Sesklo Otzaki; V_v = Presesklo; V_e = Early Sesklo; V_1 = Late Sesklo.

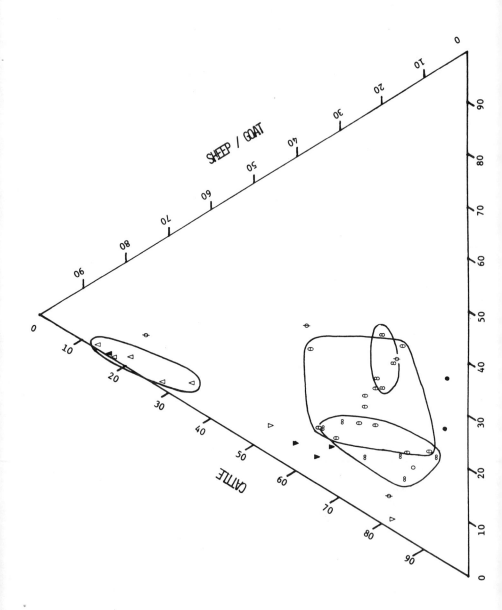

well as throughout the Bronze and Iron ages here, are all marked by a considerable reliance upon pig.

Such a trend toward the domestic pig is not surprising. Their absence in Mediterranean sites might best be explained by its relatively inefficient body temperature regulatory capacity. Pigs thrive in shaded riverine systems and forested lands of a temperate environment. They represent somewhat of a specialization in that their value lies almost exclusively in high meat yield. Unlike cattle, sheep, or goats, they have no additional economic uses. Their diet, too, is unlike the other domesticates. They do not thrive on grasses but consume nuts, tubers, and grains, and they are not transhumant animals. This specialization is suggestive of human populations who have developed a more intensive pattern of environmental modification than had been the case during early Neolithic times (Harris 1971:41, 42).

CONCLUSION

Although much of the preceding is to be viewed as speculative and open to question on a number of scores, the possibilities afforded by viewing the early food-producing populations in southern Europe in these terms are much more fruitful than the traditional explanations given. The possibility that the early Neolithic populations relied heavily upon transhumant strategies can be tested in the field. The recognition of this possibility must cause the investigator to raise different kinds of questions from those usually asked in connection with the Neolithic of Mediterranean Europe. Some energies will have to be directed to territories hitherto not considered to have been valuable to early populations. Greater importance must be afforded to the recovery and treatment of faunal and floral remains. New questions will have to be asked about the faunal samples. If the early food-producing Neolithic populations were transhumant pastoralists, the question of seasonal versus year-round will have to be approached differently from what has been done until now. As it stands, whole regions are essentially without suitable faunal studies. The most important to the current investigation is the Adriatic coast, where only grossly qualitative statements about the economy of the early settlers along the coast can be made (Benac 1973:344).

Figure 17.7. Three-pole graph plotting of proportions of domestic fauna, emphasizing sites in temperate environments. Δ = Körös; ▲ = Cardial; ▽ = Starčevo; ▼ = Starčevo–Obre; ○ = Vinča; ● = Butmir–Obre; θ = Linearbandkeramik; φ = Chalcolithic; ∞ = Bronze Age; 8 = Hallstatt.

When we consider the factors that might have caused the shifts observed in the record at the Obre sites and elsewhere, and that have been interpreted as described in this chapter, there is no certain conclusion that can be drawn. In the event that the opportunity would arise for one to investigate such matters freely in the Dinaric region, two obvious alternatives would seem to justify some attention, one involving the possible effects of an established food-producing way of life in this region upon populations (Boserup 1965; Clark 1966). Did the development of Neolithic food production here result in population growth, leading to more intensive economic strategies? Alternatively, did the extensive practice of transhumance result in the degrading of the grass cover and force an increased reliance upon more intensive economic practices?

Although the resolution of such questions will be no easy matter, the wide applicability throughout Mediterranean Europe would make any positive results achieved in the Dinaric region well worth the effort.

ACKNOWLEDGMENTS

The Obre data were acquired during the author's participation in excavations there sponsored by the Smithsonian Institution, Washington, D.C.; M. Gimbutas and A. Benac were the principal investigators.

The maps and other graphics were the work of A.-K. Bohlin; the photography was done by D. Tuttle.

REFERENCES

Barker, G.
    1975   Early Neolithic land use in Yugloslavia. *Proceedings of the Prehistoric Society* 41:85–104.
Benac, A.
    1973   Obre II—A Neolithic settlement of the Butmir group at Gornje polje; Obre I—A Neolithic settlement of the Starčevo–Impresso and Kakanj cultures at Raskršće. *Wissenschaftliche Mitteilungen des Bosnisch–Herzegowinischen Landesmuseums* (Archäologie: 3, Part A). Sarajevo. Pp. 5–191.
Bökönyi, S.
    1974   The Neolithic vertebrate fauna of Obre. In *Obre I and II. Neolithic sites in Bosnia*, edited by M. Gimbutas. *Widdenschaftliche Mitteilungen des Bosnisch–Herzegowinischen Landesmuseums* (Archäologie: 3, Part B). Sarajevo. Pp. 55–154.
Boserup, E.
    1965   *The conditions of agricultural growth: The economics of agrarian change under population pressure*. Chicago: Aldine.
Childe, V. G.
    1929   *The Danube in prehistory*. Oxford: Clarendon Press.

Clark, W. C.
1966   From extensive to intensive shifting cultivation: A succession from New Guinea. *Ethnology* 5:347–359.
Darling, F. F.
1956   Man's ecological dominance through domesticated animals on wild lands. In *Man's role in changing the face of the earth*, edited by W. L. Thomas, Jr. Chicago: Chicago Univ. Press. Pp. 778–787.
Dedijer, J.
1916   La transhumance dans les pays dinariques. *Annales de Géographie* 25 (137): 347–365.
Harris, M.
1974   *Cows, pigs, wars and witches*. New York: Vintage.
Matley, I. M.
1968   Transhumance in Bosnia and Herzegovina. *The Geographical Review* 58:231–261.
Menghin, O.
1931   *Weltgeschichte der Steinzeit*. Vienna: Anton Schroll.
Narr, K. J.
1956   Early food-producing populations. In *Man's role in changing the face of the earth*, edited by W. L. Thomas, Jr. Chicago: Chicago Univ. Press. Pp. 134–151.
Palavestra, V.
1971   Folk traditions of the ancient populations of the Dinaric region. *Wissenschaftliche Mitteilungen des Bosnisch–Herzegowinischen Landesmuseums* (Volkskunde: 3, Part B). Sarajevo. Pp. 13–98.
Payne, S.
1975   Faunal change at Franchthi Cave from 20,000 B.C. to 3,000 B.C. In *Archaeozoological studies*, edited by A. T. Clason. Amsterdam: North-Holland Publ. Pp. 120–131.
Popović, C. D.
1971   Les migrations des troupeaux en Bosnie et Herzégovine. *Wissenschaftliche Mitteilungen des Bosnisch–Herzegowinischen Landesmuseums* (Volkskunde: 1, Part B). Sarajevo. Pp. 99–116.
Renfrew, J. M.
1973   *Palaeoethnobotany*. New York: Columbia Univ. Press.
1974   Report on the carbonized cereal grains and seeds from Obre I and II and Kakanj. In *Obre I and II. Neolithic sites in Bosnia*, edited by M. Gimbutas. *Wissenschaftliche Mitteilungen des Bosnisch–Herzegowinischen Landesmuseums* (Archäologie: 3, Part B). Sarajevo. Pp. 47–53.
Sherratt, A. G.
1973   The interpretation of change in European prehistory. In *The explanation of culture change: Models in prehistory*, edited by A. C. Renfrew. London: Duckworth. Pp. 419–428.
Sterud, E. L.
1976   *The Kakanj-Butmir transition at Obre: A case study in the use of quantitative analysis*. Unpublished Ph.D. dissertation, on file, Univ. of California at Los Angeles.
Sterud, E. L. and A. K. Sterud
1974   A quantitative analysis of the material remains. In *Obre I and II. Neolithic sites in Bosnia*, edited by M. Gimbutas. *Wissenschaftliche Mitteilungen des Bosnisch–Herzegowinischen Landesmuseums* (Archäologie: 3, Part B). Sarajevo. Pp. 153–355.

Weinberg, S.
  1965   Ceramics and the supernatural: Cult and burial evidence in the Aegean world. In *Ceramics and man*, edited by F. Matson. *Viking Fund Publications in Anthropology* No. 41:187–201.
Wilkes, J. J.
  1969   *Dalmatia*. Cambridge, Mass.: Harvard Univ. Press.

PART III

Cultural
Resource
Management

No contemporary discussions of approaches in archeology can ignore the development and implications of cultural resource management (CRM). This book is no exception. Social archeology and other directions in the discipline make two major assumptions: (a) that there is an archeological data base on which they can apply their theories and methods; and (b) that this data base is available when needed without restriction so that the desired research associated with an approach can proceed without confining limitations.

The reality of the situation is that with increasing industrial development, the availability of archeological resources consistently diminishes. Although in some countries this rapid development and corresponding destruction of data is the exception and not the rule, in areas such as North America, this situation is encountered frequently.

How does the emergence of CRM as a necessary development within archeology interrelate with what we perceive as social archeology? Mainly, we view CRM as an academic and organizational framework within which increasing amounts of archeological research will operate. This framework comes equipped with some unavoidable limitations but also generates some beneficial products.

The limitations refer to various legal obligations set forth either by federal and state governments, or by the specific contracting agencies. These statutes many times limit what the archeologist may include in his research and how this research may be performed and presented. Another consideration is the various constraints issued by the contractual agreements between archeologist and sponsoring agency. In most cases, these restrict research to predefined spatial boundaries while superimposing a time framework that work schedules must meet. One other issue involves the need for specialized training of students to handle not only appropriate research questions but the management of personnel, funding, and scheduling as well as the mitigation necessary in the management of cultural resources.

The benefits accrued from CRM are many and varied. They range from the need to develop stringent and explicit research designs to the broadening of the archeological subject matter, to the encouragement of innovative and efficient methods and techniques of data recovery, analysis, and interpretation. Perhaps the most important and rewarding benefit is the preservation of at least some of the archeological data base so that contemporary and future developments in approaches to archeological research issues may have resources preserved in their original contexts from which to apply their emerging methodologies.

The chapters in this part exemplify the new directions in CRM and review many of the benefits and constraints that archeologists may encounter in their contemproary research.

In Chapter 18, Charles R. McGimsey views CRM as a concept presenting a set of challenges, specifically to (a) integrate archeological investigations into the the discipline of anthropology; (b) broaden the dimensions of the archeological profession; and (c) promote communication among a wide sector of audiences and participants.

McGimsey voices the opinion that archeologists have a responsibility and an obligation to the whole of the anthropological profession to incorporate into their research designs elements relating to all cultural resources, not just archeological ones. In this way the maximum amount of data is acquired and recorded, thereby optimizing the value of the research situation.

Under the premise that "in order for the past to be studied, it must be available for study," McGimsey discusses the remaining challenges. To ensure that responsible decisions are made concerning the preservation, or nonpreservation, of cultural resources, archeologists must expand their involvement in policy- and decision-making situations rather than participating solely in the traditional teaching and curating professions. The archeological discipline as a whole must adjust to accept these new directions as legitimate professional endeavors.

The third challenge offered by McGimsey is the obligation to foster and promote communication within the profession, with the public, and with policymaking agencies in order to "establish and maintain an acceptable level of credibility." Without this credibility, disillusionment would surely follow.

Fred Plog in Chapter 19 discusses a series of intellectual issues that arise from cultural resource assessment and management: (a) the theoretical issue of the conservation ethic; (b) the legal issue of site significance; and (c) the management issue of cost accountability. He stresses the contribution of new archeology in responding to these issues by defining problem areas, setting goals, and attempting resolutions to these research problems. A number of issues in archeology are discussed in the context of the CRM framework. Among these are the goals of research, regional archeology, areal survey, and excavation. Plog argues that unless we have general consensus on our research goals, and unless we improve and update our techniques of data recovery, we cannot effectively define and pursue mitigation measures. In this regard, Plog proposes a "goal-conscious, problem-conscious training effort," such as those exemplified in the traditions of the new archeology, as fundamental training for students and professionals concerned with CRM.

When scholars discuss CRM, most regard this framework as composed of groups of people performing similar tasks with similar management goals in mind. Thomas King, in Chapter 20, reviews the CRM framework and explains the internal branching of groups within the structure: the preservationists and the salvage archeologists. Each group operates under different premises, with important ramifications. When we examine the recent legal history of CRM, some interesting and mixed perspectives begin to emerge. King argues for a rekindling of communication between archeologists and historic preservationists so that the conservation ethic expounded by cultural resource managers may benefit from the experiences and resolutions of both groups and therefore become more fully realized.

In the final chapter of this book, Rex Wilson examines federally funded archeology programs in a historical framework and discusses their positive contributions to American archeology as well as to the wider spectrum of anthropology. Wilson outlines pertinent federal legislation, its evolution, and its present state and indicates the increasing involvement of archeologists in policymaking and funding agencies. Finally, Wilson describes the agency's recent steps to enhance and pursue communication with the archeological profession and our parent discipline, anthropology.

chapter 18

Cultural Resource Management—Archeology Plus

CHARLES R. McGIMSEY III

The concept of cultural resource management has provided archeology with the challenge of more effectively integrating its investigations and results into the whole of anthropology. It also has opened up the vistas of the archeological profession to their fullest dimensions. I would like to elaborate on these two points and conclude with a third.

The general, but nowhere specifically explicated, public philosophy that gave rise to the legal grounds upon which the concept of cultural resource management has begun to flourish is a broadly based one. The basic concern is with all resources of a cultural nature of sufficient value to warrant serious scientific consideration and the expenditure of public and private energy and funds to ensure their conservation—or, if appropriate, their recovery and/or preservation. Two of the most recent pieces of federal legislation—the Historic Preservation Act of 1966 and the National Environmental Policy Act of 1969—clearly reflect this broad philosophy. The first specifically incorporates general cultural resources along with the perhaps more specific archeological, historical, and architectural resources. The second likewise specifically includes cultural

415

Social Archeology:
Beyond Subsistence and Dating

resources within the scope and intent of the law thus ensuring their consideration during the planning process of any entity utilizing federal funding or requiring a federal permit. In this case there now is ample court precedent for the inclusion of archeological, historical, and architectural resources within the broader concept of cultural resources.

The third recent piece of federal legislation, the Archeological and Historical Preservation Act of 1974, though somewhat more narrowly directed in its concerns, does nonetheless extend its coverage to "significant scientific . . . data" as well as the more specific prehistoric, historical, and archeological resources.

Although it seems clear that archeological, historical, and architectural resources may be significant scientifically and culturally, there has been, as yet, no serious attempt to define the outer limits of "scientific" and "cultural" significance. I believe it also would be correct to say that the legal base has outpaced the acceptance of this broadly based philosophy by major elements of the immediately concerned professional community—the cultural anthropologists, historians, and others scientifically involved with the cultural resources.

Indeed, to many agencies concerned administratively with cultural resource management, the concept is accepted as applying primarily to archeological and visible historical or architectural structures. Nearly all individuals employed by such agencies to help them administer cultural resources located on lands or affected by programs for which they are responsible have been, in fact, archeologists. The voice of the archeologist has been heard throughout the land, whereas the voice of the cultural anthropologist has hardly been audible.

This situation presents archeology with a challenge and an obligation that hopefully will be viewed by all those in a position to react as an unparalleled opportunity.

In the United States the vast majority of archeologists active in teaching, research, and administration are anthropologically trained. They are aware at least that in order to be understood, man and cultural activities must be studied *in toto*, however narrow an individual researcher's immediate goals or interests might be. We need to translate this understanding into action and ensure that whenever we are responsible for activities involving cultural resource management, we accept that term in its broadest sense.

When responsible for research, archeologists must do what they can to ensure that the total research design includes appropriate cultural and historical studies, if only because the results of both may well have a significant impact on and thus need to be incorporated into the archeological interpretations, just as appropriate archeological data should be incorporated into the cultural and historical studies. Being responsible for administering cultural resources, archeologists should remember that the letter and spirit of the basic laws as well as their own professional training as anthropologists necessitates their integrating into their management programs a concern for *all* cultural resources.

Now to my second point: the vastly expanded vistas of the archeological profession.

Not very long ago an individual thought of as a professional archeologist was one who conducted research in the field as often as possible and carried out ancillary activities, normally teaching or curating, in order to eat between field trips. Many professionals still view themselves—and their profession—in that manner (as does most of the public). I submit that this is altogether too limited a view of the archeological profession and of the individual who chooses to make archeology a career—or, for that matter, who chooses it as an avocation.

It has often been said that archeology is the study of the past—and so it is, but it is far more than that. Archeology encompasses a total concern for the human past and for ensuring that a maximum amount of information meaningful to present and future generations is derived from that past and made available to those generations. This entails a great deal more than just studying the past.

In order for the past to be studied, it must be available for study. The profession cannot afford to let others assume total responsibility for assuring that an adequate portion of the resource base will be available. Determining which sites, objects, and data are to be preserved for future study, which are to be investigated now, and how much of the public's and the professional's resources are to be allocated to each entails many difficult decisions. Persons with an adequate background in archeology must be involved in making those determinations—either directly as managers or decision makers, or indirectly as members of a planning team.

Once a decision has been made to conserve a resource, individuals need to be involved who are adequately and appropriately trained (and this consciously implies training other than the traditional training in archeology). This will entail an increasing and increasingly varied amount of professional time and skills. For again, not only sites, but objects and data must be conserved. Archeology cannot afford to let land managers, museum directors, and data retrieval specialists or similar individuals trained in other disciplines assume the total or even a major portion of the responsibility for conserving our data base. All areas of conservation must be recognized as valid areas of full- or part-time professional involvement by archeologists.

As archeological research programs increase and become in many instances year-round activities, other forms of a professional career open up. Once this situation develops, and it has already developed in many areas of the country, it will be possible for an increasing number of individuals, for at least a portion of their professional careers, to carry out full-time research. Further, as programs of this nature develop, it will be necessary for some archeologists to devote a major if not all of their professional activity toward administering these programs. As was the case with the managers just discussed, full-time research and administration of research programs requires that the archeologist become conversant with and on occasion skilled in areas not now always associated with archeology or normally included in the present training of most archeologists.

But once again the archeological profession must not simply abdicate its responsibility to business managers, accountants, lawyers, planners, and legislators but must endeavor to encourage individual members of the profession to become knowledgeable administrators, so that they can assume responsibility for piloting archeological research through to a successful harbor.

Finally, the profession must recognize that those individuals who undertake to communicate the results of archeological research in a responsible manner to the public are performing a professional service of inestimable value, and the profession must make proper recognition of that fact.

The archeological profession is changing rapidly, so that the administration of archeological resources and of archeological research, teaching, full-time research, and communication of archeological information to the public must now be accepted activities of the professionally trained or serious avocational archeologist. I would also hope that individuals in the course of their careers would on occasion move back and forth among these various professional tracks—for only in this way can the profession remain healthy and avoid fatal fragmentation.

My final point is simple but somber. The archeological profession is today presented with more challenges and opportunities than at any time in its history. It also faces its gravest peril. The opportunities are to ensure that archeological (and all cultural) resources are incorporated in public and increasingly in private planning, that decisions concerning those resources are made in the context of the total public good and are based on adequate information, and, finally, that adequate investigation, recovery, conservation, and analysis are carried out on those resources that must be damaged or destroyed.

The federal legal base for accomplishing this is to a large degree already present, and the legal base is increasing, seemingly almost daily, on the state and local level. To an almost overwhelming degree, public and private entities responsible for management and program decisions are conscious of and looking to archeology to provide the appropriate information and adequate scientific response to enable them to make proper managerial decisions.

This change has taken place within the last 5 years. The next 5 years are going to be decisive ones for the profession.

If we meet our obligations by arriving at and communicating to the profession and to the public some basic guidelines with respect to such essentials as approximate costs, levels of information, performance, and results, so that we establish and maintain an appropriate level of credibility, then archeology could enter into a golden era. If we do not, and the public—particularly inasmuch as that public is represented by responsible public and private officials—becomes convinced that the profession cannot enable those officials to meet their current legal and publicly demanded archeological obligations, then those officials and the public are going to become disillusioned. The resultant backlash from that failure could be very serious indeed—adversely affecting not only the newly found sources of support for archeological research but the more traditional ones as well.

During the next year or two as never before (and as never again will be possible), the profession, and its success in implementing the concept of cultural resource management, holds the future of the past in its hands.

chapter 19

Cultural Resource Management and The "New Archeology"

FRED PLOG

The rapid growth in activities undertaken by archeologists in the name of cultural resource management is having and will continue to have a substantial impact on the discipline. For some of both cultural resource management's advocates and critics, this impact is principally a financial one. I intend to argue that the issues of funding in archeology that the emergence of cultural resource management has raised are of minimal significance in comparison with a series of deep intellectual issues—even crises—that are now before us. If archeologists are to successfully pursue the crafts of resource assessment and resource management, very specific answers to extremely difficult questions must be found.

These questions are a product of theoretical, legal, and fiscal components of cultural resource management. First, the conservation preservation ethic, which must be the guiding "theory" of cultural resource management if our ends are other than short term and pecuniary in nature, forces us to address a simple but difficult question: How can we learn the maximum about the past for the minimum of effort? It is true that the

421

Social Archeology:
Beyond Subsistence and Dating

prime directive of this ethic is preservation. But, it is impossible to regard preservation as more than an ideal, a frequently unattainable ideal.

On the one hand, we must take seriously our roles as guardians of the archeological record. On the other, as a matter of realism, we must recognize that playing a significant role in our nation's planning processes, which always have been and always will be political processes, will necessitate compromises between the preservation and growth goals of our society. It is important to remember that the intent of the legislation that has led to the emergence of cultural resource management is not the cessation of growth but more careful attention to environmental matters in the planning process. Therefore, mitigation will continue to be important. And, to conserve as well as to preserve, we must have some reason for believing that the measures we propose will have maximum effectiveness in knowing the past with minimum cost to the agencies involved. Otherwise, we will quickly and properly find ourselves too expensive to afford.

If this conservation issue is of importance within cultural resource management, it must be equally important outside of it. Nothing will make the position of the archeologist–cultural resource manager more untenable than a situation in which a conservation ethic is advocated for some purposes but not for others. Specifically, if the conservation ethic is important, it must be important for all archeologists, not just those involved in cultural resource management. Thus even non–cultural resource management, "research-oriented" archeologists must be certain that the impact they have on the archeological record as they seek and obtain new information is the *minimum feasible*. If archeological resources are rapidly disappearing, they are rapidly disappearing for all of us, and all of us must rethink the necessity of excavating in a variety of different circumstances in which we would previously have proceeded with gay abandon.

In summary, if we are to preserve and conserve archeological resources, we must have a very fine understanding of ways in which a maximum of information can be obtained with minimum cost and minimum impact on existing archeological resources.

A second set of considerations arise from the various needs to assess the significance or importance of sites. Most of us who have dealt with assessment are now familiar with the phrase ". . . is likely to yield information important to the understanding of . . . ." How many of us are in a position to evaluate with conviction the extent to which any site is unlikely to yield such information? Answering such a question involves methodological and theoretical as well as empirical concerns.

On the methodological plane, whether or not a site will yield such information depends on the kinds of techniques that we command for obtaining data from a site with its characteristics. On the empirical side, it depends on the extent to which complete, even relatively complete, information has been obtained from a particular region. On a theoretical plane, it depends on the kinds of information that archeologists as a group deem pertinent to their goals. The empirical issue is perhaps the easiest to address. Archeologists trained in the southwestern United States are aware of a number of occasions on which this area has been declared at least informally to be a "sucked orange." Yet over the years, it has continued to yield considerable new insights. I think most would agree that there is no area of North America in which as much time, effort, and money has been invested as the Southwest. Yet, even in this area the probability of obtaining new information has been and will continue to remain quite high. Thus, assessing the significance of a site is at present a difficult, close to impossible task for most areas of North America unless we are willing to take the simplistic and unrealistic position that every existing site may potentially yield such information.

Apart from the theoretical issue of the conservation ethic, apart from the legal issue of significance, we now face a nitty-gritty issue of cost accountability. How can we assure funding agencies that the information we obtain for them is the maximum that could be obtained at a particular level of funding? How can we assure them that the information they seek might not have been obtained at a far lower cost? Such assurances cannot be provided unless we are able to state with some precision the extent of archeological activites that are required to make specific statements about the archeological record of an area and/or specific statements about its prehistory. Are we actually in a position to make such claims? I think not.

There are really no firm answers that can be provided to *any* of the questions that I have raised thus far. It is fortunate that cultural resource management has forced us and will force us to address them. It is unfortunate that we did not choose to address them earlier. This choice betrays our assumption, if not belief, that archeological resources were infinite. It betrays the extent to which we pretended that the budgets we submitted to granting agencies were reasonable when we did not in fact know them to be so. For, whatever the reasons that we have not firmly addressed issues of goals, of the comprehensiveness of our understanding of particular areas, of costs, it is now clear that we must begin to address such issues.

I wish to suggest that to the minimal extent that we are able to respond to these issues at present, we are able to do so because of the people, ideas, and traditions associated with "new archeology." Yes, I consider myself to be a new archeologist. I do not, however, intend to argue that new archeology either has or will somehow magically provide us with answers and resolutions to the issues that I have raised. We are still very far away from such understanding. But, to repeat, to the minimal extent that we are able to respond to these issues at present, it is because of what new archeologists have learned. In this regard, I will defend the proposition that it is the intellectual traditions new archeologists have introduced that should form the basis of training for archeologists concerned with cultural resource management and the issues that cultural resource management raises. Specifically, I wish to address four aspects of archeological scholarship in the context of these cultural resource management–related issues: goals, "regional archeology," areal survey, and excavation.

GOALS

In recent years, a number of us have called for a more explicit discussion of the goals of archeological research. Fixing a precise date for the beginning of this period of self-examination is difficult. Minimally, it begins with the publication of Taylor's *A Study of Archaeology* (1948). But, it is reasonable to argue that the real impact of Taylor's work was not felt until 10 or 15 years after the publication of this work. In any case, it seems evident that during the last 2 decades archeology emerged from a period of several decades during which goals were not substantially questioned.

At present, there are some relatively clear elements of disagreement. Although all of us might agree that space–time systematics, paleoethnography, and processual archeology identify the broad parameters of our work, there is extensive dissension as to the extent to which each of these concerns should be evident in every piece of research. Moreover, there are finer and more specific issues over which it would be difficult if not impossible to argue that consensus exists—the relative importance of synchronic and diachronic studies, for example.

This disagreement—or at least lack of consensus—has important implications in cultural resource management. First, it is unlikely that we will make sense to any single agency with which we deal (much less all agencies) if the goals mentioned in specific assessment reports are significantly different. At a more basic level, there is no way to define effectively what we mean by mitigation in the absence of agreement on those goals. Has the impact of a particular project been mitigated if flotation samples have not been taken from a site? If pollen samples have not been taken? If only "diagnostic" artifacts have been saved? If waste flakes or minimally utilized flakes have not been saved? Clearly there would be no substantial agreement on such issues at present. Even questions as seemingly technical as the size of excavation unit and the level of detail at which vertical provenience is recorded can have an important effect of the quality of data from a given site or region that are saved. Finally, there is no basis on which we could currently even begin to decide if there is some "mini-max" strategy that would recover data relevant to some average archeologist working on some average set of problems.

My claim is not that new archeologists have somehow magically resolved the issue of archeological goals. Clearly they have not; they have only underscored the problem. The problem having been identified, a resolution is clearly necessary. And, a goal-conscious, problem-conscious training effort is necessary in order to produce archeologists working both in and out of cultural resource management who can provide clear answers to what, at present, can honestly be described only as questions.

"REGIONAL" ARCHEOLOGY

Although I grant that there is considerable room for argument on the issue, I believe that prior to the publication of some of Lewis Binford's (1964, 1965) early articles, the unit of archeological analysis and thought was a single site. Although there was general awareness of the need to generalize about organizational entities larger than those associated with a site, little attention was given to field and analytical strategies that would lead to such generalizations. That Binford's work began such a discussion is critical for a variety of issues in cultural resource management.

Most basically, the issue of the significance of a particular site or a group of sites can only be evaluated in a regional context. When we cannot specify the broad parameters of the prehistory of a region, whatever our goals, significance cannot be evaluated; it can only be guessed, guesstimated, or divined.

Yet, for most areas of the United States, our ability to speak with precision about regional characteristics is very limited. For how many areas of the U.S. can we even say with confidence what percentage of the archeological sites have been located? And, I emphasize *located*; I do not mean understood. During the last several years, I have worked in areas of the Southwest that most archeologists would have seen as rather completely known. Yet there is clear evidence that prior to recent surveys the percentage of sites in these areas that had even been identified was a maximum of 10%, often much lower. It is equally evident that the 10% of sites that were known in some areas represented an extremely biased sample of the archeological sites that existed. In what areas can we claim that the detail of our understanding of the archeological record is more substantial? Few—perhaps, none.

If we are to be successful as cultural resource managers, we must strive to free ourselves from a project-by-project assessment of cultural resources. The results of a given project cannot adequately be assessed without information on the region as an entity. Until we are in a position to assess and manage resources at the regional level, we are unlikely to do an effective job.

Again, I do not claim that the new archeology has provided us with a clear basis for doing regional archeology. I only argue that it has pointed us in a direction that is critical for successful cultural resource management and that such an understanding must be a pivotal aspect of graduate training.

SURVEYS AND AREAL SAMPLING

As was the case in the preceding discussion, one can argue *ad infinitum* about the origin of modern survey archeology. Problem-oriented surveys have a long history in the discipline. Willey's survey in the Viru Valley (1953) certainly stimulated some considerable rethinking of our survey efforts and Ruppé's discussion of kinds of surveys carried the matter further (1966). Yet, I would argue that a number of surveys carried out in the last 5 years embody significant advances in our understanding of (a) the precise nature of problems that can best be resolved; (b) the meaning of "intensity" in survey research; and (c) the role of sampling and sampling strategies in surveying. The importance of the first issue is clear: As conservation archeologists we should prefer surveys to excavation whenever possible because surveys conserve the archeological record to a more substantial degree than does excavation.

The second issue is a critical one in both resource assessment and resource management. When an archeologist undertakes such an activity, he is responsible for *all* of the resources in the project area. Clearly, *all* by yesterday's standard is not *all* by today's standard. Modern surveys have identified many more sites and a more diverse range of sites in area after area. Lofty generalizations of a generation ago have been shown to be dependent on hopelessly incomplete data bases.

To the extent that we take seriously our role as planners, the third issue is expecially critical. Certainly, we can all agree that once a project design is finalized, a 100% and very intensive survey of the area to be impacted is required. But what of the earlier stages in the planning process? Only a few years ago, we were attempting to identify some magic sampling fraction that all of us could follow. It is now evident that other issues (e.g., sample size), especially the nature of the question being asked, are equally important. We now ask for what kinds of questions and for what kinds of design activites is a 1%, a 5%, a 10%, and a 50% sample required. As a result of the work of Mueller, Plog, and others, we are beginning to obtain answers to such questions. But, we are still far away. The sampling literature is a substantial and a complex one. The precise modifications necessary to apply sampling successfully in an archeological context are unclear. It is, however, clear that 1% samples in some areas have identified more sites than "100% samples" of a decade ago did. And it is equally clear that unless we can state with some precision the sample size required for answering specific questions at specific levels of detail, we are dealing neither honestly nor fairly with funding agencies.

EXCAVATION

The issues involved in excavation are parallel to those of the preceding discussion. When do we not need to excavate a site because a surface collection has obtained the information that can be obtained? What percentage of a site must be excavated to obtain specific classes of information? For what classes of data is screening desirable? Necessary? When does a site have and not have integrity? How can we assess the impact of plowing and other disturbances on the integrity of a site? To the minimal extent that we have answers to questions such as these, the answers are in the literature of the last decade, the answers are incomplete, and the need for students trained to resolve the questions is substantial.

ETHEREAL QUESTIONS

One of the most important products of the new archeology pertains to no specific field, methodological, or theoretical issue but to our belief about the archeological record. In a variety of ways, we have become much more informed on issues related to measurement theory and the operationalization of variables. As a result, efforts are under way to precisely formulate and measure what early on in the development of cultural resource management were "ethereal" concepts and definitions.

Indirect impact is an example. All of us could spend virtually endless hours speculating about the indirect impacts resulting from the construction of a road, dam, or campground. Fortunately, we need not speculate. Given some definition of what an impact on the archeological record is, it is possible to measure the impact of a variety of different projects. Light-foot (1978) and Francis (1978) have completed such an analysis pertaining to roads in northeastern Arizona. They define a series of artifactual variables—ratios of different kinds of ceramic and lithic tools and densities of each—that are essential to the most basic inferences that archeologists make from surface materials. They demonstrate that within .5 mile of roads, the nature of artifactual materials has been significantly changed and that up to 30% of the variance in some artifactual characteristics of the area is attributable to casual collecting, which itself is related to differential access to the region resulting from the presence–absence of roads in particular areas. Although their effort is a preliminary one, it indicates the extent to which a concept such as indirect impact can become the subject of specific research efforts, the extent to which operational variables can be defined around such a concept. There are other equally problematical and "ethereal" issues in cultural resource management that will prove susceptible to field and laboratory investigation if and when research designs are constructed around them.

CONCLUSION

In summary, at a point when progress in resolving a whole series of methodological questions is beginning, it has become essential that answers and not just suggestions be obtained. Archeologists involved in assessment and management activities must be able to resolve questions such as those raised in this chapter. Inside and outside of cultural resource management, the effort to answer the questions must continue. Otherwise, we will certainly fail in shouldering the burden and realizing the opportunities of cultural resource management.

REFERENCES

Binford, Lewis
    1964   A consideration of archaeological research design. *American Antiquity 29*: 425–441.
    1965   Archaeological systematics and the study of cultural process. *American Antiquity 31*: 203–210.
Francis, Julie
    1978   The effect of casual surface collecting on variation in chipped stone artifacts. In *An analytical approach to cultural resource management: The Little Colorado Planning Unit*, edited by F. Plog. *Anthropological Research Papers No. 13*. Arizona State Univ.

Lightfoot, Kent
   1978   Casual Surface Collecting's Impact on Archeological Interpretation. In *An analytical approach to cultural resource management: The Little Colorado Planning Unit*, edited by F. Plog. *Anthropological Research Papers No. 13.*
Ruppe, Reynold
   1966   The archaeological survey: A defense. *American Antiquity 31:* 313–333.
Willey, Gordon
   1953   Prehistoric settlement patterns in the Viru Valley, Peru. *Bureau of American Ethnology Bulletin No. 155.*
Taylor, Walter
   1948   A Study of Archaeology. *Memoir Series of the American Anthropological Association No. 69.*

chapter 20

Archeology and Historic Preservation: A Case for Convergence

THOMAS F. KING

During the latter part of the nineteenth century, a rather motley group of people in the United States began to emerge as a "preservation movement." The designation was a sloppy one, it included a mixed bag of architects, archeologists, anthropologists, theologians, history buffs, and others who saw something valuable called "heritage" slipping away in the face of onslaughts by the modern world. The nascent preservation "movement" in America overlapped with the conservation movement that developed during the presidency of Theodore Roosevelt. It saw expression in the acquisition of Serpent Mound in Ohio for the Peabody Museum; in attempts to acquire and preserve the homes and birthplaces of various national, state, and local founding fathers; and in various expeditions of the USGS and BAE (Bureau of American Ethnology). It found its statutory expression in the Antiquities Act of 1906.

By the 1930s, the U.S. was a more complex place, and during the Great Depression the body of preservationists began to bifurcate. On the one hand, many architects and historians were employed in make-work programs that had them documenting, interpreting, and restoring old

431

Social Archeology:
Beyond Subsistence and Dating

buildings. On the other hand, many archeologists were employed in make-work programs digging up sites, often in advance of reservoir construction by the TVA and others.

Thus were created the two branches of what is now uneasily called cultural resource management: historic preservation and salvage archeology. The historic preservationists found their statutory expression in the Historic Sites Act of 1935, which established a broad mandate for the National Park Service to identify and protect cultural properties—to *preserve, in situ,* those things that were really of gut-wrenching historical importance to the American people. The archeologists, meanwhile, found their level in the River Basin Salvage Program and its equivalents, eventuating in the Reservoir Salvage Act of 1960, aimed at the *extraction* of data from archeological sites about to be destroyed. These are very different approaches: One stresses permanent, physical preservation of things because of their living, intrinsic importance; the other accepts the premise that cultural resources must inevitably be sacrificed to onrushing progress and attempts to get and preserve information about those resources before they go under. I do not mean to imply a necessary value judgment here; I am as uncomfortable with the historic preservationists' emphasis on things *qua* things as I am about the archeologists' itchy hands on the shovel. Nor do I mean to imply that historic preservationists do not have their salvage operations; the Historic American Building Survey (HABS) in the National Park Service, for example, very commonly conducts programs of architectural documentation of buildings that are doomed to destruction. Such salvage is not at the core of preservation, however. The basic philosophical premise of historic preservation is that all things of historic value should be saved; recognizing the impracticability of this premise, preservationists have set out to develop a variety of strategies, including the HABS salvage approach, but have gone far beyond it to maximize useful preservation in the modern world. The core premise of salvage archeology, I believe, is quite different; however much we may declare that we would really like to preserve everything, deep in our guts most archeologists really like to dig sites, and salvage, for all its unpleasantness, provides the opportunity.

This distinction between premises is an important one, and we should be aware of its ramifications. I think it is silly to make a lot of pompous declarations about "conserving the resource base" if all we really mean is that we're going to translate "salvage" into "mitigation." Instead, if we're serious about a conservation ethic, we need to get reacquainted with our long-lost preservationist siblings and see how our strategies may complement each other. The recent history of cultural resource management brings both preservationist and archeological strategies into contrast and gives rise to some rather mixed prognostications.

As we all know, in 1960 the archeological community obtained passage of the Reservoir Salvage Act, which permitted appropriations to the National Park Service for salvage purposes. In 1966, attempting to bind up the swinging steel balls of urban renewal, the preservationists obtained passage of the National Historic Preservation Act (NHPA)—a very complex but cleverly engineered piece of legislation that put the federal government in direct support of the establishment of a nationwide system for the identification, protection, and rehabilitation of historic properties. Features of the act include a national site data file called the National Register of Historic Places; a state historic preservation officer and staff in each state, with federal funds to do surveys to complete the file; a requirement that federal agencies pay attention to properties in the file during planning; and an independent watchdog, the Advisory Council on Historic Preservation, to jump on—or at least at—such agencies if they don't fulfill their functions. The contrast I pointed out before is apparent here: the NHPA creates a national structure within which many kinds of preservation activities can take place and within which a preservation community can grow. The Reservoir Salvage Act authorizes us to dig.

By the late 1960s, the federal government had so infused American life that both historic preservationists and archeologists found their earlier simple strategies inoperative. Thus were born Executive Order 11593 and the "Moss-Bennett Act," Public Law 93-291. The executive order was the preservationists' response to the fact that important properties were being destroyed faster than they could be placed on the National Register and thus brought under the protection of the NHPA; equivocal language aside, it called upon all agencies to treat historic properties as innocent until proven guilty, eligible for the National Register until proven otherwise. Moss-Bennet, on the other hand, was a salvage statute, reflecting a traditional archeological approach to the increasingly widespread federally assisted destruction of cultural resources.

Holding decent credentials as a backer of Moss-Bennett, I want to state at the outset that I think we made a mistake. This is not to say that something wasn't needed in the way of legislation to get us out from under the fiscal strictures of the Reservoir Salvage Act, but it is to say that we would have been a lot smarter to have evaluated what historic preservation was up to and tried to plug into it, instead of going our own, rather narrow-minded way.

The historic preservation laws and policies, although not without their problems, are rather smarter statutes than those developed by archeologists. Collectively, they provide for the following: (a) a plan—in essence, a research design or cluster of designs—to be developed by each state for the treatment of its cultural resources; (b) a survey of each state, resulting in systematic nomination of properties to the National Register in accordance with the plan; (c) protection of properties determined to be significant—implicitly, at least, relative to criteria developed through the plan—from damage by federal activities; (d) assistance in acquisition and long-term protection of a sample of such properties.

Granted, historic preservation laws and policies were not working very well for archeology in the early 1970s, and they're not always working well now. I do believe, however, that they provide a structure for archeological data protection that makes sense, and we would have done well to have written a statute that cured the ills of historic preservation from our point of view, rather than to have ignored historic preservation altogether and merely extended our old salvage programs into new and lusher pastures.

The deleterious effects of Moss-Bennett have been several, but two general problem areas stand out in my mind:

First, Moss-Bennett has provided a smokescreen behind which some agencies have deftly maneuvered away from their preservation responsibilities. For instance, it has been argued—and there are grounds for the argument—that once an agency has informed the secretary of the interior that its project may endanger cultural resources—without any kind of survey and without any provision for salvage, preservation, or anything else—it has discharged all its statutory obligations with respect to cultural resources and can blast away unscathed, leaving it to the secretary to scrape up the money to do something about it.

How are we to counter this? Only by insisting that, whatever Moss-Bennett may say, agencies still have definite responsibilities under the National Environmental Policy Act (NEPA), the National Historic Preservation Act (NHPA), and Executive Order 11593. It must be recognized that Moss-Bennett is a salvage statute, which provides agencies with a method of impact mitigation *after* they have fulfilled their responsibilities to locate, identify, evaluate, and if possible preserve cultural resources. This, however, brings us to the second dangerous misuse of Moss-Bennett.

Lately several archeologists have railed against use of the historic preservation statutes in archeological preservation, suggesting that we should abandon the National Register and all the statutes and regulations that are tied to it and use Moss-Bennett and NEPA as our sole sources of protective strength. This is a strange willingness to cast away weapons in the face of some pretty formidable enemies. It would leave us without the ability to stop projects pending full consideration of cultural resources, unless we wanted to litigate on the slippery courtroom flooring provided by NEPA. It would cut us off from a considerable source of strength—for us or against us—in the persons of the state historic preservation officers and the Office of the National Register. Worst, perhaps, it would divorce us from the NHPA, which provides the only explicit legal mandate anybody has to undertake the creation of systematic, regional research designs and plans for the evaluation, study, and protection of cultural resources—surely among the most sacred of the cows in the archeological milk barn. Let us suppose, for a moment, that we had a law specifying that a national system be set up for recording all archeological sites, ultimately computerizing these data and making them available for research. We might joke about the lifetimes it would take to complete such a filing system, and we might worry about its misuse, but we would surely applaud the concept and try to work with it. Suppose then that the law also required, and funded, a survey in each state to obtain information for the master file; we would surely greet this with enthusiasm. Suppose, further, that the states were required to develop research designs and plans for the identification, evaluation, and wise use of archeological sites; would this not be pleasing? Suppose then that all federal agencies were required to identify sites and develop ways of protecting or salvaging them, in consultation with the state, in advance of any action that might be archeologically damaging; would this not gain our approval? Finally, imagine that our archeological law, recognizing the frailties of state officials and federal agencies, established an independent federal review body to oversee compliance, with procedures to ensure both professional and public review. Would we not regard the whole package as nothing short of epochal?

My point, of course, is that we *have* such a law, passed, signed, and half-implemented, in the National Historic Preservation Act of 1966, as amended in 1976 and as implemented by Executive Order 11593 and the various procedures of the Advisory Council on Historic Preservation and the Office of Archeology and Historic Preservation. All we have to do is substitute the words *significant historic property* for *archeological site* and we are in business. Anti-registrants will insist that the terms are not interchangeable, and of course I agree: There are many valuable historic properties that lack archeological interest. The converse, however, is not true; it is ridiculous to think that an archeological site could be interesting but not valuable, useful for research but insignificant.

The process by which we define something as an archeological site is a process of significance determination. Is a single-component prehistoric occupation locus a site? Most would certainly say yes. What if it is represented by only five flakes in a 3-square-foot area? Most would probably hedge: Yes, it's a site, but no, I wouldn't invest the time and money necessary to deploy a survey team in such a way as to ensure the identification of such things. Why not? Because the data yield from such a site would not usually justify the effort.

Thus many products of human behavior, technically definable as archeological sites, go unrecorded because they are regarded as insignificant. But the case can be carried further: Suppose instead of flakes the site consisted of five pop-top beer cans; is it a site? No? What about five rum and port bottles, ca. 1760? Is this a site? Yes? What is the distinction; is it not information content?

My point is simple: an archeological site is recognized as such because it is thought to represent useful data about the past, but we seldom work through the recognition process, or define the bases for recognition, in any explicit way (See Thomas 1975 for an exception). The bases that we use to recognize an archeological site can also be used to recognize a National Register eligible property, but these bases must be defined and the recognition process *must* be explicated. This definition and explication is necessary to ensure that the public's historic preservation dollar is not being misspent, but I also suggest that a little rigor of this kind would not hurt the intellectual caliber of archeology as a science.

Excuses for continuation of the divorce of archeology from historic preservation, advanced in papers and conversation by archeologists, range from an ingenuous confusion of the National Register with a list of National Landmarks to a petty personal distaste for individual employees of the historic preservation agencies or for historic preservation in general. I would attribute these attitudes to mere naiveté or latent masochism were it not for the fact that they are often expressed by representatives of institutions that have traditionally made a lot of money by doing salvage. Salvage, as it used to be done, has some large advantages for the archeological empire builder; since its emphasis is on extracting all endangered data rather than applying any significance standards, what gets done is left entirely up to the individual project director. Since salvage carries no threat of stopping projects, one can be quite cozy with destructive agencies. Since what gets done is decided entirely between the sponsoring agency and the archeological institution, there are fine opportunities for deal making without being troubled about research designs, cost effectiveness, or general responsibility to the archeological community or the public.

Well, I obviously think this is wrong. I think it may be very attractive to some archeologists—including some who are honest and ethical but who happen to live in that rosy-hued place called the Southwest, where most of the land is federal and most of the projects are big enough to require modestly thoughtful environmental impact statements. In the more urban environments of the East, the irrelevance of Moss-Bennett and NEPA become much more clear, and we lean continually on the executive order, the Historic Preservation Act, and their implementing procedures.

In conclusion, I favor a rapprochement with our fellow preservationists. They are not all little old people in tennis shoes, and when you get to know them, you find that they not only share many of our problems but have challenging intellectual questions of their own. When you start thinking about historic preservation in its largest context, you find that it is a very anthropological activity, and I recommend it highly for anyone with an open enough mind to think that archeology might not solely be an enterprise dedicated to digging holes and manipulating sherds.

REFERENCES

Thomas, D. H.
1975 Nonsite sampling in archeology: Up the creek without a site? In *Sampling in archaeology*, edited by J. W. Mueller. Tucson, Ariz.: Univ. of Arizona Press.

chapter **21**

Changing Directions in the Federal Archeology Programs

REX L. WILSON

There is some apprehension today within the archeological community as to what the federal government is up to in matters of public archeology. Consequently, I will address in this chapter some of the more salient recent changes in federal posture with regard to archeology including comments on how these changes and new directions have the potential for impacting American archeology in a positive and substantial way. Further, I will outline how the federal programs may assist in the continuing development of archeology in this country. Finally, I will review the realigned—and redesigned—extramural archeological programs of the National Park Service and discuss some of the ways we plan for these programs to bring federally funded archeological research into a closer relationship with our parent discipline.

The federal government has long been associated with American archeology in a variety of ways, and it has provided considerable funding for archeological work through several agencies of the executive branch. Many archeologists of the generation preceding mine were, from the beginning of their careers, aware of federal support provided to John

439

Social Archeology:
Beyond Subsistence and Dating

Copyright © 1978 by Academic Press, Inc.
All rights of reproduction in any form reserved.
ISBN 0-12-585150-2

Wesley Powell in his explorations throughout the American Southwest. Many were directly involved during the 1930s in the government's make-work programs (most notably the Works Progress Administration) on the Macon Plateau in Georgia, in the Tennessee Valley, and in a multitude of other archeological manifestations throughout the nation. In addition to these programs, the major federal support for archeology prior to World War II was funneled through the Smithsonian Institution, the Tennessee Valley Authority, and the National Park Service.

With the close of World War II, the federal government moved rapidly ahead with long-developed and extensive plans for the construction of numerous multipurpose dams and related water resource projects throughout the nation. In many areas, construction plans were well advanced for the creation of reservoirs that had been authorized in the 1930s. Of primary concern were projects of the Corps of Engineers and the Bureau of Reclamation, projects that were revitalized as the war drew to an end. In addition to the often gargantuan dam and reservoir projects of these agencies, there were literally thousands of smaller projects being planned: canals and laterals, stream channel improvements, flood control projects, erosion control projects, watershed projects, and land leveling for irrigation activities below the dams and reservoirs. In response to the massive potential for the recovery of significant archeological information in the projects planned for the Missouri River basin, there emerged the Interagency Archeological Salvage Program. Partners in the program were the Smithsonian Institution, the Bureau of Reclamation, the Corps of Engineers, and the National Park Service. Archeological investigations were limited to federally undertaken water resource developments.

By 1970 all administrative aspects of the Interagency Archeological Salvage Program were being handled by the National Park Service, whose participation in the program was based on the Antiquities Act of 1906 and the Historic Sites Act of 1935. The Antiquities Act gave the Secretary of the Interior responsibility for protecting prehistoric and historic ruins, monuments, and objects situated on most federal lands. This responsibility has been delegated to the Director of the National Park Service. Congress declared in the Historic Sites Act of 1935 that "it is a national policy to preserve for public use historic sites, buildings and objects of national significance." The act empowers "the Secretary of the Interior through the National Park Service" to carry out this policy and authorizes the Service to conduct surveys, publish studies, and otherwise encourage the preservation of historic properties not federally owned. Finally, the Reservoir Salvage Act of 1960 gave the Department of the Interior, and through it the National Park Service, major responsibility for the preservation of archeological data that might be lost specifically through dam construction.

Spearheading and stimulating the new directions that were to follow in the 1970s was the National Historic Preservation Act of 1966. Because it provides the structure that joins together the subsequent historic preservation legislation and Executive Order 11593, its significance for archeology cannot be underestimated. Particularly significant to archeology is the provision of a means and an additional legal instrument for the protection of "districts, sites, building, structures, and objects significant in American history, architecture, archeology, or culture." An important aspect of the act is the provision for the listing of significant archeological resources or sites in the National Register of Historic Places.

Through the 1966 Act, Congress has broadened federal policy with regard to historic preservation activities to encourage the preservation of archeological or historic remains—of national, state, or local significance—by private persons and by state and local governments. For example, matching grants to the states to assist in the preparation of historic preservation plans are authorized by the 1966 Act. Section 106 of the act is especially important to American archeology. It requires that all sites and objects listed on the National Register be considered by the heads of federal agencies before they approve expenditures of federal monies on projects that may damage or destroy them. No federal project affecting a National Register property may proceed until the President's Advisory Council on Historic Preservation, also established by the 1966 Act, has been presented an opportunity to comment on the undertaking.

Another major change affecting federal involvement in American archeology occurred with the enactment of the National Environmental Policy Act. Effective on January 1, 1970, the act was signed into law "to establish a national policy for the environment, to provide for the establishment of a Council on Environmental Quality, and for other purposes." Although it is not concerned specifically with the disposition of archeological remains, it does have broad implications for a host of federal agencies and for the archeological community. The act clearly places responsibility on the federal government "to use all practicable means, consistent with other essential considerations of national policy, to improve and coordinate Federal plans, functions, programs, and resources to the end that the Nation may . . . preserve important historic, cultural, and natural aspects of our national heritage." The act further directs that all federal agencies shall employ "a systematic, interdisciplinary approach which will insure the integrated use of the natural and social sciences . . . in planning and decisionmaking which may have an impact on man's environment."

As a direct result of the enactment of the National Environmental Policy Act, federal agencies are no longer at liberty to disregard archeological values when they consider the impact of their programs on the total environment. Federal agencies now routinely fund archeological assessments of their own as part of their responsibilities for preparing environmental impact statements for their land modification projects. Consequently, the Interagency Archeological Salvage Program, coordinated by the National Park Service, no longer includes archeological surveys in advance of construction.

Further directional changes in the federal programs were occasioned by the issuance of Executive Order 11593 in the spring of 1971. It is generically related to the preceding historic preservation legislation and furthers its purposes and policies.

In essence, Executive Order 11593 requires federal agencies to "administer the cultural properties under their control in a spirit of stewardship and trusteeship for future generations," take immediate action to inventory and evaluate archeological and historic resources located on their lands, and "nominate to the Secretary of the Interior all sites . . . under their jurisdiction or control that appear to qualify for listing in the National Register of Historic Places."

Under Executive Order 11593, several coordinative responsibilities are placed on the Secretary of the Interior. These responsibilities are delegated to the National Park Service, as the principal agency of the Department of the Interior with archeological expertise. Accordingly, the Service is charged with: (a) encouraging the responsible federal agency, in consultation with State Historic Preservation Officers, to nominate to the National Register of Historic Places historic and archeological sites of established or potential significance located on federally owned properties; (b) developing criteria and procedures that can be used by federal agencies in meeting their responsibilities under Executive Order 11593; (c) preparing guidelines concerning professional methods and techniques of preserving historic properties that can be used by federal agencies, state, and local governments; and (d) providing advice to federal agencies with respect to the evaluation, preservation, and maintenance of historic properties and with providing all other assistance consistent with the intent and spirit of the executive order.

The basic purpose of the Archeological and Historic Preservation Act of 1974 (Public Law 93-291) is to make federal construction programs and all programs licensed or otherwise assisted by federal agencies, responsive to the damage they will cause to scientific, prehistoric, historic, and archeological resources once a project has been authorized. Clearly, the Congress did not intend that the act serve as a substitute for an agency's several responsibilities regarding its planning process—for example, the preparation of environmental impact statements and the observance of other requirements of the National Environmental Policy Act, the National Historic Preservation Act, and Executive Order 11593.

Policy relating to Public Law 93-291 has been developed by the Department of the Interior and is proceeding toward codification in the Code of Federal Regulations. The Department, through the National Park Service's Interagency Archeological Services, intends to implement the 1974 act in a manner consistent with existing environmental and historic preservation planning regulations that are imposed equally on all federal agencies.

The Department has taken the position that the preservation of data *in situ* is usually preferable to their preservation by removing them from historic and prehistoric sites prior to their disturbance or destruction through construction activities. In addition to making good management sense, we believe this reflects our responsibility to preserve data for future generations of researchers where possible. Using increasingly sophisticated techniques of data extraction and analysis, archeologists of the future can extract the data from their original contexts and study them at leisure. Although much of the urgency for archeological investigations in federal projects no longer obtains, it continues to be true that the study of data recovered in advance of construction activities and land-use projects is limited, sometimes severely, by current archeological methods and the constraints of funding and time. Further, we recognize that some historic and prehistoric properties may hold intangible sociocultural values for local communities, particular social groups, or the American people as a whole. Accordingly, the responsible agency must carefully assess the need and potential for preservation of historic and prehistoric values before making the decision to proceed with data recovery activities and permit destruction of the properties.

Planning processes are prescribed by the National Historic Preservation Act, the National Environmental Policy Act, and Executive Order 11593. They provide a framework within which the potential for *in situ* preservation can be determined. These processes also make possible the identification of archeological and historic properties while plans for federal undertakings are in their early phases of development. In consequence, the efficiency of any necessary data recovery activities can be significantly improved and conflicts between the undertaking and the preservation or extraction of archeological and historic data can be avoided. Moreover, when data must be recovered, these processes provide for maximum professional review of data recovery plans and hence maximize the probability that these plans will be complete and responsible.

Clearly indicated in the legislative history of Public Law 93-291 is a concern by the Congress that conflicts be avoided that might lead to delays in carrying out federal projects undertaken in the public interest. In most instances a responsible agency can avoid such conflicts by identifying potentially significant properties during the early planning stages of any proposed undertaking. Identification of significant properties should be made well in advance of the initiation of the project, commonly through preparation of environmental impact statements or other early planning documents. Having made such identifications, effective measures to mitigate damage to the properties can be taken before land modification actually gets under way. Federal responsibility for the protection of cultural resources does not end with consideration of significant values directly or indirectly threatened by federal or federally connected construction projects. It also extends to those historic and prehistoric resources situated on lands that federal agencies either own or control. Such agencies are responsible for the identification and protection of cultural resources under sections 2a and 2b of Executive Order 11593. They should institute policies to identify cultural resources on lands they administer and to minimize the possibility that such resources will be transferred or sold without evaluation and protection if necessary, damaged by ongoing activities, or allowed to deteriorate (cf. 36 CFR 800.9).

After the responsible agency has identified significant archeological or historic properties that are threatened with disturbance or destruction through federal or federally connected activities or by land and resource management policies, and when it has determined that preservation is neither prudent nor feasible, Public Law 93-291 can be applied for the recovery of important data.

Our present policy is to take all prudent and feasible measures to keep archeological remains threatened by federal projects in the ground—not to dig them up. Only if all lawful and prudent means for preservation meet with failure will we undertake to excavate or to recommend excavation.

The possibility that significant scientific, prehistoric, historic, or archeological data might be irrevocably lost or destroyed will in most situations remain speculative until planning steps required by law have been substantially completed by the responsible federal agencies. Accordingly, the Department of the Interior will typically not consider using funds appropriated for survey, recovery, protection, and preservation of any such data until such time as the concerned agency informs the Department that it is in compliance with the requirements of the National Environmental Policy Act, Executive Order 11593, and the National Historic Preservation Act of 1966 and is in a position where it may, consistent with these responsibilities, assure the Department that the loss of such data is probable. These same limitations will be expressed in coordinating guidelines being developed to structure all data recovery operations pursuant to Public Law 93-291. Every effort will be made, however, to avoid undue interference or delay of federal projects and programs consistent with this legislation and its legislative history.

The fundamental purpose of Public Law 93-291 is to expand the application of the Reservoir Salvage Act of 1960 (Public Law 86-523) to include the preservation of scientific, prehistoric, historic, and archeological data in all federal or federally assisted or licensed construction projects, not just federal dam and reservoir sites. It places coordinating responsibility with the Secretary of the Interior to ensure a relatively uniform federal data recovery program. It authorizes all federal agencies to seek future appropriations, to obligate available monies, or reprogram existing appropriations for the recovery, protection, and preservation of significant data. Finally, it permits agencies either to undertake the requisite recovery, protection, and preservation themselves in coordination with the Secretary of the Interior or to transfer a maximum of one percent of the total amount authorized to be appropriated for each project to the Secretary of the Interior for this purpose.

The Department of the Interior is presently preparing procedures to implement the Secretary of the Interior's coordination role. Particular concern is being placed on the development of professional standards to ensure that all data recovery programs under this legislation are performed in a professional manner.

Although the historic involvement of the federal government in American archeology is well known, few federal agencies in modern times have actually funded archeological investigations. Fewer still have developed archeological programs and hired archeologists. But, prompted by recent preservation legislation, several federal agencies have become increasingly sensitive to the need to preserve the nation's cultural resources. Their concern is reflected by the recent employment of archeologists in a number of agencies and in the funding support now being provided for investigations in federal or federally assisted land-altering projects.

The U.S. Forest Service serves as an excellent example of these recent developments. From a single full-time professional archeologist in 1966, by 1975 the Forest Service's archeological staff has grown to 17 full-time professionals located in central and field offices. Their part-time professional staff has grown from none in 1966 to 20 during the 1975 field season. The Forest Service is now recruiting for two additional full-time archeologists, who will be located in regional offices.

For the 1977 fiscal year the Forest Service budgeted around $1.5 million to (a) administer and operate cultural history properties on which preservation management decisions have been made; and (b) conduct and maintain professional-level cultural history surveys to establish the presence or absence of cultural values on National Forest system lands to be affected by development activities. This represented a budget increase from zero in 1966.

The Forest Service programs demonstrate a greatly heightened threshold of awareness of cultural history values among their employees at all levels of work. Payoff from this effort is reflected in a significantly increased level of voluntary compliance with the intent and spirit of the law.

We take seriously our coordinative role under recent legislation, and we are moving toward total implementation of a realigned external archeological program in the National Park Service. Changes we are making are specifically designed, in consultation with colleagues outside the federal government, as a further expression of our determination to be full partners in the archeological profession. We are building a staff of carefully selected professionals who will represent a body of expertise second to none. We intend to ensure that archeological investigations undertaken under federal auspices will be of a nature and quality equal to the best research being carried out anywhere in the country.

As a direct result of recent legislation and enlightened federal programs, we need no longer conduct the kind of archeology we have long thought of as salvage. Emergency situations will doubtless arise from time to time, to which we must react immediately. But such situations are rapidly dwindling and are becoming exceptional cases. With our new authorities we are now able to enter into long-term agreements that will set the stage for further development of archeological method and theory and will encourage programmatic and problem-oriented research under federal contract. The contracting procedures we have recently adopted are designed to assure that contracting institutions develop research strategies that not only will result in products that will satisfy the needs of the funding agency, but will have the potential for solid contributions to anthropological archeology.

In addition, our competitive negotiation process is designed to extend full consideration to small institutions and private firms as well as to large institutions, consistent with our policy of awarding contracts to those best qualified to carry out the research needed. We recognize that in recent years important trends have developed that may lead to the solution of many theoretical and methodological problems. We have joined in these efforts with the objective of improving the quality and timeliness of data recovery under authority of Public Law 93-291. The position we have taken is reinforced by federal procurement regulations recently called to our attention by legal counsel. In consequence, several serious legal defects in our traditional contracting procedure have been identified and corrected. Although cumbersome, these regulations establish a procurement system calculated to support and promote the quality improvement recognized as crucial to the archeological activities being funded by the federal government under the 1974 Act. Equally important, they are explicitly designed to promote equitability in all aspects of research procurement. Accordingly, we have discontinued sole-source contracting with the larger educational institutions and museums as basic policy. We have taken the position that a continuation of this practice, which characterized the Interagency Archeological Salvage Program for 30 years, unduly restricts the research market. Furthermore, it discourages intellectual growth and innovation and unfairly and illegally eliminates qualified small colleges and universities, private concerns, and individual archeologists from consideration for contracts. We expect, in addition, to settle the question of the suitability of commercial firms to carry out archeological mitigation under federal contract by encouraging their participation in the Interagency Archeological Program. Because the Interagency Archeological Services staff of the National Park Service is fully committed to represent the professional interests of the archeological community within the federal government, we have sought to enhance both our credibility and our interaction with the profession. We have taken and will continue to take steps calculated to expand the limited scope that once characterized our external programs. For example, we have contracted for several studies related to the general matter of land-use planning that could affect cultural resources now and in the future. Our plan was to relate predictive statements about the distribution of such resources to projected land uses that might damage or destroy them. These and other related studies will support the development of procedures for comprehensive archeological planning that can be implemented by State Historic Preservation Officers and other resource managers.

Another recent step calculated to enhance our relationships with the profession was taken through a contract with the Society for American Archaeology. We contracted with the Society for a series of seminars designed to develop concepts and recommendations from within the discipline dealing with such mutual concerns as professional standards, standards for report writing, cultural resource management, Native American versus archeologist relationships, and several others that have grown increasingly crucial over the past several years.

In order to increase meaningful communication with the archeological community and to improve the professional diversity and strength of the Interagency Archeological Services staff, we have established an internship program designed to bring practicing professionals and graduate students into the National Park Service on temporary appointments.

As our program grows in responsiveness to the needs of the discipline, we will continue to seek additional means of improving on our relationships with the profession and the public at large.

Procedures and guidelines for compliance with Executive Order 11593 and Public Law 93-291 being developed for publication are intended for the primary use of federal agencies whose programs must be in compliance with the law. These procedures include, in considerable detail, the position taken by the Department of the Interior in regard to qualifications of institutions eligible for funding support under the federal programs, professional standards for reporting on research results, and qualifications under federal contracts.

In conclusion I would observe that there has probably never been a more exciting time to be an archeologist, either inside or outside the federal government. The challenges have never been greater, and there has never been a greater opportunity on our part to contribute substantially to knowledge. We have never before had such potential for broadening our profession and bringing it into a closer alignment with our parent discipline. Our success or failure depends altogether on how much effort we are willing to invest.

POSTSCRIPT

On January 25, 1978, Secretary Cecil D. Andrus signed a Secretarial Order creating the Heritage Conservation and Recreation Service within the Department of the Interior. Pursuant to the order, all functions of the Office of Archeology and Historic Preservation, including Interagency Archeological Services, were withdrawn from the National Park Service and combined with those functions formerly within the Bureau of Outdoor Recreation.

Index

A 8
B 9
C 0
D 1
E 2
F 3
G 4
H 5
I 6
J 7

STUDIES IN ARCHEOLOGY

Consulting Editor: Stuart Struever

Department of Anthropology
Northwestern University
Evanston, Illinois